TECHNOLOGICAL
SLAVERY

TECHNOLOGICAL SLAVERY

THEODORE JOHN KACZYNSKI

VOLUME ONE

FITCH & MADISON

PUBLISHERS

Fourth edition, 2022.

Published by Fitch & Madison Publishers.

Inquiries to the publisher should be addressed to Fitch & Madison Publishers, 15150 North Hayden Road, Suite 210, Scottsdale, AZ 85260, Tel: 602-457-4800, Fax: 602-457-4802, or via e-mail at info@fitchmadison.com.

Fitch & Madison and Fitch & Madison Publishers are registered trademarks of Fitch & Madison Publishers, LLC, an Arizona limited liability company.

www.fitchmadison.com

Theodore John Kaczynski does not receive any remuneration for this book.

First Published 2008 by Éditions Xenia as *The Road to Revolution*
Second edition published 2010 by Feral House as *Technological Slavery*
Third edition published 2019 by Fitch & Madison Publishers

∞ This paper meets the requirements of

ANSI/NISO Z39.48-1992 (Permanence of Paper).

Printed in the United States of America

10 9 8 7 6 5 4 3 2

Publisher's Cataloging-in-Publication data

Kaczynski, Theodore John, 1942-,   author.
        Technological slavery , volume one / Theodore John
Kaczynski. — 4th edition.
        pages cm
        Includes bibliographical references and index.
        Library of Congress Control Number: 2021945621
        ISBN 978-1-944228-03-3

        1. Technology and civilization. 2. Technology—Social aspects.
3. Technology—Philosophy. 4. Ecology.
5. Digital media—Social aspects. 6. Thought and thinking.

T14 .K33 2022   303.48'3—dc23

Who is here so base that would be a bondman?

—Shakespeare, *Julius Caesar*

CONTENTS

PREFACE TO THE FIRST AND SECOND EDITIONS

Preface To The First And Second Editions

I have to begin by saying that I am deeply dissatisfied with this book. It should have been an organized and systematic exposition of a series of related ideas. Instead, it is an unorganized collection of writings that expound the ideas unsystematically. And some ideas that I consider important are not even mentioned. I simply have not had the time to organize, rewrite, and complete the contents of this book.

The principal reason why I have not had time is that agencies of the United States government have created unnecessary legal difficulties for me. To mention only the most important of these difficulties, the United States Attorney for the Eastern District of California has formally proposed to round up and confiscate the original and every copy of everything I have ever written and turn over all such papers to my alleged "victims" through a fictitious sale that will allow the "victims" to acquire all of the papers without having to pay anything for them. Under this plan the government would even confiscate papers that I have given to libraries, including papers that have been on library shelves for several years. The documents in which the United States Attorney has put forward this proposal are available to the public: They are Document 704 and Document 713, Case Number CR-S-96-259 GEB, United States District Court for the Eastern District of California.

At this writing (March 21, 2007), I have the assistance of lawyers in resisting the government's actions in regard to my papers. But I have learned from hard experience that it is unwise to leave everything in the hands of lawyers; one is well advised to research the legal issues oneself, keep track of what the lawyers are doing, and intervene when necessary. Such work is time-consuming, especially when one is confined in a maximum-security prison and therefore has only very limited access to law books.

I would have preferred to delay publication of the present book until I'd had time to prepare its contents properly, but it seemed advisable to publish before the government took action to confiscate all my papers. I have, moreover, another reason to avoid delay: The Federal Bureau of Prisons has proposed new regulations that would allow prison wardens to cut off almost all communications between allegedly "terrorist" prisoners and the outside world. The proposed regulations are published in the *Federal Register*, Volume 71, Number 63, pages 16520–25.

I have no idea when the new regulations may be approved, but if and when that happens it is all too possible that my communications will be cut off. Obviously it is important for me to publish while I can still communicate relatively freely, and that is why this book has to appear now in an unfinished state.

The version of "Industrial Society and Its Future" that appears in this book differs from the original manuscript only in trivial ways; spelling, punctuation, capitalization, and the like have been corrected or improved here and there. As far as I know, all earlier versions of "Industrial Society and Its Future" published in English or French contain numerous errors, such as the omission of parts of sentences and even of whole sentences, and some of these errors are serious enough so that they change or obscure the meaning of an entire paragraph.

What is much more serious is that at least one completely spurious article has been published under my name. I recently received word from a correspondent in Spain that an article titled "*La Rehabilitación del Estado por los Izquierdistas*" ("The Rehabilitation of the State by the Leftists") had been published and attributed to me. But I most certainly did not write such an article. So the reader should not assume that everything published under my name has actually been written by me. Needless to say, all writings attributed to me in the present book are authentic.

I would like to thank Dr. David Skrbina for having asked questions and raised arguments that spurred me to formulate and write down certain ideas that I had been incubating for years.

I owe thanks to a number of other people also. At the end of "The Truth About Primitive Life" I have thanked by name (and with their permission) several people who provided me with materials for that essay, and some of those people have helped me enormously in other ways as well. In particular, I owe a heavy debt of gratitude to F.B. and to Patrick S. I owe special thanks to my Spanish correspondent who writes under the pseudonym "Último Reducto"[1] and to a female friend of his, both of whom provided stimulating argument; and Último Reducto moreover has ably translated many of my writings into Spanish. I hesitate to name others to whom I owe thanks, because I'm not sure that they would want to be named publicly.

For the sake of clarity, I want to state here in summary form the four main points that I've tried to make in my writings.

1. Technological progress is carrying us to inevitable disaster. There may be physical disaster (for example, some form of environmental catastrophe), or there may be disaster in terms of human dignity (reduction of the human race to a degraded and servile condition). But disaster of one kind or another will certainly result from continued technological progress.

This is not an eccentric opinion. Among those frightened by the probable consequences of technological progress are Bill Joy, whose article "Why the Future Doesn't Need Us" is now famous, Martin Rees, author of the book *Our Final Hour*, and Richard A. Posner, author of *Catastrophe: Risk and Response*.[2] None of these three is by any stretch of the imagination radical or predisposed to find fault with the existing structure of society. Richard Posner is a conservative judge of the United States Court of Appeals for the Seventh Circuit. Bill Joy is a well-known computer wizard, and Martin Rees is the Astronomer Royal of Britain. These last two men, having devoted their lives to technology, would hardly be likely to fear it without having good reason to do so.

Joy, Rees, and Posner are concerned mainly with physical disaster and with the possibility or indeed the likelihood that human beings will be supplanted by machines. The disaster that technological progress implies for human dignity has been discussed by men like Jacques Ellul and Lewis Mumford, whose books are widely read and respected. Neither man is considered to be out on the fringe or even close to it.

2. Only the collapse of modern technological civilization can avert disaster. Of course, the collapse of technological civilization will itself bring disaster. But the longer the technoindustrial system continues to expand, the worse will be the eventual disaster. A lesser disaster now will avert a greater one later.

The development of the technoindustrial system cannot be controlled, restrained, or guided, nor can its effects be moderated to any substantial degree. This, again, is not an eccentric opinion. Many writers, beginning with Karl Marx, have noted the fundamental importance of technology in determining the course of society's development. In effect, they have recognized that it is technology that rules society, not the other way around. Ellul especially has emphasized the autonomy of technology, i.e., the fact that modern technology has taken on a life of its own and is not subject to human control. Ellul, moreover, was not the first to formulate this conclusion. Already in 1934 the Mexican thinker Samuel Ramos[3] clearly stated the principle of technological autonomy, and this insight was adumbrated as early as the 1860s by Samuel Butler.[4] Of course, no one questions the obvious fact that human individuals or groups can control technology in the sense that at a given point in time they can decide what to do with a particular item of technology. What the principle of techno-logical autonomy asserts is that the overall development of technology, and its long-term consequences for society, are not subject to human control. Hence, as long as modern technology continues to exist, there is little we can do to moderate its effects.

A corollary is that nothing short of the collapse of technological society can avert a greater disaster. Thus, if we want to defend ourselves against technology, the only action we can take that might prove effective is an effort to precipitate the collapse of technological society. Though this conclusion is an obvious consequence of the principle of technolog-ical autonomy, and though it possibly is implied by certain statements of Ellul, I know of no conventionally published writer who has explicitly recognized that our only way out is through the collapse of technological society. This seeming blindness to the obvious can only be explained as the result of timidity.

If we want to precipitate the collapse of technological society, then our goal is a revolutionary one under any reasonable definition of that term. What we are faced with, therefore, is a need for out-and-out revolution.

3. The political left is technological society's first line of defense against revolution. In fact, the left today serves as a kind of fire extin-guisher that douses and quenches any nascent revolutionary movement. What do I mean by "the left"? If you think that racism, sexism, gay rights, animal rights, indigenous people's rights, and "social justice" in general are among the most important issues that the world currently faces, then you are a leftist as I use that term. If you don't like this application of the word "leftist," then you are free to designate the people I'm referring to by some other term. But, whatever you call them, the people who extin-guish revolutionary movements are the people who are drawn indiscrim-inately to causes: racism, sexism, gay rights, animal rights, the environ-ment, poverty, sweatshops, neocolonialism… it's all the same to them. These people constitute a subculture that has been labeled "the adversary culture."[5] Whenever a movement of resistance begins to emerge, these leftists (or whatever you choose to call them) come swarming to it like flies to honey until they outnumber the original members of the movement, take it over, and turn it into just another leftist faction, thereby emasculating it. The history of "Earth First!" provides an elegant example of this process.[6]

4. What is needed is a new revolutionary movement, dedicated to the elimination of technological society, that will take measures to exclude all leftists, as well as the assorted neurotics, lazies, incompetents, charlatans, and persons deficient in self-control who are drawn to resistance movements in America today. Just what form a revolutionary movement should take remains open to discussion. What is clear is that, for a start, people who are serious about addressing the problem of technology must establish systematic contact with one another and a sense of common purpose; they must strictly separate themselves from the "adversary culture"; they must be oriented toward practical action; and they must take as their goal nothing less than the dissolution of technological civilization.

NOTES

1. Último Reducto has no connection with the Mexican fascist group that, coincidentally, has adopted the same name.

2. For information on these three works, see our List of Works Cited.

3. Ramos, pp. 104–05.

4. Jones, p. 46.

5. See Hollander as referenced in our List of Works Cited.

6. The process is ably documented by M.F. Lee (see List of Works Cited).

PREFACE TO THE
REVISED AND EXPANDED
EDITION

Preface To The Revised And Expanded Edition

I. The original *Technological Slavery* was a miscellaneous collection of letters and articles written at earlier times and hastily thrown together for publication with inadequate editing and proofreading. It was presented in that unfinished and poorly organized form because, in view of new regulations that had been proposed by the Federal Bureau of Prisons under the Bush administration, there appeared to be a danger that my communications with the outside world might be cut off before I could get the book into print. See the Preface to the First and Second Editions, fourth paragraph. Under the Obama administration, however, the proposed regulations were quietly allowed to die, or perhaps were merely forgotten, and my communications with the outside world remained open.

In view of its deficiencies, *Technological Slavery* should have been thoroughly and completely rewritten so that its ideas could now be presented in a systematic and well-organized form. But the new (as of 2017) administration in Washington seems to be shaping up as a regime of the far right, and it's all too possible that the regulations proposed earlier may be revived or that other, similar ones may be put into effect; so once again I'm faced with a danger that my communications may be cut off. I've therefore had to move quickly in preparing the revised *Technological Slavery* for publication. This has precluded a complete rewriting, but it has not precluded substantial improvements over the earlier editions.

I've decided to divide the revised *Technological Slavery* into two volumes, in part because, with the new material that is being added, a single volume might have proven somewhat unwieldy, but mainly because in this first volume I can get the most important ideas and arguments into print much more quickly than I could if I waited until all of the materials were ready for publication.

II. The present volume includes *Industrial Society and Its Future* (ISAIF), "The System's Neatest Trick," and all of the letters[1] that appeared in the second edition of *Technological Slavery*. Here and there these materials have been modified for the sake of clarity, for stylistic reasons, or to correct errors. The notes have been greatly expanded, again to correct errors, but especially to provide clarification of points made in the text, full citation of sources incompletely cited in the earlier editions, and citation of new sources in support of some of my arguments and assertions. Eight new appendices have been added that provide justification, clarification, or amplification of arguments that appear in the main text. Appendices Three and Five improve upon Afterthoughts 4 and 3, respectively, of the second edition of *Technological Slavery*.[2] In addition to the foregoing materials, the present volume includes the long and previously unpublished "Letter to Dr. P.B. on the Motivations of Scientists."

As those who have read the Preface to the First and Second Editions (above) know already, ISAIF as it first appeared in the *Washington Post* was marred by numerous, serious errors of transcription, and subsequent versions, whether published in print or on the Internet, added further errors to those of the *Washington Post*. The first reasonably accurate version of ISAIF to be published was the one that appeared in the second edition of *Technological Slavery*. Those who have not read the second edition are therefore advised to read ISAIF as it appears in the present volume, even if they have previously read it elsewhere. Readers should in any case bear in mind that ISAIF was written in 1995 and therefore is in some respects dated. Though I've made some minor changes for stylistic reasons or for clarity, I have not tried to rewrite ISAIF to bring it up to date. Corrections and major clarifications have been relegated to the notes, the number of which has been increased from 36 to 63.

Apart from ISAIF, the most important section of this book consists of my letters to David Skrbina. I've modified the text of these to a somewhat greater extent than I have that of ISAIF; even so, corrections, clarifications, and amplifications have mostly been reserved for the notes and the appendices. Six of the latter, out of eight, are related to my letters to Dr. Skrbina.

In Part III of the Preface to my book *Anti-Tech Revolution: Why and How* (2016), I discussed the fact that I had found it necessary to use many doubtful sources of information; for example, media reports and encyclopedia articles. Everything I said there applies also to my use of doubtful sources in the present work.

III. A number of people have helped me in revising and supplementing *Technological Slavery*; only the most important among them will be mentioned here. I owe thanks above all to Susan Gale, who has been far and away my best researcher in this project, as she was in the case of my book *Anti-Tech Revolution: Why and How*; she has done almost all of the typing and has served as the center around whom the whole project has been organized. After Susan, my most important researchers have been Kwani Chung, T.F., and Elizabeth Tobier. Elizabeth and T.F. have been especially generous in ordering books for me at their own expense; Dr. Susie Meister, T.N., Stephanie Tisza and two persons who prefer not to be named have likewise provided me with books at their own expense. Various people have sent me copies of articles or called my attention to information of which I've made use; among them are Lydia Eccles, Isumatag (pseudonym), Último Reducto (pseudonym), Andrea Speijer-Beek, and Dr. David Skrbina who, among other things, located the source of the Einstein quote comparing technology to an axe in the hand of a pathological criminal (see the Letter to Dr. P.B. on the Motivations of Scientists, Part III). To a correspondent who wishes to remain anonymous I owe special thanks for pointing out an error of mine respecting earthworms (pages 333 and 369 of the 2010 edition of *Technological Slavery*). Of those who have helped with proofreading, the most important have been Amber M., Lyn Kaminski, and Andrea Speijer-Beek. Dr. Julie Ault has been supportive, while Patrick S. and a gentleman who prefers not to be named have provided indispensable financial support.

To all of these people I am warmly grateful.

IV. *Note on Referencing.* In the notes that follow each section of this book, I generally cite sources of information by giving the author's last name and a page number. The reader can find the author's full name, the title of the book or article cited, the date of publication, and other necessary information by looking up the author's last name in the List of Works Cited that appears at the end of the book. When a source without named author is cited, the reader will in some cases find additional information about the source in the list of works without named author that concludes the List of Works Cited.

Two abbreviations are used repeatedly in the notes:

"ISAIF" refers to *Industrial Society and Its Future*, which appears in this volume.

"NEB" means *The New Encyclopaedia Britannica*, Fifteenth Edition. The Fifteenth Edition has been modified repeatedly, so "NEB" is always followed by a date in parentheses that indicates the particular version of NEB that is cited. For example, "NEB (2003)" means the version of *The New Encyclopaedia Britannica* that bears the copyright date 2003.

Ted Kaczynski
April 2017

NOTES

1.   Except a part of the "Excerpts from Letter to M.K."

2.   Afterthought 1 has been rendered unnecessary by the new notes 20, 25, 56 to ISAIF, Afterthought 5 by modifications in the text of the letters to Dr. Skrbina. Afterthought 2 is not relevant to the present volume.

NOTE ON THE FOURTH EDITION

Note on the Fourth Edition

The present edition of this book incorporates a number of minor improvements as well as five revisions that I consider significant. In descending order of importance:

1. In the Third Edition, Appendix Four—on Domingo Faustino Sarmiento and the gauchos—was far from adequate, because when I wrote it I lacked sufficient information. Since then I've procured two books on gaucho life by Argentinian historians, and I've rewritten Appendix Four accordingly.

2. The new Note 8 to the Extract from Letter to J.N. makes an important point that I have not made explicitly elsewhere.

3. Two of the Further Comments added at the end of ISAIF clarify significant issues.

4. In the Third Edition, the long Note 8 to Appendix Three was in part misguided. Note 8 addressed Prussia's failure to build an overseas empire, and I've written a new Note 8 which—while still tentative—addresses the same question in a way that I hope is less misguided.

5. To Appendix Two I've added a second example in support of my contention that the decisions of individuals can occasionally have an important and long-lasting effect on the course of history.

Ted Kaczynski
January 2021

LETTER TO SCIENTIFIC AMERICAN

Letter to *Scientific American* (1995)[1]

We write in reference to a piece by Russell Ruthen, "Strange Matters: Can Advanced Accelerators Initiate Runaway Reactions?," Science and the Citizen, *Scientific American*, August, 1993.

It seems that physicists have long kept behind closed doors their concern that experiments with particle accelerators might lead to a world-swallowing catastrophe. This is a good example of the arrogance of scientists, who routinely take risks affecting the public. The public commonly is not aware that risks are being taken, and often the scientists do not even admit to themselves that there are risks. Most scientists have a deep emotional commitment to their work and are not in a position to be objective about its negative aspects.

We are not so much concerned about the danger of experiments with accelerated particles. Since the physicists are not fools, we assume that the risk is small (though probably not as small as the physicists claim).[2] But scientists and engineers constantly gamble with human welfare, and we see today the effects of some of their lost gambles: ozone depletion, the greenhouse effect, cancer-causing chemicals to which we cannot avoid exposure, accumulating nuclear waste for which a sure method of disposal has not yet been found, the crowding, noise, and pollution that have followed industrialization, massive extinction of species, and so forth. For the future, what will be the consequences of genetic engineering? Of the development of superintelligent computers (if this occurs)? Of understanding of the human brain and the resulting inevitable temptation to "improve" it? No one knows.

We emphasize that negative *physical* consequences of scientific advances often are completely unforeseeable. (It probably never occurred to the chemists who developed early pesticides that they might be causing many cases of disease in humans.) But far more difficult to foresee are the negative *social* consequences of technological progress. The engineers who began the Industrial Revolution never dreamed that their work would result in the creation of an industrial proletariat[3] or the economic boom and bust cycle. The wiser ones may have guessed that contact with industrial society would disrupt other cultures around the world, but they probably never imagined the extent of the damage that these other cultures would suffer. Nor did it occur to them that in the West itself technological

21

progress would lead to a society tormented by a variety of social and psychological problems.

Every major technical advance is also a social experiment. These experiments are performed on the public by the scientists and by the corporations and government agencies that pay for their research. These elite groups get the fulfillment, the exhilaration, the sense of power involved in bringing about technological progress, while the average man gets only the consequences of their social experiments. It could be argued that in a purely physical sense the consequences are on balance positive, since life expectancy has increased. But the acceptability of risks cannot be assessed in purely actuarial terms. "[P]eople also rank risks based on... how equitably the danger is distributed, how well individuals can control their exposure and whether risk is assumed voluntarily."[4] The elite groups who create technological progress share in control of the process and assume the risks voluntarily, whereas the role of the average individual is necessarily passive and involuntary. Moreover, it is possible that at some time in the future the population explosion, environmental disaster, or the breakdown of an increasingly troubled society may lead to a sudden, drastic lowering of life expectancy.

However it may be with the *physical* consequences, there are good reasons to believe that the *social* consequences of technological progress are on balance highly negative. This matter is discussed at length in a manuscript that we are sending to the *New York Times*.[5]

The engineers who initiated the Industrial Revolution can be forgiven for not having anticipated its negative consequences. But the harm caused by technological progress is by this time sufficiently apparent so that to continue to promote it is grossly irresponsible.

NOTES

1.   Here slightly rewritten.

2.   See Kolbert, "Crash Course," pp. 69–70.

3.   However, Thomas Jefferson and James Madison may have foreseen the emergence of something along the lines of an industrial proletariat. Jefferson "predict[ed] that factory workers would one day rock governments." Randall, p. 417. Madison "envisaged a future when the majority of the people would have no property at all." He was thinking of "the great capitalists... and the members employed by them," and he suggested that the propertyless workers might some

day unite and endanger "the rights of property and the public liberty." Haraszti, p. 32. Marx and Lenin would have agreed enthusiastically.

4. Morgan, p. 35.

5. This was ISAIF.

INDUSTRIAL SOCIETY
AND ITS FUTURE (ISAIF)

Industrial Society and Its Future (ISAIF)

Introduction

1. The Industrial Revolution and its consequences have been a disaster for the human race. They have greatly increased the life expectancy of those of us who live in "advanced" countries, but they have destabilized society, have made life unfulfilling, have subjected human beings to indignities, have led to widespread psychological suffering (in the Third World to physical suffering as well) and have inflicted severe damage on the natural world. The continued development of technology will worsen the situation. It will certainly subject human beings to greater indignities and inflict greater damage on the natural world, it will probably lead to greater social disruption and psychological suffering,[1] and it may lead to increased physical suffering even in "advanced" countries.

2. The industrial-technological system may survive or it may break down. If it survives, it *may* eventually achieve a low level of physical and psychological suffering, but only after passing through a long and very painful period of adjustment and only at the cost of permanently reducing human beings and many other living organisms to engineered products and mere cogs in the social machine. Furthermore, if the system survives, the consequences will be inevitable: There is no way of reforming or modifying the system so as to prevent it from depriving people of dignity and autonomy.

3. If the system breaks down the consequences will still be very painful. But the bigger the system grows the more disastrous the results of its breakdown will be, so if it is to break down it had best break down sooner rather than later.

4. We therefore advocate a revolution against the industrial system. This revolution may or may not make use of violence; it may be sudden or it may be a relatively gradual process spanning a few decades. We can't predict any of that. But we do outline in a very general way the measures that those who hate the industrial system should take in order to prepare the way for a revolution against that form of society. This is not to be a *political* revolution. Its object will be to overthrow not governments but the economic and technological basis of the present society.

5.   In this article we give attention to only some of the negative developments that have grown out of the industrial-technological system. Other such developments we mention only briefly or ignore altogether. This does not mean that we regard these other developments as unimportant. For practical reasons we have to confine our discussion to areas that have received insufficient public attention or in which we have something new to say. For example, since there are well-developed environmental and wilderness movements, we have written very little about environmental degradation or the destruction of wild nature, even though we consider these to be highly important.

The Psychology of Modern Leftism

6.   Almost everyone will agree that we live in a deeply troubled society. One of the most widespread manifestations of the craziness of our world is leftism, so a discussion of the psychology of leftism can serve as an introduction to the discussion of the problems of modern society in general.

7.   But what is leftism? During the first half of the 20th century leftism could practically have been identified with socialism. Today the movement is fragmented and it is not clear who can properly be called a leftist. When we speak of leftists in this article we have in mind mainly socialists, collectivists, "politically correct" types, feminists, gay and disability activists, animal-rights activists and the like. But not everyone who is associated with one of these movements is a leftist. What we are trying to get at in discussing leftism is not so much a movement or an ideology as a psychological type, or rather a collection of related types. Thus, what we mean by "leftism" will emerge more clearly in the course of our discussion of leftist psychology. (Also, see paragraphs 227–230.)

8.   Even so, our conception of leftism will remain a good deal less clear than we would wish, but there doesn't seem to be any remedy for this. All we are trying to do here is indicate in a rough and approximate way the two psychological tendencies that we believe are the main driving force of modern leftism. We by no means claim to be telling the *whole* truth about leftist psychology. Also, our discussion is meant to apply to modern leftism only. We leave open the question of the extent to which our discussion could be applied to the leftists of the 19th and early 20th centuries.

9. The two psychological tendencies that underlie modern leftism we call *feelings of inferiority* and *oversocialization.* Feelings of inferiority are characteristic of modern leftism as a whole, while oversocialization is characteristic only of a certain segment of modern leftism; but this segment is highly influential.

Feelings of Inferiority

10. By "feelings of inferiority" we mean not only inferiority feelings in the strict sense but a whole spectrum of related traits: low self-esteem, feelings of powerlessness, depressive tendencies, defeatism, guilt, self-hatred, etc. We argue that modern leftists tend to have some such feelings (possibly more or less repressed), and that these feelings are decisive in determining the direction of modern leftism.

11. When someone interprets as derogatory almost anything that is said about him (or about groups with whom he identifies), we conclude that he has inferiority feelings or low self-esteem. This tendency is pronounced among minority-rights activists, whether or not they belong to the minority groups whose rights they defend. They are hypersensitive about the words used to designate minorities and about anything that is said concerning minorities. The terms "Negro," "oriental," "handicapped," or "chick" for an African, an Asian, a disabled person, or a woman originally had no derogatory connotation. "Broad" and "chick" were merely the feminine equivalents of "guy," "dude," or "fellow." The negative connotations have been attached to these terms by the activists themselves. Some animal-rights activists have gone so far as to reject the word "pet" and insist on its replacement by "animal companion." Leftish anthropologists go to great lengths to avoid saying anything about primitive peoples that could conceivably be interpreted as negative. They want to replace the word "primitive" with "nonliterate." They seem almost paranoid about anything that might suggest that any primitive culture is inferior to our own. (We do not mean to imply that primitive cultures *are* inferior to ours. We merely point out the hypersensitivity of leftish anthropologists.)

12. Those who are most sensitive about "politically incorrect" terminology are not the average black ghetto-dweller, Asian immigrant, abused woman or disabled person, but a minority of activists, many of whom do not even belong to any "oppressed" group but come from

privileged strata of society. Political correctness has its stronghold among university professors, who have secure employment with comfortable salaries, and the majority of whom are heterosexual white males from middle to upper-class families.

13. Many leftists have an intense identification with the problems of groups that have an image of being weak (women), defeated (American Indians), repellent (homosexuals), or otherwise inferior. The leftists themselves feel that these groups are inferior. They would never admit to themselves that they have such feelings, but it is precisely because they do see these groups as inferior that they identify with their problems. (We do not mean to suggest that women, Indians, etc., *are* inferior; we are only making a point about leftist psychology.)

14. Feminists are desperately anxious to prove that women are as strong and as capable as men. Clearly they are nagged by a fear that women may *not* be as strong and as capable as men.

15. Leftists tend to hate anything that has an image of being strong, good and successful. They hate America, they hate Western civilization, they hate white males, they hate rationality. The reasons that leftists give for hating the West, etc., clearly do not correspond with their real motives. They *say* they hate the West because it is warlike, imperialistic, sexist, ethnocentric and so forth, but where these same faults appear in socialist countries or in primitive cultures, the leftist finds excuses for them, or at best he *grudgingly* admits that they exist; whereas he *enthusiastically* points out (and often greatly exaggerates) these faults where they appear in Western civilization. Thus it is clear that these faults are not the leftist's real motive for hating America and the West. He hates America and the West because they are strong and successful.

16. Words like "self-confidence," "self-reliance," "initiative," "enterprise," "optimism," etc., play little role in the liberal and leftist vocabulary. The leftist is anti-individualistic, pro-collectivist. He wants society to solve everyone's problems for them, satisfy everyone's needs for them, take care of them. He is not the sort of person who has an inner sense of confidence in his ability to solve his own problems and satisfy his own needs. The leftist is antagonistic to the concept of competition because, deep inside, he feels like a loser.

17. Art forms that appeal to modern leftish intellectuals tend to focus on sordidness, defeat and despair, or else they take an orgiastic tone, throwing off rational control as if there were no hope of accomplishing

anything through rational calculation and all that were left were to immerse oneself in the sensations of the moment.

18.   Modern leftish philosophers tend to dismiss reason, science, objective reality and to insist that everything is culturally relative. It is true that one can ask serious questions about the foundations of scientific knowledge and about how, if at all, the concept of objective reality can be defined. But it is obvious that modern leftish philosophers are not simply cool-headed logicians systematically analyzing the foundations of knowledge. They are deeply involved emotionally in their attack on truth and reality. They attack these concepts because of their own psychological needs. For one thing, their attack is an outlet for hostility, and, to the extent that it is successful, it satisfies the drive for power. More importantly, the leftist hates science and rationality because they classify certain beliefs as true (i.e., successful, superior) and other beliefs as false (i.e., failed, inferior). The leftist's feelings of inferiority run so deep that he cannot tolerate any classification of some things as successful or superior and other things as failed or inferior This also underlies the rejection by many leftists of the concept of mental illness and of the utility of IQ tests. Leftists are antagonistic to genetic explanations of human abilities or behavior because such explanations tend to make some persons appear superior or inferior to others. Leftists prefer to give society the credit or blame for an individual's ability or lack of it. Thus if a person is "inferior" it is not his fault, but society's, because he has not been brought up properly.

19.   The leftist is not typically the kind of person whose feelings of inferiority make him a braggart, an egotist, a bully, a self-promoter, a ruthless competitor. This kind of person has not wholly lost faith in himself. He has a deficit in his sense of power and self-worth, but he can still conceive of himself as having the capacity to be strong, and his efforts to make himself strong produce his unpleasant behavior.[2] But the leftist is too far gone for that. His feelings of inferiority are so ingrained that he cannot conceive of himself as individually strong and valuable. Hence the collectivism of the leftist. He can feel strong only as a member of a large organization or a mass movement with which he identifies himself.

20. Notice the masochistic tendency of leftist tactics. Leftists protest by lying down in front of vehicles, they intentionally provoke police or racists to abuse them, etc. These tactics may often be effective, but many leftists use them not as a means to an end but because they *prefer* masochistic tactics. Self-hatred is a leftist trait.

21. Leftists may claim that their activism is motivated by compassion or by moral principles, and moral principle does play a role for the leftist of the oversocialized type. But compassion and moral principle cannot be the main motives for leftist activism. Hostility is too prominent a component of leftist behavior; so is the drive for power. Moreover, much leftist behavior is not rationally calculated to be of benefit to the people whom the leftists claim to be trying to help. For example, if one believes that affirmative action is good for black people, does it make sense to demand affirmative action in hostile or dogmatic terms? Obviously it would be more productive to take a diplomatic and conciliatory approach that would make at least verbal and symbolic concessions to white people who think that affirmative action discriminates against them. But leftist activists do not take such an approach because it would not satisfy their emotional needs. Helping black people is not their real goal. Instead, race problems serve as an excuse for them to express their own hostility and frustrated need for power. In doing so they actually harm black people, because the activists' hostile attitude toward the white majority tends to intensify race hatred.

22. If our society had no social problems at all, the leftists would have to *invent* problems in order to provide themselves with an excuse for making a fuss.

23. We emphasize that the foregoing does not pretend to be an accurate description of everyone who might be considered a leftist. It is only a rough indication of a general tendency of leftism.

Oversocialization

24. Psychologists use the term "socialization" to designate the process by which children are trained to think and act as society demands. A person is said to be well socialized if he believes in and obeys the moral code of his society and fits in well as a functioning part of that society. It may seem senseless to say that many leftists are oversocialized, since the leftist is perceived as a rebel. Nevertheless, the position can be defended. Many leftists are not such rebels as they seem.

25. The moral code of our society is so demanding that no one can think, feel and act in a completely moral way. For example, we are not supposed to hate anyone, yet almost everyone hates somebody at some

time or other, whether he admits it to himself or not. Some people are so highly socialized that the attempt to think, feel and act morally imposes a severe burden on them. In order to avoid feelings of guilt, they continually have to deceive themselves about their own motives and find moral explanations for feelings and actions that in reality have a non-moral origin. We use the term "oversocialized" to describe such people.[3]

26. Oversocialization can lead to low self-esteem, a sense of powerlessness, defeatism, guilt, etc. One of the most important means by which our society socializes children is by making them feel ashamed of behavior or speech that is contrary to society's expectations. If this is overdone, or if a particular child is especially susceptible to such feelings, he ends by feeling ashamed of *himself*. Moreover, the thought and the behavior of the oversocialized person are more restricted by society's expectations than are those of the lightly-socialized person. The majority of people engage in a significant amount of naughty behavior. They lie, they commit petty thefts, they break traffic laws, they goof off at work, they hate someone, they say spiteful things or they use some underhanded trick to get ahead of the other guy. The oversocialized person cannot do these things, or if he does do them he generates in himself a sense of shame and self-hatred. The oversocialized person cannot even experience, without guilt, thoughts or feelings that are contrary to the accepted morality; he cannot think "unclean" thoughts. And socialization is not just a matter of morality; we are socialized to conform to many norms of behavior that do not fall under the heading of morality. Thus the oversocialized person is kept on a psychological leash and spends his life running on rails that society has laid down for him. In many oversocialized people this results in a sense of constraint and powerlessness that can be a severe hardship. We suggest that oversocialization is among the more serious cruelties that human beings inflict on one another.

27. We argue that a very important and influential segment of the modern left is oversocialized and that their oversocialization is of great importance in determining the direction of modern leftism. Leftists of the oversocialized type tend to be intellectuals or members of the upper middle class. Notice that university intellectuals[4] constitute the most highly socialized segment of our society and also the most left-wing segment.

28. The leftist of the oversocialized type tries to get off his psychological leash and assert his autonomy by rebelling. But usually he is not strong enough to rebel against the most basic values of society. Generally

speaking, the goals of today's leftists are *not* in conflict with the accepted morality. On the contrary, the left takes an accepted moral principle, adopts it as its own, and then accuses mainstream society of violating that principle. Examples: racial equality, equality of the sexes, helping poor people, peace as opposed to war, nonviolence generally, freedom of expression, kindness to animals. More fundamentally, the duty of the individual to serve society and the duty of society to take care of the individual. All these have been deeply rooted values of our society (or at least of its middle and upper classes[5]) for a long time. These values are explicitly or implicitly expressed or presupposed in most of the material presented to us by the mainstream communications media and the educational system. Leftists, especially those of the oversocialized type, usually do not rebel against these principles but justify their hostility to society by claiming (with some degree of truth) that society is not living up to these principles.

29. Here is an illustration of the way in which the oversocialized leftist shows his real attachment to the conventional attitudes of our society while pretending to be in rebellion against it. Many leftists push for affirmative action, for moving black people into high-prestige jobs, for improved education in black schools and more money for such schools; the way of life of the black "underclass" they regard as a social disgrace. They want to integrate the black man into the system, make him a business executive, a lawyer, a scientist just like upper-middle-class white people. The leftists will reply that the last thing they want is to make the black man into a copy of the white man; instead, they want to preserve African-American culture. But in what does this preservation of African-American culture consist? It can hardly consist in anything more than eating black-style food, listening to black-style music, wearing black-style clothing and going to a black-style church or mosque. In other words, it can express itself only in superficial matters. In all *essential* respects, most leftists of the oversocialized type want to make the black man conform to white middle-class ideals. They want to make him study technical subjects, become an executive or a scientist, spend his life climbing the status ladder to prove that black people are as good as white. They want to make black fathers "responsible," they want black gangs to become nonviolent, etc. But these are exactly the values of the industrial-technological system. The system couldn't care less what kind of music a man listens to, what kind of clothes he wears or what religion he believes in as long as he studies in school, holds a respectable job, climbs the status ladder, is a "responsible" parent,

is nonviolent and so forth. In effect, however much he may deny it, the oversocialized leftist wants to integrate the black man into the system and make him adopt its values.

30. We certainly do not claim that leftists, even of the oversocialized type, *never* rebel against the fundamental values of our society. Clearly they sometimes do. Some oversocialized leftists have gone so far as to rebel against one of modern society's most important principles by engaging in physical violence. By their own account, violence is for them a form of "liberation." In other words, by committing violence they break through the psychological restraints that have been trained into them. Because they are oversocialized these restraints have been more confining for them than for others; hence their need to break free of them. But they usually justify their rebellion in terms of mainstream values. If they engage in violence they claim to be fighting against racism or the like.

31. We realize that many objections could be raised to the foregoing thumbnail sketch of leftist psychology. The real situation is complex, and anything like a complete description of it would take several volumes even if the necessary data were available. We claim only to have indicated very roughly the two most important tendencies in the psychology of modern leftism.

32. The problems of the leftist are indicative of the problems of our society as a whole. Low self-esteem, depressive tendencies and defeatism are not restricted to the left. Though they are especially noticeable in the left, they are widespread in our society. And today's society tries to socialize us to a greater extent than any previous society. We are even told by experts how to eat, how to exercise, how to make love, how to raise our kids and so forth.

The Power Process[6]

33. Human beings have a need (probably based in biology) for something that we will call the *power process*. This is closely related to the need for power (which is widely recognized) but it is not quite the same thing. The power process has four elements. The three most clear-cut of these we call goal, effort and attainment of goal. (Everyone needs to have goals whose attainment requires effort, and needs to succeed in attaining at least some of his goals.) The fourth element is more difficult to define

and may not be necessary for everyone. We call it autonomy and will discuss it later (paragraphs 42–44).

34. Consider the hypothetical case of a man who can have anything he wants just by wishing for it. Such a man has power, but he will develop serious psychological problems. At first he will have a lot of fun, but by and by he will become acutely bored and demoralized. Eventually he may become clinically depressed. History shows that leisured aristocracies tend to become decadent. This is not true of fighting aristocracies that have to struggle to maintain their power. But leisured, secure aristocracies that have no need to exert themselves usually become bored, hedonistic and demoralized, even though they have power. This shows that power is not enough. One must have goals toward which to exercise one's power.

35. Everyone has goals; if nothing else, to obtain the physical necessities of life: food, water and whatever clothing and shelter are made necessary by the climate. But the leisured aristocrat obtains these things without effort. Hence his boredom and demoralization.

36. Non-attainment of important goals results in death if the goals are physical necessities, and in frustration if non-attainment of the goals is compatible with survival. Consistent failure to attain goals throughout life results in defeatism, low self-esteem or depression.

37. Thus, in order to avoid serious psychological problems, a human being needs goals whose attainment requires effort, and he must have a reasonable rate of success in attaining his goals.

Surrogate Activities

38. But not every leisured aristocrat becomes bored and demoralized. For example, the emperor Hirohito, instead of sinking into decadent hedonism, devoted himself to marine biology, a field in which he became distinguished. When people do not have to exert themselves to satisfy their physical needs they often set up artificial goals for themselves. In many cases they then pursue these goals with the same energy and emotional involvement that they otherwise would have put into the search for physical necessities. Thus the aristocrats of the Roman Empire had their literary pretensions; many European aristocrats a few centuries ago invested tremendous time and energy in hunting, though they certainly didn't need the meat; other aristocracies have competed for status through

elaborate displays of wealth; and a few aristocrats, like Hirohito, have turned to science.

39. We use the term "surrogate activity" to designate an activity that is directed toward an artificial goal that people set up for themselves merely in order to have some goal to work toward, or, let us say, merely for the sake of the "fulfillment" that they get from pursuing the goal. Here is a rule of thumb for the identification of surrogate activities. Given a person who devotes much time and energy to the pursuit of goal X, ask yourself this: If he had to devote most of his time and energy to satisfying his biological needs, and if that effort required him to use his physical and mental faculties in a varied and interesting way, would he feel seriously deprived because he did not attain goal X? If the answer is no, then the person's pursuit of goal X is a surrogate activity. Hirohito's studies in marine biology clearly constituted a surrogate activity, since it is pretty certain that if Hirohito had had to spend his time working at interesting non-scientific tasks in order to obtain the necessities of life, he would not have felt deprived because he didn't know all about the anatomy and life-cycles of marine animals. On the other hand, the pursuit of sex and love (for example) is not a surrogate activity, because most people, even if their existence were otherwise satisfactory, would feel deprived if they passed their lives without ever having a relationship with a member of the opposite sex. (But pursuit of an excessive amount of sex, more than one really needs, can be a surrogate activity.)

40. In modern industrial society only minimal effort is necessary to satisfy one's physical needs. It is enough to go through a training program to acquire some petty technical skill, then come to work on time and exert the very modest effort needed to hold a job. The only requirements are a moderate amount of intelligence and, most of all, simple *obedience*. If one has those, society takes care of one from cradle to grave. (Yes, there is an underclass that cannot take the physical necessities for granted, but we are speaking here of mainstream society.) Thus it is not surprising that modern society is full of surrogate activities. These include scientific work, athletic achievement, humanitarian work, artistic and literary creation, climbing the corporate ladder, acquisition of money and material goods far beyond the point at which they cease to give any additional physical satisfaction, and social activism when it addresses issues that are not important for the activist personally, as in the case of white activists who work for the rights of nonwhite minorities. These are not always *pure* surrogate activities,

since for many people they may be motivated in part by needs other than the need to have some goal to pursue. Scientific work may be motivated in part by a drive for prestige, artistic creation by a need to express feelings, militant social activism by hostility. But for most people who pursue them, these activities are in large part surrogate activities. For example, the majority of scientists will probably agree that the "fulfillment" they get from their work is more important than the money and prestige they earn.

41. For many if not most people, surrogate activities are less satisfying than the pursuit of real goals (that is, goals that people would want to attain even if their need for the power process were already fulfilled). One indication of this is the fact that, in many or most cases, people who are deeply involved in surrogate activities are never satisfied, never at rest. Thus the money-maker constantly strives for more and more wealth. The scientist no sooner solves one problem than he moves on to the next. The long-distance runner drives himself to run always farther and faster. Many people who pursue surrogate activities will say that they get far more fulfillment from these activities than they do from the "mundane" business of satisfying their biological needs, but that is because in our society the effort required to satisfy the biological needs has been reduced to triviality. More importantly, in our society people do not satisfy their biological needs *autonomously* but by functioning as parts of an immense social machine. In contrast, people generally have a great deal of autonomy in pursuing their surrogate activities.

Autonomy

42. Autonomy as a part of the power process may not be necessary for every individual. But most people need a greater or lesser degree of autonomy in working toward their goals. Their efforts must be undertaken on their own initiative and must be under their own direction and control. Yet most people do not have to exert this initiative, direction and control as single individuals. It is usually enough to act as a member of a *small* group. Thus, if half a dozen people discuss a goal among themselves and make a successful joint effort to attain that goal, their need for the power process will be served. But if they work under rigid orders handed down from above that leave them no room for autonomous decision and initiative, then their need for the power process will not be served. The

same is true when decisions are made on a collective basis, if the group making the collective decision is so large that the role of each individual is insignificant.[7]

43. It is true that some individuals seem to have little need for autonomy. Either their drive for power is weak, or they satisfy it by identifying themselves with some powerful organization to which they belong. And then there are unthinking, animal types who seem to be satisfied with a purely physical sense of power (the good combat soldier, who gets his sense of power by developing fighting skills that he is quite content to use in blind obedience to his superiors).

44. But for most people it is through the power process—having a goal, making an *autonomous* effort, and attaining the goal—that self-esteem, self-confidence and a sense of power are acquired. When one does not have adequate opportunity to go through the power process the consequences are (depending on the individual and on the way the power process is disrupted) boredom, demoralization, low self-esteem, inferiority feelings, defeatism, depression, anxiety, guilt, frustration, hostility, spouse or child abuse, insatiable hedonism, abnormal sexual behavior, sleep disorders, eating disorders, etc.[8]

Sources of Social Problems

45. Any of the foregoing symptoms can occur in any society, but in modern industrial society they are present on a massive scale. We aren't the first to mention that the world today seems to be going crazy. This sort of thing is not normal for human societies. There is good reason to believe that primitive man suffered from less stress and frustration and was better satisfied with his way of life than modern man is. It is true that not all was sweetness and light in primitive societies. Abuse of women was common among the Australian aborigines, transsexuality was fairly common among some of the American Indian tribes. But it does appear that *generally speaking* the kinds of problems that we have listed in the preceding paragraph were far less common among primitive peoples than they are in modern society.

46. We attribute the social and psychological problems of modern society to the fact that that society requires people to live under conditions radically different from those under which the human race evolved

and to behave in ways that conflict with the patterns of behavior that the human race developed while living under the earlier conditions. It is clear from what we have already written that we consider lack of opportunity to properly experience the power process as the most important of the abnormal conditions to which modern society subjects people. But it is not the only one. Before dealing with disruption of the power process as a source of social problems we will discuss some of the other sources.

47. Among the abnormal conditions present in modern industrial society are excessive density of population, isolation of man from nature, excessive rapidity of social change and the breakdown of natural small-scale communities such as the extended family, the village or the tribe.

48. It is well known that crowding increases stress and aggression. The degree of crowding that exists today and the isolation of man from nature are consequences of technological progress. All pre-industrial societies were predominantly rural. The Industrial Revolution vastly increased the size of cities and the proportion of the population that lives in them, and modern agricultural technology has made it possible for the Earth to support a far denser population than it ever did before. (Also, technology exacerbates the effects of crowding because it puts increased disruptive powers in people's hands. For example, a variety of noise-making devices: power mowers, radios, motorcycles, etc. If the use of these devices is unrestricted, people who want peace and quiet are frustrated by the noise. If their use is restricted, people who use the devices are frustrated by the regulations. But if these machines had never been invented there would have been no conflict and no frustration generated by them.)

49. For primitive societies the natural world (which usually changes only slowly) provided a stable framework and therefore a sense of security. In the modern world it is human society that dominates nature rather than the other way around, and modern society changes very rapidly owing to technological change. Thus there is no stable framework.

50. The conservatives are fools: They whine about the decay of traditional values, yet they enthusiastically support technological progress and economic growth. Apparently it never occurs to them that you can't make rapid, drastic changes in the technology and the economy of a society without causing rapid changes in all other aspects of the society as well, and that such rapid changes inevitably break down traditional values.

51. The breakdown of traditional values to some extent implies the breakdown of the bonds that hold together traditional small-scale social

groups. The disintegration of small-scale social groups is also promoted by the fact that modern conditions often require or tempt individuals to move to new locations, separating themselves from their communities. Beyond that, a technological society *has to* weaken family ties and local communities if it is to function efficiently. In modern society an individual's loyalty must be first to the system and only secondarily to a small-scale community, because if the internal loyalties of small-scale communities were stronger than loyalty to the system, such communities would pursue their own advantage at the expense of the system.

52. Suppose that a public official or a corporation executive appoints his cousin, his friend or his coreligionist to a position rather than appointing the person best qualified for the job. He has permitted personal loyalty to supersede his loyalty to the system, and that is "nepotism" or "discrimination," both of which are terrible sins in modern society. Would-be industrial societies that have done a poor job of subordinating personal or local loyalties to loyalty to the system are usually very inefficient. (Look at Latin America.) Thus an advanced industrial society can tolerate only those small-scale communities that are emasculated, tamed and made into tools of the system.[9]

53. Crowding, rapid change and the breakdown of communities have been widely recognized as sources of social problems. But we do not believe they are enough to account for the extent of the problems that are seen today.

54. A few pre-industrial cities were very large and crowded, yet their inhabitants do not seem to have suffered from psychological problems to the same extent as modern man. In America today there still are uncrowded rural areas, and we find there the same problems as in urban areas, though the problems tend to be less acute in the rural areas.[10] Thus crowding does not seem to be the decisive factor.

55. On the growing edge of the American frontier during the 19th century, the mobility of the population probably broke down extended families and small-scale social groups to at least the same extent as these are broken down today. In fact, many nuclear families lived by choice in such isolation, having no neighbors within several miles, that they belonged to no community at all,[11] yet they do not seem to have developed problems as a result.

56. Furthermore, change in American frontier society was very rapid and deep. A man might be born and raised in a log cabin, outside

the reach of law and order and fed largely on wild meat; and by the time he arrived at old age he might be working at a regular job and living in an ordered community with effective law enforcement. This was a deeper change than that which typically occurs in the life of a modern individual, yet it does not seem to have led to psychological problems. In fact, 19th-century American society had an optimistic and self-confident tone, quite unlike that of today's society.[12]

57. The difference, we argue, is that modern man has the sense (largely justified) that change is *imposed* on him, whereas the 19th-century frontiersman had the sense (also largely justified) that he created change himself, by his own choice. Thus a pioneer settled on a piece of land of his own choosing and made it into a farm through his own effort. In those days an entire county might have only a couple of hundred inhabitants, and was a far more isolated and autonomous entity than a modern county is. Hence the pioneer farmer participated as a member of a relatively small group in the creation of a new, ordered community. One may well question whether the creation of this community was an improvement, but at any rate it satisfied the pioneer's need for the power process.

58. It would be possible to give other examples of societies in which there has been rapid change and/or lack of close community ties without the kind of massive behavioral aberration that is seen in today's industrial society. We contend that the most important cause of social and psychological problems in modern society is the fact that people have insufficient opportunity to go through the power process in a normal way. We don't mean to say that modern society is the only one in which the power process has been disrupted. Probably most if not all civilized societies have interfered with the power process to a greater or lesser extent. But in modern industrial society the problem has become particularly acute. Leftism, at least in its recent (mid- to late-20th century) form, is in part a symptom of deprivation with respect to the power process.

Disruption of the Power Process in Modern Society

59. We divide human drives into three groups: (1) those drives that can be satisfied with minimal effort; (2) those that can be satisfied but only at the cost of serious effort; (3) those that cannot be adequately satisfied no matter how much effort one makes. The power process is the process

of satisfying the drives of the second group. The more drives there are in the third group, the more there is frustration, anger, eventually defeatism, depression, etc.

60. In modern industrial society natural human drives tend to be pushed into the first and third groups, and the second group tends to consist increasingly of artificially created drives.

61. In primitive societies, physical necessities generally fall into group 2: They can be obtained, but only at the cost of serious effort. But modern society tends to guarantee the physical necessities to everyone[13] in exchange for only minimal effort, hence physical needs are pushed into group 1. (There may be disagreement about whether the effort needed to hold a job is "minimal"; but usually, in lower- to middle-level jobs, whatever effort is required is merely that of *obedience*. You sit or stand where you are told to sit or stand and do what you are told to do in the way you are told to do it. Seldom do you have to exert yourself seriously, and in any case you have hardly any autonomy in work, so that the need for the power process is not well served.)

62. Social needs, such as sex, love and status, often remain in group 2 in modern society, depending on the situation of the individual.[14] But, except for people who have a particularly strong drive for status, the effort required to fulfill the social drives is insufficient to satisfy adequately the need for the power process.

63. So certain artificial needs have been created that fall into group 2, hence serve the need for the power process. Advertising and marketing techniques have been developed that make many people feel they need things that their grandparents never desired or even dreamed of. It requires serious effort to earn enough money to satisfy these artificial needs, hence they fall into group 2. (But see paragraphs 80–82.) Modern man must satisfy his need for the power process largely through pursuit of the artificial needs created by the advertising and marketing industry,[15] and through surrogate activities.

64. It seems that for many people, maybe the majority, these artificial forms of the power process are insufficient. A theme that appears repeatedly in the writings of the social critics of the second half of the 20th century is the sense of purposelessness that afflicts many people in modern society. (This purposelessness is often called by other names, such as "anomie" or "middle-class vacuity.") We suggest that the so-called "identity crisis" is actually a search for a sense of purpose, often for commitment

to a suitable surrogate activity. It may be that existentialism is in large part a response to the purposelessness of modern life.[16] Very widespread in modern society is the search for "fulfillment." But we think that for the majority of people an activity whose main goal is fulfillment (that is, a surrogate activity) does not bring completely satisfactory fulfillment. In other words, it does not fully satisfy the need for the power process. (See paragraph 41.) That need can be fully satisfied only through activities that have some external goal, such as physical necessities, sex, love, status, revenge, etc.

65. Moreover, where goals are pursued through earning money, climbing the status ladder or functioning as part of the system in some other way, most people are not in a position to pursue their goals *autonomously*. Most workers are someone else's employee and, as we pointed out in paragraph 61, must spend their days doing what they are told to do in the way they are told to do it. Even most people who are in business for themselves have only limited autonomy. It is a chronic complaint of small-business persons and entrepreneurs that their hands are tied by excessive government regulation. Some of these regulations are doubtless unnecessary, but for the most part government regulations are essential and inevitable parts of our extremely complex society. A large portion of small business today operates on the franchise system. It was reported in the *Wall Street Journal* a few years ago that many of the franchise-granting companies require applicants for franchises to take a personality test that is designed to *exclude* those who have creativity and initiative, because such persons are not sufficiently docile to go along obediently with the franchise system.[17] This excludes from small business many of the people who most need autonomy.

66. Today people live more by virtue of what the system does *for* them or *to* them than by virtue of what they do for themselves. And what they do for themselves is done more and more along channels laid down by the system. Opportunities tend to be those that the system provides, the opportunities must be exploited in accord with rules and regulations,[18] and techniques prescribed by experts must be followed if there is to be a chance of success.

67. Thus the power process is disrupted in our society through a deficiency of real goals and a deficiency of autonomy in the pursuit of goals. But it is also disrupted because of those human drives that fall into group 3: the drives that one cannot adequately satisfy no matter how

much effort one makes. One of these drives is the need for security. Our lives depend on decisions made by other people, we have no control over these decisions and usually we do not even know the people who make them. ("We live in a world in which relatively few people—maybe 500 or 1,000—make the important decisions."—Philip B. Heymann of Harvard Law School[19]). Our lives depend on whether safety standards at a nuclear power-plant are properly maintained; on how much pesticide is allowed to get into our food or how much pollution into our air; on how skillful (or incompetent) our doctor is; whether we lose or get a job may depend on decisions made by government economists or corporation executives; and so forth. Most individuals are not in a position to secure themselves against these threats to more than a very limited extent. The individual's search for security is therefore frustrated, which leads to a sense of powerlessness.

68. It may be objected that primitive man is physically less secure than modern man, as is shown by his shorter life-expectancy; hence modern man suffers from less, not more than the amount of insecurity that is normal for human beings. But psychological security does not closely correspond with physical security. What makes us *feel* secure is not so much objective security as a sense of confidence in our ability to take care of ourselves. Primitive man, threatened by a fierce animal or by hunger, can fight in self-defense or travel in search of food. He has no certainty of success in these efforts, but he is by no means helpless against the things that threaten him. The modern individual on the other hand is threatened by many things against which he is helpless: nuclear accidents, carcinogens in food, environmental pollution, war, increasing taxes, invasion of his privacy by large organizations, nationwide social or economic phenomena that may disrupt his way of life.

69. It is true that primitive man is powerless against some of the things that threaten him; disease for example. But he can accept the risk of disease stoically. It is part of the nature of things, it is no one's fault, unless it is the fault of some imaginary, impersonal demon.[20] But threats to the modern individual tend to be *man-made*. They are not the results of chance but are *imposed* on him by other persons whose decisions he, as an individual, is unable to influence. Consequently he feels frustrated, humiliated and angry.

70. Thus primitive man for the most part has his security in his own hands (either as an individual or as a member of a *small* group), whereas the security of modern man is in the hands of persons or organizations

that are too remote or too large for him to be able personally to influence them. So modern man's drive for security tends to fall into groups 1 and 3; in some areas (food, shelter, etc.) his security is assured at the cost of only trivial effort, whereas in other areas he *cannot* attain security. (The foregoing greatly simplifies the real situation, but it does indicate in a rough, general way how the condition of modern man differs from that of primitive man.)

71. People have many transitory drives or impulses that are necessarily frustrated in modern life, hence fall into group 3. One may become angry, but modern society cannot permit fighting. In many situations it does not even permit verbal aggression. When going somewhere one may be in a hurry, or one may be in a mood to travel slowly, but one generally has no choice but to move with the flow of traffic and obey the traffic signals. One may want to do one's work in a different way, but usually one can work only according to the rules laid down by one's employer. In many other ways as well, modern man is strapped down by a network of rules and regulations (explicit or implicit) that frustrate many of his impulses and thus interfere with the power process. Most of these regulations cannot be dispensed with, because they are necessary for the functioning of industrial society.

72. Modern society is in certain respects extremely permissive. In matters that are irrelevant to the functioning of the system we can generally do what we please. We can believe in any religion we like (as long as it does not encourage behavior that is dangerous to the system). We can go to bed with anyone we like (as long as we practice "safe sex"). We can do anything we like as long as it is *unimportant*. But in all *important* matters the system tends increasingly to regulate our behavior.

73. Behavior is regulated not only through explicit rules and not only by the government. Control is often exercised through indirect coercion or through psychological pressure or manipulation, and by organizations other than the government, or by the system as a whole. Most large organizations use some form of propaganda[21] to manipulate public attitudes or behavior. Propaganda is not limited to "commercials" and advertisements, and sometimes it is not even consciously intended as propaganda by the people who make it. For instance, the content of entertainment programming is a powerful form of propaganda. An example of indirect coercion: There is no law that says we have to go to work every day and follow our employer's orders. Legally there is nothing to prevent us from going to live in the wild like primitive people or from going into business for ourselves.

But in practice there is very little wild country left, and there is room in the economy for only a limited number of small-business owners. Hence most of us can survive only as someone else's employee.

74. We suggest that modern man's obsession with longevity, and with maintaining physical vigor and sexual attractiveness to an advanced age, is a symptom of unfulfillment resulting from deprivation with respect to the power process. The "mid-life crisis" also is such a symptom. So is the lack of interest in having children that is fairly common in modern society but almost unheard-of in primitive societies.

75. In primitive societies life is a succession of stages. The needs and purposes of one stage having been fulfilled, there is no particular reluctance about passing on to the next stage. A young man goes through the power process by becoming a hunter, hunting not for sport or for fulfillment but to get meat that is necessary for food. (In young women the process is more complex, with greater emphasis on social power; we won't discuss that here.) This phase having been successfully passed through, the young man has no reluctance about settling down to the responsibilities of raising a family. (In contrast, some modern people indefinitely postpone having children because they are too busy seeking some kind of "fulfillment." We suggest that the fulfillment they need is adequate experience of the power process—with real goals instead of the artificial goals of surrogate activities.) Again, having successfully raised his children, going through the power process by providing them with the physical necessities, the primitive man feels that his work is done and he is prepared to accept old age[22] (if he survives that long) and death. Many modern people, on the other hand, are disturbed by the prospect of physical deterioration and death, as is shown by the amount of effort they expend in trying to maintain their physical condition, appearance and health. We argue that this is due to unfulfillment resulting from the fact that they have never put their physical powers to any practical use, have never gone through the power process using their bodies in a serious way. It is not the primitive man, who has used his body daily for practical purposes, who fears the deterioration of age, but the modern man, who has never had a practical use for his body beyond walking from his car to his house. It is the man whose need for the power process has been satisfied during his life who is best prepared to accept the end of that life.

76. In response to the arguments of this section someone will say, "Society must find a way to give people the opportunity to go through

the power process." This won't work for those who need autonomy in the power process. For such people the value of the opportunity is destroyed by the very fact that society gives it to them. What they need is to find or make their own opportunities. As long as the system *gives* them their opportunities it still has them on a leash. To attain autonomy they must get off that leash.

How Some People Adjust

77. Not everyone in industrial-technological society suffers from psychological problems. Some people even profess to be quite satisfied with society as it is. We now discuss some of the reasons why people differ so greatly in their response to modern society.

78. First, there doubtless are innate differences in the strength of the drive for power. Individuals with a weak drive for power may have relatively little need to go through the power process, or at least relatively little need for autonomy in the power process. These are docile types who would have been happy as plantation darkies in the Old South. (We don't mean to sneer at the "plantation darkies" of the Old South. To their credit, most of the slaves were *not* content with their servitude. We do sneer at people who *are* content with servitude.)

79. Some people may have some exceptional drive, in pursuing which they satisfy their need for the power process. For example, those who have an unusually strong drive for social status may spend their whole lives climbing the status ladder without ever getting bored with that game.

80. People vary in their susceptibility to advertising and marketing techniques. Some people are so susceptible that, even if they make a great deal of money, they cannot satisfy their constant craving for the shiny new toys that the marketing industry dangles before their eyes. So they always feel hard-pressed financially even if their income is large, and their cravings are frustrated.

81. Some people have low susceptibility to advertising and marketing techniques. These are the people who aren't interested in money. Material acquisition does not serve their need for the power process.

82. People who have medium susceptibility to advertising and marketing techniques are able to earn enough money to satisfy their craving for goods and services, but only at the cost of serious effort (putting

in overtime, taking a second job, earning promotions, etc.). Thus material acquisition serves their need for the power process. But it does not necessarily follow that their need is fully satisfied. They may have insufficient autonomy in the power process (their work may consist in following orders) and some of their drives may be frustrated (e.g., security, aggression). (We are guilty of oversimplification in paragraphs 80–82 because we have assumed that the desire for material acquisition is entirely a creation of the advertising and marketing industry. Of course, it's not that simple.)

83. Some people partly satisfy their need for power by identifying themselves with a powerful organization or a mass movement. An individual lacking goals or power joins a movement or an organization, adopts its goals as his own, then works toward those goals. When some of the goals are attained, the individual, even though his personal efforts have played only an insignificant part in the attainment of the goals, feels (through his identification with the movement or organization) as if he had gone through the power process. This phenomenon was exploited by the Fascists, Nazis and Communists. Our society uses it too, though less crudely. Example: Manuel Noriega was an irritant to the U.S. (goal: punish Noriega). The U.S. invaded Panama (effort) and punished Noriega (attainment of goal). The U.S. went through the power process and many Americans, because of their identification with the U.S., experienced the power process vicariously. Hence the widespread public approval of the Panama invasion; it gave people a sense of power.[23] We see the same phenomenon in armies, corporations, political parties, humanitarian organizations, religious or ideological movements. In particular, leftist movements tend to attract people who are seeking to satisfy their need for power. But for most people, identification with a large organization or a mass movement does not fully satisfy the need for power.

84. Another way in which people satisfy their need for the power process is through surrogate activities. As we explained in paragraphs 38–40, a surrogate activity is an activity that is directed toward an artificial goal that the individual pursues for the sake of the "fulfillment" that he gets from pursuing the goal, not because he needs to attain the goal itself. For instance, there is no practical motive for building enormous muscles, hitting a little white ball into a hole or acquiring a complete series of postage stamps. Yet many people in our society devote themselves with passion to bodybuilding, golf or stamp-collecting. Some people are more "other-directed" than others, and therefore will more readily attach

importance to a surrogate activity simply because the people around them treat it as important or because society tells them it is important. That is why some people get very serious about essentially trivial activities such as sports, or bridge, or chess, or arcane scholarly pursuits, whereas others who are more clear-sighted never see these things as anything but the surrogate activities that they are, and consequently never attach enough importance to them to satisfy their need for the power process in that way. It only remains to point out that in many cases a person's way of earning a living is also a surrogate activity. Not a *pure* surrogate activity, since part of the motive for the activity is to gain the physical necessities and (for some people) social status and the luxuries that advertising makes them want. But many people put into their work far more effort than is necessary to earn whatever money and status they require, and this extra effort constitutes a surrogate activity. This extra effort, together with the emotional investment that accompanies it, is one of the most potent forces acting toward the continual development and perfecting of the system, with negative consequences for individual freedom. (See paragraph 131.) Especially, for the most creative scientists and engineers, work tends to be largely a surrogate activity. This point is so important that it deserves a separate discussion, which we shall give in a moment (paragraphs 87–92).

85. In this section we have explained how many people in modern society do satisfy their need for the power process to a greater or lesser extent. But we think that for the majority of people the need for the power process is not fully satisfied. In the first place, those who have an insatiable drive for status, or who get firmly "hooked" on a surrogate activity, or who identify strongly enough with a movement or an organization to satisfy their need for power in that way, are exceptional personalities. Others are not fully satisfied with surrogate activities or by identification with an organization. (See paragraphs 41, 64.) In the second place, too much control is imposed by the system through explicit regulation or through socialization, which results in a deficiency of autonomy, and in frustration due to the impossibility of attaining certain goals and the necessity of restraining too many impulses.

86. But even if most people in industrial-technological society were well satisfied, we (FC) would still be opposed to that form of society, because (among other reasons) we consider it demeaning to fulfill one's need for the power process through surrogate activities or through identification with an organization, rather than through pursuit of real goals.

The Motives of Scientists

87.   Science and technology provide the most important examples of surrogate activities. Some scientists claim that they are motivated by "curiosity" or by a desire to "benefit humanity." But it is easy to see that neither of these can be the principal motive of most scientists. As for "curiosity," that notion is simply absurd. Most scientists work on highly specialized problems that are not the object of any normal curiosity. For example, is an astronomer, a mathematician or an entomologist curious about the properties of isopropyltrimethylmethane? Of course not. Only a chemist is curious about such a thing, and he is curious about it only because chemistry is his surrogate activity. Is the chemist curious about the appropriate classification of a new species of beetle? No. That question is of interest only to the entomologist, and he is interested in it only because entomology is his surrogate activity. If the chemist and the entomologist had to exert themselves seriously to obtain the physical necessities, and if that effort exercised their abilities in an interesting way but in some nonscientific pursuit, then they wouldn't give a damn about isopropyltrimethylmethane or the classification of beetles. Suppose that lack of funds for postgraduate education had led the chemist to become an insurance broker instead of a chemist. In that case he would have been very interested in insurance matters but would have cared nothing about isopropyltrimethylmethane. In any case it is not normal to put into the satisfaction of mere curiosity the amount of time and effort that scientists put into their work. The "curiosity" explanation of the scientists' motive just doesn't stand up.

88.   The "benefit of humanity" explanation doesn't work any better. Some scientific work has no conceivable relation to the welfare of the human race—most of archaeology or comparative linguistics, for example. Some other areas of science present obviously dangerous possibilities. Yet scientists in these areas are just as enthusiastic about their work as those who develop vaccines or study air pollution. Consider the case of Dr. Edward Teller, who had an obvious emotional involvement in promoting nuclear power-plants. Did this involvement stem from a desire to benefit humanity? If so, then why didn't Dr. Teller get emotional about other "humanitarian" causes? If he was such a humanitarian then why did he help to develop the hydrogen bomb? As with many other scientific achievements, it is very

much open to question whether nuclear power-plants actually do benefit humanity. Does the cheap electricity outweigh the accumulating waste and the risk of accidents? Dr. Teller saw only one side of the question. Clearly his emotional involvement with nuclear power arose not from a desire to "benefit humanity" but from the personal fulfillment he got from his work and from seeing it put to practical use.

89. The same is true of scientists generally. With possible rare exceptions, their motive is neither curiosity nor a desire to benefit humanity but the need to go through the power process: to have a goal (a scientific problem to solve), to make an effort (research) and to attain the goal (solution of the problem). Science is a surrogate activity because scientists work mainly for the fulfillment they get out of the work itself.

90. Of course, it's not that simple. Other motives do play a role for many scientists. Money and status, for example. Some scientists may be persons of the type who have an insatiable drive for status (see paragraph 79) and this may provide much of the motivation for their work. No doubt the majority of scientists, like the majority of the general population, are more or less susceptible to advertising and marketing techniques and need money to satisfy their craving for goods and services. Thus science is not a *pure* surrogate activity. But it is in large part a surrogate activity.

91. Also, science and technology constitute a powerful mass movement, and many scientists gratify their need for power through identification with this mass movement. (See paragraph 83.)

92. Thus science marches on blindly, without regard to the real welfare of the human race or to any other standard, obedient only to the psychological needs of the scientists and of the government officials and corporation executives who provide the funds for research.[24]

The Nature of Freedom

93. We are going to argue that industrial-technological society cannot be reformed in such a way as to prevent it from progressively narrowing the sphere of human freedom. But because "freedom" is a word that can be interpreted in many ways, we must first make clear what kind of freedom we are concerned with.

94. By "freedom" we mean the opportunity to go through the power process—with real goals, not the artificial goals of surrogate activities—and

without interference, manipulation or supervision from anyone, especially from any large organization. Freedom means being in control (either as an individual or as a member of a *small* group) of the life-and-death issues of one's existence: food, clothing, shelter and defense against whatever threats there may be in one's environment. Freedom means having power; not the power to control other people but the power to control the circumstances of one's own life.[25] One does not have freedom if anyone else (especially a large organization) has power over one, no matter how benevolently, tolerantly and permissively that power may be exercised. It is important not to confuse freedom with mere permissiveness. (See paragraph 72.)

95.   It is said that we live in a free society because we have a certain number of constitutionally guaranteed rights. But these are not as important as they seem. The degree of personal freedom that exists in a society is determined more by the economic and technological structure of the society than by its laws or its form of government.[26] Most of the Indian nations of New England were monarchies,[27] and many of the cities of the Italian Renaissance were controlled by dictators. But in reading about these societies one gets the impression that they allowed far more personal freedom than our society does. In part this was because they lacked efficient mechanisms for enforcing the ruler's will: There were no modern, well-organized police forces, no rapid long-distance communications, no surveillance cameras, no dossiers of information about the lives of average citizens. Hence it was relatively easy to evade control.

96.   As for our constitutional rights, consider for example that of freedom of the press. We certainly don't mean to knock that right; it is a very important tool for limiting concentration of political power and for keeping those who do have political power in line by publicly exposing any misbehavior on their part. But freedom of the press is of very little use to the average citizen as an individual. The mass media are mostly under the control of large organizations that are integrated into the system. Anyone who has a little money can have something printed, or can distribute it on the Internet or in some such way, but what he has to say will be swamped by the vast volume of material put out by the media, hence will have no practical effect. To make an impression on society with words is therefore almost impossible for most individuals and small groups. Take us for example. If we had never done anything violent and had submitted the present writings to a publisher, they probably would not have been

accepted. If they had been accepted and published, they probably would not have attracted many readers, because it's more fun to watch the entertainment put out by the media than to read a sober essay. Even if these writings had had many readers, most of those readers would soon have forgotten what they had read as their minds were flooded by the mass of material to which the media expose them. In order to get our message before the public with some chance of making a lasting impression, we've had to kill people.

97. Constitutional rights are useful up to a point, but they do not serve to guarantee much more than what might be called the bourgeois conception of freedom. According to the bourgeois conception, a "free" man is essentially an element of a social machine and has only a certain set of prescribed and delimited freedoms; freedoms that are designed to serve the needs of the social machine more than those of the individual. Thus the bourgeois's "free" man has economic freedom because that promotes growth and progress; he has freedom of the press because public criticism restrains misbehavior by political leaders; he has a right to a fair trial because imprisonment at the whim of the powerful would be bad for the system. This was clearly the attitude of Simón Bolívar. To him, people deserved liberty only if they used it to promote progress (progress as conceived by the bourgeois).[28] Other bourgeois thinkers have taken a similar view of freedom as a mere means to collective ends. Chester C. Tan explains the philosophy of the Kuomintang leader Hu Han-Min: "An individual is granted rights because he is a member of society and his community life requires such rights. By community Hu meant the whole society or the nation."[29] And Tan states that according to Carsun Chang (Chang Chun-Mai, head of the State Socialist Party in China) freedom had to be used in the interest of the state and of the people as a whole.[30] But what kind of freedom does one have if one can use it only as someone else prescribes? Our conception of freedom is not that of Bolívar, Hu, Chang or other bourgeois theorists. The trouble with such theorists is that they have made the development and application of social theories their surrogate activity. Consequently the theories are designed to serve the needs of the theorists more than the needs of any people who may be unlucky enough to live in a society on which the theories are imposed.

98. One more point to be made in this section: It should not be assumed that a person has enough freedom just because he *says* he has enough. Freedom is restricted in part by psychological controls of which

people are unconscious, and moreover many people's ideas of what constitutes freedom are governed more by social convention than by their real needs. For example, it's likely that many leftists of the oversocialized type would say that most people, including themselves, are socialized too little rather than too much, yet the oversocialized leftist pays a heavy psychological price for his high level of socialization.

Some Principles of History

99. Think of history as the sum of two components: an erratic component that consists of unpredictable events that follow no discernible pattern, and a regular component that consists of long-term historical trends. Here we are concerned with the long-term trends.

100. *First Principle.* If a *small* change is made that affects a long-term historical trend, then the effect of that change will almost always be transitory—the trend will soon revert to its original state. (Example: A reform movement designed to clean up political corruption in a society rarely has more than a short-term effect; sooner or later the reformers relax and corruption creeps back in. The level of political corruption in a given society tends to remain constant, or to change only slowly with the evolution of the society. Normally, a political cleanup will be permanent only if accompanied by widespread social changes; a *small* change in the society won't be enough.) If a small change in a long-term historical trend appears to be permanent, it is only because the change acts in the direction in which the trend is already moving, so that the trend is not altered but only pushed a step ahead.

101. The first principle is almost a tautology. If a trend were not stable with respect to small changes, it would wander at random rather than following a definite direction; in other words, it would not be a long-term trend at all.

102. *Second Principle.* If a change is made that is sufficiently large to alter permanently a long-term historical trend, then it will alter the society as a whole. In other words, a society is a system in which all parts are interrelated, and you can't permanently change any important part without changing all other parts as well.

103. *Third Principle.* If a change is made that is large enough to alter permanently a long-term trend, then the consequences for the society as a

whole cannot be predicted in advance. (Unless various other societies have passed through the same change and have all experienced the same consequences, in which case one can predict on empirical grounds that another society that passes through the same change will be likely to experience similar consequences.)

104. *Fourth Principle.* A new kind of society cannot be designed on paper. That is, you cannot plan out a new form of society in advance, then set it up and expect it to function as it was designed to do.

105. The third and fourth principles result from the complexity of human societies. A change in human behavior will affect the economy of a society and its physical environment; the economy will affect the environment and vice versa, and the changes in the economy and the environment will affect human behavior in complex, unpredictable ways; and so forth. The network of causes and effects is far too complex to be untangled and understood.

106. *Fifth Principle.* People do not consciously and rationally choose the form of their society. Societies develop through processes of social evolution that are not under rational human control.

107. The fifth principle is a consequence of the other four.

108. To illustrate: By the first principle, generally speaking an attempt at social reform either acts in the direction in which the society is developing anyway (so that it merely accelerates a change that would have occurred in any case) or else it has only a transitory effect, so that the society soon slips back into its old groove. To make a lasting change in the direction of development of any important aspect of a society, reform is insufficient and revolution is required. (A revolution does not necessarily involve an armed uprising or the overthrow of a government.) By the second principle, a revolution never changes only one aspect of a society, it changes the whole society; and by the third principle changes occur that were never expected or desired by the revolutionaries. By the fourth principle, when revolutionaries or utopians set up a new kind of society, it never works out as planned.

109. The American Revolution does not provide a counterexample. The American "Revolution" was not a revolution in our sense of the word, but a war of independence followed by a rather far-reaching political reform. The Founding Fathers did not change the direction of development of American society, nor did they aspire to do so. They only freed the development of American society from the retarding effect of British rule. Their

political reform did not change any basic trend, but only pushed American political culture along its natural direction of development. British society, of which American society was an offshoot, had been moving for a long time in the direction of representative democracy. And prior to the War of Independence the Americans were already practicing a significant degree of representative democracy in the colonial assemblies. The political system established by the Constitution was modeled on the British system and on the colonial assemblies. With major alterations, to be sure—there is no doubt that the Founding Fathers took a very important step. But it was a step along the road that the English-speaking world was already traveling. The proof is that Britain and all of its colonies that were populated predominantly by people of British descent ended up with systems of representative democracy essentially similar to that of the United States. If the Founding Fathers had lost their nerve and declined to sign the Declaration of Independence, our way of life today would not have been significantly different. Maybe we would have had somewhat closer ties to Britain, and would have had a Parliament and Prime Minister instead of a Congress and President. No big deal. Thus the American Revolution provides not a counterexample to our principles but a good illustration of them.

110. Still, one has to use common sense in applying the principles. They are expressed in imprecise language that allows latitude for interpretation, and exceptions to them can be found. So we present these principles not as inviolable laws but as rules of thumb, or guides to thinking, that may provide a partial antidote to naïve ideas about the future of society. The principles should be borne constantly in mind, and whenever one reaches a conclusion that conflicts with them one should carefully reexamine one's thinking and retain the conclusion only if one has good, solid reasons for doing so.

Industrial-Technological Society Cannot Be Reformed

111. The foregoing principles help to show how hopelessly difficult it would be to reform the industrial system in such a way as to prevent it from progressively narrowing our sphere of freedom. There has been a consistent tendency, going back at least to the Industrial Revolution, for technology to strengthen the system at a high cost in individual freedom and local autonomy. Hence any change designed to protect freedom from

technology would be contrary to a fundamental trend in the development of our society. Consequently, such a change either would be a transitory one— soon swamped by the tide of history—or, if large enough to be permanent, would alter the nature of our whole society. This by the first and second principles. Moreover, since society would be altered in a way that could not be predicted in advance (third principle) there would be great risk. Changes large enough to make a lasting difference in favor of freedom would not be initiated because it would be realized that they would gravely disrupt the system. So any attempts at reform would be too timid to be effective. Even if changes large enough to make a lasting difference were initiated, they would be retracted when their disruptive effects became apparent. Thus, permanent changes in favor of freedom could be brought about only by persons prepared to accept radical, dangerous and unpredictable alteration of the entire system. In other words, by revolutionaries, not reformers.

112.   People anxious to rescue freedom without sacrificing the supposed benefits of technology will suggest naïve schemes for some new form of society that would reconcile freedom with technology. Apart from the fact that people who make such suggestions seldom propose any practical means by which the new form of society could be set up in the first place, it follows from the fourth principle that even if the new form of society could once be established, it either would collapse or would give results very different from those expected.

113.   So even on very general grounds it seems highly improbable that any way of changing society could be found that would reconcile freedom with modern technology. In the next few sections we will give more specific reasons for concluding that freedom and technological progress are incompatible.

Restriction of Freedom is Unavoidable in Industrial Society

114.   As explained in paragraphs 65–67, 70–73, modern man is strapped down by a network of rules and regulations, and his fate depends on the actions of persons remote from him whose decisions he cannot influence. This is not accidental or a result of the arbitrariness of arrogant bureaucrats. It is necessary and inevitable in any technologically advanced society. The system *has to* regulate human behavior closely in order to function. At work, people have to do what they are told to do, when they are told

to do it and in the way they are told to do it, otherwise production would be thrown into chaos. Bureaucracies *have to* be run according to rigid rules. To allow any substantial personal discretion to lower-level bureaucrats would disrupt the system and lead to charges of unfairness due to differences in the way individual bureaucrats exercised their discretion. It is true that some restrictions on our freedom could be eliminated, but *generally speaking* the regulation of our lives by large organizations is necessary for the functioning of industrial-technological society. The result is a sense of powerlessness on the part of the average person. It may be, however, that formal regulations will tend increasingly to be replaced by psychological tools that make us want to do what the system requires of us. (Propaganda,[31] educational techniques, "mental health" programs, etc.)

115.   The system *has to* force people to behave in ways that are increasingly remote from the natural pattern of human behavior. For example, the system needs scientists, mathematicians and engineers. It can't function without them. So heavy pressure is put on children to excel in these fields. It isn't natural for an adolescent human being to spend the bulk of his time sitting at a desk absorbed in study.[32] A normal adolescent wants to spend his time in active contact with the real world. Among primitive peoples the things that children are trained to do tend to be in reasonable harmony with natural human impulses. Among the American Indians, for example, boys were trained in active outdoor pursuits—just the sort of things that boys like. But in our society children are pushed into studying technical subjects, which most do grudgingly.

116.   Because of the constant pressure that the system exerts to modify human behavior, there is a gradual increase in the number of people who cannot or will not adjust to society's requirements: welfare leeches, youth-gang members, cultists, anti-government rebels, radical environmentalist saboteurs, dropouts and resisters of various kinds.

117.   In any technologically advanced society the individual's fate *must* depend on decisions that he personally cannot influence to any great extent. A technological society cannot be broken down into small, autonomous communities, because production depends on the cooperation of very large numbers of people and machines. Such a society *must* be highly organized and decisions *have to* be made that affect very large numbers of people. When a decision affects, say, a million people, then each of the affected individuals has, on the average, only a one-millionth share in making the decision. What usually happens in practice is that decisions are

made by public officials or corporation executives, or by technical special-ists, but even when the public votes on a decision the number of voters ordinarily is too large for the vote of any one individual to be significant.[33] Thus most individuals are unable to influence measurably the major deci-sions that affect their lives. There is no conceivable way to remedy this in a technologically advanced society. The system tries to "solve" this problem by using propaganda to make people *want* the decisions that have been made for them, but even if this "solution" were completely successful in making people feel better, it would be demeaning.

118.   Conservatives and some others advocate more "local autonomy." Local communities once did have autonomy, but such autonomy becomes less and less possible as local communities become more and more enmeshed with and dependent on large-scale systems like public utilities, computer networks, highway systems, the mass communi-cations media and the modern health-care system. Also operating against autonomy is the fact that technology applied in one location often affects people at other locations far away. Thus pesticide or chemical use near a creek may contaminate the water supply hundreds of miles downstream, and the greenhouse effect affects the whole world.

119.   The system does not and cannot exist to satisfy human needs. Instead, it is human behavior that has to be modified to fit the needs of the system. This has nothing to do with the political or social ideology that may pretend to guide the technological system. It is not the fault of capitalism and it is not the fault of socialism. It is the fault of technology, because the system is guided not by ideology but by technical necessity.[34] Of course, the system does satisfy many human needs, but generally speaking it does this only to the extent that it is to the advantage of the system to do it. It is the needs of the system that are paramount, not those of the human being. For example, the system provides people with food because the system couldn't function if everyone starved; it attends to people's psychological needs whenever it can *conveniently* do so, because it couldn't function if too many people became depressed or rebellious. But the system, for good, solid, practical reasons, must exert constant pressure on people to mold their behavior to the needs of the system. Too much waste accumulating? The government, the media, the educational system, environmentalists, everyone inundates us with a mass of propaganda about recycling. Need more technical personnel? A chorus of voices exhorts kids to study science. No one stops to ask whether it is inhumane to force adolescents to spend the bulk of their time studying

subjects that most of them hate. When skilled workers are put out of a job by technical advances and have to undergo "retraining," no one asks whether it is humiliating for them to be pushed around in this way. It is simply taken for granted that everyone must bow to technical necessity. And for good reason: If human needs were put before technical necessity there would be economic problems, unemployment, shortages or worse. The concept of "mental health" in our society is defined largely by the extent to which an individual behaves in accord with the needs of the system and does so without showing signs of stress.

120. Efforts to make room for a sense of purpose and for autonomy within the system are no better than a joke. For example, one company, instead of having each of its employees assemble only one section of a telephone book, had each assemble a whole telephone book, and this was supposed to give them a sense of purpose and achievement. Some companies have tried to give their employees more autonomy in their work, but for practical reasons this usually can be done only to a very limited extent, and in any case employees are never given autonomy as to ultimate goals—their "autonomous" efforts can never be directed toward goals that they select personally, but only toward their employer's goals, such as the survival and growth of the company. Any company would soon go out of business if it permitted its employees to act otherwise. Similarly, in any enterprise within a socialist system, workers must direct their efforts toward the goals of the enterprise, otherwise the enterprise will not serve its purpose as part of the system. Once again, for purely technical reasons it is not possible for most individuals or small groups to have much autonomy in industrial society. Even the small-business owner commonly has only limited autonomy. Apart from the necessity of government regulation, he is restricted by the fact that he must fit into the economic system and conform to its requirements. For instance, when someone develops a new technology, the small-business person often has to use that technology whether he wants to or not, in order to remain competitive.

The "Bad" Parts of Technology Cannot Be Separated from the "Good" Parts

121. A further reason why industrial society cannot be reformed in favor of freedom is that modern technology is a unified system in which

all parts are dependent on one another. You can't get rid of the "bad" parts of technology and retain only the "good" parts. Take modern medicine, for example. Progress in medical science depends on progress in chemistry, physics, biology, computer science and other fields. Advanced medical treatments require expensive, high-tech equipment that can be made available only by a technologically progressive, economically rich society. Clearly you can't have much progress in medicine without the whole technological system and everything that goes with it.

122. Even if medical progress could be maintained without the rest of the technological system, it would by itself bring certain evils. Suppose for example that a cure for diabetes is discovered. People with a genetic tendency to diabetes will then be able to survive and reproduce as well as anyone else. Natural selection against genes for diabetes will cease and such genes will spread throughout the population. (This may be occurring to some extent already, since diabetes, while not curable, can be controlled through the use of insulin.) The same thing will happen with many other diseases susceptibility to which is affected by genetic factors (e.g., childhood cancer), resulting in massive genetic degradation of the population.[35] The only solution will be some sort of eugenics program or extensive genetic engineering of human beings, so that man in the future will no longer be a creation of nature, or of chance, or of God (depending on your religious or philosophical opinions), but a manufactured product.

123. If you think that big government interferes in your life too much *now*, just wait till the government starts regulating the genetic constitution of your children. Such regulation will inevitably follow the introduction of genetic engineering of human beings, because the consequences of unregulated genetic engineering would be disastrous.[36]

124. The usual response to such concerns is to talk about "medical ethics." But a code of ethics would not serve to protect freedom in the face of medical progress; it would only make matters worse. A code of ethics applicable to genetic engineering would be in effect a means of regulating the genetic constitution of human beings. Somebody (probably the upper middle class, mostly) would decide that such and such applications of genetic engineering were "ethical" and others were not, so that in effect they would be imposing their own values on the genetic constitution of the population at large. Even if a code of ethics were chosen on a completely democratic basis, the majority would be imposing their own values on any minorities who might have a different idea of what constituted an "ethical"

use of genetic engineering. The only code of ethics that would truly protect freedom would be one that prohibited *any* genetic engineering of human beings, and you can be sure that no such code will ever be applied in a technological society. No code that reduced genetic engineering to a minor role could stand up for long, because the temptation presented by the immense power of biotechnology would be irresistible, especially since to the majority of people many of its applications will seem obviously and unequivocally good (eliminating physical and mental diseases, giving people the abilities they need to get along in today's world). Inevitably, genetic engineering will be used extensively, but only in ways consistent with the needs of the industrial-technological system.

Technology is a More Powerful Social Force than the Aspiration for Freedom

125. It is not possible to make a *lasting* compromise between technology and freedom, because technology is by far the more powerful social force and continually encroaches on freedom through *repeated* compromises. Imagine the case of two neighbors, each of whom at the outset owns the same amount of land, but one of whom is more powerful than the other. The powerful one demands a piece of the other's land. The weak one refuses. The powerful one says, "Okay, let's compromise. Give me half of what I asked." The weak one has little choice but to give in. Some time later the powerful neighbor demands another piece of land, again there is a compromise, and so forth. By forcing a long series of compromises on the weaker man, the powerful one eventually gets all of his land. So it goes in the conflict between technology and freedom.

126. Let us explain why technology is a more powerful social force than the aspiration for freedom.

127. A technological advance that appears not to threaten freedom often turns out to threaten it very seriously later on. For example, consider motorized transport. A walking man formerly could go where he pleased, go at his own pace without observing any traffic regulations, and was independent of technological support systems. When motor vehicles were introduced they appeared to increase man's freedom. They took no freedom away from the walking man, no one had to have an automobile if he didn't want one, and anyone who did choose to buy an automobile

could travel much faster and farther than a walking man. But the introduction of motorized transport soon changed society in such a way as to
restrict greatly man's freedom of locomotion. When automobiles became
numerous, it was found necessary to regulate their use extensively. In a car,
especially in densely populated areas, one cannot just go where one likes
at one's own pace; one's movement is governed by the flow of traffic and
by various traffic laws. One is tied down by various obligations: license
requirements, driver test, renewing registration, insurance, maintenance
required for safety, monthly payments on purchase price. Moreover, the
use of motorized transport is no longer optional. Since the introduction
of motorized transport the arrangement of our cities has changed in such
a way that the majority of people no longer live within walking distance
of their place of employment, shopping areas and recreational opportunities, so that they *have to* depend on the automobile for transportation.
Or else they must use public transportation, in which case they have even
less control over their own movement than when driving a car. Even the
walker's freedom is now greatly restricted. In the city he continually has to
stop to wait for traffic lights that are designed mainly to serve auto traffic.
In the country, motor traffic makes it dangerous and unpleasant to walk
along the highway. (Note this important point that we have just illustrated
with the case of motorized transport: When a new item of technology is
introduced as an option that an individual can accept or not as he chooses,
it does not necessarily *remain* optional. In many cases the new technology
changes society in such a way that people eventually find themselves *forced*
to use it.)

128.   While technological progress *as a whole* continually narrows
our sphere of freedom, each new technical advance *considered by itself*
appears to be desirable. Electricity, indoor plumbing, rapid long-distance
communications... how could one argue against any of these things, or
against any other of the innumerable technical advances that have made
modern society? It would have been absurd to resist the introduction of
the telephone, for example. It offered many advantages and no disadvantages. Yet, as we explained in paragraphs 59–76, all these technical
advances taken together have created a world in which the average man's
fate is no longer in his own hands or in the hands of his neighbors and
friends, but in those of politicians, corporation executives and remote,
anonymous technicians and bureaucrats whom he as an individual has
no power to influence.[37] The same process will continue in the future.

Take genetic engineering, for example. Few people will resist the introduction of a genetic technique that eliminates a hereditary disease. It does no apparent harm and prevents much suffering. Yet a large number of genetic improvements taken together will make the human being into an engineered product rather than a free creation of chance (or of God, or whatever, depending on your religious beliefs).

129. Another reason why technology is such a powerful social force is that, within the context of a given society, technological progress marches in only one direction; it can never be reversed. Once a technical innovation has been introduced, people usually become dependent on it, so that they can never again do without it, unless it is replaced by some still more advanced innovation. Not only do people become dependent as individuals on a new item of technology, but, even more, the system as a whole becomes dependent on it. (Imagine what would happen to the system today if computers, for example, were eliminated.) Thus the system can move in only one direction, toward greater technologization. Technology repeatedly forces freedom to take a step back but technology can never take a step back—short of the overthrow of the whole technological system.

130. Technology advances with great rapidity and threatens freedom at many different points at the same time (crowding, rules and regulations, increasing dependence of individuals on large organizations, propaganda and other psychological techniques, genetic engineering, invasion of privacy through surveillance devices and computers, etc.). To hold back any *one* of the threats to freedom would require a long and difficult social struggle. Those who want to protect freedom are overwhelmed by the sheer number of new attacks and the rapidity with which they develop, hence they become apathetic and no longer resist. To fight each of the threats separately would be futile. Success can be hoped for only by fighting the technological system as a whole; but that is revolution, not reform.

131. Technicians (we use this term in its broad sense to describe all those who perform a specialized task that requires training) tend to be so involved in their work (their surrogate activity) that when a conflict arises between their technical work and freedom, they almost always decide in favor of their technical work. This is obvious in the case of scientists, but it also appears elsewhere: Educators, humanitarian groups, conservation organizations do not hesitate to use propaganda[38] or other psychological techniques to help them achieve their laudable ends. Corporations and government agencies, when they find it useful, do not hesitate to collect information

about individuals without regard to their privacy. Law-enforcement agencies are frequently inconvenienced by the constitutional rights of suspects and often of completely innocent persons, and they do whatever they can do legally (or sometimes illegally) to restrict or circumvent those rights. Most of these educators, government officials and law officers believe in freedom, privacy and constitutional rights, but when these conflict with their work, they usually feel that their work is more important.

132. It is well known that people generally work better and more persistently when striving for a reward than when attempting to avoid a punishment or negative outcome. Scientists and other technicians are motivated mainly by the rewards they get through their work. But those who oppose technological invasions of freedom are working to avoid a negative outcome, consequently there are few who work persistently and well at this discouraging task. If reformers ever achieved a signal victory that seemed to set up a solid barrier against further erosion of freedom through technical progress, most would tend to relax and turn their attention to more agreeable pursuits. But the scientists would remain busy in their laboratories, and technology as it progressed would find ways, in spite of any barriers, to exert more and more control over individuals and make them always more dependent on the system.

133. No social arrangements, whether laws, institutions, customs, or ethical codes, can provide permanent protection against technology. History shows that all social arrangements are transitory; they all change or break down eventually. But technological advances are permanent within the context of a given civilization. Suppose for example that it were possible to arrive at some social arrangement that would prevent genetic engineering from being applied to human beings, or prevent it from being applied in such a way as to threaten freedom and dignity. Still the technology would remain, waiting. Sooner or later the social arrangement would break down. Probably sooner, given the pace of change in our society. Then genetic engineering would begin to invade our sphere of freedom, and this invasion would be irreversible (short of a breakdown of technological civilization itself). Any illusions about achieving anything permanent through social arrangements should be dispelled by what is currently [as of 1995] happening with environmental legislation. A few years ago it seemed that there were secure legal barriers preventing at least *some* of the worst forms of environmental degradation. A change in the political wind, and those barriers begin to crumble.

134. For all of the foregoing reasons, technology is a more powerful social force than the aspiration for freedom. But this statement requires an important qualification. It appears that during the next several decades the industrial-technological system will be undergoing severe stresses due to economic and environmental problems, and especially due to problems of human behavior (alienation, rebellion, hostility, a variety of social and psychological difficulties). We hope that the stresses through which the system is likely to pass will cause it to break down, or at least will weaken it sufficiently so that a revolution against it becomes possible. If such a revolution occurs and is successful, then at that particular moment the aspiration for freedom will have proven more powerful than technology.

135. In paragraph 125 we used an analogy of a weak neighbor who is left destitute by a strong neighbor who takes all his land by forcing on him a series of compromises. But suppose now that the strong neighbor gets sick, so that he is unable to defend himself. The weak neighbor can force the strong one to give him his land back, or he can kill him. If he lets the strong man survive and only forces him to give the land back, he is a fool, because when the strong man gets well he will again take all the land for himself. The only sensible alternative for the weaker man is to kill the strong one while he has the chance. In the same way, while the industrial system is sick we must destroy it. If we compromise with it and let it recover from its sickness, it will eventually wipe out all of our freedom.

Simpler Social Problems Have Proved Intractable

136. If anyone still imagines that it would be possible to reform the system in such a way as to protect freedom from technology, let him consider how clumsily and for the most part unsuccessfully our society has dealt with other social problems that are far more simple and straightforward. Among other things, the system has failed to stop environmental degradation, political corruption, drug trafficking or domestic abuse.

137. Take our environmental problems, for example. Here the conflict of values is straightforward: economic expedience now versus saving some of our natural resources for our grandchildren.[39] But on this subject we get only a lot of blather and obfuscation from the people who have power, and nothing like a clear, consistent line of action, and we keep on piling up environmental problems that our grandchildren will

have to live with. Attempts to resolve the environmental issue consist of struggles and compromises between different factions, some of which are ascendant at one moment, others at another moment. The line of struggle changes with the shifting currents of public opinion. This is not a rational process, nor is it one that is likely to lead to a timely and successful solution to the problem. Major social problems, if they get "solved" at all, rarely or never are solved through any rational, comprehensive plan. They just work themselves out through a process in which various competing groups pursuing their own (usually short-term) self-interest[40] arrive (mainly by luck) at some more or less stable modus vivendi. In fact, the principles we formulated in paragraphs 100–06 make it seem doubtful that rational, long-term social planning can *ever* be successful.

138. Thus it is clear that the human race has at best a very limited capacity for solving even relatively straightforward social problems. How then is it going to solve the far more difficult and subtle problem of reconciling freedom with technology? Technology presents clear-cut material advantages, whereas freedom is an abstraction that means different things to different people, and its loss is easily obscured by propaganda and fancy talk.

139. And note this important difference: It is conceivable that our environmental problems (for example) may some day be settled through a rational, comprehensive plan, but if this happens it will be only because it is in the long-term interest of the system to solve these problems. But it is *not* in the interest of the system to preserve freedom or small-group autonomy. On the contrary, it is in the interest of the system to bring human behavior under control to the greatest possible extent.[41] Thus, while practical considerations may eventually force the system to take a rational, prudent approach to environmental problems, equally practical considerations will force the system to regulate human behavior ever more closely (preferably by indirect means that will disguise the encroachment on freedom). This isn't just our opinion. Eminent social scientists (e.g., James Q. Wilson) have stressed the importance of "socializing" people more effectively.

Revolution is Easier than Reform

140. We hope we have convinced the reader that the system cannot be reformed in such a way as to reconcile freedom with technology. The

only way out is to dispense with the industrial-technological system alto-gether. This implies revolution, not necessarily an armed uprising, but certainly a radical and fundamental change in the nature of society.

141. People tend to assume that because a revolution involves a much greater change than reform does, it is more difficult to bring about than reform is. Actually, under certain circumstances, revolution is much easier than reform. The reason is that a revolutionary movement can inspire an intensity of commitment that a reform movement cannot inspire. A reform movement merely offers to solve a particular social problem. A revolutionary movement offers to solve all problems at one stroke and create a whole new world; it provides the kind of ideal for which people will take great risks and make great sacrifices. For this reason it would be much easier to overthrow the whole technological system than to put effective, permanent restraints on the development or application of any one segment of technology, such as genetic engineering, for example. Not many people will devote them-selves with single-minded passion to imposing and maintaining restraints on genetic engineering, but under suitable conditions large numbers of people may devote themselves passionately to a revolution against the industri-al-technological system. As we noted in paragraph 132, reformers seeking to limit certain aspects of technology would be working to avoid a negative outcome. But revolutionaries work to gain a powerful reward—fulfillment of their revolutionary vision—and therefore work harder and more persistently than reformers do.

142. Reform is always restrained by the fear of painful consequences if changes go too far. But once a revolutionary fever has taken hold of a society, people are willing to undergo unlimited hardships for the sake of their revolution. This was clearly shown in the French and Russian Revolutions. It may be that in such cases only a minority of the population is really committed to the revolution, but this minority is sufficiently large and active so that it becomes the dominant force in society. We will have more to say about revolution in paragraphs 180–205.

Control of Human Behavior

143. Since the beginning of civilization, organized societies have had to put pressures on human beings for the sake of the functioning of the social organism. The kinds of pressures vary greatly from one society

to another. Some of the pressures are physical (poor diet, excessive labor, environmental pollution), some are psychological (noise, crowding, forcing human behavior into the mold that society requires). In the past, human nature has been approximately constant, or at any rate has varied only within certain bounds. Consequently, societies have been able to push people only up to certain limits. When the limit of human endurance has been passed, things start going wrong: rebellion, or crime, or corruption, or evasion of work, or depression and other mental problems, or an elevated death rate, or a declining birth rate or something else, so that either the society breaks down, or its functioning becomes too inefficient and it is (quickly or gradually, through conquest, attrition or evolution) replaced by some more efficient form of society.[42]

144. Thus human nature has in the past put certain limits on the development of societies. People could be pushed only so far and no farther. But today this may be changing, because modern technology is developing ways of modifying human beings.

145. Imagine a society that subjects people to conditions that make them terribly unhappy, then gives them drugs to take away their unhappiness. Science fiction? It is already happening to some extent in our own society. It is well known that the rate of clinical depression has been greatly increasing in recent decades. We believe that this is due to disruption of the power process, as explained in paragraphs 59–76. But even if we are wrong, the increasing rate of depression is certainly the result of *some* conditions that exist in today's society. Instead of removing the conditions that make people depressed, modern society gives them antidepressant drugs. In effect, antidepressants are a means of modifying an individual's internal state in such a way as to enable him to tolerate social conditions that he would otherwise find intolerable. (Yes, we know that depression is often of purely genetic origin. We are referring here to those cases in which environment plays the predominant role.)

146. Drugs that affect the mind are only one example of the methods of controlling human behavior that modern society is developing. Let us look at some of the other methods.

147. To start with, there are the techniques of surveillance. Hidden video cameras are now used in most stores and in many other places, computers are used to collect and process vast amounts of information about individuals. Information so obtained greatly increases the effectiveness of physical coercion (i.e., law enforcement).[43] Then there are

the methods of propaganda, for which the mass communications media provide effective vehicles. Efficient techniques have been developed for winning elections, selling products, influencing public opinion. The entertainment industry serves as an important psychological tool of the system, possibly even when it is dishing out large amounts of sex and violence. Entertainment provides modern man with an essential means of escape. While absorbed in television, videos, etc., he can forget stress, anxiety, frustration, dissatisfaction. Many primitive peoples, when they don't have any work to do, are quite content to sit for hours at a time doing nothing at all, because they are at peace with themselves and their world. But most modern people must be constantly occupied or entertained, otherwise they get "bored," i.e., they get fidgety, uneasy, irritable.[44]

148. Other techniques strike deeper than the foregoing. Education is no longer a simple affair of paddling a kid's behind when he doesn't know his lessons and patting him on the head when he does know them. It is becoming a scientific technique for controlling the child's development. Sylvan Learning Centers, for example, have had great success in motivating children to study, and psychological techniques are also used with more or less success in many conventional schools. "Parenting" techniques that are taught to parents are designed to make children accept the fundamental values of the system and behave in ways that the system finds desirable. "Mental health" programs, "intervention" techniques, psychotherapy and so forth are ostensibly designed to benefit individuals, but in practice they usually serve as methods for inducing individuals to think and behave as the system requires. (There is no contradiction here; an individual whose attitudes or behavior bring him into conflict with the system is up against a force that is too powerful for him to conquer or escape from, hence he is likely to suffer from stress, frustration, defeat. His path will be much easier if he thinks and behaves as the system requires. In that sense the system is acting for the benefit of the individual when it brainwashes him into conformity.) Child abuse in its gross and obvious forms is disapproved in most if not all cultures. Tormenting a child for a trivial reason or no reason at all is something that appalls almost everyone. But many psychologists interpret the concept of abuse much more broadly. Is spanking, when used as part of a rational and consistent system of discipline, a form of abuse? The question will ultimately be decided by whether or not spanking tends to produce behavior that makes a person fit in well with the existing system of society. In practice, the word "abuse" tends

to be interpreted to include any method of child-rearing that produces behavior inconvenient for the system. Thus, when they go beyond the prevention of obvious, senseless cruelty, programs for preventing "child abuse" are directed toward the control of human behavior on behalf of the system.

149. Presumably, research will continue to increase the effectiveness of psychological techniques for controlling human behavior. But we think it is unlikely that psychological techniques alone will be sufficient to adjust human beings to the kind of society that technology is creating. Biological methods probably will have to be used. We have already mentioned the use of drugs in this connection. Neurology may provide other avenues for modifying the human mind. Genetic engineering of human beings is already beginning to occur in the form of "gene therapy," and there is no reason to assume that such methods will not eventually be used to modify those aspects of the body that affect mental functioning.

150. As we mentioned in paragraph 134, industrial society seems likely to be entering a period of severe stress, due in part to problems of human behavior and in part to economic and environmental problems. And a considerable proportion of the system's economic and environmental problems result from the way human beings behave. Alienation, low self-esteem, depression, hostility, rebellion; children who won't study, youth gangs, illegal drug use, rape, child abuse, other crimes, unsafe sex, teen pregnancy, population growth, political corruption, race hatred, ethnic rivalry, bitter ideological conflict (e.g., pro-choice vs. pro-life), political extremism, terrorism, sabotage, anti-government groups, hate groups. All these threaten the very survival of the system. The system will therefore be *forced* to use every practical means of controlling human behavior.

151. The social disruption that we see today is certainly not the result of mere chance. It can only be a result of the conditions of life that the system imposes on people. (We have argued that the most important of these conditions is disruption of the power process.) If the system succeeds in imposing sufficient control over human behavior to ensure its own survival, a new watershed in human history will have been passed. Whereas formerly the limits of human endurance have imposed limits on the development of societies (as we explained in paragraphs 143, 144), industrial-technological society will be able to pass those limits by modifying human beings, whether by psychological methods or biological methods or both. In the future, social systems will not be adjusted to suit

the needs of human beings. Instead, human beings will be adjusted to suit the needs of the system.[45]

152.   Generally speaking, technological control over human behavior will probably not be introduced with a totalitarian intention or even through a conscious desire to restrict human freedom.[46] Each new step in the assertion of control over the human mind will be taken as a rational response to a problem that faces society, such as curing alcoholism, reducing the crime rate or inducing young people to study science and engineering. In many cases, there will be a humanitarian justification. For example, when a psychiatrist prescribes an antidepressant for a depressed patient, he is clearly doing that individual a favor. It would be inhumane to withhold the drug from someone who needs it. When parents send their children to Sylvan Learning Centers to have them manipulated into becoming enthusiastic about their studies, they do so from concern for their children's welfare. It may be that some of these parents wish that one didn't have to have specialized training to get a job and that their kid didn't have to be brainwashed into becoming a computer nerd. But what can they do? They can't change society, and their child may be unemployable if he doesn't have certain skills. So they send him to Sylvan.

153. Thus control over human behavior will be introduced not by a calculated decision of the authorities but through a process of social evolution (*rapid* evolution, however). The process will be impossible to resist, because each advance, considered by itself, will appear to be beneficial, or at least the evil involved in making the advance will seem to be less than that which would result from not making it. (See paragraph 127.) Propaganda for example is used for many good purposes, such as discouraging child abuse or race hatred.[47] Sex education is obviously useful, yet the effect of sex education (to the extent that it is successful) is to take the shaping of sexual attitudes away from the family and put it into the hands of the state as represented by the public school system.

154. Suppose a biological trait is discovered that increases the likelihood that a child will grow up to be a criminal, and suppose some sort of gene therapy can remove this trait.[48] Of course, most parents whose children possess the trait will have them undergo the therapy. It would be inhumane to do otherwise, since the child would probably have a miserable life if he grew up to be a criminal. But many or most primitive societies have a low crime rate in comparison with that of our society, even though they have neither high-tech methods of child-rearing nor harsh systems of

punishment. Since there is no reason to suppose that more modern men than primitive men have innate predatory tendencies, the high crime rate of our society must be due to the pressures that modern conditions put on people, to which many cannot or will not adjust. Thus a treatment designed to remove potential criminal tendencies is at least in part a way of re-engineering people so that they suit the requirements of the system.

155. Our society tends to regard as a "sickness" any mode of thought or behavior that is inconvenient for the system, and this is plausible, because when an individual doesn't fit into the system it causes pain to the individual as well as problems for the system. Thus the manipulation of an individual to adjust him to the system is seen as a "cure" for a "sickness" and therefore as good.

156. In paragraph 127 we pointed out that if the use of a new item of technology is *initially* optional, it does not necessarily *remain* optional, because the new technology tends to change society in such a way that it becomes difficult or impossible for an individual to function without using that technology. This applies also to the technology of human behavior. In a world in which most children are put through a program to make them enthusiastic about studying, a parent will almost be forced to put his kid through such a program, because if he does not, then the kid will grow up to be, comparatively speaking, an ignoramus and therefore unemployable. Or suppose a biological treatment is discovered that, without undesirable side-effects, will greatly reduce the psychological stress from which so many people suffer in our society. If large numbers of people choose to undergo the treatment, then the general level of stress in society will be reduced, so that it will be possible for the system to increase the stress-producing pressures. This will lead more people to undergo the treatment; and so forth, so that eventually the pressures may become so heavy that few people will be able to survive without undergoing the stress-reducing treatment. In fact, something like this seems to have happened already with one of our society's most important psychological tools for enabling people to reduce (or at least temporarily escape from) stress, namely, mass entertainment (see paragraph 147). Our use of mass entertainment is "optional": No law requires us to watch television, listen to the radio, read magazines. Yet mass entertainment is a means of escape and stress-reduction on which most of us have become dependent. Everyone complains about the trashiness of television, but almost everyone watches it. A few have kicked the TV habit, but it would be a rare person who could get along today without using *any* form of

mass entertainment. (Yet until quite recently in human history most people got along very nicely with no other entertainment than that which each local community created for itself.) Without the entertainment industry the system probably would not have been able to get away with putting as much stress-producing pressure on us as it does.

157.   Assuming that industrial society survives, it is likely that technology will eventually acquire something approaching complete control over human behavior. It has been established beyond any rational doubt that human thought and behavior have a largely biological basis. As experimenters have demonstrated, feelings such as hunger, pleasure, anger and fear can be turned on and off by electrical stimulation of appropriate parts of the brain. Memories can be destroyed by damaging parts of the brain or they can be brought to the surface by electrical stimulation. Hallucinations can be induced or moods changed by drugs. There may or may not be an immaterial human soul, but if there is one it clearly is less powerful than the biological mechanisms of human behavior. For if that were not the case then researchers would not be able so easily to manipulate human feelings and behavior with drugs and electrical currents.

158.   It presumably would be impractical for all people to have electrodes inserted in their heads so that they could be controlled by the authorities. But the fact that human thoughts and feelings are so open to biological intervention shows that the problem of controlling human behavior is mainly a technical problem; a problem of neurons, hormones and complex molecules; the kind of problem that is accessible to scientific attack. Given the outstanding record of our society in solving technical problems, it is overwhelmingly probable that great advances will be made in the control of human behavior.

159. Will public resistance prevent the introduction of technological control of human behavior? It certainly would if an attempt were made to introduce such control all at once. But since technological control will be introduced through a long sequence of small advances, there will be no rational and effective public resistance. (See paragraphs 127, 132, 153.)

160.   To those who think that all this sounds like science fiction, we point out that yesterday's science fiction is today's fact. The Industrial Revolution has radically altered man's environment and way of life, and it is only to be expected that as technology is increasingly applied to the human body and mind, man himself will be altered as radically as his environment and way of life have been.

Human Race at a Crossroads

161. But we have gotten ahead of our story. It is one thing to develop in the laboratory a series of psychological or biological techniques for manipulating human behavior and quite another to integrate these techniques into a functioning social system. The latter problem is the more difficult of the two. For example, while the techniques of educational psychology doubtless work quite well in the "lab schools" where they are developed, it is not necessarily easy to apply them effectively throughout our educational system. We all know what many of our schools are like. The teachers are too busy [as of 1995] taking knives and guns away from the kids to subject them to the latest techniques for making them into computer nerds. Thus, in spite of all its technical advances relating to human behavior, the system to date has not been impressively successful in controlling human beings. The people whose behavior is fairly well under the control of the system are those of the type that might be called "bourgeois." But there are growing numbers of people who in one way or another are rebels against the system: welfare leeches, youth gangs, cultists, satanists, Nazis, radical environmentalists, militiamen, etc.

162. The system is currently engaged in a desperate struggle to overcome certain problems that threaten its survival, among which the problems of human behavior are the most important. If the system succeeds in acquiring sufficient control over human behavior quickly enough, it will probably survive. Otherwise it will break down. We think the issue will most likely be resolved within the next several decades, say forty to a hundred years.

163. Suppose the system survives the crisis of the next several decades. By that time it will have to have solved, or at least brought under control, the principal problems that confront it, in particular that of "socializing" human beings; that is, making people sufficiently docile so that their behavior no longer threatens the system. That being accomplished, it does not appear that there would be any further obstacle to the development of technology, and it would presumably advance toward its logical conclusion, which is complete control over everything on Earth, including human beings and all other important organisms. The system may become a unitary, monolithic organization, or it may be more or less fragmented and consist of a number of organizations coexisting in a

relationship that includes elements of both cooperation and competition, just as today the government, the corporations and other large organizations both cooperate and compete with one another. Human freedom mostly will have vanished, because individuals and small groups will be impotent vis-à-vis large organizations armed with supertechnology and an arsenal of advanced psychological and biological tools for manipulating human beings, besides instruments of surveillance and physical coercion. Only a small number of people will have any real power, and even these probably will have only very limited freedom, because their behavior too will be regulated; just as today our politicians and corporation executives can retain their positions of power only as long as their behavior remains within certain fairly narrow limits.

164. Don't imagine that the system will stop developing further techniques for controlling human beings and nature once the crisis of the next few decades is over and increasing control is no longer necessary for the system's survival. On the contrary, once the hard times are over the system will increase its control over people and nature more rapidly, because it will no longer be hampered by difficulties of the kind that it is currently experiencing. Survival is not the principal motive for extending control. As we explained in paragraphs 87–90, technicians and scientists carry on their work largely as a surrogate activity; that is, they satisfy their need for power by solving technical problems. They will continue to do this with unabated enthusiasm, and among the most interesting and challenging problems for them to solve will be those of understanding the human body and mind and intervening in their development. For the "good of humanity," of course.

165. But suppose on the other hand that the stresses of the coming decades prove to be too much for the system. If the system breaks down there may be a period of chaos, a "time of troubles" such as those that history has recorded at various epochs in the past. It is impossible to predict what would emerge from such a time of troubles, but at any rate the human race would be given a new chance. The greatest danger is that industrial society may begin to reconstitute itself within the first few years after the breakdown. Certainly there will be many people (power-hungry types especially) who will be anxious to get the factories running again.

166. Therefore two tasks confront those who hate the servitude to which the industrial system is reducing the human race. First, we must work to heighten the social stresses within the system so as to increase the

likelihood that it will break down or be weakened sufficiently so that a revolution against it becomes possible. Second, it is necessary to develop and propagate an ideology that opposes technology and the industrial system. Such an ideology can become the basis for a revolution against industrial society if and when the system becomes sufficiently weakened. And such an ideology will help to ensure that, if and when industrial society breaks down, its remnants will be smashed beyond repair, so that the system cannot be reconstituted. The factories should be destroyed, technical books burned, etc.

Human Suffering

167. The industrial system will not break down purely as a result of revolutionary action. It will not be vulnerable to revolutionary attack unless its own internal problems of development lead it into very serious difficulties. So if the system breaks down it will do so either spontaneously, or through a process that is in part spontaneous but helped along by revolutionaries. If the breakdown is sudden, many people will die, since the world has become so grossly overpopulated that it cannot even feed itself any longer without advanced technology. Even if the breakdown is gradual enough so that reduction of the population can occur more through lowering of the birth rate than through elevation of the death rate,[49] the process of de-industrialization probably will be very chaotic and involve much suffering. It is naive to think it likely that technology can be phased out in a smoothly managed, orderly way, especially since the technophiles will fight stubbornly at every step. Is it therefore cruel to work for the breakdown of the system? Maybe, but maybe not. In the first place, revolutionaries will not be able to break the system down unless it is already in enough trouble so that there would be a good chance of its eventually breaking down by itself anyway; and the bigger the system grows, the more disastrous the consequences of its breakdown will be; so it may be that revolutionaries, by hastening the onset of the breakdown, will be reducing the extent of the disaster.

168. In the second place, one has to balance struggle and death against the loss of freedom and dignity. To many of us, freedom and dignity are more important than a long life or avoidance of physical pain. Besides, we all have to die sometime, and it may be better to die fighting for survival, or for a cause, than to live a long but empty and purposeless life.

169. In the third place, it is not at all certain that survival of the system will lead to less suffering than the breakdown of the system would. The system has already caused, and is continuing to cause, immense suffering all over the world. Ancient cultures, that for hundreds or thousands of years gave people a satisfactory relationship with each other and with their environment, have been shattered by contact with industrial society, and the result has been a whole catalog of economic, environmental, social and psychological problems. One of the effects of the intrusion of industrial society has been that over much of the world traditional controls on population have been thrown out of balance. Hence the population explosion, with all that that implies. Then there is the psychological suffering that is widespread throughout the supposedly fortunate countries of the West (see paragraphs 44, 45). No one knows [as of 1995] what will happen as a result of ozone depletion, the greenhouse effect and other environmental problems that cannot yet be foreseen. And, as nuclear proliferation has shown, new technology cannot be kept out of the hands of dictators and irresponsible Third World nations. Would you like to speculate about what Iraq or North Korea will do with genetic engineering?

170. "Oh!" say the technophiles, "Science is going to fix all that! We will conquer famine, eliminate psychological suffering, make everybody healthy and happy!" Yeah, sure. That's what they said two hundred years ago. The Industrial Revolution was supposed to eliminate poverty, make everybody happy, etc. The actual result has been quite different. The technophiles are hopelessly naive (or self-deceiving) in their understanding of social problems. They are unaware of (or choose to ignore) the fact that when large changes, even seemingly beneficial ones, are introduced into a society, they lead to a long sequence of other changes, most of which are impossible to predict (paragraph 103). The result is disruption of the society. So it is very probable that in their attempts to end poverty and disease, engineer docile, happy personalities and so forth, the technophiles will create social systems that are terribly troubled, even more so than the present one. For example, the scientists boast that they will end famine by creating new, genetically engineered food plants. But this will allow the human population to keep expanding indefinitely, and it is well known that crowding leads to increased stress and aggression. This is merely one example of the *predictable* problems that will arise. We emphasize that, as past experience has shown, technical progress will lead to other new

problems that *cannot* be predicted in advance (paragraph 103). In fact, ever since the Industrial Revolution, technology has been creating new problems for society far more rapidly than it has been solving old ones. Thus it will take a long and difficult period of trial and error for the technophiles to work the bugs out of their Brave New World (if they ever do). In the meantime there will be great suffering. So it is not at all clear that the survival of industrial society would involve less suffering than the breakdown of that society would. Technology has gotten the human race into a fix from which there is not likely to be any easy escape.

The Future[50]

171. But suppose now that industrial society does survive the next several decades and that the bugs do eventually get worked out of the system, so that it functions smoothly. What kind of system will it be? We will consider several possibilities.

172. First let us postulate that the computer scientists succeed in developing intelligent machines that can do all things better than human beings can do them. In that case presumably all work will be done by vast, highly organized systems of machines and no human effort will be necessary. Either of two cases might occur. The machines might be permitted to make all of their own decisions without human oversight, or else human control over the machines might be retained.

173. If the machines are permitted to make all their own decisions we can't make any conjecture as to the results, because it is impossible to guess how such machines might behave. We only point out that the fate of the human race would be at the mercy of the machines. It might be argued that the human race would never be foolish enough to hand over all power to the machines. But we are suggesting neither that the human race would voluntarily turn power over to the machines nor that the machines would willfully seize power. What we do suggest is that the human race might easily permit itself to drift into a position of such dependence on the machines that it would have no practical choice but to accept all of the machines' decisions. As society and the problems that face it become more and more complex and as machines become more and more intelligent, people will let machines make more and more of their decisions for them, simply because machine-made decisions will bring better results

than man-made ones. Eventually a stage may be reached at which the decisions necessary to keep the system running will be so complex that human beings will be incapable of making them intelligently. At that stage the machines will be in effective control. People won't be able to just turn the machines off, because they will be so dependent on them that turning them off would amount to suicide.

174. On the other hand, it is possible that human control over the machines may be retained. In that case the average man may have control over certain private machines of his own, such as his car or his personal computer, but control over large systems of machines will be in the hands of a tiny elite—just as it is today, but with two differences. Due to improved techniques the elite will have greater control over the masses; and because human work will no longer be necessary the masses will be superfluous, a useless burden on the system. If the elite is ruthless they may simply decide to exterminate the mass of humanity. If they are humane they may use propaganda or other psychological or biological techniques to reduce the birth rate until the mass of humanity becomes extinct, leaving the world to the elite. Or, if the elite consists of soft-hearted liberals, they may decide to play the role of good shepherds to the rest of the human race. They will see to it that everyone's physical needs are satisfied, that all children are raised under psychologically hygienic conditions, that everyone has a wholesome hobby to keep him busy, and that anyone who may become dissatisfied undergoes "treatment" to cure his "problem." Of course, life will be so purposeless that people will have to be biologically or psychologically engineered either to remove their need for the power process or to make them "sublimate" their drive for power into some harmless hobby. These engineered human beings may be happy in such a society, but they most certainly will not be free. They will have been reduced to the status of domestic animals.

175. But suppose now that the computer scientists do not succeed in developing strong artificial intelligence, so that human work remains necessary. Even so, machines will take care of more and more of the simpler tasks so that there will be an increasing surplus of human workers at the lower levels of ability. (We see this happening already. There are many people who find it difficult or impossible to get work, because for intellectual or psychological reasons they cannot acquire the level of training necessary to make themselves useful in the present system.) On those who are employed, ever-increasing demands will be placed: They will need

more and more training, more and more ability, and will have to be ever
more reliable, conforming and docile, because they will be more and more
like cells of a giant organism. Their tasks will be increasingly specialized,
so that their work will be, in a sense, out of touch with the real world,
being concentrated on one tiny slice of reality. The system will have to use
any means that it can, whether psychological or biological, to engineer
people to be docile, to have the abilities that the system requires and to
"sublimate" their drive for power into some specialized task. But the statement that the people of such a society will have to be docile may require
qualification. The society may find competitiveness useful, provided that
ways are found of directing competitiveness into channels that serve the
needs of the system. We can imagine a future society in which there is
endless competition for positions of prestige and power. But no more than
a very few people will ever reach the top, where the only real power is (see
end of paragraph 163). Very repellent is a society in which a person can
satisfy his need for power only by pushing large numbers of other people
out of the way and depriving them of *their* opportunity for power.

176. One can envision scenarios that incorporate aspects of more
than one of the possibilities that we have just discussed. For instance, it may
be that machines will take over most of the work that is of real, practical
importance, but that human beings will be kept busy by being given relatively unimportant work. It has been suggested, for example, that a great
development of the service industries might provide work for human beings.
Thus people would spend their time shining each other's shoes, driving each
other around in taxicabs, making handicrafts for one another, waiting on
each other's tables, etc. This seems to us a thoroughly contemptible way
for the human race to end up, and we doubt that many people would find
fulfilling lives in such pointless busy-work. They would seek other, dangerous
outlets (drugs, crime, "cults," hate groups) unless they were biologically or
psychologically engineered to adapt them to such a way of life.

177. Needless to say, the scenarios outlined above do not exhaust
all the possibilities. They only indicate the kinds of outcomes that seem
to us most likely. But we can envision no plausible scenarios that are any
more palatable than the ones we've just described. It is overwhelmingly
probable that if the industrial-technological system survives the next forty
to one hundred years, it will by that time have developed certain general
characteristics: Individuals (at least those of the "bourgeois" type, who are
integrated into the system and make it run, and who therefore have all the

power) will be more dependent than ever on large organizations; they will be more "socialized" than ever and their physical and mental qualities to a significant extent (possibly to a very great extent) will be those that are engineered into them rather than being the results of chance (or of God's will, or whatever); and whatever may be left of wild nature will be reduced to remnants preserved for scientific study and kept under the supervision and management of scientists (hence it will no longer be truly wild). In the long run (say a few centuries from now) it is likely that neither the human race nor any other important organisms will exist as we know them today, because once you start modifying organisms through genetic engineering there is no reason to stop at any particular point, so that the modifications will probably continue until man and other organisms have been utterly transformed.

178. Whatever else may be the case, it is certain that technology is creating for human beings a new physical and social environment radically different from the spectrum of environments to which natural selection has adapted the human race physically and psychologically. If man is not adjusted to this new environment by being artificially re-engineered, then he will be adapted to it through a long and painful process of natural selection. The former is far more likely than the latter.

179. It would be better to dump the whole stinking system and take the consequences.

Strategy

180. The technophiles are taking us all on an utterly reckless ride into the unknown. Many people understand something of what technological progress is doing to us, yet take a passive attitude toward it because they think it is inevitable. But we don't think it is inevitable. We think it can be stopped, and we will give here some indications of how to go about stopping it.

181. As we stated in paragraph 166, the two main tasks for the present are to promote social stress and instability in industrial society and to develop and propagate an ideology that opposes technology and the industrial system. When the system becomes sufficiently stressed and unstable, a revolution against technology may be possible. The pattern would be similar to that of the French and Russian Revolutions. French

society and Russian society, for several decades prior to their respective revolutions, showed increasing signs of stress and weakness. Meanwhile, ideologies were being developed that offered a new world-view that was quite different from the old one. In the Russian case, revolutionaries were actively working to undermine the old order. Then, when the old system was put under sufficient additional stress (by financial crisis in France, by military defeat in Russia) it was swept away by revolution. What we propose is something along the same lines.

182. It will be objected that the French and Russian Revolutions were failures. But most revolutions have two goals. One is to destroy an old form of society and the other is to set up the new form of society envisioned by the revolutionaries. The French and Russian revolutionaries failed (fortunately!) to create the new kind of society of which they dreamed, but they were quite successful in destroying the old society. We have no illusions about the feasibility of creating a new, ideal form of society. Our goal is only to destroy the existing form of society.

183. But an ideology, in order to gain enthusiastic support, must have a positive ideal as well as a negative one; it must be *for* something as well as *against* something. The positive ideal that we propose is Nature. That is, *wild* nature: those aspects of the functioning of the Earth and its living things that are independent of human management and free of human interference and control. And with wild nature we include human nature, by which we mean those aspects of the functioning of the human individual that are not subject to regulation by organized society but are products of chance, or free will, or God (depending on your religious or philosophical opinions).

184. Nature makes a perfect counter-ideal to technology for several reasons. Nature (that which is outside the power of the system) is the opposite of technology (which seeks to expand indefinitely the power of the system). Most people will agree that nature is beautiful; certainly it has tremendous popular appeal. The radical environmentalists *already* hold an ideology that exalts nature and opposes technology.[51] It is not necessary for the sake of nature to set up some chimerical utopia or any new kind of social order. Nature takes care of itself: It was a spontaneous creation that existed long before any human society, and for countless centuries many different kinds of human societies coexisted with nature without doing it an excessive amount of damage. Only with the Industrial Revolution did the effect of human society on nature become really

devastating. To relieve the pressure on nature it is not necessary to create any special kind of social system, it is only necessary to get rid of industrial society. Granted, this will not solve all problems. Industrial society has already done tremendous damage to nature and it will take a very long time for the scars to heal. Besides, even pre-industrial societies can do significant damage to nature. Nevertheless, getting rid of industrial society will accomplish a great deal. It will relieve the worst of the pressure on nature so that the scars can begin to heal. It will remove the capacity of organized society to keep increasing its control over nature (including human nature). Whatever kind of society may exist after the demise of the industrial system, it is certain that most people will live close to nature, because in the absence of advanced technology there is no other way that people *can* live. To feed themselves they must be peasants, or herdsmen, or fishermen, or hunters, etc. And, generally speaking, local autonomy should tend to increase, because lack of advanced technology and rapid communications will limit the capacity of governments or other large organizations to control local communities.

185. As for the negative consequences of eliminating industrial society—well, you can't eat your cake and have it too. To gain one thing you have to sacrifice another.

186. Most people hate psychological conflict. For this reason they avoid doing any serious thinking about difficult social issues, and they like to have such issues presented to them in simple, black-and-white terms: *this* is all good and *that* is all bad. The revolutionary ideology should therefore be developed on two levels.[52]

187. On the more sophisticated level the ideology should address itself to people who are intelligent, thoughtful and rational. The object should be to create a core of people who will be opposed to the industrial system on a rational, thought-out basis, with full appreciation of the problems and ambiguities involved, and of the price that has to be paid for getting rid of the system. It is particularly important to attract people of this type, as they are capable people and will be instrumental in influencing others. These people should be addressed on as rational a level as possible. Facts should never intentionally be distorted and intemperate language should be avoided. This does not mean that no appeal can be made to the emotions, but in making such appeal care should be taken to avoid misrepresenting the truth or doing anything else that would destroy the intellectual respectability of the ideology.

188. On a second level, the ideology should be propagated in a simplified form that will enable the unthinking majority to see the conflict of technology vs. nature in unambiguous terms. But even on this second level the ideology should not be expressed in language that is so cheap, intemperate or irrational that it alienates people of the thoughtful and rational type. Cheap, intemperate propaganda sometimes achieves impressive short-term gains, but it will be more advantageous in the long run to keep the loyalty of a small number of intelligently committed people than to arouse the passions of an unthinking, fickle mob who will change their attitude as soon as someone comes along with a better propaganda gimmick. However, propaganda of the rabble-rousing type may be necessary when the system is nearing the point of collapse and there is a final struggle between rival ideologies to determine which will become dominant when the old world-view goes under.

189. Prior to that final struggle, the revolutionaries should not expect to have a majority of people on their side. History is made by active, determined minorities, not by the majority, which seldom has a clear and consistent idea of what it really wants. Until the time comes for the final push toward revolution,[53] the task of revolutionaries will be less to win the shallow support of the majority than to build a small core of deeply committed people. As for the majority, it will be enough to make them aware of the existence of the new ideology and remind them of it frequently; though of course it will be desirable to get majority support to the extent that this can be done without weakening the core of seriously committed people.

190. Any kind of social conflict helps to destabilize the system, but one should be careful about what kind of conflict one encourages. The line of conflict should be drawn between the mass of the people and the power-holding elite of industrial society (politicians, scientists, upper-level business executives, government officials, etc.). It should *not* be drawn between the revolutionaries and the mass of the people. For example, it would be bad strategy for the revolutionaries to condemn Americans for their habits of consumption. Instead, the average American should be portrayed as a victim of the advertising and marketing industry, which has suckered him into buying a lot of junk that he doesn't need and that is very poor compensation for his lost freedom. Either approach is consistent with the facts. It is merely a matter of attitude whether you blame the advertising industry for manipulating the public or blame the public

for allowing itself to be manipulated. As a matter of strategy one should generally avoid blaming the public.

191. One should think twice before encouraging any other social conflict than that between the power-holding elite (which wields technology) and the general public (over which technology exerts its power). For one thing, other conflicts tend to distract attention from the important conflicts (between power-elite and ordinary people, between technology and nature); for another thing, other conflicts may actually tend to encourage technologization, because each side in such a conflict wants to use technological power to gain advantages over its adversary. This is clearly seen in rivalries between nations. It also appears in ethnic conflicts within nations. For example, in America many black leaders are anxious to gain power for African-Americans by placing black individuals in the technological power-elite. They want there to be many black government officials, scientists, corporation executives and so forth. In this way they are helping to absorb the African-American subculture into the technological system. Generally speaking, one should encourage only those social conflicts that can be fitted into the framework of the conflicts of power-elite vs. ordinary people, technology vs. nature.

192. But the way to discourage ethnic conflict is *not* through militant advocacy of minority rights (see paragraphs 21, 29). Instead, the revolutionaries should emphasize that although minorities do suffer more or less disadvantage, this disadvantage is of peripheral significance. Our real enemy is the industrial-technological system, and in the struggle against the system, ethnic distinctions are of no importance.

193. The kind of revolution we have in mind will not necessarily involve an armed uprising against any government. It may or may not involve physical violence, but it will not be a *political* revolution. Its focus will be on technology and economics, not politics.

194. Probably the revolutionaries should even *avoid* assuming political power, whether by legal or illegal means, until the industrial system is stressed to the danger point and has proven itself to be a failure in the eyes of most people. Suppose for example that some "green" party should win control of the United States Congress in an election. In order to avoid betraying or watering down their own ideology they would have to take vigorous measures to turn economic growth into economic shrinkage. To the average man the results would appear disastrous: There would be massive unemployment, shortages of commodities, etc. Even if the grosser

ill effects could be avoided through superhumanly skillful management, still people would have to begin giving up the luxuries to which they have become addicted. Dissatisfaction would grow, the "green" party would be voted out of office and the revolutionaries would have suffered a severe setback. For this reason the revolutionaries should not try to acquire political power until the system has gotten itself into such a mess that any hardships will be seen as resulting from the failures of the industrial system itself and not from the policies of the revolutionaries. The revolution against technology will probably have to be a revolution by outsiders, a revolution from below and not from above.

195. The revolution must be international and worldwide. It cannot be carried out on a nation-by-nation basis. Whenever it is suggested that the United States, for example, should cut back on technological progress or economic growth, people get hysterical and start screaming that if we fall behind in technology the Japanese will get ahead of us. Holy robots! The world will fly off its orbit if the Japanese ever sell more cars than we do! (Nationalism is a great promoter of technology.) More reasonably, it is argued that if the relatively democratic nations of the world fall behind in technology while nasty, dictatorial nations like China, Vietnam and North Korea continue to progress, eventually the dictators may come to dominate the world. That is why the industrial system should be attacked in all nations simultaneously, to the extent that this may be possible. True, there is no assurance that the industrial system can be destroyed at approximately the same time all over the world, and it is even conceivable that the attempt to overthrow the system could lead instead to the domination of the system by dictators. That is a risk that has to be taken. And it is worth taking, since the difference between a "democratic" industrial system and one controlled by dictators is small compared with the difference between an industrial system and a non-industrial one.[54] It might even be argued that an industrial system controlled by dictators would be preferable, because dictator-controlled systems usually have proven inefficient, hence they are presumably more likely to break down. Look at Cuba.

196. Revolutionaries might consider favoring measures that tend to bind the world economy into a unified whole. Free trade agreements like NAFTA (North American Free Trade Agreement) and GATT (General Agreement on Tariffs and Trade) are probably harmful to the environment in the short run, but in the long run they may perhaps be advantageous because they foster economic interdependence between nations. It

will be easier to destroy the industrial system on a worldwide basis if the world economy is so unified that its breakdown in any one major nation will lead to its breakdown in all industrialized nations.

197. Some people take the line that modern man has too much power, too much control over nature; they argue for a more passive attitude on the part of the human race. At best these people are expressing themselves unclearly, because they fail to distinguish between power for *large organizations* and power for *individuals* and *small groups*. It is a mistake to argue for powerlessness and passivity, because people *need* power. Modern man as a collective entity—that is, the industrial system—has immense power over nature, and we (FC) regard this as evil. But modern *individuals* and *small groups of individuals* have far less power than primitive man ever did. Generally speaking, the vast power of "modern man" over nature is exercised not by individuals or small groups but by large organizations. To the extent that the average modern *individual* can wield the power of technology, he is permitted to do so only within narrow limits and only under the supervision and control of the system. (You need a license for everything and with the license come rules and regulations.) The individual has only those technological powers with which the system chooses to provide him. His *personal* power over nature is slight.

198. Primitive *individuals* and *small groups* actually had considerable power over nature; or maybe it would be better to say power *within* nature. When primitive man needed food he knew how to find and prepare edible roots, how to track game and take it with homemade weapons. He knew how to protect himself from heat, cold, rain, dangerous animals, etc. But primitive man did relatively little damage to nature because the *collective* power of primitive society was negligible compared to the *collective* power of industrial society.

199. Instead of arguing for powerlessness and passivity, one should argue that the power of the *industrial system* should be broken, and that this will greatly *increase* the power and freedom of *individuals* and *small groups*.

200. Until the industrial system has been thoroughly wrecked, the destruction of that system must be the revolutionaries' *only* goal. Other goals would distract attention and energy from the main goal. More importantly, if the revolutionaries permit themselves to have any other goal than the destruction of technology, they will be tempted to use technology as a tool for reaching that other goal. If they give in to that temptation, they will fall right back into the technological trap, because modern

technology is a unified, tightly organized system, so that, in order to retain *some* technology, one finds oneself obliged to retain *most* technology, hence one ends up sacrificing only token amounts of technology.

201. Suppose for example that the revolutionaries took "social justice" as a goal. Human nature being what it is, social justice would not come about spontaneously; it would have to be enforced. In order to enforce it the revolutionaries would have to retain central organization and control. For that they would need rapid long-distance transportation and communication, and therefore all the technology needed to support the transportation and communication systems. To feed and clothe poor people they would have to use agricultural and manufacturing technology. And so forth. So that the attempt to ensure social justice would force them to retain most parts of the technological system. Not that we have anything against social justice, but it must not be allowed to interfere with the effort to get rid of the technological system.

202. It would be hopeless for revolutionaries to try to attack the system without using *some* modern technology. If nothing else they must use the communications media to spread their message. But they should use modern technology for only *one* purpose: to attack the technological system.

203. Imagine an alcoholic sitting with a barrel of wine in front of him. Suppose he starts saying to himself, "Wine isn't bad for you if used in moderation. Why, they say small amounts of wine are even good for you! It won't do me any harm if I take just one little drink... ." Well, you know what is going to happen. Never forget that the human race with technology is just like an alcoholic with a barrel of wine.

204. Revolutionaries should have as many children as they can.[55] There is strong scientific evidence that social attitudes are to a significant extent inherited. No one suggests that a social attitude is a direct outcome of a person's genetic constitution, but it appears that personality traits are partly inherited and that certain personality traits tend, within the context of our society, to make a person more likely to hold this or that social attitude. Objections to these findings have been raised, but the objections are feeble and seem to be ideologically motivated. In any event, no one denies that children tend on the average to hold social attitudes similar to those of their parents. From our point of view it doesn't matter much whether the attitudes are passed on genetically or through childhood training. In either case they *are* passed on.

205. The trouble is that many of the people who are inclined to rebel against the industrial system are also concerned about the population problem, hence they are apt to have few or no children. In this way they may be handing the world over to the sort of people who support or at least accept the industrial system. To ensure the strength of the next generation of revolutionaries the present generation should reproduce itself abundantly. In doing so they will be worsening the population problem only slightly. And the most important problem is to get rid of the industrial system, because once the industrial system is gone the world's population necessarily will decrease (see paragraph 167); whereas, if the industrial system survives, it will continue developing new techniques of food production that may enable the world's population to keep increasing almost indefinitely.

206. With regard to revolutionary strategy, the only points on which we absolutely insist are that the single, overriding goal must be the elimination of modern technology, and that no other goal can be allowed to compete with this one. For the rest, revolutionaries should take an empirical approach. If experience indicates that some of the recommendations made in the foregoing paragraphs are not going to give good results, then those recommendations should be discarded.

Two Kinds of Technology

207. An argument likely to be raised against our proposed revolution is that it is bound to fail, because (it is claimed) throughout history technology has always progressed, never regressed, hence technological regression is impossible. But this claim is false.

208. We distinguish between two kinds of technology, which we will call *small-scale technology* and *organization-dependent technology*. Small-scale technology is technology that can be used by small-scale communities without outside assistance. Organization-dependent technology is technology that depends on large-scale social organization. We are aware of no significant cases of regression in small-scale technology.[56] But organization-dependent technology *does* regress when the social organization on which it depends breaks down. Example: When the Roman Empire fell apart the Romans' small-scale technology survived because any clever village craftsman could build, for instance, a water wheel, any skilled

smith could make steel by Roman methods, and so forth. But the Romans' organization-dependent technology *did* regress. Their aqueducts fell into disrepair and were never rebuilt. Their techniques of road construction were lost. The Roman system of urban sanitation was forgotten, so that not until rather recent times did the sanitation of European cities equal that of ancient Rome.[57]

209. The reason why technology has seemed always to progress is that, until perhaps a century or two before the Industrial Revolution, most technology was small-scale technology. But most of the technology developed since the Industrial Revolution is organization-dependent technology. Take the refrigerator, for example. Without factory-made parts or the facilities of a modern machine shop, it would be virtually impossible for a handful of local craftsmen to build a refrigerator. If by some miracle they did succeed in building one it would be useless to them without a reliable source of electric power. So they would have to dam a stream and build a generator. Generators require large amounts of copper wire. Imagine trying to make that wire without modern machinery. And where would they get a gas suitable for refrigeration? It would be much easier to build an icehouse or preserve food by drying or pickling, as was done before the invention of the refrigerator.

210. So it is clear that if the industrial system were once thoroughly broken down, refrigeration technology would quickly be lost. The same is true of other organization-dependent technology. And once this technology had been lost for a generation or so it would take centuries to rebuild it, just as it took centuries to build it the first time around. Surviving technical books would be few and scattered. An industrial society, if built from scratch without outside help, can only be built in a series of stages: You need tools to make tools to make tools to make tools … . A long process of economic development and progress in social organization is required. And, even in the absence of an ideology opposed to technology, there is no reason to believe that anyone would be interested in rebuilding industrial society. The enthusiasm for "progress" is a phenomenon peculiar to the modern form of society, and it seems not to have existed prior to the 17th century or thereabouts.[58]

211. In the late Middle Ages there were four main civilizations that were about equally "advanced": Europe, the Islamic world, India, and the Far East (China, Japan, Korea). Three of those civilizations remained more or less stable, and only Europe became dynamic. No one knows why

Europe became dynamic at that time; historians have their theories, but these are only speculation. At any rate, it is clear that rapid development toward a technological form of society occurs only under special conditions. So there is no reason to assume that a long-lasting technological regression cannot be brought about.

212. Would society *eventually* develop again toward an industrial-technological form? Maybe, but there is no use in worrying about it, since we can't predict or control events five hundred or a thousand years in the future. Those problems will have to be dealt with by the people who will live at that time.

The Danger of Leftism

213. Because of their need for rebellion and for membership in a movement, leftists or persons of similar psychological type often are attracted to a rebellious or activist movement whose goals and membership are not initially leftist. The resulting influx of leftish types can easily turn a non-leftist movement into a leftist one, so that leftist goals replace or distort the original goals of the movement.

214. To avoid this, a movement that exalts nature and opposes technology must take a resolutely anti-leftist stance and must avoid all collaboration with leftists. Leftism is in the long run inconsistent with wild nature, with human freedom and with the elimination of modern technology. Leftism is collectivist; it seeks to bind together the entire world (both nature and the human race) into a unified whole. But this implies management of nature and of human life by organized society, and it requires advanced technology. You can't have a united world without rapid long-distance transportation and communication, you can't make all people love one another without sophisticated psychological techniques, you can't have a "planned society" without the necessary technological base. Above all, leftism is driven by the need for power, and the leftist seeks power on a collective basis, through identification with a mass movement or an organization. Leftism is unlikely ever to give up technology, because technology is too valuable a source of collective power.

215. The anarchist[59] too seeks power, but he seeks it on an individual or small-group basis; he wants individuals and small groups to be able to control the circumstances of their own lives. He opposes technology

because it makes small groups dependent on large organizations.

216. Some leftists may seem to oppose technology, but they will oppose it only as long as they are outsiders and the technological system is controlled by non-leftists. If leftism ever becomes dominant in society, so that the technological system becomes a tool in the hands of leftists, they will enthusiastically use it and promote its growth. In doing this they will be repeating a pattern that leftism has shown again and again in the past. When the Bolsheviks in Russia were outsiders, they vigorously opposed censorship and the secret police, they advocated self-determination for ethnic minorities, and so forth; but as soon as they came into power themselves, they imposed a tighter censorship and created a more ruthless secret police than any that had existed under the tsars, and they oppressed ethnic minorities at least as much as the tsars had done. In the United States, during the 1960s when leftists were a minority in our universities, leftist professors were vigorous proponents of academic freedom, but today, in those of our universities where leftists have become dominant, they have shown themselves ready to take away everyone else's academic freedom. (This is "political correctness.") The same will happen with leftists and technology: They will use it to oppress everyone else if they ever get it under their own control.

217. In earlier revolutions, leftists of the most power-hungry type, repeatedly, have first cooperated with non-leftist revolutionaries, as well as with leftists of a more libertarian inclination, and later have double-crossed them to seize power for themselves. Robespierre did this in the French Revolution, the Bolsheviks did it in the Russian Revolution, the communists did it in Spain in 1938, and Castro and his followers did it in Cuba. Given the past history of leftism, it would be utterly foolish for non-leftist revolutionaries today to collaborate with leftists.

218. Various thinkers have pointed out that leftism is a kind of religion. Leftism is not a religion in the strict sense, because leftist doctrine does not postulate the existence of any supernatural being. But, for the leftist, leftism plays a psychological role much like that which religion plays for some people. The leftist *needs* to believe in leftism; it plays a vital role in his psychological economy. His beliefs are not easily modified by logic or facts. He has a deep conviction that leftism is morally Right with a capital R, and that he has not only a right but a duty to impose leftist morality on everyone. (However, many of the people we are referring to as "leftists" do not think of themselves as leftists and would not describe their

system of beliefs as leftism. We use the term "leftism" because we don't know of any better word to designate the spectrum of related creeds that includes the feminist, gay rights, political correctness, etc., movements, and because these movements have a strong affinity with the old left. See paragraphs 227–230.)

219. Leftism is a totalitarian force. Wherever leftism is in a position of power it tends to invade every private corner and force every thought into a leftist mold. In part this is because of the quasi-religious character of leftism; everything contrary to leftist beliefs represents Sin. More importantly, leftism is a totalitarian force because of the leftists' drive for power. The leftist seeks to satisfy his need for power through identification with a social movement, and he tries to go through the power process by helping to pursue and attain the goals of the movement (see paragraph 83). But no matter how far the movement has gone in attaining its goals the leftist is never satisfied, because his activism is a surrogate activity (see paragraph 41). That is, the leftist's real motive is not to attain the ostensible goals of leftism; in reality he is motivated by the sense of power he gets from struggling for and then reaching a social goal.[60] Consequently, the leftist is never satisfied with the goals he has already attained; his need for the power process leads him always to pursue some new goal. The leftist wants equal opportunities for minorities. When that is attained he insists on statistical equality of achievement by minorities. And as long as anyone harbors in some corner of his mind a negative attitude toward some minority, the leftist has to re-educate him. And ethnic minorities are not enough; no one can be allowed to have a negative attitude toward homosexuals, disabled people, fat people, old people, ugly people, and on and on and on. It's not enough that the public should be informed about the hazards of smoking; a warning has to be stamped on every package of cigarettes. Then cigarette advertising has to be restricted if not banned. The activists will never be satisfied until tobacco is outlawed, and after that it will be alcohol, then junk food, etc. Activists have fought gross child abuse, which is reasonable. But now they want to stop all spanking. When they have done that they will want to ban something else they consider unwholesome, then another thing and then another. They will never be satisfied until they have complete control over all child-rearing practices. And then they will move on to another cause.

220. Suppose you asked leftists to make a list of *all* the things that were wrong with society, and then suppose you instituted *every* social

change that they demanded. It is safe to say that within a couple of years the majority of leftists would find something new to complain about, some new social "evil" to correct, because, once again, the leftist is motivated less by distress at society's ills than by the need to satisfy his drive for power by imposing his solutions on society.

221.   Because of the restrictions placed on their thought and behavior by their high level of socialization, many leftists of the oversocialized type cannot pursue power in the ways that other people do. For them the drive for power has only one morally acceptable outlet, and that is in the struggle to impose their morality on everyone.

222.   Leftists, especially those of the oversocialized type, are True Believers in the sense of Eric Hoffer's book, *The True Believer*. But not all True Believers are of the same psychological type as leftists. Presumably a true-believing Nazi, for instance, is very different psychologically from a true-believing leftist.[61] Because of their capacity for single-minded devotion to a cause, True Believers are a useful, perhaps a necessary, ingredient of any revolutionary movement. This presents a problem with which we must admit we don't know how to deal. We aren't sure how to harness the energies of the True Believer to a revolution against technology. At present all we can say is that no True Believer will make a safe recruit to the revolution unless his commitment is exclusively to the destruction of technology. If he is committed also to another ideal, he may want to use technology as a tool for pursuing that other ideal. (See paragraphs 200, 201.)

223.   Some readers may say, "This stuff about leftism is a lot of crap. I know John and Jane who are leftish types, and they don't have all these totalitarian tendencies." It's quite true that many leftists, possibly even a numerical majority, are decent people who sincerely believe in tolerating others' values (up to a point) and wouldn't want to use high-handed methods to reach their social goals. Our remarks about leftism are not meant to apply to every individual leftist, but to describe the general character of leftism as a movement. And the general character of a movement is not necessarily determined by the numerical proportions of the various kinds of people involved in the movement.

224.   The people who rise to positions of power in leftist movements tend to be leftists of the most power-hungry type,[62] because power-hungry people are those who strive hardest to get into positions of power. Once the power-hungry types have captured control of the movement, there

are many leftists of a gentler breed who inwardly disapprove of many of the actions of the leaders, but cannot bring themselves to oppose them. They *need* their faith in the movement, and because they cannot give up this faith they go along with the leaders. True, *some* leftists do have the guts to oppose the totalitarian tendencies that emerge, but they generally lose, because the power-hungry types are better organized, are more ruthless and Machiavellian, and have taken care to build themselves a strong power-base.

225. These phenomena appeared clearly in Russia and other countries that were taken over by leftists. Similarly, before the breakdown of communism in the USSR, leftish types in the West would seldom criticize that country. If prodded they would admit that the USSR did many wrong things, but then they would try to find excuses for the communists and begin talking about the faults of the West. They always opposed Western military resistance to communist aggression. Leftish types all over the world vigorously protested the U.S. military action in Vietnam, but when the USSR invaded Afghanistan they did nothing. Not that they approved of the Soviet actions; but because of their leftist faith, they just couldn't bear to put themselves in opposition to communism. Today, in those of our universities where "political correctness" has become dominant, there are probably many leftish types who privately disapprove of the suppression of academic freedom, but they go along with it anyway.

226. Thus, the fact that many individual leftists are personally mild and fairly tolerant people by no means prevents leftism as a whole from having a totalitarian tendency.

227. Our discussion of leftism has a serious weakness. It is still far from clear what we mean by the word "leftist." There doesn't seem to be much we can do about this. Leftism today is fragmented into a whole spectrum of activist movements. Yet not all activist movements are leftist, and some activist movements (e.g., radical environmentalism) seem to include both personalities of the leftist type and personalities of thoroughly un-leftist types who ought to know better than to collaborate with leftists. Varieties of leftists fade out gradually into varieties of non-leftists, and we ourselves would often be hard-pressed to decide whether a given individual is or is not a leftist. To the extent that it is defined at all, our conception of leftism is defined by the discussion of it that we have given in this article, and we can only advise the reader to use his own judgment in deciding who is a leftist.

228. But it will be helpful to list some criteria for diagnosing leftism. These criteria cannot be applied in a cut and dried manner. Some individuals may meet some of the criteria without being leftists, some leftists may not meet any of the criteria. Again, you just have to use your judgment.

229.   The leftist is oriented toward large-scale collectivism. He emphasizes the duty of the individual to serve society and the duty of society to take care of the individual. He has a negative attitude toward individualism. He often takes a moralistic tone. He tends to be for gun control, for sex education and other psychologically "enlightened" educational methods, for social planning, for affirmative action, for multiculturalism. He tends to identify with victims. He tends to be against competition and against violence, but he often finds excuses for those leftists who do commit violence. He is fond of using the common catch-phrases of the left, like "racism," "sexism," "homophobia," "capitalism," "imperialism," "neocolonialism," "genocide," "social change," "social justice," "social responsibility." Maybe the best diagnostic trait of the leftist is his tendency to sympathize with the following movements: feminism, gay rights, ethnic rights, disability rights, animal rights, political correctness. Anyone who strongly sympathizes with *all* of these movements is almost certainly a leftist.[63]

230. The more dangerous leftists, that is, those who are most power-hungry, are often characterized by arrogance or by a dogmatic approach to ideology. However, the most dangerous leftists of all may be certain oversocialized types who avoid irritating displays of aggressiveness and refrain from advertising their leftism, but work quietly and unobtrusively to promote collectivist values, "enlightened" psychological techniques for socializing children, dependence of the individual on the system, and so forth. These crypto-leftists (as we may call them) approximate certain bourgeois types as far as practical action is concerned, but differ from them in psychology, ideology and motivation. The ordinary bourgeois tries to bring people under control of the system in order to protect his way of life, or he does so simply because his attitudes are conventional. The crypto-leftist tries to bring people under control of the system because he is a True Believer in a collectivistic ideology. The crypto-leftist is differentiated from the average leftist of the oversocialized type by the fact that his rebellious impulse is weaker and he is more securely socialized. He is differentiated from the ordinary well-socialized bourgeois by the fact that there is some deep lack within him that makes it necessary for him

to devote himself to a cause and immerse himself in a collectivity. And maybe his (well-sublimated) drive for power is stronger than that of the average bourgeois.

Final Note

231. Throughout this article we've made imprecise statements and statements that ought to have had all sorts of qualifications and reservations attached to them; and some of our statements may be flatly false. Lack of sufficient information and the need for brevity have made it impossible for us to formulate our assertions more precisely or add all the necessary qualifications. And, of course, in a discussion of this kind one must rely heavily on intuitive judgment, and that can sometimes be wrong. So we don't claim that this article expresses more than a crude approximation to the truth.

232. All the same, we are reasonably confident that the general outlines of the picture we have painted here are roughly correct. Just one possible weak point needs to be mentioned. We have portrayed leftism in its modern form as a phenomenon peculiar to our time and as a symptom of the disruption of the power process. But we might possibly be wrong about this. Oversocialized types who try to satisfy their drive for power by imposing their morality on everyone have certainly been around for a long time. But we *think* that the decisive role played by feelings of inferiority, low self-esteem, powerlessness, identification with victims by people who are not themselves victims, is a peculiarity of modern leftism. Identification with victims by people not themselves victims can be seen to some extent in 19th-century leftism and early Christianity, but as far as we can make out, symptoms of low self-esteem, etc., were not nearly so evident in these movements, or in any other movements, as they are in modern leftism. But we are not in a position to assert confidently that no such movements have existed prior to modern leftism. This is a significant question to which historians ought to give their attention.

NOTES

1. (¶ 1) (Added 2016) See in this volume: Letter to Dr. Skrbina of Nov. 23, 2004, Part III.E.

2.   (¶ 19) We are not asserting that all, or even most, bullies and ruthless competitors suffer from feelings of inferiority.

3.   (¶ 25) During the Victorian period many oversocialized people suffered from serious psychological problems as a result of repressing or trying to repress their sexual feelings. Freud apparently based his theories on people of this type. Today the focus of socialization has shifted from sex to aggression.

4.   (¶ 27) Not necessarily including specialists in engineering or the "hard" sciences.

5.   (¶ 28) There are many individuals of the middle and upper classes who resist some of these values, but usually their resistance is more or less covert. Such resistance appears in the mass media only to a very limited extent. The main thrust of propaganda in our society is in favor of the stated values. The principal reason why these values have become, so to speak, the official values of our society is that they are useful to the industrial system. Violence is discouraged because it disrupts the functioning of the system. Racism is discouraged because ethnic conflicts also disrupt the system, and discrimination wastes the talents of minority-group members who could be useful to the system. Poverty must be "cured" because the underclass causes problems for the system and contact with the underclass lowers the morale of the other classes. Women are encouraged to have careers because their talents are useful to the system and, more importantly, because by having regular jobs women become integrated into the system and tied directly to it rather than to their families. This helps to weaken family solidarity. (The leaders of the system say they want to strengthen the family, but what they really mean is that they want the family to serve as an effective tool for socializing children in accord with the needs of the system. We argue in paragraphs 51, 52 that the system cannot afford to let the family or other small-scale social groups be strong or autonomous.)

6.   (¶¶ 33–37) (Added 2016) See in this volume: Letter to Dr. Skrbina of Oct. 12, 2004, Part I; and Appendix One.

7.   (¶ 42) It may be argued that the majority of people don't want to make their own decisions, but want leaders to do their thinking for them. There is an element of truth in this. People like to make their own decisions in small matters, but making decisions on difficult, fundamental questions requires facing up to psychological conflict, and most people hate psychological conflict. Hence they tend to lean on others in making difficult decisions. But it does not follow that they like to have decisions imposed on them without having any opportunity to influence those decisions. The majority of people are natural followers, not leaders, but they like to have direct personal access to their leaders, they want to be able to influence the leaders and participate to some extent in making even the difficult decisions. At least to that degree they need autonomy.

8.   (¶ 44) (Supplemented 2016) Some of the symptoms listed are similar

to those shown by caged animals. See Morris, passim, especially pp. 160–225. To explain how these symptoms arise from deprivation with respect to the power process: Common-sense understanding of human nature tells one that lack of goals whose attainment requires effort leads to boredom and that boredom, long continued, often leads eventually to depression. Failure to attain goals leads to frustration and lowering of self-esteem. Frustration leads to anger, anger to aggression, often in the form of spouse or child abuse. It has been shown that long-continued frustration commonly leads to depression and that depression tends to cause anxiety, guilt, sleep disorders, eating disorders, and bad feelings about oneself. Those who are tending toward depression seek pleasure as an anti-dote; hence insatiable hedonism and excessive sex, with perversions as a means of getting new kicks. Boredom too tends to cause excessive pleasure-seeking since, lacking other goals, people often use pleasure as a goal. The foregoing is a simplification. Reality is more complex, and of course deprivation with respect to the power process is not the *only* cause of the symptoms described. By the way, when we mention depression we do not necessarily mean depression that is severe enough to be treated by a psychiatrist. Often only mild forms of depression are involved. And when we speak of goals we do not necessarily mean long-term, thought-out goals. For many or most people through much of human history, the goals of a hand-to-mouth existence (merely providing oneself and one's family with food and other necessities from day to day) have been quite sufficient.

9.   (¶ 52) (Modified 2016) A partial exception may be made for a few passive, inward-looking groups, such as the Amish, which have little effect on the wider society. Apart from these, some genuine small-scale communities do exist in America today. For instance, youth gangs and "cults." Everyone regards them as dangerous, and so they are, because the members of these groups are loyal primarily to one another rather than to the system, hence the system cannot control them. Or take the gypsies. The gypsies commonly get away with theft and fraud because their loyalties are such that they can always get other gypsies to give testimony that "proves" their innocence. See, e.g., Maas, pp. 78–79. Obviously the system would be in serious trouble if too many people belonged to such groups. For some relevant examples, see Appendix Seven. Also see Carrillo, pp. 46–47.

10.   (¶ 54) (Added 2016) Actually, it's open to question whether the problems tend to be less acute in rural areas. Compare *The Week*, Oct. 17, 2008, p. 14, "The myth of small-town superiority" with *The Economist*, June 25, 2011, p. 94, "A New York state of mind." The main point stands in any case: that crowding is not the decisive factor.

11.   (¶ 55) (Added 2016) E.g.: "In a fashion that men and women of the twentieth century will never fully understand, farmers of the Mississippi valley and the Plains states [in the 1830s or 1840s] had begun to feel 'crowded.' One

farmer said that the reason he had to emigrate from western Illinois was that 'people were settling right under his nose,' although his nearest neighbor was twelve miles away." Schlissel, p. 20, citing Bright, p. 246. See also Dick, p. 25.

12. (¶ 56) Yes, we know that 19th-century America had its problems, and serious ones, but for the sake of brevity we have to express ourselves in simplified terms.

13. (¶ 61) We leave aside the "underclass." We are speaking of the mainstream.

14. (¶ 62) Some social scientists, educators, "mental health" professionals and the like are doing their best to push the social drives into group 1 by trying to see to it that everyone has a satisfactory social life.

15. (¶ 63) Is the drive for endless material acquisition really an artificial creation of the advertising and marketing industry? Certainly there is no innate human drive for material acquisition. There have been many cultures in which people have desired little material wealth beyond what was necessary to satisfy their basic physical needs (Australian aborigines, traditional Mexican peasant culture, some African cultures). On the other hand, there have also been many pre-industrial cultures in which material acquisition has played an important role. So we can't claim that today's acquisition-oriented culture is exclusively a creation of the advertising and marketing industry. But it is clear that the advertising and marketing industry has had an important part in creating that culture. The big corporations that spend millions on advertising wouldn't be spending that kind of money without solid proof that they were getting it back in increased sales.

(Added 2016) In searching for a summer job in 1958, I answered a classified ad that led me to an office in Chicago. From there I was taken with several other teenagers to a suburban neighborhood, where we were all turned loose to sell magazine subscriptions from door to door. None of us succeeded in selling even one. Afterward the man in charge told us frankly, "Our job is to make people buy things they don't want and don't need." He then explained that the same neighborhood would be covered later by experienced professional salesmen who would sell numerous subscriptions where we had sold none at all. Evidently the objective of our excursion had not actually been to sell subscriptions; maybe it was simply to test out the youths in question. Whatever the objective may have been, the foregoing account illustrates the fact that professionals can and do manipulate people into buying things they don't really want.

As ISAIF was originally written, the incident described here was altered to avoid any risk that the author could be identified; the present account is accurate.

16. (¶ 64) The problem of purposelessness seems to have become less serious during the last 15 years or so [this refers to the 15 years preceding 1995], because people now feel less secure physically and economically than they did earlier, and the need for security provides them with a goal. But purposelessness

has been replaced by frustration over the difficulty of attaining security. We emphasize the problem of purposelessness because the liberals and leftists would wish to solve our social problems by having society guarantee everyone's security; but if that could be done it would only bring back the problem of purposelessness. The real issue is not whether society provides well or poorly for people's security; the trouble is that people are dependent on the system for their security rather than having it in their own hands. This, by the way, is part of the reason why some people get worked up about the right to bear arms; possession of a gun puts that aspect of their security in their own hands.

17.   (¶ 65) (Added 2016) The following item appeared in *The Missoulian*, May 25, 1988, under the title "Small businesses, take heart": "… 'But if you're a true entrepreneur, you may not qualify for a franchise. Franchise Development Inc. of Pittsburgh says its clients have been using 2½-hour psychological tests to ferret out those with strong entrepreneurial qualities, such as creativity and independence—just the people who become "troublemakers" by refusing to work within the franchise system.' *Wall Street Journal*."

18.   (¶ 66) Conservatives' efforts to decrease the amount of government regulation are of little benefit to the average man. For one thing, only a fraction of the regulations can be eliminated because most regulations are necessary. For another thing, most of the deregulation affects business rather than the average individual, so that its main effect is to take power from the government and give it to private corporations. What this means for the average man is that government interference in his life is replaced by interference from big corporations, which may be permitted, for example, to dump more chemicals that get into his water supply and give him cancer. The conservatives are just taking the average man for a sucker, exploiting his resentment of Big Government to promote the power of Big Business.

19.   (¶ 67) (Added 2016) Quoted by Anthony Lewis, *New York Times*, April 21, 1995.

20.   (¶ 69) (Added 2016) Último Reducto has pointed out that many primitive peoples attribute sickness not to an "impersonal demon," but to witchcraft. If someone becomes seriously ill attempts are made to identify the supposed "witch," who is then killed. See, e.g., Ross, p. 154. Pre-industrial peoples believed in magic and witchcraft because such beliefs provided them with an explanation for otherwise incomprehensible negative events and with an illusion of power to ward off such events. A discussion of beliefs that serve a similar purpose in the modern world would be of considerable interest, but this is not the place for it.

21.   (¶ 73) When someone approves of the purpose for which propaganda is being used in a given case, he generally calls it "education" or applies to it some similar euphemism. But propaganda is propaganda regardless of the purpose for which it is used.

22.   (¶ 75) (Added 2016) I may have gone too far here. Among the Mbuti

Pygmies, according to Turnbull, *Wayward Servants*, p. 127, "[The elder age group] is an age group to which a man or a woman resigns himself [sic] with some reluctance... ." It still does seem true, however, that any reluctance to grow old among primitives is far exceeded by the reluctance of many modern people, as shown by the lengths to which some of the latter will go in an effort to maintain youthfulness.

23.   (¶ 83) We are not expressing approval or disapproval of the Panama invasion. We only use it to illustrate a point.

24.   (¶¶ 87–92) (Added 2016) The discussion here of the motives of scientists is certainly inadequate. For a more thorough discussion, see the Letter to Dr. P.B. on the Motivations of Scientists, which appears elsewhere in this volume.

25.   (¶ 94) (Added 2016) Último Reducto has pointed out that this definition of freedom requires refinement and/or explanation, inasmuch as people have never had full control over the circumstances of their own lives. They have not, for example, been able to control bad weather, which in some circumstances can lead to the failure of food supplies. I think the necessary refinement and explanation of the definition can be provided, but this is not the place for it.

26.   (¶ 95) When the American colonies were under British rule there were fewer and less effective legal guarantees of freedom than there were after the American Constitution went into effect, yet there was more personal freedom in pre-industrial America, both before and after the War of Independence, than there was after the Industrial Revolution took hold in this country. We quote Graham & Gurr, Chapt. 12 by Roger Lane, pp. 476–78: "The progressive heightening of standards of propriety, and with it the increasing reliance on official law enforcement [in 19th-century America]... were common to the whole society... [T]he change in social behavior is so long term and so wide-spread as to suggest a connection with the most fundamental of contemporary social processes; that of industrial urbanization itself. ...Massachusetts in 1835 had a population of some 660,940, eighty-one percent rural, overwhelmingly pre-industrial and native born. Its citizens were used to considerable personal freedom. Whether teamsters, farmers or artisans, they were all accustomed to setting their own schedules, and the nature of their work made them physically independent of each other. ...Individual problems, sins or even crimes, were not generally cause for wider social concern. ...But the impact of the twin movements to the city and to the factory, both just gathering force in 1835, had a progressive effect on personal behavior throughout the 19th century and into the 20th. The factory demanded regularity of behavior, a life governed by obedience to the rhythms of clock and calendar, the demands of foreman and supervisor. In the city or town, the needs of living in closely packed neighborhoods inhibited many actions previously unobjectionable. Both blue- and white-collar employees in larger establishments were mutually dependent on their fellows; as one man's work fit into another's,

so one man's business was no longer his own. The results of the new organization of life and work were apparent by 1900, when some 76 percent of the 2,805,346 inhabitants of Massachusetts were classified as urbanites. Much violent or irregular behavior which had been tolerable in a casual, independent society was no longer acceptable in the more formalized, cooperative atmosphere of the later period. …The move to the cities had, in short, produced a more tractable, more socialized, more 'civilized' generation than its predecessors."

27.   (¶ 95) (Added 2016) Último Reducto has pointed out that the correct anthropological term here would be "chiefdoms" rather than "monarchies," but for our purposes this makes no difference.

28.   (¶ 97) (Added 2016) Bolívar wrote: "No liberty is legitimate, except when aimed at the honour of mankind and the improvement of his lot." Trend, p. 114. See Appendix Six.

29.   (¶ 97) (Added 2016) Tan, p. 202.

30.   (¶ 97) (Added 2016) Ibid., p. 259.

31.   (¶ 114) See Note 21.

32.   (¶ 115) (Added 2016) "The whining schoolboy, with his satchel and shining morning face, creeps like a snail unwillingly to school." Shakespeare, *As You Like It*, Act 2, Scene 7 (here slightly altered).

33.   (¶ 117) Apologists for the system are fond of citing cases in which elections have been decided by one or two votes, but such cases are rare.

34.   (¶ 119) "Today, in technologically advanced lands, men live very similar lives in spite of geographical, religious, and political differences. The daily lives of a Christian bank clerk in Chicago, a Buddhist bank clerk in Tokyo, and a Communist bank clerk in Moscow are far more alike than the life of any one of them is like that of any single man who lived a thousand years ago. These similarities are the result of a common technology… ." De Camp, p. 17. The lives of the three bank clerks are not *identical*. Ideology does have *some* effect. But all technological societies, in order to survive, must evolve along *approximately* the same trajectory.

35.   (¶ 122) For a further example of undesirable consequences of medical progress, suppose a reliable cure for cancer is discovered. Even if the treatment is too expensive to be available to any but the elite, it will greatly reduce their incentive to stop the escape of carcinogens into the environment.

36.   (¶ 123) Just think, an irresponsible genetic engineer might create a lot of terrorists.

37.   (¶ 128) Since many people may find paradoxical the notion that a large number of good things can add up to a bad thing, we illustrate with an analogy. Suppose Mr. A is playing chess with Mr. B. Mr. C, a grand master, is looking over Mr. A's shoulder. Mr. A of course wants to win his game, so if Mr. C points out a good move for him to make, he is doing Mr. A a favor. But suppose

now that Mr. C tells Mr. A how to make *all* of his moves. In each particular instance he does Mr. A a favor by showing him his best move, but by making *all* of his moves for him he spoils his game, since there is no point in Mr. A's playing the game at all if someone else makes all his moves. The situation of modern man is analogous to that of Mr. A. The system makes an individual's life easier for him in innumerable ways, but in doing so it deprives him of control over his own fate.

38. (¶ 131) See Note 21.

39. (¶ 137) Here we are considering only the conflict of values within the mainstream. For the sake of simplicity we leave out of the picture "outsider" values like the idea that wild nature is more important than human economic welfare.

40. (¶ 137) Self-interest is not necessarily *material* self-interest. It can consist in fulfillment of some psychological need, for example, by promoting one's own ideology or religion.

41. (¶ 139) A qualification: It is in the interest of the system to permit a certain prescribed degree of freedom in some areas. For example, economic freedom (with suitable limitations and restraints) has proven effective in promoting economic growth. But only planned, circumscribed, limited freedom is in the interest of the system. The individual must always be kept on a leash, even if the leash is sometimes long. (See paragraphs 94, 97.)

42. (¶ 143) We don't mean to suggest that the efficiency or the potential for survival of a society has always been inversely proportional to the amount of pressure or discomfort to which the society subjects people. That certainly is not the case. There is good reason to believe that many primitive societies subjected people to less pressure than European society did, but European society proved far more efficient than any primitive society and always won out in conflicts with such societies because of the advantages conferred by technology.

43. (¶ 147) If you think that more effective law enforcement is unequivocally good because it suppresses crime, then remember that crime as defined by the system is not necessarily what *you* would call crime. Today [this refers to 1995], smoking marijuana is a "crime," and, in some places in the U.S., so is possession of an unregistered handgun. Tomorrow, possession of *any* firearm, registered or not, may be made a crime, and the same thing may happen with disapproved methods of child-rearing, such as spanking. In some countries, expression of dissident political opinions is a crime, and there is no certainty that this will never happen in the U.S., since no constitution or political system lasts forever. If a society needs a large, powerful law-enforcement establishment, then there is something gravely wrong with that society; it must be subjecting people to severe pressures if so many refuse to follow the rules, or follow them only because forced. Many societies in the past have gotten by with little or no formal law-enforcement.

44.   (¶ 147) (Added 2016, modified 2019) A psychological study has found that for most modern people, "simply being alone with their own thoughts for 15 min" is a highly aversive experience. See Wilson, Reinhard, et al. Compare this with the statements of the Eskimo mentioned by Durant, Chapt. II, p. 6, and the Indians described by Ferris, Chapt. LXI, as pacing in front of their lodges. See also Kaczynski, *Technological Slavery* (2010), p. 406.

45.   (¶ 151) To be sure, past societies have had means of influencing human behavior, but these have been primitive and of low effectiveness compared with the technological means that are now being developed.

46.   (¶ 152) (Supplemented 2016) However, some psychologists have publicly expressed opinions indicating their contempt for human freedom. E.g., "I believe that the day has come when we can combine sensory deprivation with drugs, hypnosis and astute manipulation of reward and punishment to gain almost absolute control over an individual's behavior. ...We should reshape our society so that we all would be trained from birth to do what society wants us to do." James V. McConnell, quoted in an article titled "Behavior Control: Boon or Bane?," in the Chicago *Sun Times*, March 7, 1971. And the mathematician Claude Shannon was quoted in *Omni*, Aug. 1987, as saying: "I visualize a time when we will be to robots what dogs are to humans, and I'm rooting for the machines."

47.   (¶ 153) See Note 21.

48.   (¶ 154) This is no science fiction! After writing paragraph 154 we came across an article in *Scientific American* according to which scientists are actively developing techniques for identifying possible future criminals and for treating them by a combination of biological and psychological means. Some scientists advocate compulsory application of the treatment, which may be available in the near future. See W.W. Gibbs, as referenced in our List of Works Cited. Maybe you think this is okay because the treatment would be applied to those who might become violent criminals. But of course it won't stop there. Next, a treatment will be applied to those who might become drunk drivers (they endanger human life too), then perhaps to people who spank their children, then to environmentalists who sabotage logging equipment, eventually to anyone whose behavior is inconvenient for the system.

(Added 2016) The foregoing was written in 1995, but, as far as I know, compulsory treatments to prevent children from growing up to be criminals have not yet begun. This fact illustrates two points that I did not fully understand in 1995:

First, that invasions of our freedom and dignity tend to come from unexpected directions. An apparent threat to our freedom and dignity very often is never realized, or takes much longer to be realized than anyone has expected;

the erosion of our freedom and dignity continues, but in ways that no one has foreseen. For example, in 1970 "strong" (i.e., human-like) artificial intelligence, which would have put excessive power into the hands of those who possessed it, was expected within 15 years or so. Darrach, p. 58. But it has not yet arrived. On the other hand, most people nowadays have become so absorbed in and dependent on computerized electronic media that the technology industry has acquired enormous power over them in a way that no one dreamed of in 1970.

The second point is that where methods for controlling human behavior require intelligent monitoring or treatment of individuals, they are excessively difficult to apply effectively throughout an entire population. Thus our criminal-justice system, to the extent that it operates by attempting to manipulate actual or potential offenders on an individualized basis, is expensive and ineffective as a tool for controlling the behavior of the criminal population as a whole. The same can be said of our educational system to the extent that it tries to manipulate students individually. Present-day society therefore relies primarily on methods that can be applied on a mass basis and without taking account of individual differences, such as ubiquitous electronic surveillance that intimidates potential offenders and facilitates physical coercion, or propaganda in the widest sense of the term, for which the educational system serves as an effective vehicle.

49. (¶ 167) (Added 2016) I now think a gradual breakdown is so unlikely that we need not take that possibility into consideration. See Kaczynski, *Anti-Tech Revolution*, Chapt. Two.

50. (¶¶ 171–78) (Added 2016) I've now moved well beyond the speculations put forward here. For a far more probable vision of the future, see ibid.

51. (¶ 184) A further advantage of nature as a counter-ideal to technology is that, in many people, nature inspires the kind of reverence that is associated with religion, so that nature could perhaps be idealized on a religious basis. It is true that in many societies religion has served as a support and justification for the established order, but it is also true that religion has often provided a basis for rebellion. Thus it may be useful to introduce a religious element into the rebellion against technology, the more so because Western society today has no strong religious foundation. Religion nowadays either is used as cheap and transparent support for narrow, short-sighted selfishness (some conservatives use it this way), or even is cynically exploited to make easy money (by many evangelists), or has degenerated into crude irrationalism (fundamentalist Protestant sects, "cults"), or is simply stagnant (Catholicism, mainline Protestantism). The nearest thing to a strong, widespread, dynamic religion that the West has seen in recent times has been the quasi-religion of leftism, but leftism today is fragmented and has no clear, unified, inspiring goal. Thus there is a religious vacuum in our society that could perhaps be filled by a religion focused on nature in opposition to technology. But it would be a mistake to try to concoct artificially a religion to fill this role. Such

an invented religion would probably be a failure. Take the "Gaia" religion for example. Do its adherents *really* believe in it or are they just play-acting? If they are just play-acting their religion will be a flop in the end. It is probably best not to try to introduce religion into the conflict of nature vs. technology unless you *really* believe in that religion yourself and find that it arouses a deep, strong, genuine response in many other people.

52. (¶¶ 186–88) (Added 2016) Since writing these paragraphs in 1995, I've been gratified to find these two points confirmed by authors who are much better qualified than I am to deal with this subject: ISAIF's distinction between two levels of ideology corresponds roughly to Plekhanov's and Lenin's distinction between "propaganda" and "agitation." See NEB (2003), Vol. 26, "Propaganda," p. 171; Ulam, p. 34&n21; Selznick, pp. 9–10; Lenin, *What is to be Done?*, Chapt. III, Part B; pp. 101–02 in Christman. Alinsky, pp. 27–28, 78, 133–34, stresses the importance of presenting issues in black-and-white terms in the process of agitation, with all the good on one side and all the evil on the other.

53. (¶ 189) (Modified 2016) Assuming that such a final push occurs. It's conceivable though highly unlikely that the industrial system might be eliminated in a somewhat gradual or piecemeal fashion. (See paragraphs 4, 167 and Note 49.)

54. (¶ 195) The economic and technological structure of a society are far more important than its political structure in determining the way the average man lives. (See paragraphs 95, 119 and Notes 26, 34.)

55. (¶ 204) (Added 2016) I now retract this sentence. The advice to revolutionaries to have many children may possibly have had some merit in 1995, but I now believe that the final and decisive stage of the struggle against the system will have to be conducted by people who have already been born, though perhaps with some help from the first generation that follows them. The problem with having children is that potential revolutionaries who do so usually become so involved in family matters that they are of little use as revolutionaries.

56. (¶ 208) (Added 2016) Último Reducto has pointed out some examples of regression of small-scale technology in primitive societies, but even if such examples can be found in civilized societies they will not affect our argument.

57. (¶ 208) (Added 2016) See NEB (2003), Vol. 15, "Building Construction," p. 317.

58. (¶ 210) (Added 2016) See Bury, pp. 58–60, 64–65, 113.

59. (¶ 215) This statement refers to our particular brand of anarchism. A wide variety of social attitudes have been called "anarchist," and it may be that many who consider themselves anarchists would not accept our statement of paragraph 215. It should be noted, by the way, that there is a nonviolent anarchist movement whose members probably would not accept FC as anarchist and certainly would not approve of FC's violent methods.

(Added 2016) In 1995 I described FC as "anarchist" because I thought it would be advantageous to have some recognized political identity. At that time I knew very little about anarchism. Since then I've learned that anarchists, at least those of the U.S. and the U.K., are nothing but a lot of hopelessly ineffectual bunglers and dreamers, useless for any purpose. Needless to say, I now disavow any identification as an anarchist.

60.   (¶ 219) Many leftists are motivated also by hostility, but the hostility probably results in part from a frustrated need for power.

61.   (¶ 222) (Added 2016) This statement will perhaps be disputed. See Hoffer, § 14. Also, Rothfels, p. 63, notes that after Hitler's seizure of power in 1933 many Communists defected to become Nazis, and vice versa after 1945 in the Soviet zone of occupied Germany. But those who switched from one party to the other under such circumstances were not necessarily True Believers. More likely they were opportunists who joined whatever party seemed to be on the winning side at any given time. Be that as it may, even if true-believing Nazis and Communists of the first half of the 20th century were of identical psychological type, and even if one grants that all True Believers have *some* psychological traits in common, this writer finds it implausible to suppose that there are no major psychological differences between the typical Nazi and the typical true-believing leftist of recent decades in North America and Western Europe.

62.   (¶ 224) (Added 2016) My use of the term "power-hungry" has caused some confusion inasmuch as I've stressed the fact that everyone needs power, hence, many readers assume that everyone should be considered power-hungry. However, the term "power-hungry" is conventionally applied only to those who seek power over other people, as in the form of political or financial power, or any power to command. Those who seek power in the form, for example, of intellectual, artistic, or athletic prowess, or manual skills, or, say, the skills needed to live independently of the technological system, are not necessarily power-hungry in the usual sense of the term.

63.   (¶ 229) It is important to understand that we mean someone who sympathizes with these movements as they exist today in our society. One who believes that women, homosexuals, etc., should have equal rights is not necessarily a leftist. The feminist, gay rights, etc., movements that exist in our society have the particular ideological tone that characterizes leftism, and if one believes, for example, that women should have equal rights it does not necessarily follow that one must sympathize with the feminist movement as it exists today.

FURTHER COMMENTS (ADDED 2020)

In reference to paragraph 11, "broad," "chick," etc. In answer to this, a correspondent remarked that he would be offended if he were referred to or addressed as "dude," so some clarification is required. In many contexts, "dude" can be offensive *to the individual so addressed,* and even prior to the advent of leftist hypersensitivity "broad" or "chick" could be offensive *to the individual to whom those terms were applied.* The difference is that leftists now interpret the terms "broad" and "chick" as insulting to the entire female sex, even when those terms are applied only to particular individuals. No one feels that the entire male sex is insulted when a particular individual is called "dude."

In reference to paragraph 20, "Self-hatred is a leftist trait." It's worth noting that *The Organizer's Manual* (see List of Works Cited—Works Without Named Author), which was written by and for leftists, on page 33 portrays leftist ideology as a means of avoiding self-hatred.

In reference to paragraphs 38–41, surrogate activities. A distinction should be made between individual and collective surrogate activities. To take an example, if an individual runs long distances, not as a member of a running club and without expectation of running competitively, and runs more than is necessary for the promotion of health, then he or she engages in a purely individual surrogate activity. But if an individual runs as a member of a running club in competition with other members of the club, then an important part of his or her motive may be to win status among the members of the club. For the club collectively, running is a pure surrogate activity because its only purpose is to give the members of the club an opportunity to experience the power process. But for the individual member of the club running may not be a pure surrogate activity, because its purpose may be, at least in part, to achieve status within the club. This point is important in connection with the discussion of science as a surrogate activity (paragraphs 87–92). Science is, in part, a *collective* surrogate activity, because most individual scientists are motivated to a significant degree by a desire to achieve status among other scientists (which is not the same thing as achieving status in society at large).

In reference to the last paragraph of Note 48. This paragraph may soon lose its validity, because sophisticated computer algorithms are beginning to make individualized manipulation possible without individualized decision-making by human beings.

POSTSCRIPT
TO ISAIF

Postscript (2007) to ISAIF

ISAIF, *Industrial Society and its Future*, has been criticized as "unoriginal," but this misses the point. ISAIF was never intended to be original. Its purpose was to set forth certain points about modern technology in clear and relatively brief form, so that those points could be read and understood by people who would never work their way through a difficult text such as Jacques Ellul's *Technological Society*.

The accusation of unoriginality is in any case irrelevant. Is it important for the future of the world to know whether Ted Kaczynski is original or unoriginal? Obviously not! But it is indeed important for the future of the world to know whether modern technology has us on the road to disaster, whether anything short of revolution can avert that disaster, and whether the political left is an obstacle to revolution. So why have critics, for the most part, ignored the substance of the arguments raised in ISAIF and wasted words on matters of negligible importance, such as the author's putative lack of originality and the defects of his style? Clearly, the critics can't answer the substance of ISAIF's reasoning, so they try to divert their own and others' attention from its arguments by attacking irrelevant aspects of ISAIF.

One doesn't need to be original to recognize that technological progress is taking us down the road to disaster, and that nothing short of the overthrow of the entire technological system will get us off that road. In other words, only by accepting a massive disaster now can we avoid a far worse disaster later. But most of our intellectuals—and here I use that term in a broad sense—prefer not to face up to this frightening dilemma because, after all, they are not very brave, and they find it more comfortable to spend their time perfecting society's solutions to problems left over from the 19th century, such as those of social inequality, colonialism, cruelty to animals, and the like.

I haven't read everything that's been written on the technology problem, and it's possible that ISAIF may have been preceded by some other text that expounded the problem in equally brief and accessible form. But even so it would not follow that ISAIF was superfluous. However familiar its points may be to social scientists, those points still have not come to the attention of many other people who ought to be aware of them. More importantly, the available knowledge on this subject is not being *applied*. I don't think many of our intellectuals nowadays would deny that there *is* a technology problem, but nearly all of them decline to address it. At best they discuss particular problems created by technological progress, such as global warming or the spread of nuclear weapons. The technology problem as a whole is simply ignored.

It follows that the facts about technological progress and its consequences for society cannot be repeated too often. Even the most intelligent people may refuse to face up to a painful truth until it has been drummed into their heads again and again.

I should add that, as with ISAIF, no claim of originality is made for this book as a whole. The fact that I've cited authority for many of the ideas about human society that are presented here shows that those ideas are not new, and probably most of the other ideas too have previously appeared somewhere in print.

If there is anything new in my approach, it is that I've taken revolution seriously as a practical proposition. Many radical environmentalists and "green" anarchists talk of revolution, but as far as I am aware none of them have shown any understanding of how real revolutions come about, nor do they seem to grasp the fact that the exclusive target of revolution must be technology itself, not racism, sexism, or homophobia. A very few serious thinkers have suggested revolution against the technological system; for example, Ellul, in his *Autopsy of Revolution*. But Ellul only dreams of a revolution that would result from a vaguely defined, spontaneous spiritual transformation of society, and he comes very close to admitting that the proposed spiritual transformation is impossible. I on the other hand think it plausible that the preconditions for revolution may be developing in modern society, and I mean a real revolution, not fundamentally different in character from other revolutions that have occurred in the past. But this revolution will not become a reality without a well-defined revolutionary movement guided by suitable leaders—leaders who have a rational understanding of what they are doing, not enraged adolescents acting solely on the basis of emotion.

THE SYSTEM'S
NEATEST TRICK

The System's Neatest Trick (2002)

> The supreme luxury of the society of technical necessity will be to grant the bonus of useless revolt and of an acquiescent smile.
>
> —Jacques Ellul[1]

The System has played a trick on today's would-be revolutionaries and rebels. The trick is so cute that if it had been consciously planned one would have to admire it for its almost mathematical elegance.

1. *What the System is Not*

Let's begin by making clear what the System is not. The System is not George W. Bush and his advisors and appointees, it is not the cops who maltreat protestors, it is not the CEOs of the multinational corporations, and it is not the Frankensteins in their laboratories who criminally tinker with the genes of living things. All of these people are servants of the System, but in themselves they do not constitute the System. In particular, the personal and individual values, attitudes, beliefs, and behavior of any of these people may be significantly in conflict with the needs of the System.

To illustrate with an example, the System requires respect for property rights, yet CEOs, cops, scientists, and politicians sometimes steal. (In speaking of stealing we don't have to confine ourselves to actual lifting of physical objects. We can include all illegal means of acquiring property, such as cheating on income tax, accepting bribes, and any other form of graft or corruption.) But the fact that CEOs, cops, scientists, and politicians sometimes steal does not mean that stealing is part of the System. On the contrary, when a cop or a politician steals something he is rebelling against the System's requirement of respect for law and property. Yet, even when they are stealing, these people remain servants of the System as long as they publicly maintain their support for law and property.

Whatever illegal acts may be committed by politicians, cops, or CEOs as individuals, theft, bribery, and graft are not part of the System but diseases of the System. The less stealing there is, the better the System

119

functions, and that is why the servants and boosters of the System always advocate obedience to the law in public, even if they may sometimes find it convenient to break the law in private.

Take another example. Although the police are the System's enforcers, police brutality is not part of the System. When the cops beat the crap out of a suspect they are not doing the System's work, they are only letting out their own anger and hostility. The System's goal is not brutality or the expression of anger. As far as police work is concerned, the System's goal is to compel obedience to its rules and to do so with the least possible amount of disruption, violence, and bad publicity. Thus, from the System's point of view, the ideal cop is one who never gets angry, never uses any more violence than necessary, and as far as possible relies on manipulation rather than force to keep people under control. Police brutality is only another disease of the System, not part of the System. For proof, look at the attitude of the media. The mainstream media almost universally condemn police brutality. Of course, the attitude of the mainstream media represents, as a rule, the consensus of opinion among the powerful classes in our society as to what is good for the System.

What has just been said about theft, graft, and police brutality applies also to issues of discrimination and victimization such as racism, sexism, homophobia, poverty, and sweatshops. All of these are bad for the System. For example, the more that black people feel themselves scorned or excluded, the more likely they are to turn to crime and the less likely they are to educate themselves for careers that will make them useful to the System.

Modern technology, with its rapid long-distance transportation and its disruption of traditional ways of life, has led to the mixing of populations, so that nowadays people of different races, nationalities, cultures, and religions have to live and work side by side. If people hate or reject one another on the basis of race, ethnicity, religion, sexual preference, etc., the resulting conflicts interfere with the functioning of the System. Apart from a few old fossilized relics of the past like Jesse Helms,[2] the leaders of the System know this very well, and that is why we are taught in school and through the media to believe that racism, sexism, homophobia, and so forth are social evils to be eliminated.

No doubt some of the leaders of the System, some of the politicians, scientists, and CEOs, privately feel that a woman's place is in the home, or that homosexuality and interracial marriage are repugnant. But even if the majority of them felt that way it would not mean that racism, sexism, and homophobia were part of the System—any more than the existence of stealing among the leaders means that stealing is part of the System. Just as the System must promote respect for law and property for the sake of its own security, the System must also discourage racism and other forms of victimization, for the same reason. That is why the System, notwithstanding any private deviations by individual members of the elite, is basically committed to suppressing discrimination and victimization. For proof, look again at the attitude of the mainstream media. In spite of occasional timid dissent by a few of the more daring and reactionary commentators, media propaganda overwhelmingly favors racial and gender equality and acceptance of homosexuality and interracial marriage.[3]

The System needs a population that is meek, nonviolent, domesticated, docile, and obedient. It needs to avoid any conflict or disruption that could interfere with the orderly functioning of the social machine. In addition to suppressing racial, ethnic, religious, and other group hostilities, it also has to suppress or harness for its own advantage all other tendencies that could lead to disruption or disorder, such as machismo, aggressive impulses, and any inclination to violence. Naturally, traditional racial and ethnic antagonisms die slowly, machismo, aggressiveness, and violent impulses are not easily suppressed, and attitudes toward sex and gender identity are not transformed overnight. Therefore there are many individuals who resist these changes, and the System is faced with the problem of overcoming their resistance.[4]

2. *How the System Exploits the Impulse to Rebel*

All of us in modern society are hemmed in by a dense network of rules and regulations. We are at the mercy of large organizations such as corporations, governments, labor unions, universities, churches, and political parties, and consequently we are powerless. As a result of the servitude, the powerlessness, and the other indignities that the System inflicts on us, there is widespread frustration, which leads to an impulse to rebel. And this is where the System plays its neatest trick: Through a brilliant sleight of hand, it turns rebellion to its own advantage.

Many people do not understand the roots of their own frustration, hence their rebellion is directionless. They know that they want to rebel, but they don't know what they want to rebel against. Luckily, the System is able to fill their need by providing them with a list of standard and stereotyped grievances in the name of which to rebel: racism, homophobia, women's issues, poverty, sweatshops... the whole laundry-bag of "activist" issues. Huge numbers of would-be rebels take the bait. In fighting racism, sexism, etc., etc., they are only doing the System's work for it. In spite of this, they imagine that they are rebelling against the System. How is this possible?

First, in the 1950s the System was not yet committed to equality for black people, women and homosexuals, so that action in favor of these causes really was a form of rebellion. Consequently these causes came to be conventionally regarded as rebel causes. They have retained that status today simply as a matter of tradition; that is, because each rebel generation imitates the preceding generations.

Second, there are still significant numbers of people, as I pointed out earlier, who resist the social changes that the System requires, and some of these people even are authority figures such as cops, judges, or politicians. These resisters provide a target for the would-be rebels, someone for them to rebel against. Commentators like Rush Limbaugh help the process by ranting against the activists: Seeing that they have made someone angry fosters the activists' illusion that they are rebelling.

Third, in order to bring themselves into conflict even with that majority of the System's leaders who fully accept the social changes that the System demands, the would-be rebels insist on solutions that go farther than what the System's leaders consider prudent, and they show exaggerated anger over trivial matters. For example, they demand payment of reparations to black people, and they often become enraged at any criticism of an "oppressed" group, no matter how cautious and reasonable.

In this way the activists are able to maintain the illusion that they are rebelling against the System. But the illusion is absurd. Agitation against racism, sexism, homophobia and the like no more constitutes rebellion against the System than does agitation against political graft and corruption. Those who work against graft and corruption are not rebelling but acting as the System's enforcers: They are helping to keep the politicians obedient to the rules of the System. Those who work against racism, sexism, and homophobia similarly are acting as the System's enforcers: They help the System to suppress the deviant racist, sexist, and homophobic attitudes that cause problems for the System.

But the activists don't act only as the System's enforcers. They also serve as a kind of lightning rod that protects the System by drawing public resentment away from the System and its institutions. For example, there were several reasons why it was to the System's advantage to get women out of the home and into the workplace. In the 1950s, if the System, as represented by the government or the media, had begun out of the blue a propaganda campaign designed to make it socially acceptable for women to center their lives on careers rather than on the home, the natural human resistance to change would have caused widespread public resentment. What actually happened was that the changes were spearheaded by radical feminists, behind whom the System's institutions trailed at a safe distance. The resentment of the more conservative members of society was directed primarily against the radical feminists rather than against the System and its institutions, because the changes sponsored by the System seemed slow and moderate in comparison with the more radical solutions advocated by feminists, and even these relatively slow changes were seen as having been forced on the System by pressure from the radicals.

3. *The System's Neatest Trick*

So, in a nutshell, the System's neatest trick is this:

(a) For the sake of its own efficiency and security, the System needs to bring about deep and radical social changes to match the changed conditions resulting from technological progress.

(b) The frustration of life under the circumstances imposed by the System leads to rebellious impulses.

(c) Rebellious impulses are co-opted by the System in the service of the social changes it requires; activists "rebel" against the old and outmoded values that are no longer of use to the System and in favor of the new values that the System needs us to accept.

(d) In this way rebellious impulses, which otherwise might have been dangerous to the System, are given an outlet that is not only harmless to the System, but useful to it.

(e) Much of the public resentment resulting from the imposition of social changes is drawn away from the System and its institutions and is directed instead at the radicals who spearhead the social changes.[5]

Of course, this trick was not planned in advance by the System's leaders, who are not conscious of having played a trick at all. The way it works is something like this:

In deciding what position to take on any issue, the editors, publishers, and owners of the media must consciously or unconsciously balance several factors. They must consider how their readers or viewers will react to what they print or broadcast about the issue, they must consider how their advertisers, their peers in the media, and other powerful persons will react, and they must consider the effect on the security of the System of what they print or broadcast.

These practical considerations will usually outweigh whatever personal feelings they may have about the issue. The personal feelings of the media leaders, their advertisers, and other powerful persons are varied. They may be liberal or conservative, religious or atheistic. The only universal common ground among the leaders is their commitment to the System, its security, and its power. Therefore, within the limits imposed by what the public is willing to accept, the principal factor determining the attitudes propagated by the media is a rough consensus of opinion among the media leaders and other powerful people as to what is good for the System.

Thus, when an editor or other media leader sets out to decide what attitude to take toward a movement or a cause, his first thought is whether the movement includes anything that is good or bad for the System. Maybe he tells himself that his decision is based on moral, philosophical, or religious grounds, but it is an observable fact that in practice the security of the System takes precedence over all other factors in determining the attitude of the media.

For example, if a news-magazine editor looks at the militia movement, he may or may not sympathize personally with some of its grievances and goals, but he also sees that there will be a strong consensus among his advertisers and his peers in the media that the militia movement is potentially dangerous to the System and therefore should be discouraged. Under these circumstances he knows that his magazine had *better* take a negative attitude toward the militia movement. The negative attitude of the media presumably is part of the reason why the militia movement has died down.

When the same editor looks at radical feminism he sees that some of its more extreme solutions would be dangerous to the System, but he also sees that feminism holds much that is useful to the System. Women's participation in the business and technical world integrates them and their families better into the System. Their talents are of service to the System in business and technical matters. Feminist emphasis on ending domestic abuse and rape also serves the System's needs, since rape and abuse, like other forms of violence, are dangerous to the System. Perhaps most important, the editor recognizes that the pettiness and meaninglessness of modern housework and the social isolation of the modern housewife can lead to serious frustration for many women; frustration that will cause problems for the System unless women are allowed an outlet through careers in the business and technical world.

Even if this editor is a macho type who personally feels more comfortable with women in a subordinate position, he knows that feminism, at least in a relatively moderate form, is good for the System. He knows that his editorial posture must be favorable toward moderate feminism, otherwise he will face the disapproval of his advertisers and other powerful people. This is why the mainstream media's attitude has been generally supportive of moderate feminism, mixed toward radical feminism, and consistently hostile only toward the most extreme feminist positions.

Through this process, rebel movements that are dangerous to the System are subjected to negative propaganda, while rebel movements that are believed to be useful to the System are given cautious encouragement in the media. Unconscious absorption of media propaganda influences would-be rebels to "rebel" in ways that serve the interests of the System.

The university intellectuals also play an important role in carrying out the System's trick. Though they like to fancy themselves independent thinkers, the intellectuals are (allowing for individual exceptions) the most oversocialized, the most conformist, the tamest and most domesticated, the most pampered, dependent, and spineless group in America today. As a result, their impulse to rebel is particularly strong. But, because they are incapable of independent thought, real rebellion is impossible for them. Consequently they are suckers for the System's trick, which allows them to irritate people and enjoy the illusion of rebelling without ever having to challenge the System's basic values.

Because they are the teachers of young people, the university intellectuals are in a position to help the System play its trick on the young, which they do by steering young people's rebellious impulses toward the standard, stereotyped targets: racism, colonialism, women's issues, etc.

Young people who are not college students learn through the media, or through personal contact, of the "social justice" issues for which students rebel, and they imitate the students. Thus a youth culture develops in which there is a stereotyped mode of rebellion that spreads through imitation of peers—just as hairstyles, clothing styles, and other fads spread through imitation.

4. The Trick Is Not Perfect

Naturally, the System's trick does not work perfectly. Not all of the positions adopted by the "activist" community are consistent with the needs of the System. In this connection, some of the most important difficulties that confront the System are related to the conflict between two different types of propaganda that the System has to use, integration propaganda and agitation propaganda.[6]

Integration propaganda is the principal mechanism of socialization in modern society. It is propaganda that is designed to instill in people the attitudes, beliefs, values, and habits that they need to have in order to be safe and useful tools of the System. It teaches people to repress permanently or to sublimate those emotional impulses that are dangerous to the System. Its focus is on long-term attitudes and deep-seated values of broad applicability, rather than on attitudes toward specific, current issues.

Agitation propaganda plays on people's emotions so as to bring out certain attitudes or behaviors in specific, current situations. Instead of teaching people to suppress dangerous emotional impulses, it seeks to stimulate certain emotions for well-defined purposes localized in time.

The System needs an orderly, docile, cooperative, passive, dependent population. Above all it requires a nonviolent population, since it needs the government to have a monopoly on the use of physical force. For this reason, integration propaganda has to teach us to be horrified, frightened, and appalled by violence, so that we will not be tempted to use it even when we are very angry. (By "violence" I mean physical attacks on human beings.) More generally, integration propaganda has to teach us soft, cuddly values that emphasize nonaggressiveness, interdependence, and cooperation.

On the other hand, in certain contexts the System itself finds it useful or necessary to resort to brutal, aggressive methods to achieve its own objectives. The most obvious example of such methods is warfare.

In wartime the System relies on agitation propaganda: In order to win public approval of military action, it plays on people's emotions to make them feel frightened and angry at their real or supposed enemy. In this situation there is a conflict between integration propaganda and agitation propaganda. Those people in whom the cuddly values and the aversion to violence have been most deeply planted can't easily be persuaded to approve a bloody military operation. Here the System's trick backfires to some extent. The activists, who have been "rebelling" all along in favor of the values of integration propaganda, continue to do so during wartime. They oppose the war effort not only because it is violent but because it is "racist," "colonialist," "imperialist," etc., all of which are contrary to the soft, cuddly values taught by integration propaganda.

The System's trick also backfires where the treatment of animals is concerned. Inevitably, many people extend to animals the soft values and the aversion to violence that they are taught with respect to humans. They are horrified by the slaughter of animals for meat and by other practices harmful to animals, such as the reduction of chickens to egg-laying machines kept in tiny cages or the use of animals in scientific experiments. Up to a point, the resulting opposition to mistreatment of animals may be useful to the System: Because a vegan diet is more efficient in terms of resource-utilization than an omnivorous one is,[7] veganism, if widely adopted, will help to ease the burden placed on the Earth's limited resources by the growth of the human population. But activists' insistence on ending the use of animals in scientific experiments is squarely in conflict with the System's needs, since for the foreseeable future there is not likely to be any workable substitute for living animals as research subjects.

All the same, the fact that the System's trick does backfire here and there does not prevent it from being on the whole a remarkably effective device for turning rebellious impulses to the System's advantage.

It has to be conceded that the trick described here is not the only factor determining the direction that rebellious impulses take in our society. Many people today feel weak and powerless (for the very good reason that the System really does make us weak and powerless), and therefore identify obsessively with victims, with the weak and the oppressed. That is part of the reason why victimization issues, such as racism, sexism, homophobia, and neocolonialism have become standard activist issues. On this subject see ISAIF, ¶¶ 10–23.

5. *An Example*

I have with me an anthropology textbook in which I've noticed several nice examples of the way in which university intellectuals help the System with its trick by disguising conformity as criticism of modern society. In the cutest of these examples the author, William A. Haviland, quotes in "adapted" form an article by one Rhonda Kay Williamson, an intersexed person (that is, a person born with both male and female physical characteristics).[8]

Williamson states that the American Indians not only accepted intersexed persons but especially valued them.[9] She contrasts this attitude with the Euro-American attitude, which she equates with the attitude that her own parents adopted toward her. Williamson's parents mistreated her cruelly. They held her in contempt for her intersexed condition. They told her she was "cursed and given over to the devil," and they took her to charismatic churches to have the "demon" cast out of her. She was even given napkins into which she was supposed to "cough out the demon."

But it is absurd to equate this with the modern Euro-American attitude. It may approximate the Euro-American attitude of 150 years ago, but nowadays almost any American educator, psychologist, or mainstream clergyman would be horrified at that kind of treatment of an intersexed person. The media would never dream of portraying such treatment in a favorable light. Average middle-class Americans today may not be as accepting of the intersexed condition as the Indians were, but few would fail to recognize the cruelty of the way in which Williamson was treated.

Williamson's parents obviously were deviants, religious kooks whose attitudes and beliefs were way out of line with the values of the System. Thus, while putting on a show of criticizing modern Euro-American society, Williamson really is attacking only deviant minorities and cultural laggards who have not yet adapted to the dominant values of present-day America.

Haviland portrays cultural anthropology as iconoclastic, as challenging the assumptions of modern Western society.[10] This is so far contrary to the truth that it would be funny if it weren't so pathetic. The mainstream of modern American anthropology is abjectly subservient to the values and assumptions of the System. When today's anthropologists pretend to challenge the values of their society, typically they challenge only the values of the past—obsolete and outmoded values now held by no one but deviants and laggards who have not kept up with the cultural changes that the System requires of us.

Haviland's use of Williamson's article illustrates this very well, and it represents the general slant of Haviland's book. Haviland plays up ethnographic facts that teach his readers politically correct lessons, but he understates or omits altogether ethnographic facts that are politically incorrect. Thus, while he quotes Williamson's account to emphasize the Indians' acceptance of intersexed persons, he does not mention, for example, that among many of the Indian tribes, women who committed adultery had their noses cut off,[11] whereas no such punishment was inflicted on male adulterers; or that among the Crow Indians a warrior who was struck by a stranger had to kill the offender immediately, else he was irretrievably disgraced in the eyes of his tribe;[12] nor does Haviland discuss the habitual use of torture by the Indians of the eastern United States.[13] Of course, facts of that kind represent violence, machismo, and gender-discrimination, hence they are inconsistent with the present-day values of the System and tend to get censored out as politically incorrect.

Yet I don't doubt that Haviland is perfectly sincere in his belief that anthropologists challenge the assumptions of Western society. The capacity for self-deception of our university intellectuals will easily stretch that far.

To conclude, I want to make clear that I'm not suggesting that it is good to cut off noses for adultery, or that any other abuse of women should be tolerated, nor would I want to see anybody scorned or rejected because they were intersexed or because of their race, religion, sexual orientation, etc., etc., etc. But in our society today these matters are, at most, issues of reform. The System's neatest trick consists in having turned powerful rebellious impulses, which otherwise might have taken a revolutionary direction, to the service of these modest reforms.

NOTES

1. Ellul, *Technological Society*, p. 427.

2. The late Jesse Helms was a reactionary U.S. politician who was viewed by liberals as an arch-villain.

3. Even the most superficial review of the mass media in modern industrialized countries, or even in countries that merely aspire to modernity, will confirm that the System is committed to eliminating discrimination in regard to race, religion, gender, sexual orientation, etc., etc., etc. It would be easy to find thousands of examples that illustrate this, but here we cite only three, from three

disparate countries.

United States: "Public Displays of Affection," *U.S. News & World Report*, Sept. 9, 2002, pp. 42–43. This article provides a nice example of the way propaganda functions. It takes an ostensibly objective or neutral position on homosexual partnerships, giving some space to the views of those who oppose public acceptance of homosexuality. But anyone reading the article, with its distinctly sympathetic treatment of a homosexual couple, will be left with the impression that acceptance of homosexuality is desirable and, in the long run, inevitable. Particularly important is the photograph of the homosexual couple in question: A physically attractive pair has been selected and has been photographed attractively. No one with the slightest understanding of propaganda can fail to see that the article constitutes propaganda in favor of acceptance of homosexuality. And bear in mind that *U.S. News & World Report* is a right-of-center magazine.

Russia: "Putin Denounces Intolerance," *The Denver Post*, July 26, 2002, p. 16A. "MOSCOW—President Vladimir Putin strongly denounced racial and religious prejudice on Thursday... 'If we let this chauvinistic bacteria [sic] of either national or religious intolerance develop, we will ruin the country', Putin said in remarks prominently replayed on Russian television on Thursday night." Etc., etc.

Mexico: "Persiste racismo contra indígenas" ("Racism against indigenous people persists"), *El Sol de México*, Jan. 11, 2002, p. 1/B. Photo caption: "In spite of efforts to give dignity to the indigenous people of our country, they continue to suffer discrimination... ." The article reports on the efforts of the bishops of Mexico to combat discrimination, but says that the bishops want to "purify" indigenous customs in order to liberate the women from their traditionally inferior status. *El Sol de México* is reputed to be a right-of-center newspaper.

Anyone who wanted to take the trouble could multiply these examples a thousand times over. The evidence that the System itself is set on eliminating discrimination and victimization is so obvious and so massive that one boggles at the radicals' belief that fighting these evils is a form of rebellion. One can only attribute it to a phenomenon well known to professional propagandists: People tend to block out, to fail to perceive or to remember, information that conflicts with their ideology. See NEB (1997), Vol. 26, "Propaganda," p. 176.

4.   In this section I've said something about what the System is *not*, but I haven't said what the System *is*. A friend of mine has pointed out that this may leave the reader nonplussed, so I'd better explain that for the purposes of this article it isn't necessary to have a precise definition of what the System is. I couldn't think of any way of defining the System in a single, well-rounded sentence and I didn't want to break the continuity of the article with a long, awkward, and unnecessary digression addressing the question of what the System is, so I left that question unanswered. I don't think my failure to answer it will seriously impair the reader's understanding of the point that I want to make in this article.

5.   "The System's Neatest Trick" was written in 2002. At the present writing (2016) it seems that part (e) of the System's trick is no longer working. Political correctness has become so deeply entrenched in almost every aspect of our society that—especially after eight years of a left-wing president—"the radicals who spearhead the social changes" are no longer distinguishable from the System itself. To put it another way, the System itself is now perceived as the agency that forces social changes on American society. Consequently, those who are offended by the changes turn their resentment against the System itself. This is an important part of the reason, perhaps the main reason, why Donald Trump has attracted a large and passionate following.

6.   Ellul, *Propaganda*, discusses the concepts of "integration propaganda" and "agitation propaganda."

7.   (Added 2016) Actually it is debatable whether a vegan diet is more efficient than an omnivorous one in terms of resource-utilization.

8.   Haviland, pp. 132–36.

9.   I assume that this statement is accurate. It certainly reflects the Navaho attitude. See Reichard, p. 141. Reichard's book was originally copyrighted in 1950, well before American anthropology became heavily politicized, so I see no reason to suppose that its information is slanted.

10.   Haviland, p. 12.

11.   This is well known. See, e.g., Debo, p. 225; Marquis, p. 97; Vestal, p. 6; NEB (1997), Vol. 13, "American Peoples, Native," p. 380; Kroeber, p. 13.

12.   O. Russell, p. 147.

13.   Use of torture by the Indians of the eastern U.S. is well known. See, e.g., Wissler, pp. 131, 140, 145, 165, 282; Campbell, p. 135; NEB (1997), Vol. 13, "American Peoples, Native," p. 385; Axtell, passim, e.g., pp. 48, 86. Dick, p. 258, confirms use of torture by the Indians of the northeastern U.S., but says it "almost never" was used by those of the southeastern part of the country. Here Dick is in conflict with Wissler, pp. 145, 165 (the Cherokee and the Natchez, both southeastern tribes, tortured prisoners).

EXTRACTS FROM LETTERS
TO DAVID SKRBINA

Extracts from Letters to David Skrbina

In some respects my ideas have evolved since I wrote these letters. Where anything in the letters conflicts with what I subsequently wrote in Anti-Tech Revolution: Why and How, *the latter represents my current view.*

Letter to David Skrbina,
January 2, 2004

I've been able to identify only three ways (apart from modest reforms) in which human beings' intentions concerning the future of their own society can be realized successfully: (i) Intelligent administration can prolong the life of an existing social order. (E.g., if 19th-century Russian tsars had been a great deal less competent than they were, tsarism might have broken down earlier than it did. If Nicholas II had been a great deal more competent than he was, tsarism might have lasted a few decades longer.) (ii) Revolutionary action can bring about, or at least hasten, the breakdown of an existing social order. (E.g., if there had been no revolutionary movement in Russia, a new tsar would doubtless have been appointed on the abdication of Nicholas II and tsarism would have survived for a while.) (iii) An existing social order can sometimes be extended to encompass additional territory. (E.g., the social order of the West was successfully extended to Japan following World War II.)

If I'm right, and if we want to exert any rational influence (beyond modest reforms) on the future of our own society, then we have to choose one of the foregoing alternatives.

Letter to David Skrbina,
August 29, 2004

You sent me a copy of Bill Joy's article "Why the Future Doesn't Need Us,"[1] and you said you would be interested in my assessment of it. I read the article soon after it came out. I had already read elsewhere of most of the technological hazards described by Joy, but I considered his article useful because it gave further information about such hazards. Also, the fact that even a distinguished technophile like Bill Joy is scared about where technology is taking us should help to persuade people that the dangers of technology are real. Apart from that I was unimpressed by Joy's article. I assume that his technical expertise is solid, but it seems to me that his understanding of human nature and of how human societies work is at a naïve level. A couple of people who wrote to me about the article expressed similarly unenthusiastic opinions of it.

To give an example of what I consider to be Joy's naiveté, he writes:

> Verifying compliance will also require that scientists and engineers adopt a strong code of ethical conduct…and that they have the courage to whistleblow as necessary, even at high personal cost…. [T]he Dalai Lama argues that the most important thing is for us to conduct our lives with love and compassion for others, and that our societies need to develop a stronger notion of universal responsibility and of our interdependency….

If Bill Joy thinks that anything will be accomplished by this kind of preaching, then he is out of touch with reality. This part of his article would be funny if what is at stake weren't so desperately serious.

I've reread Joy's article to see if I were missing anything, but I found that my impression of it was the same as before. Of course, it's possible that the article has merits that I've overlooked.

*   *   *

I don't particularly consider small-scale technology to be acceptable; it's simply inevitable. See ISAIF, ¶¶ 207–212. I see no way of getting rid of it. People can't use organization-dependent technology if the social organization breaks down. E.g., you can't drive a car if the refineries aren't producing gasoline. But how could people be prevented from using small-scale technology? E.g., working steel, building a water-wheel, or ploughing and planting fields?

You ask whether I would consider a primitive steam-engine to be small-scale technology. To give a confident answer I would have to know more than I do about primitive steam-engines and their possible applications, but I think that steam-engines probably cannot be small-scale technology. "[Newcomen steam-engines'] heavy fuel consumption made them uneconomical when used where coal was expensive, but in the British coalfields they performed an essential service by keeping deep mines clear of water…."[2] An autonomous local community, without outside assistance, would find it very difficult to build an adequate steam-engine, and the engine probably would be of little use to such a community. Considering the effort required to build and maintain the engine, to produce oil to lubricate it, and to collect firewood to fuel it, any work the engine might do for a small community could probably be done more efficiently with human or animal muscle-power. Steam engines very likely could have been invented much earlier than they were, but—I would guess—they would have been of little use until certain 17th- and 18th-century economic and technological developments offered work for which steam engines were appropriate.

*   *   *

I'm quite sure that it will be impossible to control post-revolutionary conditions, but I think you're right in saying that a "positive social vision" is necessary. However, the social ideal I would put forward is that of the nomadic hunting-and-gathering society.

First, I would argue that in order to be successful a revolutionary movement *has* to be extremist. Trotsky wrote: "The different stages of a revolutionary process [are] certified by a change of parties in which the more extreme always supersedes the less… ."[3] Theodore Abel maintained that it was advisable for a movement to adopt as its goal the opposite of the evil that the movement was intended to combat.[4] The nomadic hunting-and-gathering society recommends itself as a social ideal because it is at the opposite extreme of human culture from the technological society.

Second, if one takes the position that certain appurtenances of civilization must be saved, e.g., cultural achievements up to the 17th century, then one will be tempted to make compromises when it comes to eliminating the technoindustrial system, with the possible or probable result that one will not succeed in eliminating the system at all. If the system breaks down, what will happen to the art museums with their priceless paintings and statues? Or to the great libraries with their vast stores of books? Who will take care of the artworks and books when there are no organizations large enough and rich enough to hire curators and librarians, as well as policemen to prevent looting and vandalism? And what about the educational system? Without an organized system of education, children will grow up uncultured and perhaps illiterate. Clearly, anyone who feels it is important to preserve human cultural achievements up to the 17th century will be very reluctant to see a complete breakdown of the system, hence will look for a compromise solution and will not take the frankly reckless measures that are necessary to knock our society off its present technologically-determined course of development. Therefore, only those who are willing to dispense with the achievements of civilization can be effective revolutionaries.

Third, to most people, a hunting-and-gathering existence will appear much more attractive than that offered by pre-industrial civilization. Even many modern people enjoy hunting, fishing, and gathering wild fruits and nuts. I think few would enjoy such tasks as ploughing, hoeing, or threshing. And in civilized societies, the common people have usually been exploited in one way or another by the upper classes: If they were not slaves or serfs, then they often were hired laborers or tenant-farmers subject to the domination of landowners. Pre-industrial civilized societies often suffered from disastrous epidemics or famines, and the common people in many cases had poor nutrition. In contrast, hunter-gatherers, except in the far north, generally had good nutrition.[5] Famines among them were probably rare.[6] They were relatively little troubled by infectious diseases until such diseases were introduced among them by more "advanced" peoples.[7] Slavery and well-developed social hierarchies could exist among *sedentary* hunter-gatherers, but (apart from the tendency of women to be in some degree subordinate to men), *nomadic* hunter-gatherer societies typically (not always) were characterized by social equality, and normally did not practice slavery.[8]

Just in case you've read anarcho-primitivist writings that portray the hunter-gatherer lifestyle as a kind of politically correct Garden of Eden where no one ever had to work more than three hours a day, men and women were equal, and all was love, cooperation and sharing, that's just a lot of nonsense, and at your request I'll prove it with numerous citations to the literature.[9] But even when one discounts the anarcho-primitivists' idealized vision and takes a hard-headed look at the facts, nomadic hunter-gatherer societies seem a great deal more attractive than pre-industrial civilized ones. I imagine that your chief objection to hunter-gatherer societies as opposed to (for example) late medieval or Renaissance European civilization would be their relatively very modest level of cultural achievement (in terms of art, music, literature, scholarship, etc.). But I seriously doubt that more than a small fraction of the population of modern industrial society cares very much about that kind of cultural achievement.

Hunter-gatherer society moreover has proved its appeal as a social ideal: Anarcho-primitivism seems to have gained wide popularity. One can hardly imagine equal success for a movement taking as its ideal—for example—late medieval society. Of course, one has to ask to what extent the success of anarcho-primitivism is dependent on its idealized portrayal of hunter-gatherer societies. My guess, or at least my hope, is that certain inconvenient aspects of hunter-gatherer societies (e.g., male dominance, hard work) would turn off the leftists, the neurotics, and the lazies but that such societies, depicted realistically, would remain attractive to the kind of people who could be effective revolutionaries.

I don't think that a worldwide return to a hunting-and-gathering economy would actually be a plausible outcome of a collapse of industrial society. No ideology will persuade people to starve when they can feed themselves by planting crops, so presumably agriculture will be practiced wherever the soil and climate are suitable for it. Reversion to hunting and gathering as the sole means of subsistence could occur only in regions unsuitable for agriculture, e.g., the subarctic, arid plains, or rugged mountains.

*   *   *

I'm not terribly interested in questions of values of the kind you discuss here, such as "herd values" versus the "will to power." As I see it, the overwhelmingly dominant problem of our time is that technology threatens either to destroy the world or to transform it so radically that all past questions of human values will simply become irrelevant, because the human race, as we have known it, will no longer exist. I don't mean that the human race necessarily will become physically extinct (though that is a possibility), but that the way human beings function socially and psychologically will be transformed so radically as to make traditional questions of values practically meaningless. The old-fashioned conformist will become as obsolete as the old-fashioned individualist.

Since this is the most critical juncture in the history of the human race, all other issues must be subordinated to the problem of stopping the technological juggernaut before it is too late. If I advocate a break with conventional morality, I do so not because I disapprove of the herd mentality, but because conventional morality acts as a brake on the development of an effective revolutionary movement. Furthermore, any effective revolutionary movement probably has to make use of the herd mentality. Imitativeness is part of human nature, and one has to work with it rather than preach against it.

Possibly you misinterpret my motives for emphasizing the "power process." The purpose of doing so is not to exalt the "will to power." There are two main reasons for discussing the power process. First, discussion of the power process is necessary for the analysis of the psychology of the people whom I call "leftists." Second, it is difficult to get people excited about working to avoid a future evil. It is less difficult to get people excited about throwing off a *present* evil. Discussion of the power process helps to show people how a great deal of *present* dissatisfaction and frustration results from the fact that we live in a technological society.

I should admit, though, that I personally am strongly inclined to individualism. Ideally, I shouldn't allow my individualistic predilections to influence my thinking on revolutionary strategy but should arrive at my conclusions objectively. The fact that you have spotted my individualistic leanings may mean that I have not been as objective as I should have been.

But even leaving aside all questions of "political" utility and considering only my personal predilections, I have little interest in philosophical questions such as the desirability or undesirability of the "herd mentality." The mountains of Western Montana offered me nearly everything I needed or wanted. If those mountains could have remained just as they were when I first moved to Montana in 1971, I would have been satisfied. The rest of the world could have had a herd mentality, or an individualistic mentality or whatever, and it would have been all the same to me. But, of course, under modern conditions there was no way the mountains could have remained isolated from the rest of the world. Civilization moved in and squeezed me, so...

*   *   *

Yes, growth in the population of nations and increasing racial/ethnic diversity no doubt affected social values. But increasing racial/ethnic diversity was unquestionably a consequence of technological events, namely, the development of relatively safe and efficient sailing ships, along with economic (therefore also technological) factors that provided incentives to trade, travel, and migrate widely. Presumably, population growth too was dependent on technological factors, such as improvements in agriculture that made it possible to feed more people.

*   *   *

I'll draw a distinction between a revolutionary movement and a reform movement. The distinction is not valid in all situations, but I think it is valid in the present situation.

The objective of a revolutionary movement, as opposed to a reform movement, is not to make piecemeal corrections of various evils of the social order. The objectives of a revolutionary movement are (i) to build its own strength, and (ii) to increase the tension within the social order until those tensions reach the breaking-point.

Correcting this or that social evil is likely to *decrease* the tensions within the social order. This is the reason for the classic antagonism between revolutionary movements and reform movements. Generally speaking, correction of a given social evil serves the purposes of a revolutionary movement only if it (a) constitutes a victory for the revolutionary movement that enhances the movement's prestige, (b) represents a humiliating defeat for the existing social order, (c) is achieved by methods that, if not illegal, are at least offensive to the existing order, and (d) is widely perceived as a step toward dissolution of the existing order.

In the particular situation that the world faces today, there may be also another case in which partial or piecemeal correction of a social evil may be useful: It may buy us time. For example, if progress in biotechnology is slowed, a biological catastrophe will be less likely to occur before we have time to overturn the system.

*   *   *

To address specifically your argument that a focus on population reduction is appropriate, at least as an "ancillary approach," I disagree for two reasons: (I) An effort to reduce population would be futile. (II) Even if it could be achieved, population reduction would accomplish nothing against the system. For these reasons, a focus on population reduction would waste time and energy that should be devoted to efforts that are more useful.

(I) If you were as old as I am and had watched the development of our society for fifty years, I don't think you would suggest a campaign against population growth. It has been tried and it has failed. Back in the 1960s and early 1970s, concern about "the population problem" was "in." There was even a national organization called "Zero Population Growth" whose goal was its name. Of course, it never accomplished anything. In those days, the fact that population was a problem was a new discovery, but nowadays it's "old hat," people are blasé, and it's much harder to get people aroused about population than it was back in the 1960s. Especially since the latest predictions are that world population will level off at about nine billion some time around the middle of this century. Such predictions are unreliable, but they nevertheless reduce anxiety about runaway population growth.

In any case, you could never get large numbers of people to have fewer children simply by pointing out to them the problems caused by overpopulation. As professional propagandists are well aware, reason by itself is of little use for influencing people on a mass basis.[10] To have any substantial effect, you would have to resort to the system's own techniques of propaganda. By dirtying its hands in this way, an anti-system movement would perhaps discredit itself. Anyhow, it's wildly improbable that such a movement could be rich enough to mount an effective worldwide or even nationwide campaign to persuade people to have fewer children. "Propaganda that aims to induce major changes is certain to take great amounts of time, resources, patience, and indirection, except in times of revolutionary crisis when old beliefs have been shattered... ."[11] The *Encyclopaedia Britannica Macropaedia* article "Propaganda" provides a good glimpse of the technical basis of modern propaganda, hence an idea of the vast amount of money you would need in order to make any substantial impression on the birthrate through persuasion. "Many of the bigger and wealthier propaganda agencies...conduct 'symbol campaigns' and 'image building' operations with mathematical calculation, using quantities of data that can be processed only by computers... ,"[12] etc., etc. (This should lay to rest your suggestion that "Propaganda can be opposed by counter-propaganda." Unless you have billions of dollars at your disposal, there's no way you can defeat the system in a head-on propaganda contest. A revolutionary movement has to find other means of making an impact.)

How difficult it would be to reduce the birthrate can be seen from the fact that the Chinese government has been trying to do that for years.

According to the latest reports I've heard (several years ago), they've had only very limited success, even though they have vastly greater resources than any revolutionary movement could hope to have.[13]

Furthermore, a campaign against having children could be a kind of suicide for a movement. The people who were with you wouldn't have children, your opponents *would* have children. Since the political orientation of children tends statistically to resemble that of their parents, your movement would get weaker with each generation.

And, to put it bluntly, a revolutionary movement needs an enemy, it needs someone or something to hate.[14] If you are working against overpopulation, then who is your enemy? Pregnant women? I don't think that would work very well.

(II) Even assuming you could reduce the birthrate, a population decline would be of little use and might well be counterproductive. I fail to understand your statement that population growth "seems to drive the whole technoindustrial process forward at an accelerating rate." Population increase no doubt is an important stimulus for economic growth, but it's hardly a decisive factor. In developed countries, economic growth probably occurs more through increasing demand for goods and services on the part of each individual than through an increase in the number of individuals. In any case, do you seriously believe that scientists would stop developing supercomputers and biological technology if the population started to decline? Of course, scientists need financial support from large organizations such as corporations and governments. But the large organizations' support for research is driven not by population growth but by competition for power among the large organizations.

So I think we can say that population is a dependent variable, technology is the independent variable. It's not primarily population growth that drives technology, but technology that makes population growth possible. Furthermore, because overcrowding makes people uncomfortable and increases stress and aggression, a reduction of population would tend to decrease the tensions in our society, hence would be contrary to the interests of a revolutionary movement, which, as already noted, needs to *increase* social tension. Even in the unlikely event that a victory on the population issue could be achieved, I don't think it would satisfy any of the conditions (b), (c), (d) that I listed earlier in this letter. Arguably, population decline could "buy us time" in the sense I've mentioned, but when this is weighed against the other factors I've just described I think the balance comes down

decisively against an effort to reduce population. But a revolutionary movement can make use of the population issue by pointing to overpopulation as
one of the negative consequences of technological progress.

*   *   *

I don't think the U.S. situation is as unique as you do. In any case, I
wouldn't emphasize the U.S. situation, because there are too many people
who are too ready to focus on the U.S. as the world's villain. I'm not a
patriot and not particularly interested in defending the U.S. But obsessive
anti-Americanism distracts attention from the technology problem just
as the issues of sexism, racism, etc., do. Given the present global technological and economic situation, if the U.S. weren't playing the role of the
world's bully, then probably some other country or group of countries
would be doing so. And if the Russians, for example, were playing that
role, I suspect they would play rougher than the U.S. does.

I'm not sure exactly what you mean by your final remark that there
are "many roads to revolution." But I would argue that a revolutionary
movement can't afford to be diverse and eclectic. It must be flexible, and
up to a point must allow for dissent within the movement. But a revolutionary movement needs to be unified, with a clear doctrine and goals. I
believe that a catchall movement that tries to embrace simultaneously all
roads to revolution will fail. A couple of cases in point:

A.   Under the Roman Empire there were several salvational religious movements analogous to Christianity. You'll find a discussion of this
in Jerome Carcopino's *Daily Life in Ancient Rome*. It seems that, with the
exception of Christianity, all of these religious movements were syncre-
tistic and mutually tolerant; one could belong to more than one of them.
Only Christianity required exclusive devotion.[15] And I don't have to tell
you which religion became in the end the dominant religion of Europe.

B.   In the early stage of the Russian Revolution of 1917, the Social
Revolutionary Party was dominant; the Bolshevik Party was small and
isolated. But the Social Revolutionary Party was a catchall party that took
in everyone who was vaguely in favor of the revolution. "To vote for the
Social Revolutionaries meant to vote for the revolution in general, and
involved no further obligation."[16] The Bolsheviks, in contrast, were reasonably unified and developed a program of action with clear goals. "The
Bolsheviks acted, or strove to act... like uncompromising revolutionists."[17]

And in the end it was the Bolsheviks, not the Social Revolutionaries, who determined the outcome of the revolution.

Letter to David Skrbina, September 18, 2004

I think that as a preliminary to answering your letter of July 27, it would be a good idea for me to give a more detailed outline of the "road to revolution" that I envision. The "road" is of course speculative. It's impossible to foretell the course of events, so any movement aspiring to get rid of the technoindustrial system will have to be flexible and proceed by trial and error. It's nevertheless necessary to give a *tentative* indication of the route to be followed, because without some idea of where it is going the movement will flounder around aimlessly. Also, an outline of at least a *possible* route to revolution helps to make the idea of revolution seem plausible. Probably the biggest current obstacle to the creation of an effective revolutionary movement is the mere fact that most people (at least in the U.S.) don't see revolution as a plausible possibility.

In the first place, I believe that illegal action will be indispensable. I wouldn't be allowed to mail this letter if I appeared to be trying to incite illegal action, so I will say only this much about it: A revolutionary movement should consist of two separate and independent sectors, an illegal, underground sector, and a legal sector. I'll say nothing about what the illegal sector should do. The legal sector (if only for its own protection) should carefully avoid any connection with the illegal sector.

With the possible exceptions listed in my letter of August 29, 2004, the function of the legal sector would not be to correct any evils of technology. Instead, its function would be to prepare the way for a future revolution, to be carried out when the right moment arrives.

Advance preparation is especially important in view of the fact that the occasion for revolution may arrive at any time and quite unexpectedly. The spontaneous insurrection in St. Petersburg in February 1917 took all of Russia by surprise. It is safe to say that this insurrection (if it had occurred at all) would have been no more than a massive but purposeless outburst of frustration if the way to revolution had not been prepared in advance. As it happened, there was already in existence a strong revolutionary movement that was in a position to provide leadership, and the revolutionaries moreover had for a long time been educating (or indoctrinating) the workers of St. Petersburg so that when the latter revolted they were not merely expressing senseless anger, but were acting purposefully and more or less intelligently.[18]

In order to prepare the way for revolution, the legal sector of the movement should:

(I) Build its own strength and cohesiveness. Increasing its *numbers* will be far less important than collecting members who are loyal, capable, deeply committed, and prepared for practical action. (The example of the Bolsheviks is instructive here.[19])

(II) Develop and disseminate an ideology that will (a) show people what dangers the advance of technology presents for the future; (b) show people that many of their present problems and frustrations derive from the fact that they live in a technological society; (c) show people that there have existed past societies that have been more or less free of these problems and frustrations; (d) offer as a positive ideal a life close to nature; and (e) present revolution as a realistic alternative.[20]

The utility of (II) is as follows:

As matters stand at the moment, revolution in the stable parts of the industrialized world is impossible. A revolution could occur only if something happened to shake the stability of industrial society. It is easy to imagine events or developments that could shake the system in this way. To take just one example, suppose a virus created in an experimental laboratory escaped and wiped out, say, a third of the population of the industrialized world. If this happened *now,* it hardly seems possible that it could lead to revolution. Instead of blaming the technoindustrial system as a whole for the disaster, people would blame only the carelessness of a particular laboratory. Their reaction would be not to dump technology, but to try to pick up the pieces and get the system running again—though doubtless they would enact laws requiring much stricter supervision of biotechnological research in the future.

The difficulty is that people see problems, frustrations, and disasters in isolation rather than seeing them as manifestations of the one central problem of technology. If Al Qaeda should set off a nuclear bomb in Washington, D.C., people's reaction will be, "Get those terrorists!" They will forget that the bomb could not have existed without the previous development of nuclear technology. When people find their culture or their economic welfare disrupted by the influx of large numbers of immigrants, their reaction is to hate the immigrants rather than take account of the fact that massive population movements are an inevitable consequence of economic developments that result from technological progress. If there is a worldwide depression, people will blame it merely on someone's economic mismanagement, forgetting that in earlier times, when small communities were largely self-sufficient, their welfare did not depend on the decisions of government economists. When people are upset about the decay of traditional values or the loss of local autonomy, they preach against "immorality" or get angry at "big government," without any apparent awareness that the loss of traditional values and of local autonomy is an unavoidable result of technological progress.

But if a revolutionary movement can show a sufficient number of people how the foregoing problems and many others all are outgrowths of one central problem,[21] namely, that of technology, and if the movement can successfully carry out the other tasks listed under (II), then, in case of a shattering event such as the epidemic mentioned above,[22] or a worldwide depression, or an accumulation of diverse factors that make life difficult or insecure, a revolution against the technoindustrial system may be possible.

Furthermore, the movement does not have to wait passively for a crisis that may weaken the system. Quite apart from any activities of the illegal sector, the dissension sown by the legal sector of the movement may help to bring on a crisis. For example, the Russian Revolution was precipitated by the tsarist regime's military disasters in World War I, and the revolutionary movement may have helped to create those disasters, since "[i]n no other belligerent country were political conflicts waged as intensively during the war as in Russia, preventing the effective mobilization of the rear."[23]

In carrying out the task (II) described above, the movement will of course use rational argument. But as I pointed out in my letter of August 29, 2004, reason by itself is a very weak tool for influencing human behavior on a mass basis. You have to work also with the non-rational aspects of human behavior. But in doing so you can't rely on the system's own techniques of propaganda. As I argued in my letter of August 29, 2004, you can't defeat the system in a head-on propaganda contest. Instead, you have to circumvent the system's superiority in psychological weaponry by making use of certain advantages that a revolutionary movement will have over the system. These advantages would include the following:

(i) It seems to be felt by many people that there is a kind of spiritual emptiness in modern life. I'm not sure exactly what this means, but "spiritual emptiness" would include at least the system's apparent inability to provide any positive values of wide appeal other than hedonistic ones or the simple worship of technological progress for its own sake. Evidence that many people find these values unsatisfactory is provided by the existence within modern society of groups that offer alternative systems of values— values that sometimes are in conflict with those of the system. Such groups would include fundamentalist churches and other, smaller cults that are still farther from the mainstream, as well as deviant political movements on the left and on the right. A successful revolutionary movement would have to do much better than these groups and fill the system's spiritual vacuum with values that can appeal to rational, self-disciplined people.

(ii) Wild nature still fascinates people. This is shown by the popularity of magazines like *National Geographic,* tourism to such (semi-)wild places as remain, and so forth. But, notwithstanding all the nature magazines, the guided wilderness tours, the parks and preserves, etc., the system's propaganda is unable to disguise the fact that "progress" is destroying wild nature. I think that many people continue to find this seriously disturbing, even apart from the practical consequences of environmental destruction, and their feelings on this subject provide a lever that a revolutionary movement can utilize.

(iii) Most people feel a need for a sense of community, or for belonging to what sociologists call a "reference group." The system tries to satisfy this need to the extent that it is able: Some people find their reference group in a mainstream church, a Boy Scout troop, a "support group," or the like. That these system-provided reference groups are for many people unsatisfactory is indicated by the proliferation of independent groups that lie outside the mainstream or even are antagonistic toward it. These include, inter alia, cults, gangs, and politically dissident groups. Possibly the reason why many people find the system-provided reference groups unsatisfactory is the very fact that these groups are appendages of the system. It may be that people need groups that are "their own thing," i.e., that are autonomous and independent of the system.

A revolutionary movement should be able to form reference groups that would offer values more satisfying than the system's hedonism. Wild nature perhaps would be the central value, or one of the central values.

In any case, where people belong to a close-knit reference group, they become largely immune to the system's propaganda to the extent that that propaganda conflicts with the values and beliefs of the reference group.[24] The reference group thus is one of the most important tools by means of which a revolutionary movement can overcome the system's propaganda.

(iv) Because the system needs an orderly and docile population, it must keep aggressive, hostile, and angry impulses under firm restraint. There is a good deal of anger toward the system itself, and the system needs to keep this kind of anger under especially tight control. Suppressed anger therefore is a powerful psychological force that a revolutionary movement should be able to use against the system.

(v) Because the system relies on cheap propaganda and requires willful blindness to the grim prospect that continued technological progress offers, a revolutionary movement that develops its ideas carefully and rationally may gain a decisive advantage by having reason on its side. I've pointed out previously that reason *by itself* is a very weak tool for influencing people in the mass. But I think nevertheless that if a movement gives ample attention to the non-rational factors that affect human behavior, it may profit enormously in the long run by having its key ideas established on a solidly rational foundation. In this way the movement will attract rational, intelligent people who are repelled by the system's propaganda and its distortion of reality. Such a movement may draw a smaller number of people than one that relies on a crude appeal to the irrational, but I maintain that a modest number of high-quality people will accomplish more in the long haul than a large number of fools. Bear in mind that rationality does not preclude a deep commitment or a powerful emotional investment.

Compare Marxism with the irrational religious movements that have appeared in the U.S. The religious movements achieved little or nothing of lasting importance, whereas Marxism shook the world. Marxism to be sure had its irrational elements: To many people belief in Marxism served as an equivalent of religious faith. But Marxism was far from being wholly irrational, and even today historians recognize Marx's contribution to the understanding of the effect of economic factors on history. From the perspective of the 19th and early 20th centuries, Marxism was plausible and highly relevant to the problems of the time, hence it attracted people of an entirely different stamp from those who were drawn to religious revivals.

It's possible however that faith in Marxism as dogma may have played an essential role in the success of the Russian revolutionary movement. It may be that a movement should not try to impose too rigid a rationality on its adherents, but should leave room for faith. If the movement's ideology has an underlying rational basis, I would guess that it should be able to attract rational and intelligent people notwithstanding a certain amount of non-rational or irrational ideological superstructure. This is a delicate question, and the answer to it can be worked out only through trial and error. But I still maintain that a largely rational basis for its position should give a revolutionary movement a powerful advantage vis-à-vis the system.

In any case, the kind of people who constitute the movement will be of decisive importance. The biggest mistake that such a movement could make would be to assume that the more people it has, the better, and to encourage everyone who might be interested to join it. This is exactly the mistake that was made by the original Earth First! As it was originally constituted in the early 1980s, Earth First! may have had the makings of a genuine revolutionary movement. But it indiscriminately invited all comers, and—of course!—the majority of comers were leftish types. These swamped the movement numerically and then took it over, changing its character. The process is documented by M.F. Lee (see the List of Works Cited). I do not believe that Earth First! as *now* constituted is any longer a potentially revolutionary movement.

The green anarchist/anarcho-primitivist movement, in addition to attracting leftish types, manifests another kind of personnel problem: It has attracted too many people who are mentally disorganized and seriously deficient in self-control, so that the movement as a whole has an irrational and sometimes childish character, as a result of which I think it is doomed to failure. Actually there are some very good ideas in the green anarchist/anarcho-primitivist movement, and I believe that in certain ways that movement takes the right approach. But the movement has been ruined by an excessive influx of the wrong kinds of people.

So a critically important problem facing a nascent revolutionary movement will be to keep out the leftists, the disorganized, irrational types, and other unsuitable persons who come flocking to any rebel movement in America today.

Probably the hardest part of building a movement is the very first step: One has to collect a handful of strongly committed people of the right sort. Once that small nucleus has been formed, it should be easier to attract additional adherents. A point to bear in mind, however, is that a group will not attract and hold adherents if it remains a mere debating society. One has to get people involved in practical projects if one wants to hold their interest. This is true whether one intends to build a revolutionary movement or one directed merely toward reform. The first project for the initial handful of people would be library research and the collection of information from other sources. Information to be collected would include, for example, historical data about the ways in which social changes have occurred in past societies, and about the evolution of political, ideological, and religious movements in those societies; information about the development of such movements in our own society during recent decades; results of scholarly studies of collective behavior; and data concerning the kinds of people involved in Earth First!, green anarchism, anarcho-primitivism, and related movements today. Once the group had gathered sufficient information it could design a provisional program of action, perhaps modifying or discarding many of the ideas I've outlined on the preceding pages.

But for anyone who seriously wants to do something about the technology problem, the initial task is quite clear: It is to build a nucleus for a new movement that will keep itself strictly separate from the leftists and the irrational types who infest the existing anti-technological movement.

Letter to David Skrbina,
October 12, 2004

I. I'll begin by summarizing some information from Martin E.P. Seligman, *Helplessness: On Depression, Development, and Death.* Here I have to rely on memory, because I do not have a copy of Seligman's book, nor do I have extensive notes on it.[25] Seligman arrived at the following conclusions through experiments with animals:

Take an animal, subject it repeatedly to a painful stimulus, and each time block its efforts to escape from the stimulus. The animal becomes frustrated. Repeat the process enough times, and the state of frustration gives way to one of depression. The animal just gives up. The animal has now acquired "learned helplessness." If at a later time you subject the animal to the same painful stimulus, it will not try to escape from the stimulus even if it could easily do so.

Learned helplessness can be unlearned. I don't recall the details, but the general idea is that the animal gets over learned helplessness by making *successful* efforts.

Both learning and unlearning of helplessness occur within the specific area of behavior in which the animal is trained. For example, if an animal acquires learned helplessness through repeated frustration of its efforts to escape from electrical shocks, it will not necessarily show learned helplessness in relation to efforts to get food. But learned helplessness does to some extent carry over from one area to another: If an animal acquires learned helplessness in relation to electrical shocks, subsequently it will more easily become discouraged when its efforts to get food are frustrated. The same principles apply to *un*learning of helplessness.

An animal can be partly "immunized" to learned helplessness: If an animal is given prior experience in overcoming obstacles through effort, it will be much more resistant to learned helplessness (hence also to depression) than an animal that has not had such experience. For example, if caged pigeons are able to get food only by pushing a lever on an apparatus that gives them one grain of wheat or the like for each push of the lever, then they will later acquire learned helplessness much less easily than pigeons that have not had to work for their food.

My memory of the following is not very clear, but I think Seligman indicates that laboratory rats and wild rats differ in that wild rats are far more energetic and persistent than laboratory ones in trying to save themselves in a desperate situation. Presumably the wild rats have been immunized to learned helplessness through successful efforts made in the course of their earlier lives.

At any rate, it does appear that purposeful effort plays an essential role in the psychological economy of animals.[26]

I first read Seligman's book in the late 1980s. The book originally came out in 1975, and I haven't had much opportunity to read later work on learned helplessness. But the theory is believed to be valid also for human beings, and I think it is the subject of continuing work.

I don't necessarily accept a psychological theory just because some psychologists say it's true. There's a lot of nonsense in the field, and even experimental psychologists sometimes draw silly conclusions from their data. But the theory of learned helplessness squares very neatly with my own personal experience and with my impressions of human nature gained from observation of others.

The need for purposeful, successful effort implies a need for competence, or a need to be able to exercise control, because one's goals can't be attained if one does not have the competence, or the power to exercise control, that is necessary to reach the goals. Seligman writes:

> Many theorists have talked about the need or drive to master events in
> the environment. In a classic exposition, R.W. White (1959) proposed the
> concept of *competence*. He argued that the basic drive for control had been
> overlooked by learning theorists and psychoanalytic thinkers alike. The
> need to master could be more pervasive than sex, hunger, and thirst in
> the lives of animals and men.... J.L. Kavanau (1967) has postulated that
> the drive to resist compulsion is more important to wild animals than sex,
> food, or water. He found that captive white-footed mice spent inordinate
> time and energy just resisting experimental manipulation. If the experi-
> menters turned the lights up, the mouse spent his time setting them down.
> If the experimenters turned the lights down, the mouse turned them up.[27]

This suggests a need not only for power but for autonomy. In fact,
such a need would seem to be implied by the need to attain goals through
effort; for if one's efforts are undertaken in subordination to another
person, then those efforts will be directed toward the other person's goals
rather than toward one's own goals.

Yet the inconvenient fact is that human individuals seem to differ
greatly in the degree of autonomy that they need. For some people the
drive for autonomy is very powerful, while at the other extreme there are
people who seem to need no autonomy at all, but prefer to have someone
else do their thinking for them. It may be that these people, automatically
and without even willing it, accept as their own goals whatever goals are
set up for them by those whose authority they recognize. Another view
might be that for some reason certain people need purposeful effort that
exercises their powers of thinking and decision-making, while other people
need only to exercise their physical and their strictly routine mental capa-
bilities. Yet another hypothesis would be that those who prefer to have
others set their goals for them are persons who have acquired learned
helplessness in the area of thinking and decision-making.

So the question of autonomy remains somewhat problematic. In
any case, it's clear how ISAIF's concept of the power process is related to
the foregoing discussion. As ISAIF explains in ¶ 33, the need for the power
process consists in a need to have goals, to make efforts toward those goals,
and to succeed in attaining at least some of the goals; and most people
need a greater or lesser degree of autonomy in pursuing their goals.

If one has had insufficient experience of the power process, then one has not been "immunized" to learned helplessness, hence one is more susceptible to helplessness and consequently to depression. Even if one has been immunized, long-continued inability to attain goals will cause frustration and will lead eventually to depression. As any psychologist will tell you, frustration causes anger, and depression tends to produce guilt feelings, self-hatred, anxiety, sleep disorders, eating disorders, and other symptoms. (See ISAIF, ¶ 44 and Note 8.) Thus, if the theory of learned helplessness is correct, then ISAIF's definition of "freedom" in terms of the power process is not arbitrary but is based on biological needs of humans and of animals.

This picture has support in other quarters. The zoologist Desmond Morris, in his book *The Human Zoo*, describes some of the abnormal behavior shown by wild animals when they are confined in cages, and he explains the prevalence of abnormal behavior (e.g., child abuse and sexual perversion) among modern people by comparing present-day humans to zoo animals: Modern society is our "cage."[28] Morris shows no awareness of the theory of learned helplessness, but much of what he says dovetails very nicely with that theory. He even mentions "substitute activities" that are equivalent to ISAIF's "surrogate activities."[29]

The need for power, autonomy, and purposeful activity is perhaps implicit in some of Ellul's work. Shortly after my trial, a Dr. Michael Aleksiuk sent me a copy of his book *Power Therapy*, which contains ideas closely related to that of the power process. A major theme of Kenneth Keniston's study *The Uncommitted* is the sense of purposelessness that afflicts many people in the modern world, and he mentions an "instinct of workmanship," meaning a need to do purposeful work.[30] In the first part of his book *Growing Up Absurd*, Paul Goodman discusses as a source of social problems the fact that men no longer need to do hard, demanding work that is essential for survival.[31] Reviewing a book by Gerard Piel, Nathan Keyfitz wrote:

> Among other signs of the lack of adaptation [in modern society] is... purposelessness. Our ancestors, whose work was hard and often dangerous, always necessary simply to keep alive, seemed to know what they were here for. Now 'anomie and preoccupation with the isolated self recur as a central theme of U.S. popular culture. That they find resonance in every other industrial country suggests that the solving of the economic problem brings on these quandaries everywhere.'[32]

Thus, I argue that the power process is not a luxury but a fundamental need in human psychological development, and that disruption of the power process is a critically important problem in modern society. Because of my lack of access to good library facilities, I haven't been able to explore the relevant psychological literature to any significant extent, but for anyone interested in modern social problems such an exploration should be well worth the time it would cost.

In answering your letters I'm not going to stick rigidly with the definition of freedom given in ISAIF, ¶ 94, but I will assume throughout that the kind of freedom that really matters is the freedom to do things that have important practical consequences, and that the freedom to do things merely for pleasure, or for "fulfillment," or in pursuit of surrogate activities, is relatively insignificant. See ISAIF, ¶ 72.

"Human dignity" is a very vague term and a broadly inclusive one. But I will assume that one essential element of human dignity is the capacity to exert oneself in pursuit of important, practical goals that one has selected either by oneself or as a member of a small, autonomous group. Thus, both freedom and dignity, as I will use those terms, are closely involved with the power process and with the associated biological need.

II. You ask for a "core reason" why things are getting worse. There are two core reasons.

A. Until roughly ten thousand years ago, all people lived as hunter-gatherers, and that is the way of life to which we are adapted physically and mentally. Many of us, including some Europeans,[33] lived as hunter-gatherers much more recently than ten thousand years ago. We may have undergone some genetic changes since becoming agriculturalists, but those changes are not likely to have been massive.[34] Hunter-gatherers who survived into modern times were people very much like ourselves.

As technology has advanced over the millennia, it has increasingly altered our way of life, so that we've had to live under conditions that have diverged more and more from the conditions to which we are adapted. This growing maladaptation subjects us to an ever-increasing strain. The problem has become particularly acute since the Industrial Revolution, which has been changing our lives more profoundly than any earlier development in human history. Consequently, we are suffering more acutely than ever from maladaptation to the circumstances in which we live. (Robert Wright has developed this thesis in an article that you might be interested to read.[35])

I argue that the most important single maladaptation involved derives from the fact that our present circumstances deprive us of the opportunity to experience the power process properly. In other words, we lack freedom as the term is defined in ISAIF, ¶ 94.

The argument that "people now have more freedom than ever" is based on the fact that we are allowed to do almost anything we please *as long as it has no practical consequences*. See ISAIF, ¶ 72. Where our actions have practical consequences that may be of concern to the system (and few important practical consequences are not of concern to the system), our behavior, generally speaking, is closely regulated. Examples: We can believe in any religion we like, have sex with any consenting adult partner, take a plane to China or Timbuktu, have the shape of our nose changed, choose any from a huge variety of books, movies, musical recordings, etc., etc., etc. But these choices normally have no important practical consequences. Moreover, they do not require any serious effort on our part. We don't change the shape of our own nose, we pay a surgeon to do it for us. We don't go to China or Timbuktu under our own power, we pay someone to fly us there.

On the other hand, within our own home city, we can't go from point A to point B without our movement being controlled by traffic regulations, we can't buy a firearm without undergoing a background check, we can't change jobs without having our background scrutinized by prospective employers, most people's jobs require them to work according to rules, procedures, and schedules prescribed by their employers, we can't start a business without getting licenses and permits, observing numerous regulations, and so forth.

Moreover, we live at the mercy of large organizations whose actions determine the circumstances of our existence, such as the state of the economy and the environment, whether there will be a war or a nuclear accident, what kind of education our children will receive and what media influences they will be exposed to. Etc., etc., etc.

In short, we have more freedom than ever before to *have fun*, but we can't intervene significantly in the life-and-death issues that hang over us. Such issues are kept firmly under the control of large organizations. Hence our deprivation with respect to the power process, which requires that we have *serious* goals and the power to reach those goals through our own effort.

B. The second "core reason" why things are getting worse is that there is no way to prevent technology from being used in harmful ways, especially because the ultimate consequences of any given application of technology commonly cannot be predicted. Therefore, harm cannot be foreseen until it is too late.

Of course, the consequences of primitive man's actions may often have been unpredictable, but because his powers were limited, the negative consequences of his actions also were limited. As technology becomes more and more powerful, the unforeseeable consequences even of its well-intentioned use—let alone the consequences of its irresponsible or malicious use—become more and more serious, and introduce into the world a growing instability that is likely to lead eventually to disaster. See Bill Joy's article, "Why the Future Doesn't Need Us," and Martin Rees, *Our Final Hour*.

III.A. *"Objective" factors in history.* I assert that the course of history, in the large, is normally determined primarily by "objective" factors rather than by human intentions or by the decisions of individuals. Human intentions or the decisions of individuals may occasionally make a major, long-term difference in the course of history, but when this happens the results do not fulfill the intentions of the individuals or groups that have made the decisions. Some exceptions, however, can be identified. Human intentions can sometimes be realized in the following three ways (see my letter of January 2, 2004): (i) Intelligent administration may prolong the life of an existing social order. (ii) It may be possible to cause, or at least to hasten, the breakdown of an existing social order. (iii) An existing social order can sometimes be extended so as to encompass additional territory.[36]

I need to explain what the foregoing means. Human intentions often are realized, even for a long period, with respect to some particular factor in society. But, in such cases, human intentions for the society as a whole are not realized.

For example, in the Soviet Union the Communists achieved some of their goals, such as rapid industrialization, full employment, and a significant reduction in social inequality, but the society they created was very different from what the Bolsheviks had originally intended.[37] (And in the *long* run the socialist system failed altogether.) Since the onset of the Industrial Revolution in the 18th century, people have succeeded in achieving material abundance, but the result is certainly not the kind of society that was envisioned by 18th-century proponents of progress.[38] (And today people like Bill Joy and Martin Rees fear that industrial society may not survive much longer.) The Prophet Mohammed succeeded in establishing his new religion as the faith of millions of people; that religion has flourished for nearly fourteen centuries and may well do so for many centuries more. But: "At the end of the rule of the 'rightly guided' caliphs, the Prophet's dream of ushering in a new era of equality and social justice remained unfulfilled... ;"[39] nor has that dream been fulfilled today.

To explain further what I mean when I say that history is generally guided by "objective" factors and not by human intentions or human will, I'll use an example that presents the issue in simplified form.

Given three factors:

(i) the presence of hunting-and-gathering bands at the eastern extremity of Siberia;

(ii) the presence of good habitat for humans at the western extremity of Alaska; and

(iii) the existence of a land-bridge across what is now the Bering Strait,
the occupation of the Americas by human beings was a historical inevitability and was in a certain sense independent of human intention and of human will.

Of course, human intentions were involved. In order for the Americas to be occupied, some hunting-and-gathering band at some point had to choose intentionally to move eastward across the land-bridge. But the occupation of the Americas did not depend on the intentions of any one hunting-and-gathering band—or any dozen bands—because, given the three conditions listed above, it was inevitable that *some* band sooner or later would move across the land-bridge. It is in this sense that major, long-term historical developments normally result from the operation of "objective" factors and are independent of human intentions.

The foregoing does not mean that history is rigidly deterministic in the sense that the actions of individuals and small groups can *never* have an important, long-term effect on the course of events. For example, if the period during which the Bering Strait could be crossed had been short, say fifty or a hundred years, then the decision of a single hunting-and-gathering band to cross or not to cross to Alaska might have determined whether Columbus would find the Americas populated or uninhabited. But even in this case the occupation of the Americas would not have been a realization of the intentions of the single band that made the crossing. The intention of that band would have been only to move into one particular patch of desirable habitat, and it could have had no idea that its action would lead to the occupation of two great continents.

B. *Natural selection.* A principle to bear in mind in considering the "objective" factors in history is the law of what I call "natural selection": Social groups (of any size, from two or three people to entire nations) having the traits that best suit them to survive and propagate themselves, are the social groups that best survive and propagate themselves. This of course is an obvious tautology, so it tells us nothing new. But it does serve to call our attention to factors that we might otherwise overlook. I have not seen the term "natural selection" used elsewhere in connection with this principle,[40] but the principle itself has not gone unnoticed. In the *Encyclopaedia Britannica* we find:

> These processes were not inevitable in the sense that they corresponded to any 'law' of social change. They had the tendency, however, to spread whenever they occurred. For example, once the set of transformations known as the agrarian revolution had taken place anywhere in the world, their extension over the rest of the world was predictable. Societies that adopted these innovations grew in size and became more powerful. As a consequence, other societies had only three options: to be conquered and incorporated by a more powerful agrarian society; to adopt the innovations; or to be driven away to the marginal places of the globe. Something similar might be said of the Industrial Revolution and other power-enhancing innovations, such as bureaucratization and the introduction of more destructive weapons.[41]

Notice that there is a difference between the "natural selection" that operates among human groups and the natural selection that we are familiar with in biology. In biology, more successful organisms simply replace less successful ones and are not imitated by them. But in human affairs less successful groups tend to try to imitate more successful ones. That is, they try to adopt the social forms or practices that appear to have made the latter groups successful. Thus, certain social forms and practices propagate themselves not only because groups having those forms and practices tend to replace other groups, but also because other groups adopt those forms and practices in order to avoid being replaced. So it is probably more correct to describe natural selection as operating on social forms and practices rather than as operating on groups of people.

The principle of natural selection is beyond dispute because it is a tautology. But the principle could produce misleading conclusions if applied carelessly: For example, the principle does not a priori exclude human will as a factor guiding history.

C. *Human will versus "objective" forces of history.* In Western Europe, until recently, bellicosity—a readiness and ability to make war—was an advantageous trait in terms of "natural selection": Militarily successful nations increased their power and their territory at the expense of other nations that were less successful in war. However, I think this is no longer true, because there is a strong consensus in Western Europe today that war between two Western European nations is absolutely unacceptable. Any nation that initiated such a war would be pounced upon by all the rest of Western Europe and soundly defeated. Thus, in Western Europe, bellicosity (at least as directed against other Western European nations), is now a *dis*advantageous trait in terms of natural selection, and it is so because of the human will to avoid war in Western Europe. This shows that human will can be a "selective force" involved in the process of "natural selection" as it operates in human affairs.[42]

However (to the extent that it does not rely on the U.S. for protection), Western Europe as a whole still needs to be prepared for war, because outside Western Europe there exist other entities (nations or groups of nations) that might well make war on Western Europe if they thought they could get away with it. As it is, if any nation outside Western Europe made war on a Western European nation, and if the latter were unable to defend itself adequately, the rest of Western Europe would help it to defeat the aggressor. Thus, by eliminating *internal* warfare and acquiring a certain degree of unity, Western Europe has become more formidable in war against any outside entity.

What has happened in Western Europe is simply a continuation of a process that has been going on for thousands of years: Smaller political entities group together (whether voluntarily or through conquest) to form a larger political entity that eliminates internal warfare and thereby becomes a more successful competitor in war against other political entities. Size does not always guarantee survival (e.g., consider the breakup of the Roman Empire), but in the course of history smaller political entities generally have tended to coalesce to form larger and therefore militarily more powerful ones; and this process is not dependent on human intention but results from "natural selection."

Thus, when we take a relatively localized view of history and consider only Western Europe over the last several decades, human will appears to be an important factor in the process of natural selection, but when we take a broader view and look at the whole course of history, human will appears insignificant: "Objective" factors have determined the replacement of smaller political entities by larger ones.

Of course, it's conceivable that human will might some day eliminate war altogether. A world government might not even be necessary. It would be enough that there should exist a strong worldwide consensus, similar to the consensus now existing in Western Europe, that war was unacceptable and that any nation initiating a war should be promptly crushed by all the other nations. Bellicosity would then become a highly disadvantageous trait in terms of natural selection. And, since the whole world would be encompassed by the consensus, there would be no outside competitor left against whom it might be necessary to make war.

But you can see how difficult it is to reach the necessary consensus. Efforts to end war have been going on at least since the end of World War I with the League of Nations, and outside of Western Europe there has been little progress in that regard. Moreover, even if conventional warfare could be ended through an international consensus, organized violence might well continue, because there are forms of organized violence (e.g., guerrilla warfare, terrorism) that would be extremely difficult to suppress even if vigorously opposed by every nation on Earth.

The purpose of the foregoing discussion is not to prove that it is never possible for human will to change the course of history. If I didn't believe it were possible, then I wouldn't waste my time writing letters like this one. But we have to recognize how powerful the "objective" forces of history are and how limited is the scope for human choice. A realistic appraisal will help us to discard solutions that appear desirable but are impossible to put into practice, and concentrate our attention on solutions that may be less than ideal but perhaps have a chance of success.

D. *Democracy as a product of "objective" forces.* In your letter of July 27, 2004, you and your colleague offer "democracy" as an example of an improvement in the human condition brought about by "human action."

I assume that by "democracy" you mean representative democracy, i.e., a system of government in which people elect their own leaders. And I assume that in referring to "human action" you mean that representative democracy became the dominant form of government in the modern world through a process that more or less fits the following model: problem perceived—solution devised—solution implemented—problem solved. If this is what you mean, then I think you are wrong.

I think the problem of political oppression has been perceived for thousands of years. Presumably, people have resented political oppression ever since the beginning of civilization; this is indicated by numerous peasant revolts and the like that have been recorded in history. If representative democracy is the solution to the problem of political oppression, then the solution, too, has long been known and sometimes implemented. The idea and the practice of representative democracy go back at least to ancient Athens, and may well go back to prehistoric times, for some of the aborigines of southeastern Australia practiced representative democracy.[43] About 550–350 BC, "the region in which Buddhism arose was noted for a system of tribal democracy or republicanism. When a serious question demanded attention…, the male inhabitants would meet to decide upon a course of action, often electing a temporary ruler."[44] Sixteenth-century Cossacks had "a military organization of a peculiarly democratic kind, with a general assembly (*rada*) as the supreme authority and elected officers, including the commander in chief… ."[45] Seventeenth-century buccaneers elected their own captains, who could be deposed by the crew at any time when an enemy was not in sight.[46] Fifteenth-century Geneva had a democratic government, though perhaps not strictly speaking a representative democracy, since the legislative body consisted of all citizens.[47] In addition to fully democratic systems, there have been some partially democratic ones. Under the Roman Republic, for example, public officials were elected by the assembled people, but the aristocratic Senate was the dominant political force.[48]

Thus, representative democracy has been tried with varying degrees of success at many times and places. Nevertheless, among pre-industrial civilized societies the dominant forms of government remained the monarchical, oligarchic, aristocratic, and feudal ones, and representative democracy was only a sporadic phenomenon. Clearly, under the conditions of pre-industrial civilization, democracy was not as well adapted for survival and propagation as other forms of government were. This could have been due to internal weakness (instability, or a tendency to transmute into other forms of government), or to external weakness (a democratic government may have been unsuccessful in competing economically or militarily with its more authoritarian rivals).

Whatever it was that made pre-industrial democracy weak, the situation changed with the advent of the Industrial Revolution. Suddenly people began to admire the (semi-) democratic systems of Britain and the United States, and attempts were made to imitate those systems. If Britain had been economically poor and militarily weak, and if the United States had been a stagnant backwater, would their systems have been admired and imitated? Not likely! Britain was economically and militarily the most successful nation in Europe, and the United States was a young but dynamically growing country, hence these two countries excited the admiration and envy of the propertied classes in other countries. It was the propertied classes, not the laboring classes, who were primarily responsible for the spread of democracy. That's why Marxists always referred to the democratic revolutions as "bourgeois revolutions."

The democracies had to survive repeated contests with authoritarian systems, and they did survive, largely because of their economic and technological vigor. They won World Wars I and II, and they didn't do so because soldiers were more willing to fight for a democratic than for an authoritarian government. No one has ever questioned the bravery or the fighting spirit of the German and Japanese soldiers.[49] The democracies won mainly because of their industrial might.[50]

Notice that fascism was popular, even to some extent in the U.S.,[51] between the two World Wars. (Here I use the term "fascism" in its generic sense, not referring specifically to Mussolini's Fascists.) After World War II, fascism lost its popularity. Why? Because the fascists lost the war. If the fascists had won, fascism undoubtedly would have been admired and imitated.[52]

During much of the Cold War, "socialism" was the watchword throughout the Third World. It represented the state of bliss to which most politically-conscious people there aspired. But that lasted only as long as the Soviet Union appeared to be more dynamic and vigorous than the U.S. When it became clear that the Soviet Union and other socialist countries could not keep up with the West economically or technologically, socialism lost its popularity, and the new watchwords were "democracy" and "free market."[53]

Thus democracy has become the dominant political form of the modern world not because someone decided that we needed a more humane form of government, but because of an "objective" fact, namely, that under the conditions created by industrialization, democratic systems are more vigorous technologically and economically than other systems.[54]

Bear in mind that, as technology continues to progress, there is no guarantee that representative democracy will always be the political form best adapted to survive and propagate itself. Democracy may be replaced by some more successful political system. In fact, it could be argued that this has already happened. It could plausibly be maintained that, notwithstanding the continuation of democratic forms such as reasonably honest elections, our society is really governed by the elites that control the media and lead the political parties. Elections, it might be claimed, have been reduced to contests between rival groups of propagandists and image-makers.

Letter to David Skrbina,
November 23, 2004

III. Are things bad and getting worse, and is technology primarily responsible?

A. Arguments that technology has made things bad and is making them worse are presented throughout ISAIF, as well as in the writings of Jacques Ellul, Lewis Mumford, Kirkpatrick Sale, and others. Your colleague has not addressed these arguments in any specific way. The only substantive arguments that he offers are the four examples of ways in which things are allegedly getting better. I would be perfectly justified in dismissing these four examples by pointing out that neither I nor any responsible commentator has claimed that technology makes *everything* worse—everyone knows that technology does some good things. I could then simply refer your colleague to ISAIF, Ellul, etc., for arguments that the evil done by technology outweighs the good, and challenge him to answer those arguments, which so far he has not attempted to do.

Nevertheless, I will consider the four examples in detail (below) because they offer scope for interesting discussion, and I will make your colleague's question about whether things are bad and getting worse into an opportunity to supplement some of the arguments offered in ISAIF and elsewhere.

B. Obviously, any determination as to whether things are bad and getting worse, and, if so, how bad, involves value judgments, so the question will have no answer that will be provably correct independently of the system of values that is applied.

I should mention by the way that in order to justify revolution it is not necessary, in my opinion, to prove that things will get worse: With respect to concerns that could be grouped under the very broad rubric of "freedom and dignity," things are *already* bad enough to justify revolution. This is another value-judgment, and I feel safe in assuming that it would be a waste of time to try to persuade your colleague to agree with it. Even so, I do not think it will be an idle exercise to call attention here to some facts that are relevant to the questions of whether things are bad and whether they are getting worse.

C. First let me point out that the answers to your questions as to whether there is a core reason why things are getting worse, and when the downhill trend began, are found in my letter of October 12, 2004.

D. Your colleague suggests that "things have *always* been bad for human society," and that "we have no rational reason to expect anything better than simply staying one step ahead of death." This is a highly pessimistic attitude, even a defeatist one, and on the basis of my readings about primitive societies I would be rather surprised if such an attitude had been current in any primitive society prior to the time when the society was damaged by the intrusion of civilization. But I actually agree that we have no rational reason to expect anything better than simply staying one step ahead of death—because simply staying one step ahead of death is just fine. We've been adapted by a couple of million years of evolution to a life in which our survival has depended on the success of our daily efforts—efforts that typically were strenuous and demanded considerable skill. Such efforts represented the perfect fulfillment of the power process, and, though the evidence admittedly is anecdotal, such evidence as I've encountered strongly suggests that people thrive best under rugged conditions in which their survival demands serious efforts—provided that their efforts are reasonably successful, and that they make those efforts as free and independent men and women, not under the demeaning conditions of servitude. A few examples:

W.A. Ferris, who lived in the Rocky Mountains as a fur trapper during the 1840s, wrote that the "Free Men" (hunters and trappers not connected with an organized fur-company) lead[ ] a venturous and dangerous life, governed by no laws save their own wild impulses, and bound[ ] their desires and wishes to what their own good rifles and traps may serve them to procure.... [T]he toil, the danger, the loneliness, the deprivation of this condition of being, fraught with all its disadvantages, and replete with peril, is, they think, more than compensated by the lawless freedom, and the stirring excitement, incident to their situation and pursuits.... Yet so attached to [this way of life] do they become, that few ever leave it, and they deem themselves, nay are, ... far happier than the indwellers of towns and cities....[55]

Ferris reported that during his own rugged and dangerous life in the mountains he usually felt "resolute, cheerful, contented."[56]

Gontran de Poncins wrote of the Eskimos with whom he lived about 1939–1940:

[T]he Eskimo is constantly on the march, driven by hunger... .[57]

[T]hese Eskimos afforded me decisive proof that happiness is a disposition of the spirit. Here was a people living in the most rigorous climate in the world, ...haunted by famine...; shivering in their tents in the autumn, fighting the recurrent blizzard in the winter, toiling and moiling fifteen hours a day merely in order to get food and stay alive. ...[T]hey ought to have been melancholy men, men despondent and suicidal; instead, they were a cheerful people, always laughing, never weary of laughter.[58]

The 19th-century Argentine educator and politician Sarmiento wrote of the gaucho of his time:

His moral character shows the effects of his habit of overcoming obstacles and the power of nature; he is strong, haughty, energetic... he is happy in the midst of his poverty and his privations, which are not such for him, who has never known greater enjoyments or desired anything higher... .[59]

Sarmiento was not romanticizing the gaucho. On the contrary, he wanted to replace what he called the "barbarism" of the gaucho with "civilization."[60]

These examples are by no means exceptional. There's plenty more in the literature that suggests that people thrive when they have to exert themselves in order to "stay one step ahead of death," and I've encountered very little that indicates the opposite.

E. It would be instructive to compare the psychological state of primitive man with that of modern man, but such a comparison is difficult because, to my knowledge, there were hardly any systematic studies of psychological conditions in primitive societies prior to the time when the latter were disrupted by the intrusion of civilization. The evidence known to me is almost exclusively anecdotal and/or subjective.

Osborne Russell, who lived in the Rocky Mountains in the 1830s and 1840s, wrote:

> Here we found a few Snake Indians comprising 6 men 7 women and 8 or 10 children who were the only Inhabitants of this lonely and secluded spot. They were all neatly clothed in dressed deer and Sheep skins of the best quality and seemed to be perfectly contented and happy. ...I almost wished I could spend the remainder of my days in a place like this where happiness and contentment seemed to reign in wild romantic splendor....[61]

Such impressions of very primitive peoples are not uncommon and are worth noting. But they represent only superficial observations and almost certainly overlook interpersonal conflicts that would not be evident to a traveler merely passing through. Colin Turnbull, who studied the Mbuti pygmies of Africa thoroughly, found plenty of quarrelling and fighting among them.[62] Nevertheless, his impression of their social and psychological life was on the whole very favorable; he apparently believed that hunter-gatherers were "untroubled by the various neuroses that accompany progress."[63] He also wrote that the Mbuti "were a people who had found in the forest something that made their life more than just worth living, something that made it, with all its hardships and problems and tragedies, a wonderful thing full of joy and happiness and free of care."[64] Turnbull's book *The Forest People* has been called "romantic," but Schebesta, who studied the Mbuti a couple of decades earlier than Turnbull, and who as far as I know has never been accused of romanticism, expressed a similar opinion of the pygmies:

> How many and varied are the dangers, but also the joyous experiences, on their hunting excursions and their innumerable travels through the primeval forest![65]

Thus the pygmies stand before us as one of the most natural of human races, as people who live exclusively in accord with nature and without any violation of their organism. In this they show an unusually sturdy natural-ness and heartiness, an unparalleled cheerfulness and freedom from care.[66]

This "freedom from care," or as we would say nowadays, freedom from stress, seems to have been generally characteristic of peoples at the hunting-and-gathering stage or not far beyond it. Poncins's account makes evident the absence of psychological stress among the Eskimos with whom he lived:

[The Eskimo] had proved himself stronger than the storm. Like the sailor at sea, he had met it tranquilly, it had left him unmoved. …In mid-tempest this peasant of the Arctic, by his total impassivity, had lent me a little of his serenity of soul.[67]

Of course he would not worry. He was an Eskimo.[68]

[My Eskimos'] minds were at rest, and they slept the sleep of the unworried.[69]

In discussing the reasons why many whites during colonial times voluntarily chose to live with the Indians, the historian James Axtell cites two white converts to Indian life who referred to "the absence [among the Indians] of those cares and corroding solicitudes which so often prevail [among the whites]."[70] As we would put it, the absence of anxiety and stress. Axtell notes that while many whites chose to live as Indians, very few Indians made the transition in the opposite direction.[71] Information from other sources confirms the attractiveness of Indian life to many whites.[72]

What I've just said about anxiety and stress probably applies to depression as well, though here I'm on shaky ground since I've encoun-tered very little explicit information about depression in primitive soci-eties. Robert Wright, without citing his source, states that "when a Western anthropologist tried to study depression among the Kaluli of New Guinea, he couldn't find any."[73] Though Schebesta met thousands of Mbuti pygmies,[74] he heard of only one case of suicide among them—a case that probably did not result from depression—and he never found or heard of any case of mental illness (*Geisteskrankheit*), though he did find three persons who were either feeble-minded (*schwachsinnig*) or peculiar (*Sonderling*).[75]

Needless to say, stress and depression were not completely absent from every hunting-and-gathering society. Depression and suicide could occur among Poncins's Eskimos, at least among the old people.[76] The Ainu (hunter-gatherers who were nearly sedentary[77]) suffered from such anxiety about following correct ritual procedure that it often led to serious psychological disorders.[78] But look at the psychological condition of modern man:

> A study has shown that 45 percent of Chinese urban residents are at health risk due to stress... ,[79]

and the problem of stress in more "advanced" countries may be even worse.[80]

> There is certainly a lot of anxiety going around. Anxiety disorder... is the most common mental illness in the U.S. In its various forms... it afflicts 19 million Americans....[81]

> According to the Surgeon General, almost 21 percent of children age 9 and up have a mental disorder, including depression, attention deficit hyperactivity disorder, and bipolar disorder.[82]

> The state of college students' mental health continues to decline. ...The number of freshmen reporting less than average emotional health has been steadily rising since 1985... 76 percent of students felt 'overwhelmed' last year while 22 percent were sometimes so depressed they couldn't function. ...85 percent of [college counseling-center] directors surveyed noted an increase in severe psychological problems over the past five years....[83]

> Rates of major depression in every age group have steadily increased in several of the developed countries since the 1940s. ...Rates of depression, mania and suicide continue to rise as each new birth cohort ages....[84]

> In the U.S., ...the suicide rate in the age group between 15 and 24 tripled between 1950 and 1990; suicide is the third leading cause of death in this age group,[85]

and the American suicide rate continues to rise today.[86]

> A new UC Berkeley study reports that Mexican immigrants to the United
> States have only about half as many psychiatric disorders as U.S.-born
> Mexican Americans.[87]

One could go on and on.

F. Psychological problems of course represent only one of the ways
in which "things are bad and getting worse." I will discuss a few of the
other ways later. I want to make clear, however, that statistics on mental
disorders, environmental damage, or other such problems fail to touch
certain central issues. Though improbable, it's conceivable that the system
might some day succeed in eliminating most mental disorders, cleaning up
the environment, and solving all its other problems. But the human individual, however well the system may take care of him, will be powerless
and dependent. In fact, the better the system takes care of him, the more
dependent he will be. He will have been reduced to the status of a domestic
animal. See ISAIF, ¶ 174 & Note 16. A conscientious owner may keep his
house-dog in perfect physical and psychological health. But would you
want to be a well-cared-for domestic pet? Maybe your colleague would
be willing to accept that status, but I would choose an independent and
autonomous existence, no matter how hard, in preference to comfortable
dependence and servitude.

G. Your colleague's argument that things are getting better because
"Humanity is 'flourishing'… based on sheer numbers" makes no sense.
One of the principal objections to the technological society is that its
food-producing capacity has allowed the world to become grotesquely
overcrowded. I don't think I need to explain to you the disadvantages of
overcrowding.

H. As for your colleague's claim that the "overall material standard of living seems to be increasing," the way that works is that the technoindustrial system simply defines the term "high standard of living" to
mean the kind of living that the system itself provides, and the system then
"discovers" that the standard of living is high and increasing. But to me
and to many, many other people a high material standard of living consists
not in cars, television sets, computers, or fancy houses, but in open spaces,
forests, wild plants and animals, and clear-flowing streams. As measured
by that criterion our material standard of living is falling rapidly.

IV. Your colleague claims that reform offers a better chance of success than revolution. He claims that "we… would act… to restrict technology as it becomes necessary," and that such action represents "the general pattern." You and your colleague offer four examples to illustrate this general pattern: "slavery," "political oppression," "sanitation and waste disposal," and "air and water pollution."

A. Let's take "political oppression" first.

1. As I argued in my letter to you of October 12, 2004, representative democracy replaced authoritarian systems not through human choice or human planning but as a result of "objective" factors that were not under rational human control. Thus the spread of democracy is not an instance of the "general pattern" that you propose.

2. Political oppression has existed virtually since the beginning of civilization, i.e., for several thousand years. An alternative to authoritarian political systems—representative democracy—has been known at least since the days of ancient Athens. Yet, even under the most generous view, the time at which democracy became the world's dominant political form could not possibly be placed earlier than the 19th century. Thus, even after a workable solution was known, it took well over 2,000 years for the problem of political oppression to be (arguably) solved. If it takes 2,000 years for our present technology-related problems to be solved, we may as well forget about it, because it will be far, far too late. So your example of political oppression gives us no reason whatever to be hopeful that our technology-related problems can be solved in a peaceful and orderly way, and in time.

3. You admit that the replacement of authoritarian systems by democratic ones often occurred through revolution, but you claim that "many times it did not (e.g. England, Spain, S. Africa, Eastern European communist bloc)." However, you're wrong about England and South Africa; or, at best, you can claim you are right about them only by insisting on strict adherence to a technical definition of the term "revolution."

England developed into a full-fledged democracy through a process that took roughly 6½ centuries. Since the process took so long, one can't say it was a revolution. But the process certainly did involve violence and armed insurrection. The first step toward democracy in England was Magna Carta, which became law circa 1225 only through a revolt of the barons and an ensuing civil war (arguably a revolution).[88] At least one other step toward democracy in England required a very violent insurrection,

1642–49 (again, arguably a revolution), and the "revolution" of 1688 was nonviolent only because of the accidental fact that James II declined to fight.[89]

As for South Africa, democracy there *for whites only* goes back to the 19th century and was peacefully established,[90] but whites never comprised more than a fifth of the population,[91] and I assume that what you have in mind is the recent extension of democracy to the entire population. This, however, occurred at least in part through violent revolutionary action.[92] If the process was not a revolution, then it was saved from being one only by the fact that the government decided to grant democracy to all races through a negotiated settlement rather than let the situation get further out of hand.[93]

In most of the principal nations of Western Europe, democracy was established through revolution and/or war: In England, partly through violent insurrection, as noted above; in France, through revolution (1789, 1830, 1848) and war (1870); in Germany and Italy democracy was imposed from the outside through warfare (World War II). Among the larger Western European nations, only Spain achieved democracy peacefully, in the late 1970s, after Franco's death in 1975. But Spanish democracy clearly was only a spin-off of the democracy that had been established by violence throughout the rest of Western Europe. Spain was an outlier of a thoroughly democratized, powerful, and economically highly successful Western Europe, so it was only to be expected that Spain would follow the rest of Western Europe and become democratic. Would Spain have become democratic if the rest of Western Europe had been fascist? Probably not. So you can't maintain that the democratization of Spain occurred independently of the violence that established democracy throughout the rest of Western Europe.

The same can be said of much of that part of the "Eastern European communist bloc" that actually has become democratic and done so peacefully. Countries like Poland[94] and the Czech Republic lie on the fringes of Western Europe and are very heavily influenced by it. When one looks at Eastern European countries less closely linked with Western Europe, the status of democracy there seems considerably less secure. As far as I know, Serbia has become democratic, but it did not achieve democracy peacefully. I suppose you realize what is happening in Russia: "President Putin continues to move his country away from democracy... ," etc.[95] As for Belarus: "Belarussian President Alexander Lukashenko said... that he won a mandate from voters to stay in power in a... referendum scrapping presidential term limits. But foreign observers said the vote process was marred by violations.... That allows the authoritarian president... who has led the nation since 1994, to run again in 2006."[96] "Lukashenko [is] often branded as Europe's last dictator...."[97] In Ukraine, the future of democracy is still uncertain.

So your purported examples of democracy peacefully achieved look rather unimpressive. You would have done better to cite the Netherlands and the Scandinavian countries.[98] The Netherlands' evolution toward democracy was quite peaceful,[99] though seemingly influenced by the violence elsewhere in Europe in 1848.[100] Sweden's evolution toward democracy began early in the 18th century and apparently was entirely peaceful.[101] Norway's democratization seems to have been equally nonviolent;[102] though Norway much of the time was not an independent nation. In Denmark on the other hand I think the absolute monarchy was abolished only as a result of the 1848 revolutions; however, Denmark's progress toward democracy thereafter was reasonably orderly.[103] Note that all of the foregoing countries, as well as England, are Germanic countries. Predominantly Germanic Switzerland, too, adopted democracy readily,[104] though the 1848 revolutions apparently played an important role.[105] Compare this with the often violent and for a long time unsuccessful struggles toward democracy of the Latin and Slavic countries. Germanics seem to take to democracy relatively easily, a point that I will have occasion to mention later. (It's true that in Germany itself the first attempt at democracy—the Weimar Republic—failed, but this can be attributed to peculiarly difficult conditions, namely, the Versailles treaty and disastrous economic problems.)

But what happened in particular countries is somewhat beside the point. Consider the worldwide democratization process as a whole: Democracy was an indigenous and partly violent development in England. It was established in America through a violent insurrection. As I pointed out in my letter of October 12, 2004, democracy became the world's dominant political form only because of the economic and technological success of the democracies, especially the English-speaking countries. And this economic and technological success was achieved not only through industrialization at home but also through worldwide expansion that involved violent displacement of native peoples in North America, Australia, and New Zealand, and economic exploitation elsewhere that was often enforced by violence. The democracies repeatedly had to defend themselves in war against authoritarian systems, notably in World Wars I and II, and they won those wars only because of the vast economic and industrial power that they had built, and built in part through violent conquest and exploitation all over the world.

Thus, democracy became the world's dominant political form through a process that involved violent insurrection and extensive warfare, including predatory warfare against weaker peoples who were to be displaced or exploited.

It should also be noted that democracy, as a political form, cannot be viewed in isolation; it is just one element of a whole cultural complex that is associated with industrialization and that we call "modernity." Usually democracy (in its present-day form) can be successfully and lastingly implanted in a country only when that country has become culturally modernized. (Costa Rica is a probable exception.[106]) In my letter of October 12, 2004, I maintained that democracy had become the world's dominant political form because it was the political form most conducive to economic and technological success under conditions of industrialization. It might possibly be argued that it is not democracy itself, but other elements of the associated cultural complex that are mainly responsible for economic and technological success. Singapore achieved outstanding economic success without democracy; Spain achieved good and Taiwan achieved excellent economic success even before they were democratized. I still think that democracy as a political form is an important element of the cultural complex that confers success in an industrialized world. But whether it is or not, the fact remains that modern democracy is not a detached phenomenon but a part of a cultural complex that *tends* to be transmitted as a whole.

When a country becomes democratized peacefully, what typically happens is that either the country is so impressed by the success and dominance of the leading democracies that it willingly tries to absorb their culture, including democracy;[107] or else, due to the economic dominance of the democracies, economic forces compel the country to permit the infiltration of modern culture, and once the country has become sufficiently assimilated culturally and economically, it will be capable of democracy. But in either case the peaceful advent of democracy in any country in modern times (say, since 1900) is usually a consequence of the fact that the cultural complex of which democracy is a part has already become economically and technologically dominant throughout the world. And, as noted above, democracy and modernity have achieved this dominance, in important part, through violence.

So your example of democracy—as an allegedly *nonviolent* reform designed to solve the problem of political oppression—is clearly invalid. I want to make clear that my intention in the foregoing discussion has not been to indict democracy morally, but simply to show that it does not serve your purpose as an example of nonviolent reform.

B.   Much of what I've said about the spread of democracy applies also to the elimination of slavery. Since the arguments applicable to slavery are analogous to those I've given in the case of democracy, I'll only sketch them briefly. First note that rejection of slavery, like democracy and industrialization, is a feature of the cultural complex that we call "modernity."

1.   I would argue that slavery was (partly[108]) eliminated only because, in the modern world, there are more efficient means of getting people to work. In other words, slavery, due to its economic inefficiency, has been eliminated from the industrialized world by "natural selection" (see my letter of October 12, 2004), not primarily by human will. True, much slavery was eliminated through conscious humanitarian efforts,[109] but those efforts could not have had any great success if slave societies had been more efficient economically than the industrializing countries where the antislavery efforts originated. Hence, the basic cause of the elimination of slavery was economic, not humanitarian.[110]

2.   Slavery was widespread for thousands of years before it was (partly) eliminated in modern times. As I pointed out above, we can't afford to wait thousands of years for a solution to our technology-related problems, so your example of slavery gives us no reason to hope for a timely and peaceful solution to those problems.

3.   The elimination of slavery was by no means a nonviolent process. Slavery was expunged from Haiti through bloody revolution.[111] Slave revolts occurred repeatedly in at least some slave societies,[112] and, while these revolts rarely achieved lasting success, it seems safe to assume that they contributed to the economic inefficiency of slavery that led to its eventually being superseded by more efficient systems. Moreover, even when a slave rebellion was crushed, fear of future revolts could lead to the elimination of slavery in the territory where the rebellion had taken place.[113] Slavery was often eliminated through violent intervention from outside the slave-holding society. For example, slavery in the American South was ended by the Civil War, the bloodiest conflict in U.S. history,

and the Arab slave trade in East Africa was closed down in 1889 only after war between the slave-dealers and the colonial powers.[114]

So your example of slavery gives us no reason to hope for a *peaceful* solution to anything.

C. Before I address your other two examples, I want to point out that in focusing on isolated, formal features of societies—on whether governments were representative democracies or whether human beings were technically owned as property—you distract attention from more important questions: How much personal freedom did people have in practice and how satisfactory were their lives?

If I had to live in a specified society, would I rather live as a slave or as a non-slave? Of course, I would rather live as a non-slave. Would I prefer that the society's government should be democratic or authoritarian? *All else being equal,* I would prefer that the government should be democratic. For example, if I were to live in Spain I would rather live in Spain as it was in 1980, after democratization, than in Spain as it was in 1974, when Franco was still alive. If I had to live in Rome in AD 100, I would rather live there as a freeman than as a slave.

When the questions are framed as above, democracy and the elimination of slavery appear to be unequivocally beneficial. But, as we've seen, democracy and the elimination of slavery have prevailed not as isolated and detached features but as part of the cultural complex that we call "modernity." So what we really need to ask is: How does the quality of life in modern society compare with that in earlier societies that may have had authoritarian governments or practiced slavery? Here the answer is not so obvious.

Slavery has taken a wide variety of forms, some of which were very brutal, as everyone knows. But: "Various Greek and Roman authors report on how Etruscan slaves dressed well and how they often owned their own homes. They easily became liberated and rapidly rose in status once they were freed."[115] In as much of Spanish America as came under Simón Bolívar's observation, the slave-owner "has made his slave the companion of his indolence"; he "does not oppress his domestic servant with excessive labor: he treats him as a comrade…."[116] "The slave… vegetates in a state of neglect… enjoying, so to speak, his idleness, the estate of his lord, and many of the advantages of liberty; … he considers himself to be in his natural condition, as a member of his master's family…."[117] Such examples are not rare exceptions,[118] and it will immediately occur to you to ask whether under these conditions slaves might not have been better off than modern wage-workers. But I would go farther and argue that even under the harsher forms of servitude many slaves and serfs had more freedom—the kind of freedom that really counts—than modern man does. This, however, is not the place to make that argument. (See my letter of October 12, 2004, and points (a), (b), and (c) of Letter to J.N., in this volume.)

I could make a much stronger argument that nominally free (non-slave, non-serf, etc.) people living under authoritarian systems of past ages often had greater personal freedom—of the kind that counts—than the average citizen of a modern democracy does. Again, this is not the place to make such an argument.

But I do want to suggest here that democracy (as that term is understood in the modern world) could actually be regarded as a sign of servitude in the following sense: A modern democracy is able to maintain an adequate level of social order with a relatively decentralized power structure and relatively mild instruments of physical coercion only because sufficiently many people are willing to abide by the rules more or less voluntarily. In other words, democracy demands an orderly and obedient population. As the historian von Laue put it, "Industrial society... requires an incredible docility at the base of its freedoms."[119] I suggest that this is why the Germanic countries adjusted to democracy so easily: Germanic cultures tended to produce more disciplined, obedient, authority-respecting people than the comparatively unruly Latin and Slavic cultures did. The Latins of Europe achieved stable democracies only after experience of industrialized living trained them to a sufficient level of social discipline, and over part of the Slavic world there still is insufficient social discipline for stable democracy. Social discipline is even more insufficient in Latin America, Africa, and the Arabic countries. Democracy succeeded so well in Japan precisely because the Japanese are an especially obedient, conforming, orderly people.

Thus, it could be argued that modern democracy represents not freedom but subjection to a higher level of social discipline,[120] a discipline that is more psychological and based less on physical coercion than old-fashioned authoritarian systems were.

I can't leave the subject of democracy without inviting you to comment on this passage of Nietzsche: "Liberal institutions immediately cease to be liberal as soon as they are attained: subsequently there is

nothing more thoroughly harmful to freedom than liberal institutions. …
As long as they are still being fought for, these same institutions produce
quite different effects; they then in fact promote freedom mightily. …For
what is freedom? That one has the will to self-responsibility. …That one
has become more indifferent to hardship, toil, privation, even to life. That
one is ready to sacrifice men to one's cause, oneself not excepted." *Twilight
of the Idols (Götzen-Dämmerung)*, § 38 (translation of R.J. Hollingdale).[121]

D. Now let's look at your third example, "Sanitation and waste
disposal." It's not clear to me why you chose this particular example. It's
just another one of the innumerable technical improvements that have
been devised during the last few centuries, and you could equally well
have cited any of the others. Of course, none of the responsible opponents
of technology has ever denied that technology does some good things, so
your example tells us nothing new.

Poor sanitation and inefficient waste disposal were bad for the
system *and* bad for people, so the interests of the system coincided with the
interests of human beings, and it was therefore only to be expected that
an effective solution to the problem would be developed. But the fact that
solutions are found in cases where the interests of the system *coincide* with
the interests of human beings gives us no reason to hope for solutions in
cases where the interests of the system *conflict* with those of human beings.

For instance, consider what happens when skilled craftsmen are
put out of work by technical improvements that make them superfluous.
I recently received a letter from a professional gravestone sculptor who
provided me with a concrete example of this. He had spent much of his life
developing skills that were rendered useless a few years ago by some sort of
laser-guided device that carved gravestones automatically. He's in his forties,
unable to find work, and obviously depressed. This sort of thing has been
going on ever since the beginning of the Industrial Revolution, and it will
continue to go on because in this situation the interests of the system conflict
with those of human beings, so human beings have to give way. Where
is the solution that, according to your theory, society is supposed to have
developed? As far as I know, only two solutions have been implemented: (i)
welfare; and (ii) retraining programs. My guess is that organized retraining
programs cover only a fraction of all workers displaced by technology; at
any rate, they apparently hadn't covered the gravestone sculptor who wrote
to me. But what if they did cover him? "Okay, John, you're 45 years old
and the craft you've practiced all your life has just been rendered obsolete

by Consolidated Colossal Corporation's new laser-guided stonecutter. But smile and be optimistic, because we're going to put you through a training program to teach you how to operate a ball-bearing-polishing machine... ." Your colleague may think this is consistent with human dignity, but I don't, and I'm pretty sure the above-mentioned gravestone sculptor wouldn't think it was consistent with human dignity either.

It's worth mentioning, by the way, that improved sanitation too seems to have had unanticipated negative consequences. Sanitation no doubt is one of the most important factors in the dramatic, worldwide reduction in infant mortality rates, which presumably has played a major role in the population explosion. In addition, there is evidence that modern sanitation has brought about a sharp increase in autoimmune disorders such as allergies, inflammatory bowel disease, and type 1 diabetes. Furthermore, while the poliomyelitis virus has probably been around since time immemorial, *paralytic* polio was relatively rare prior to the Industrial Revolution. Only after industrialization were there epidemics of paralytic polio that left large numbers of people disabled for life, and it is hypothesized that these epidemics were a result of improved sanitation.[122]

E. Your fourth example is "air and water pollution." You claim that the (partial) solution to this problem has been acceptable "as defined by the majority."

1. Assuming for the sake of argument that the solution actually has been acceptable to the majority, that means nothing. The great majority of Germans supported Hitler "until the very end."[123]

The majority's opinions about society's problems are to a great extent irrational, for at least two reasons: (i) The majority's outlook is shaped, to a considerable degree, by propaganda. (ii) Most people put very little serious effort into thinking about society's problems. This is not an elitist sneer at the "unthinking masses." The average man's refusal to think seriously about large-scale problems is quite sensible: Such thought is useless to him personally because he himself can't do anything to solve such problems. In fact, some psychologists and physicians have advised people to avoid thinking about problems that they are powerless to solve, because such thinking only causes unnecessary stress and anxiety. The point is, however, that the majority's putative acceptance of existing levels of air and water pollution is largely irrelevant.

2. And how do you know that existing levels of air and water pollution are acceptable to the majority? Have you taken a survey? Maybe

you simply assume that existing levels of pollution are acceptable to the majority because there currently is very little public agitation over pollution. Though the meaning of the term "acceptable" is not at all clear in this context, it can by no means be assumed that the level of active public resistance is an accurate index of what the public feels is "acceptable." I think most historians would agree that active, organized public resistance is most likely to occur not necessarily when conditions are worst, but when people find new hope that resistance will bring success, or when some other new circumstance or event prods them into action.[124] So the absence of public resistance by no means proves that the majority is satisfied.

3. What the system has done is to alleviate the most visible and obvious signs of pollution, such as murky, stinking rivers and air darkened by smog. Since these symptoms are directly experienced by the average man, they presumably are the ones most likely to arouse public discontent; and while their (partial) cure may inconvenience certain industries it does not significantly impede the progress of the system as a whole. The most successful industrialized countries, for the present, have easily enough economic surplus to cover the cost of controlling the aforementioned visible forms of pollution. But this may not be true of backward countries that are struggling to catch up with the more advanced ones. For example, the air pollution in China is notoriously horrible, and the air is perhaps worse in Egypt and India.[125]

In fact, if you look beyond the comforting improvements in air-pollution indices over our cities as reported by the EPA and consider the worldwide pollution situation as a whole, it appears that what the system has done to alleviate the problem is almost negligible. The following by the way goes also to support the argument that things are bad and getting worse:

Acid rain (due to certain forms of air pollution) is still damaging our forests. At least up to a few years ago (and perhaps even today) the Russians were still dumping their nuclear waste in the Arctic Ocean. The public (in the U.S.) has been warned not to eat too much fish, because fish are contaminated with mercury and PCBs (from water pollution, obviously). For the foregoing I can't cite a source; I'm depending on memory. But:

The indigenous populations of Greenland and Arctic Canada are being poisoned by toxic industrial chemicals that drift north by wind and water, polluting their food supplies. On January 13, 2004, *The Los Angeles Times* told its readers that the pollutants, which include PCBs and 200 other hazardous compounds, get into the native food chains through zooplankton. 'The bodies of Artic people... contain the highest human concentrations of industrial chemicals and pesticides found anywhere on Earth—levels so extreme that the breast milk and tissues of some Greenlanders could be classified as hazardous wastes,' the *Times*' Marla Cone reports.[126]

In the mid-1980s, some researchers in the northern Midwest, Canada, and Scandinavia began reporting alarming concentrations of mercury in freshwater fish. ...[T]he skies already hold so much mercury that even if industrial emissions of the metal ended tomorrow, significant fallout of the pollutant might persist for decades....[127]

Measurable levels of cancer-causing pesticides have been found in the drinking water of 347 towns and cities. Creation and use of toxic chemicals continues at a rate far faster than our capacity to learn how safe extended exposures to these substances are. ...The U.S. Environmental Protection Agency was mandated to test existing pesticides—just one class of chemicals—for health risks by 1972, but the job still isn't completed today, and regulators are falling further behind.[128]

The new residents [on grounds of former U.S. Clark Air Base, in the Philippines] dug wells, planted crops... unaware that the ground water they drank and bathed in, the soil their rice and sweet potatoes grew in, and the creeks and ponds they fished in were contaminated by toxic substances dumped during a half century of U.S. tenure. Within a few years, health workers began tracking a rise in spontaneous abortions, still-births, and birth defects, kidney, skin, and nervous disorders; cancers, and other conditions.... Today, the Pentagon acknowledges polluting major overseas bases, but insists that the United States isn't obligated to clean them up.[129]

(On the bright side: "Air-pollution emissions have dropped 7.8% since 2000 [what pollutants are measured, and where, is unstated].... Critics say the drop in water-quality complaints reflects laggard enforcement...."[130])

Anyone who wanted to search the media could go on and on citing things of this sort. And if what I've seen is any indication, he would find vastly more on the negative than on the positive side.

Perhaps the biggest pollution problem of all is global warming, which scientists now agree is due at least in part to human production of "greenhouse gases," carbon dioxide in particular.[131] It's not just a matter of temperatures rising a few degrees; the consequences of global warming are extremely serious. They include the spread of disease,[132] extreme weather conditions, such as storms, tornados, and floods,[133] possible extinction of arctic species such as the polar bear,[134] disruption of the way of life of arctic residents,[135] rising sea levels that will flood parts of the world,[136] and drought.[137] "More of the Earth is turning to dust[.] 'It's a creeping catastrophe,' says a U.N. spokesman. Desertification's pace has doubled since the 1970s...."[138] However, global warming is only one of the causes of desertification.[139]

Your colleague's proposed "general pattern" doesn't work here, because you can't just turn something like global warming around when enough people become concerned about it. No matter what measures are taken now, we will be stuck with the consequences of global warming for (at least!) a matter of centuries. In fact, some scientists fear that human modification of the atmosphere may soon "throw a switch" that will trigger a dramatic, disastrous, and irreversible change in the Earth's climate.[140]

Since it is in the system's own interest to keep pollution and global warming under control, it is conceivable that solutions may be found that will prevent these problems from becoming utterly disastrous. But what will be the cost to human beings? In particular, what will be the cost to human freedom and dignity, which so often get in the way of the system's technical solutions?

Letter to David Skrbina,
January 3, 2005

First point (freedom). I and some other people place an extremely high value on freedom; and I do so because today there is an acute shortage of freedom as I've defined it. If I had grown up in a society in which there was an abundance of freedom but an acute shortage of (for example) physical necessities, I might well have been willing to sacrifice some of my freedom for physical necessities. Poncins says that the Eskimos he knew considered it a reward and not a punishment to be imprisoned, because in prison they were fed and kept warm without having to exert themselves.[141]

Second point (autonomy/freedom). I wouldn't say flatly that medieval peasants (for example) had more freedom than we have today, but I think one could make a strong argument that they did have more of the kind of freedom that really counts. (See my letter of October 12, 2004, and points (a), (b), and (c) of Letter to J.N., in this volume.)

Third point (surrogate activities). I've never said that surrogate activities "must be abandoned." Also, the line between surrogate activities and purposeful activities often is not easy to draw. See ISAIF, ¶¶ 40, 84, 90. And surrogate activities are not peculiar to modern society. What is true is that surrogate activities have come to play an unusual, disproportionate, and exaggerated role in modern society. In any case, I don't see that anything would be accomplished by attacking surrogate activities. But I think that the concept of surrogate activity is important for an understanding of the psychology of modern man.

Fourth point (revolution). In the present historical context a successful revolution would consist in bringing about the complete dissolution of the technoindustrial system.

Fifth point (revolution is demanded). Yes, revolution is demanded. I've never said, and I certainly do not believe, that a revolutionary movement must be peaceful and nonviolent. I have simply declined to discuss the violent aspects of revolution, because I don't want to give the authorities an excuse to cut off my communications with you on the ground that I'm "inciting violence." I do think that a revolutionary movement should have one *branch* that will avoid all violent or otherwise illegal activities in order to be able to function openly and publicly. I've never said that a revolution should be led by a "small group," which to me would mean ten, twenty, fifty, or at most a hundred people. I do think that the active and effective part of a revolutionary movement would comprise only a small fraction of the entire population. Finally, I've never said that the revolution should be led by intellectuals. Of course, that would depend on what one means by an "intellectual." I suppose that term is most commonly taken to include college and university faculty in the humanities and social sciences, and persons in closely related occupations, such as professional writers who write on serious subjects. When the word "intellectual" is understood in that sense, it is my impression that very, very few if any present-day intellectuals are potential members of a revolutionary movement. I can imagine that some intellectuals could play a very important role in formulating, articulating, and disseminating ideas that would subsequently form part of the basis for a revolutionary movement. But in reading *The New York Review, The London Review,* and *The Times Literary Supplement* over the last several years I've found virtually *no* mention of the technology problem. It's as if the intellectuals were willfully avoiding what is obviously the most critical issue of our time. That's why I'm so pleased to find at least two intellectuals—yourself and your unnamed colleague— who take a serious interest in the technology problem.

Sixth point (avoidance of stress-reduction). I decidedly disagree with your sentence that says: "In fact, [revolutionaries] should actively OPPOSE such actions… ." Absolutely not! Let's take minority rights, for example. The big problem there is that the fuss over minority rights absorbs the rebellious energies of would-be radicals and distracts attention from the critical issue of technology. By *opposing* equal rights for non-whites, women, homosexuals, etc., revolutionaries would merely intensify the conflict over minority rights and thus distract even more attention from the issue of technology. What revolutionaries have to do is show people that the fuss over minority rights is largely irrelevant.

Further, the principle that revolutionaries should work to increase the tensions in society is merely a general rule of thumb, not a rigid law that can be applied mechanically. One has to give separate consideration to each individual case. Are the social tensions arising from discrimination against minorities useful from a revolutionary point of view? Clearly not! For example, if black people are harassed by police, then their attention will be focused on that problem and they will have no time for the technology problem. Thus, again, problems of minority rights distract attention from the technology problem, and we would be better off if all minority problems had already been solved, because the associated tensions are *not* productive. See ISAIF, ¶¶ 190–92.

For another example, suppose revolutionaries were to oppose political action designed to reduce pollution. In that case people concerned about pollution would become hostile toward the revolutionaries. Further, tension between opponents of pollution and the system would be *reduced*, because opponents of pollution would attribute continued pollution in part to the obstructive behavior of the revolutionaries. They would say, "The problem is those damned extremists! If it weren't for them, we would be able to swing the system around and reduce pollution." So, instead of *opposing* reformist efforts to reduce pollution, revolutionaries have to emphasize: (i) that such efforts can never really solve the pollution problem, but only alleviate it to a limited extent; (ii) that pollution is only one of many grave problems associated with the technoindustrial system; and (iii) that it is futile to try to attack all of these problems separately and individually—the only effective solution is to bring down the whole system.

The tensions that are useful are the tensions that pit people against the technoindustrial system. Other tensions—e.g., racial tensions, which pit different racial groups against each other rather than against the system—are counterproductive and actually relieve the tension against the system, because they serve as a distraction. See ISAIF, ¶¶ 190–92.

*   *   *

You write that "we should seek *optimum levels* of technology and social order." Several other people who have written to me have raised similar questions about an optimal or acceptable level of technology. My position is that we have *only two choices*. It's like flipping a light-switch. Either your light is on or your light is off, and there's nothing more to be said. Similarly, with only minor reservations and qualifications, we have only two choices at the present point in history: We can either allow the technoindustrial system to continue on its present course, or we can destroy the technoindustrial system. In the first case, technology will eventually swallow everything. In the second case, technology will find its own level as determined by circumstances over which we have no control. Consequently, it is idle to speak of finding an "optimal" level of technology. Any conclusion we might reach about an "optimal" level of technology would be useless, because we would have no means of applying that conclusion in the real world. The same is true of any "optimal" level of social order.

*   *   *

I've read the pieces by Jacques Ellul and Ivan Illich that you sent me. Illich wrote: "If within the very near future man cannot set limits to the interference of his tools with the environment and practice effective birth control, the next generations will experience the gruesome apocalypse predicted by many ecologists."[142] Illich wrote that in 1973, and the "apocalypse" is not yet upon us. I think it's safe to say that the system will break down *eventually*—if only because every previous civilization has broken down eventually—and the breakdown when it comes will no doubt be gruesome, but I see no reason to believe that the system is now on the brink of collapse. Dire predictions made by "ecologists" in the 1960s have proven to be exaggerated and/or premature.

To me, a lot of what Illich writes is completely incomprehensible. E.g., on page 109 he says: "When business is normal the procedural opposition between corporations and clients usually heightens the legitimacy of the latter's dependence."[143] Can you explain what this sentence means? I find it hopelessly obscure.

As for Ellul, "Anarchy from a Christian Standpoint, 1. What is Anarchy?,"[144] I think he's all wrong. It would take too much time to discuss all the ways in which I think he's wrong, so I'll just mention a couple of points. First, he's wrong in claiming that, in history, violence has proven to be an ineffective tactic. Actually violence has been effective or ineffective, depending on the historical circumstances of each particular case. See the study by Kirkham, Levy & Crotty, in which they concluded that, in history, systematic assassination had been "effective in achieving the long-range goals sought, although not so in advancing the short-term goals or careers of the terrorists themselves."[145] On this subject the authors go farther than I would.

Second, Ellul writes: "[The] two great characteristics [of people], no matter what their society or education, are covetousness and a desire for power. We find these traits always and everywhere." It's not completely clear to me what Ellul means by "covetousness." But he writes that covetousness "can never be assuaged or satisfied, for once one thing is acquired it directs its attention to something else." So Ellul evidently has in mind a desire to accumulate property indefinitely. If my interpretation of his meaning is correct, then Ellul is dead wrong about covetousness. There have been many societies in which the desire to accumulate property has been absent. E.g., most if not all nomadic hunting-and-gathering societies. To take a concrete case, the Mbuti pygmies: According to Schebesta, "No urge for possession… seems to dwell in them"; "there is also the fact that among the Mbuti, any intention to pile up supplies, or at all to accumulate wealth, is lacking."[146]

The need for power undoubtedly is universal, but it does not have to take the form of a desire to dominate other people, as Ellul seems to assume. It may well be true that an impulse to dominance is innate in humans, especially in males, but I think Ellul greatly overestimates its strength. Moreover, there have existed societies in which any impulse to dominance has been kept well under control: Among the Bushmen studied by Richard Lee, no one was allowed to set himself up above the rest.[147] The same was true of the Mbuti Pygmies,[148] who according to Schebesta lacked any inclination to be domineering.[149]

Letter to David Skrbina,
March 17, 2005

I. WHY REFORM WILL FAIL

You and your colleague make a series of related assertions: We "would act... to restrict technology as it becomes necessary." "People in the future will likely act to mitigate technological advances or effects that begin to significantly undermine their well-being." Success in "adequately over-coming technologically-induced adversities" will be more likely through reform than through revolution. There's a "general pattern: A technical problem arises and... [eventually]... a compromise solution is implemented that reduces the level of harm to a 'generally acceptable level.' "

In my letter of November 23, 2004, I answered these claims in part. Addressing your four examples of the purported "general pattern," I argued that even assuming that the achieved solutions to the problems were adequate ones (which in three of the four cases was debatable at best): (i) The "solutions" came about largely through the operation of "objective" factors and independently of human will. (ii) In two of the four cases (political oppression, slavery) the solutions were reached, in important part, through warfare and violent revolution, hence could not fairly be characterized as reform. (iii) In the same two of the four cases, the solutions were not reached until thousands of years after the problems arose. In other words, the solutions did not happen when we needed them, but when the "objective" conditions were by chance right for them.

I.A. The most important point in the foregoing is:

1. The course of history, in the large, is generally determined not by human choice but by "objective" factors, especially by the kind of "natural selection" that I discussed in my letter of October 12, 2004. Consequently, we can't achieve a long-lasting solution to a major social problem by superficial

tinkering designed merely to correct particular symptoms. If a solution is possible at all, it can be reached only by finding a way to change the underlying "objective" factors that are responsible for the existing situation.

There are several other reasons why acceptable solutions to the problems of the technological society will not be reached through the "general pattern" of compromise and reform that you and your colleague propose.

2. Generally speaking, reform is possible only in cases where the interests of the system coincide with the interests of human beings. Where the interests of the system conflict with those of human beings, there is no meaningful reform.[150] E.g., sanitation has improved because it is in the system's interest to avoid epidemics. But nothing has been done about the unsatisfactory nature of modern work, because if most people worked as independent artisans rather than as cogs in the system, the economic efficiency of the system would be drastically impaired.

"Natural selection" is at work here: Systems that compromise their own power and efficiency for the sake of "human values" are at a competitive disadvantage vis-à-vis systems that put power and efficiency first. Hence, the latter expand while the former fall behind.

3. You claim that people will act to mitigate problems "that begin to significantly undermine their well-being." But often, once a problem begins to significantly undermine people's well-being, it is too late to solve the problem; or even if the problem can be solved the cost of solving it may be unacceptably high. For example, it is too late to solve the problem of the greenhouse effect (global warming). Whatever is done now, we will be stuck with its consequences for centuries to come. We can hope to "solve" the problem only to the extent of keeping the effect within certain limits, and it's not clear that even that much can be done without drastic cuts in energy consumption that will have unacceptable economic consequences.

Apparently the threat represented by nuclear weapons has not undermined people's well-being enough to lead to the abolition of these weapons. If there is ever a major nuclear war, people's well-being will be undermined very dramatically; but then it will be too late.

Right now biotechnicians are playing with fire. The escape from the laboratory of some artificially-created organisms or genetic material could have disastrous consequences, yet nothing is being done to restrain the biotechnicians. If there is ever a major biological disaster, people's well-being will indeed be undermined, but then it will be too late to correct the problem. For example, the so-called "killer bees" are a hybrid of South American and African bees that escaped from a research facility somewhere in South America. Once the bees had escaped, all efforts to stop them proved futile. They have spread over much of South America and into the U.S. and have killed hundreds of people.[151] With the experimentation in biotechnology that is now going on, something much, much worse could happen.

4. Often a bad thing cannot be fixed because its specific cause is not known. Consider for example the steady increase in the rate of mental disorders that I discussed in my letter of November 23, 2004. It seems almost certain that this increase is in some way an outgrowth of technological progress, since the entire lifestyle of modern man is essentially determined by his technology. But no one knows *specifically* why the rate of mental disorders has been increasing. My personal opinion is that the high rate of depression has a great deal to do with deprivation with respect to the power process,[152] but even if I'm right that still leaves a great deal unanswered, e.g., in regard to mania and anxiety disorders.

Again, it is believed that the rate of mortality due to cancer has increased by a factor of more than *ten* since the late 19th century,[153] and that this is not a result merely of the aging of the population. This too is almost certainly in some way an outcome of the technoindustrial lifestyle, but, while some causes of cancer are known, the reason for the overall massive increase in the incidence of this disease is still a mystery.

5. Even where a problem can be solved, the solution itself often is offensive to human dignity. For example, because the causes of depression, mania, and attention-deficit disorder either are unknown or cannot be removed without excessive cost to the system, these problems are "solved" by giving the patients drugs. So the system makes people sick by subjecting them to conditions that are not fit for human beings to live in, and then it restores their ability to function by feeding them drugs. To me, this is a colossal insult to human dignity.

6. Where a problem is of long standing people may fail to realize even that there is a problem, because they have never known anything better. For example, when I returned for a time to the city after living for an extended period in the mountains of Montana, I realized upon readjusting to urban existence that all my life, until I escaped to the mountains, I had been subject to chronic stress. To be sure, it was stress at a *relatively* low level, a level at which people habituated to urban living are not aware

of stress because they've always been subject to it and don't know how it would feel to be free of it. It was only through my experiences in the mountains that I learned how good it felt to escape from chronic stress altogether. My brother reported a similar reaction after spending long periods alone in the desert.

7. Some problems are insoluble because of the very nature of modern technology. For example, the transfer of power from individuals and small groups to large organizations is inevitable in a technological society for several reasons, one of which is that many essential operations in the functioning of the technological system can be carried out only by large organizations. E.g., if petroleum were not refined on a large scale, the production of gasoline would be so costly and laborious that the automobile would not be a practical means of transportation.

8. Your formulations, as quoted on the first page of this letter, rely on such terms as "well-being," "adversities," and "generally acceptable level" of "harm." These terms may be subject to a variety of interpretations, but I assume that what you mean is that when conditions make people sufficiently uncomfortable they will act to reduce their discomfort to an acceptable level. I deny that this is consistently true, but even if it were true it would not solve the problem as I see it.

One of the most dangerous features of the technoindustrial system is precisely its power to make people comfortable (or at least reduce their discomfort to a relatively acceptable level) in circumstances under which they should *not* be comfortable, e.g., circumstances that are offensive to human dignity, or destructive of the life that evolved on Earth over hundreds of millions of years, or that may lead to disaster at some future time. Drugs (as I've just discussed, I.A.5) can alleviate the discomfort of depression and attention-deficit disorder, propaganda can reconcile the majority to environmental destruction, and the entertainment industry gives people forgetfulness so that they won't worry too much about nuclear weapons or about the fact that they may be replaced by computers a few decades from now.

So comfort is not the main issue. On the contrary, one of our most important worries should be that people may be made comfortable with almost anything, including conditions that we would consider horrifying. Perhaps you've read Aldous Huxley's *Brave New World*, a vision of a society in which nearly everyone was supremely comfortable; yet Huxley intended this vision to repel the reader, as being inconsistent with human dignity.

9. What happens is that social norms, and people themselves, change progressively over time in response to changes in society. This occurs partly through a spontaneous process of adaptation and partly through the agency of propaganda and educational techniques; in the future, biotechnology too may alter human beings. The result is that people come to accept conditions that earlier generations would have considered inconsistent with freedom or intolerably offensive to human dignity.

For example, failure or inability to retaliate for an injury was traditionally seen as intensely shameful. To the ancient Romans it was "the lowest depth of shame to submit tamely to wrongs."[154] To 17th-century Spaniards, a man who had been subjected to a wrong was degraded and could redeem himself only by taking revenge.[155] It is probably safe to assume that similar values prevailed throughout Western Europe at the time, and this same attitude—that to be wronged is a shame that can be wiped away only through revenge—persists today in the Middle East.[156] In the United States, well into the 19th century, duels were fought over points of "honor." We all know about the famous duel in which Aaron Burr killed Alexander Hamilton, and Andrew Jackson, before he became President, killed a man in a duel.[157] In Europe too, throughout the 19th century, men of fame and distinction were involved in dueling.[158]

Today, however, "revenge" is a bad word. Dueling and private retaliation not only are illegal, but by well-socialized people are seen as immoral. We are expected to submit meekly to an injury or humiliation unless a legal remedy is available through the courts; and such remedies usually are available—if at all—only to those who are wealthy enough to hire lawyers at a rate of some hundreds of dollars per hour. Of course, it's easy to see why modern society's need for social order makes it imperative to suppress dueling and private revenge.

Prior to the advent of the Industrial Revolution in England and America, police forces were intentionally kept weak because people saw police as a threat to their freedom. People relied for protection not primarily on the police but on themselves, their families, and their friends. Effective law enforcement came to be regarded as desirable only as a result of the social changes that the Industrial Revolution brought.[159] Today, needless to say, hardly any respectable middle-class person sees the presence of strong police forces as an infringement of his freedom.

I'm not trying to persuade you to advocate the abolition of police or to approve of dueling and private revenge. My point is simply that attitudes regarding what is consistent with human dignity and freedom have changed in the past in response to the needs of the system, and will continue to change in the future, also in response to the needs of the system. Thus, even if future generations are able to "solve" social problems to the extent necessary to secure what *they* conceive of as human dignity and freedom, their solutions may be totally incompatible with what we would want for our posterity.

10. When a problem persists for a long time without substantial progress toward a solution, most people just give up and become passive with respect to it. (Note the connection with "learned helplessness.") This of course is one of the mechanisms that help bring people to accept what they formerly regarded as intolerable indignities, as I described above.

For example, back in the late '50s or early '60s, Vance Packard published a book titled *The Hidden Persuaders*, which was an exposé of the manipulative techniques that advertisers used to sell products or political candidates to consumers or voters. When the book first appeared it received a great deal of attention, and my recollection is that the most common reaction among intellectuals and other thinking people was: "Isn't this scandalous? What is the world coming to when people's attitudes, voting choices, and buying habits can be manipulated by a handful of skilled professional propagandists?" At that time I was in my late teens and was naïve enough to believe that, as a result of Packard's book and the attention it received, something would be done about manipulative advertising. Obviously nothing was done about it, and nowadays if anyone published a book about manipulative advertising it wouldn't get much attention. The reaction of most well-informed people would be: "Yeah, sure, we know all that. It's too bad... but what can you do?" They would then drop the unpleasant subject and talk or think about something else. They have lapsed into passive resignation.

Of course, nothing could be done about manipulative advertising because it would have cost the system too much to do anything about it. However insulting it may be to human dignity, the system needs propaganda, and, as always happens when the needs of the system come into conflict with human dignity, the system's needs take precedence. (See I.A.2 above.)

11. There is the "problem of the commons": It may be to everyone's advantage that everyone should take a certain course of action, yet it may be to the advantage of each particular individual to take the *opposite* course

of action. For example, in modern society, it is to everyone's advantage that everyone should pay a portion of his income to support the functions of government, but it is to the advantage of each particular individual to keep all of his income for himself. (That's why payment of taxes has to be compulsory.)

Similarly, I know people who think the technological society is horrible, that the automobile is a curse, and that we would all be better off if no one used modern technology. Yet they drive cars themselves and use all the usual technological conveniences. And why shouldn't they? If individual X refuses to drive a car, the technological system will go on as before; X's refusal to drive a car will accomplish nothing and will cost him a great deal of inconvenience. For the same reason, X in most cases will not participate in an effort to form a movement designed to remedy some problem of the technological society, because his participation would cost him time and energy, and there is at most a minimal chance that his own personal effort would make the difference between success and failure for the movement. People take action on social problems, even the most important ones, only under special circumstances.[160]

12. Most people, most of the time, are not particularly foresighted, and take little account of social dangers that lie decades in the future. As a result, preventive measures commonly are postponed until it is too late.

The greenhouse effect was predicted way back in 1896 by the Swedish chemist Svante Arrhenius,[161] and during the 1960s the danger of global warming was a subject of public discussion. Yet no one tried to do anything about it until recently, when it was already too late to avoid many of its consequences.

The problem of the disposal of nuclear waste was obvious as soon as the first nuclear power-plants were set up decades ago. No one knew of a safe way to dispose of the waste, but it was simply assumed that a solution to the problem would eventually be found and the development of nuclear power-generation was pushed ahead. Worse still, nuclear power-generation was intentionally introduced to third-world countries under the "Atoms for Peace" program without any apparent consideration of the obvious question whether their often irresponsible little governments would dispose of the wastes safely or whether they would use their nuclear capability for the development of weapons.

Today, in this country, nuclear wastes are still piling up, and there is every reason to think that they will keep piling up indefinitely. And there is still no generally accepted solution to the problem of disposing of these wastes, which will remain dangerous for many thousands of years. It is claimed that the disposal site at Yucca Mountain in Nevada is safe, but this is widely disputed. Experience has shown again and again that technological solutions, excepting only the most minor innovations, need to be tested before they can be relied on. Usually they work only after they have been corrected through trial and error. The Nevada disposal site is an experiment the result of which won't be known for thousands of years—when it will be too late. Simply on the basis of the demonstrated unreliability of *untested* technological solutions, I would guess it's more likely than not that the Nevada disposal site will prove a failure. (See Appendix Five.)

Of course, most people would rather stick future generations with the difficult and perhaps insoluble problem of dealing with our nuclear waste, than accept any substantial reduction in the availability of electricity now.

If the nuclear-waste problem in the U.S. is worrisome, you can imagine how some of these irresponsible little third-world countries are disposing of their nuclear waste. Not to mention the fact that some of them have made or are trying to make nuclear bombs. So much for the foresight of the presumably intelligent people who promoted nuclear power-generation several decades ago.

13. The threatening aspects of technology often are balanced by temptingly attractive features. And once people have given in to the temptation of accepting an attractive but dangerous technological innovation, there is no turning back—short of a breakdown of technological civilization. See ISAIF, ¶ 129. Biotechnology can increase agricultural production and provide new medicines; in the future it will probably help to eliminate genetic diseases and allow parents to give their children desired traits. As computers grow faster and more sophisticated, they give people more and more powers that they would not otherwise have. The latest electronic entertainment media give people new and exciting kicks.

Your claim that people will correct problems when these make them sufficiently uncomfortable, even if it were true, would have no clear application to such cases. Technological innovations make people comfortable in some ways and uncomfortable in other ways, and, while the comforts are obvious and direct, the discomforts often are indirect and not obvious. It may be difficult or impossible even to recognize and prove the connection between the technology and the discomfort. E.g., people directly experience the fun that they get from computers and electronic enter-tainment media, but it is by no means obvious that exposure of children to computers and electronic media may cause attention-deficit disorder. Some research suggests such an effect, but it remains an open question whether the effect is real.

14. Most people, most of the time, follow the path of least resistance. That is, they do what will make them comfortable for the present and the near future. This tendency deters people from addressing the underlying causes of the discomforts of modern life.

The underlying problems are difficult to attack and can be corrected only at a certain price, so most people take the easy way out and utilize one of the avenues of escape that offer them quick alleviation of their discomfort. For those who are not satisfied simply with immersion in the pleasures provided by the entertainment industry, there are surrogate activities and there are religions, as well as ideologies that serve psycho-logical needs in the same way that religions do. For many who suffer from a sense of powerlessness, it will be more effective to strive for a position of power within the system than to try to change the system. And for those who do struggle against the system, it will be easier and more rewarding to concentrate on one or a few limited issues in regard to which there is a reasonable chance of victory than to address the intractable problems that are the real sources of their discontent.

Consider for example the kook variety of Christianity that has become a serious political force in recent years. I'm referring to people who believe that the world will end within forty years and that sort of thing (see enclosed article by Bill Moyers).[162] It seems fairly obvious that these people retreat into their fantasy world in order to escape from the anxi-eties and frustrations of modern life. Who needs to worry about nuclear war or about the environment when the world will end soon anyway, and all the true believers will go to heaven? For those who are disturbed by the decay of traditional morality, it is much easier to fight abortion and gay marriage than to recognize that rapid technological change neces-sarily leads to rapid changes in social values. The "causes" to which left-ists devote themselves represent a similar form of escapism. See ISAIF, ¶¶ 219–222 and "The System's Neatest Trick," in this volume. Through recourse to these various forms of escapism, people avoid confronting the real sources of their discontent.

15. Technological progress brings too many problems too rapidly.

Even if we make the extremely optimistic assumption that any one of the problems could be solved through reform, it is unrealistic to suppose that *all* of the most important problems can be solved through reform, and solved in time. Here is a partial list of problems: War (with modern weapons, not comparable to earlier warfare), nuclear weapons, accumulation of nuclear waste, other pollution problems of many different kinds, global warming, ozone depletion, exhaustion of some natural resources, overpopulation and crowding, genetic deterioration of humans due to relaxation of natural selection, abnormally high rate of extinction of species, risk of disaster from biotechnological tinkering, possible or probable replacement of humans by intelligent machines, biological engineering of humans (an insult to human dignity[163]), dominance of large organizations and power- lessness of individuals, surveillance technology that makes individuals still more subject to the power of large organizations,[164] propaganda and other manipulative psychological techniques, psychoactive medications,[165] mental problems of modern life, including, inter alia, stress, depression, mania, anxiety disorders, attention-deficit disorder, addictive disorders, domestic abuse, and generalized incompetence.

The solution of any *one* of the foregoing problems (if possible at all) would require a long and difficult struggle. If your colleague thinks that *all* of these problems can be solved, and solved in time, by attacking each problem separately, then he's dreaming. The only way out is to attack the underlying source of all these problems, which is the technoindustrial system itself.

16. In a complex, highly-organized system like modern industrial society, you can't change just one thing. Everything is connected to every- thing else, and you can't make a major change in any one thing without changing the whole system. This applies not only to the physical compo- nents of the system, but to the whole mind-set, the whole system of values and priorities that characterizes the technological society.

If you try to fix things by addressing each problem separately, your reforms can't go far enough to fix any one of the problems, because if you make changes that are far-reaching enough to fix problem X, those changes will have unacceptable consequences in other parts of the system. As pointed out in ISAIF, ¶¶ 121–24, you can't get rid of the bad parts of technology and still retain the good parts.

Consider for example the problem of manipulative advertising and propaganda in general. Any serious restriction on manipulative advertising would entail interference with the advertisers' First Amendment right to free expression, so a radical restructuring of our First Amendment jurisprudence would be required. The news media are supported by advertising. If there were a drastic decline in advertising, who would support the vast network that collects information around the world and funnels it to the TV-viewer and the newspaper-reader? Maybe the government would support it, but then the government could control the news we receive, and you know what that implies. Even more important, with an end to manipulative advertising there would probably be a major drop in consumption, so the economy would go to hell. You can imagine the consequences of that as well as I can.

Since the problems can't be solved one at a time, you have to think in terms of changing the entire system, including the whole mind-set and system of values associated with it.

17. What you ask for has no precedent in history. Societies sometimes fix problems of relatively limited scope; e.g., a country that has suffered a military defeat may be able to reorganize its army on new principles and win the next battle. But historically, short of a radical transformation of the entire social fabric (i.e., revolution), it has proven impossible for societies to solve deep-lying problems of the kind we face today. I challenge you and your colleague to produce even one example from history of a society that has solved through piecemeal reform problems of the number and seriousness of those that I've listed above (see I.A.15).

I.B. If, in spite of the foregoing, you still think that reform will work, just look at our past record. To take only a few of the most conspicuous examples:

1. *Environmental destruction.* People damaged their environment to some degree even at the hunting-and-gathering stage. Forests were burned, either through recklessness or because burned-over lands produced more food for hunter-gatherers.[166] Early hunters may have exterminated some species of large game.[167] As technology increased man's power, environmental destruction became more serious. For example, it is well known that the Mediterranean region was largely deforested by pre-modern civilizations.[168] But forests are only one part of the picture: Pre-industrial societies had no radioactive waste, no chemical factories, no diesel engines, and the damage they did to their environment was minor in comparison with what is being done today. In spite of the feeble palliative measures that are now being taken, the overall picture is clear: For thousands of

years, the damage that humans have done to their environment has been steadily increasing. As for reform—there *is* an environmental movement, but its successes have been very modest in relation to the magnitude of the problem.

2. *War.* War existed among nomadic hunter-gatherers, and could be nasty.[169] But as civilization and military technology advanced, war became more and more destructive. By the 20th century it was simply horrible. As Winston Churchill put it, "War, which used to be cruel and magnificent, has now become cruel and squalid."[170] Private efforts to end war began at least as early as the 1790s,[171] and efforts by governments began at least as early as the end of World War I with the League of Nations. You can see how little has been accomplished.

3. *Psychological problems incident to modern life.* I discussed these in my letter of November 23, 2004. But the presence of such problems was already evident early in the 20th century in the neurotic tendency of the arts. In reading a history of Spanish literature recently, I was struck by the way the neurotic made its appearance as the historian moved from the 19th to the 20th century. E.g.: "The poetry of Dámaso Alonso [born in 1898]... is a cry... of anguish and anger; *an explosion of impotent rage against his own misery and against the pain of the world around him.*"[172] Artists of this type can't be dismissed simply as individuals with psychological problems peculiar to themselves, because the fact that their work has been accepted and admired among intellectuals is an indication that the neurosis is fairly widespread. And what has been done about the psychological problems of modern times? Drugs, psychotherapy—in my view insults to human dignity. Where is the reform movement that, according to your theory, is supposed to fix things?

4. *Propaganda.* As I mentioned above (see I.A.10), the problem of propaganda was well publicized by Vance Packard circa 1960, and the problem was certainly recognized by others (e.g., Harold Lasswell) long before that. And what has been done to correct this insult to human dignity? Nothing whatsoever.

5. *Domination of our lives by large organizations.* This is a matter of fundamental importance, and nothing effective has been done to alleviate the problem. As I've pointed out (see I.A.7), nothing *can* be done about this problem in the context of a technological society.

6. *Nuclear Weapons.* This is perhaps the star exhibit. Of all our technologically induced problems, the problem of nuclear weapons should

be the easiest to solve through reform: The danger presented by these weapons is in no way subtle—it is obvious to anyone with a normal IQ. While such things as genetic engineering and superintelligent computers promise benefits that may seem to offset their menace, nuclear weapons offer no benefits whatever—only death and destruction. With the exception only of a tiny minority of dictators, military men, and politicians who see nuclear weapons as enhancing their own power, virtually every thinking person agrees that the world would be better off without nuclear weapons. Yet nuclear weapons have been around since 1945, and almost no progress has been made toward eliminating them. On the contrary, they proliferate: The U.S., Russia, Britain, France; then China, Israel, India, Pakistan; now North Korea, and in a few years probably Iran...

If reform can't solve the problem of nuclear weapons, then how can it solve the far more subtle and difficult problems among those that modern technology has created?

So it's clear that reform isn't working, and there's no reason to hope that it will ever work. Obviously it's time to try something else.

II. WHY REVOLUTION MAY SUCCEED

II.A. There are several reasons why revolution may succeed where reform has made no progress.

1. Until circa 1980 I used to think the situation was hopeless, largely because of people's thoughtlessness and passivity and their tendency to take the easy way out. (See I.A.6, 8–14, above.) Up to that point I had never read much history. But then I read Thomas Carlyle's history of the French Revolution, and it opened my eyes to the fact that, in time of revolution, the usual rules do not apply: People behave differently. Subsequent reading about revolutions, especially the French and Russian ones, confirmed that conclusion. Once a revolutionary fever has taken hold of a country, people throw off their passivity and are willing to make the greatest efforts and endure the greatest hardships for the sake of their revolution. In such cases it may be that only a minority of the population is gripped by the revolutionary fever, but that minority is sufficiently large and energetic so that it becomes the dominant force in the country. See ISAIF, ¶ 142.

2. Long before that large and dominant revolutionary minority develops, that is, long before the revolution actually begins, an avowedly

revolutionary movement can shake a much smaller minority out of its apathy and learned helplessness and inspire it to passionate commitment and sacrifice in a way that a moderate and "reasonable" reform effort cannot do. See ISAIF, ¶ 141. This small minority may then show remarkable stamina and long-term determination in preparing the way for revolution. The Russian revolutionary movement up to 1917 provides a notable example of this.

3.   The fact that revolutions are usually prepared and carried out by minorities is important, because the system's techniques of propaganda almost always enable it to keep the attitudes and behavior of the majority within such limits that they do not threaten the system's basic interests. As long as society is governed through the usual democratic processes—elections, public-opinion polls, and other numerical indices of majority choice—no reform movement that threatens the system's basic interests can succeed,[173] because the system can always contrive to have the majority on its side. Fifty-one percent who are just barely interested enough to cast a vote will always defeat forty-nine percent, no matter how serious and committed the latter may be. But in revolution a minority, if sufficiently determined and energetic, can outweigh the relatively inert majority.

4.   Unlike reformers, revolutionaries are not restrained by fear of negative consequences (see I.A.16, above). Consider for example the emission of greenhouse gases and/or creation of nuclear waste associated with the generation of electric power. Because it is unthinkable that anyone should have to do without electricity, the reformers are largely stymied; they can only hope that a technological solution will be found in time. But revolutionaries will be prepared to shut down the power plants regardless of consequences.

5.   As noted above (see I.A.15), reformers have to fight a number of different battles, the loss of any one of which could lead either to physical disaster or to conditions intolerably offensive to human dignity. Revolutionaries whose goal is the overthrow of the technoindustrial system have only *one* battle to fight and win.

6.   As I've argued (see I.A.1), history is guided mainly by "objective" circumstances, and if we want to change the course of history we have to change the "objective" circumstances to that end. The dominant "objective" circumstances in the world today are those created by the technoindustrial system. If a revolutionary movement could bring about the collapse of the technoindustrial system, it would indeed change the "objective" circumstances dramatically.

7. As I've pointed out (see I.A.17), your proposed solution through piecemeal reform has no historical precedents. But there are numerous precedents for the elimination through revolution of an existing form of society. Probably the precedent most apposite to our case is that of the Russian Revolution, in which a revolutionary movement systematically prepared the way for revolution over a period of decades, so that when the right moment arrived the revolutionaries were ready to strike.

8. Even if you believe that adequate reforms are possible, you should still favor the creation of an effective revolutionary movement. It's clear that the necessary reforms—if such are possible—are not currently being carried out. Often the system needs a hard kick in the pants to get it started on necessary reforms, and a revolutionary movement can provide that kick in the pants.

Further, if it is an error to attempt revolution—that is, if adequate reforms are possible—then the error should be self-correcting: As soon as the system has carried through the necessary reforms, the revolutionary movement will no longer have a valid cause, so it will lose support and peter out. For example, in Western Europe during the 19th and the early 20th century the labor movement was revolutionary in nature, but the revolutionary impulse of the working class subsequently faded because the condition of the workers was sufficiently alleviated through reforms;[174] this in contrast to what happened in Russia, where the tsarist regime's stubborn resistance to reform led to revolution.

II.B. You write: "Perhaps it would be useful to focus on specific actions necessary to alter our present technological path rather than to use loaded terms like 'revolution,' which may alienate as many, or more, supporters of change as it would galvanize adherents. Or so my colleague suggests."

1. Once one has decided that the overthrow of the technoindustrial system is necessary, there is no reason to shrink from using the word "revolution." If a person is prepared to embrace a goal as radical as that of overthrowing the technoindustrial system, he is hardly likely to be alienated by the term "revolution."

Furthermore, if you want to build a movement dedicated to such a radical goal, you can't build it out of lukewarm people. You need people who are passionately committed, and you must be careful to avoid allowing your movement to be swamped by a lot of well-meaning do-gooders who may be attracted to it because they are concerned about the environment and all that, but will shrink from taking radical measures. So you *want* to alienate the lukewarm do-gooders. You need to keep them away from your movement.

A mistake that most people make is to assume that the more followers you can recruit, the better. That's true if you're trying to win an election. A vote is a vote regardless of whether the voter is deeply committed or just barely interested enough to get to the polls. But when you're building a revolutionary movement, the number of people you have is far less important than the quality of your people and the depth of their commitment. Too many lukewarm or otherwise unsuitable people will ruin the movement. As I pointed out in an earlier letter, at the outset of the Russian Revolution of 1917 the Social Revolutionary party was numerically dominant because it was a catchall party to which anyone who was vaguely in favor of revolution could belong.[175] The more radical Bolsheviks were numerically far inferior, but they were deeply committed and had clear goals. The Social Revolutionaries proved ineffective, and it was the Bolsheviks who won out in the end.

2. This brings me to your argument that if the nomadic hunting-and-gathering (NHG) society is taken as the social ideal, the pool of potential revolutionaries would be minimal. You yourself (same page of same letter) suggested a possible answer to this, namely, that the NHG ideal might "draw in the most committed activists," and that is essentially the answer that I would give. As I've just argued, level of commitment is more important than numbers. But I would also mention that of all societies of biologically modern humans, the nomadic hunting-and-gathering ones were those that suffered least from the chief problems that modern society brings to the world, such as environmental destruction, dangerous technological powers, dominance of large organizations over individuals and small groups. This fact certainly weighs in favor of the NHG ideal. Moreover, I think you greatly underestimate the number of potential revolutionaries who would be attracted by such an ideal. I may say more about that in a later letter.

III. NECESSITY OF REVOLUTION

You challenge me to present evidence that "the situation is so urgent that truly revolutionary action is demanded," and you write: "If in fact the situation is as serious as you portray, then surely there would be other rational thinkers who would come to the same conclusion. Where are the other intelligent voices that see this reality, and likewise conclude that revolution is the only option?" But there are two separate issues here: The seriousness and urgency of the situation is one question and the call for revolution is another.

III.A. I shouldn't have to offer you any evidence on the seriousness and urgency of the situation, because others have already done that. You're familiar with Bill Joy's article. Jared Diamond and Richard Posner (U.S. Circuit Judge, conservative, pro-government) have written books about the risk of catastrophe.[176] The British Astronomer Royal, Sir Martin Rees, estimates that "the odds are no better than fifty-fifty that our present civilization on Earth will survive to the end of the present century." Among other terrifying possibilities, experiments with particle accelerators at extremely high energies could conceivably lead to a catastrophe that would destroy our whole planet almost instantly, and eventually the entire universe.[177] I don't think your colleague will dismiss any of the foregoing people as "raving anarchists."

The people mentioned in the preceding paragraph warn of dangers in the hope that these can be forestalled. I think there are many others who see the situation as hopeless and believe that disaster is inevitable. Several years ago someone sent me what seemed to be a responsible article titled "Planet of Weeds."[178] I didn't actually read the article, I only glanced through it, but I think the thesis was that our civilization would cause the extinction of most life on Earth, and that when our civilization was dead—and the human race with it—the organisms that would survive would be the weed-like ones, i.e., those that could grow and reproduce quickly under adverse conditions. Many of the original members of Earth First!—before it was taken over by the leftists—were political conservatives and I don't think your colleague could reasonably dismiss them as "raving anarchists." Their view was that the collapse of industrial civilization through environmental disaster was inevitable in the relatively near future. They felt that it was impossible to prevent the disaster, and their goal was merely to save some remnants of wilderness that could serve as "seeds" for the regeneration of life after industrial society was gone.[179]

So I think there are significant numbers of intelligent and rational people who see the situation as more serious and urgent than I do. The people I've mentioned up to this point have considered mainly the risk of physical disaster. Ellul and others have addressed the issues of human dignity, and if my recollections of his book *Autopsy of Revolution* are correct, Ellul felt that there was at most a minimal chance of avoiding a complete and permanent end to human freedom and dignity. So Ellul too saw the situation as worse than I see it.

III.B. Why then is rational advocacy of revolution so rare? There are several reasons that have nothing to do with the degree of urgency or seriousness of the situation.

1. In mainstream American society today, it is socially unacceptable to advocate revolution. Anyone who does so risks being classified as a "raving anarchist" merely by virtue of the fact that he advocates revolution.

2. Many would shrink from advocating revolution simply because of the physical risk that they would run if a revolution actually occurred. Even if they survived the revolution, they would likely have to endure physical hardship. We live in a soft society in which most people are much more fearful of death and hardship than the members of earlier societies were. (The anthropologist Turnbull records the contempt that traditional Africans have for modern man's weakness in the face of pain and death.[180])

3. Most people are extremely reluctant to accept fundamental changes in the pattern of life to which they are adapted. They prefer to cling to familiar ways even if they know that those ways will lead to disaster fifty years in the future. Or even forty, twenty, or ten years. Turnbull observes that "few of us would be willing to sacrifice" modern "achievements," "even in the name of survival."[181] Instead of "achievements" he should have said "habitual patterns of living." Jared Diamond has pointed out that societies often cling stubbornly to their established ways of life even when the price of doing so is death.[182] This alone is enough to explain why calls for revolution are hardly ever heard outside of the most radical fringe.

4. Even people who might otherwise accept a radical change in their way of life may be frightened at the prospect of having to get by without the technological apparatus on which they feel themselves to be dependent. For instance, I know of a woman in the Upper Peninsula of Michigan who hates the technological system with a passion and hopes for its collapse. But in a letter to me dated August 19, 2004, she wrote: "A lightning strike on June 30 'fried' our power inverter at the cabin. For three weeks I lived without electricity. ... I realized how much I was dependent. I grew to hate the night. I think that humans will do whatever possible to preserve the electrical power grids...."

5. Many people (e.g., the original Earth First!ers whom I mentioned above, III.A) think the system will collapse soon anyway, in which case no revolution will be necessary.

6. Finally, there is hopelessness and apathy. The system seems so all-powerful and invulnerable that nothing can be done against it. There's no point in advocating a revolution that is impossible. This, rather than that revolution is unnecessary or too extreme, is the objection I've heard from some people. But it is precisely the general assumption that revolution is impossible that makes it impossible in fact. If enough people could be made to *believe* that revolution were possible, then it would *be* possible. One of the first tasks of a nascent revolutionary movement would be to get itself taken seriously.

III.C. Your colleague insists that "the case for revolution needs to be demonstrated virtually *beyond doubt*, because it is so extreme and serious." I disagree. The possible or probable consequences of continued technological progress include the extinction of the human race or even of all of the more complex forms of life on Earth; or the replacement of humans by intelligent machines; or a transformation of the human race that will entail the permanent loss of all freedom and dignity as these have traditionally been conceived. These consequences are so much more extreme and serious than those to be expected from revolution that I don't think we need to be 100% certain, or even 90% certain, that revolution is really necessary in order to justify such action.[183]

Anyway, the standard that your colleague sets for the justification of revolution ("virtually beyond doubt") is impossibly high. Since major wars are just as dangerous and destructive as revolutions, he would have to apply the same standard to warfare. Does your colleague believe, for example, that the Western democracies acted unjustifiably in fighting World War II? If not, then how would he justify World War II under the "virtually beyond doubt" standard?

III.D. Even if we assume that it is not known at present whether revolution will ever be necessary or justifiable, the time to begin building a revolutionary movement is now. If we wait too long and it turns out that revolution *is* necessary, we may find that it is too late.

Revolutions can occur spontaneously. (For example, the way for the French Revolution was not consciously prepared in advance.) But that is a matter of chance. If we don't want merely to hope for luck, then we have to start preparing the way for revolution decades in advance as the Russian revolutionaries did, so that we will be ready when the time is ripe.

I suggest that as time goes by, the system's tools for forestalling or suppressing revolution get stronger. Suppose that revolution is delayed until after computers have surpassed humans in intelligence. Presumably the most intelligent computers will be in the hands of large organizations such as corporations and governments. At that point revolution may become impossible, because the government's computers will be able to outsmart revolutionaries at every step.

Revolutions often depend for their success on the fact that the revolutionaries have enough support in the army or among the police so that at least some elements of these remain neutral or aid the revolutionaries. The revolutionary sympathies of soldiers certainly played an important part in the French and Russian Revolutions. But the armies and police forces of the future may consist of robots, which presumably will not be susceptible to subversion.

This is not science fiction. "[E]xperts said that between 2011 and 2015, every household will have a robot doing chores such as cleaning and laundering."[184] [This is one among many examples of overoptimistic predictions by technical experts; as of March 2016 the prediction has not yet come true. But it does indicate the general direction in which we are moving. For example, self-driving cars are now (2016) a reality, even though until a dozen years ago most robotics experts believed that such cars were impossible.[185]] The Honda company already claims to have "an advanced robot with unprecedented humanlike abilities. ASIMO walks forward and backward, turns corners, and goes up and down stairs with ease.... The future of this exciting technology is even more promising. ASIMO has the potential to respond to simple voice commands, recognize faces.... [O]ne day, ASIMO could be quite useful in some very important tasks. Like assisting the elderly, and even helping with household chores. In essence, ASIMO might serve as another set of eyes, ears and legs for all kinds of people in need."[186] Police and military applications of robots are an obvious next step, and in fact the U.S. military is already developing robotized fighting machines for use in combat.[187]

So if we're going to have a revolution we had better have it before technology makes revolution impossible. If we wait until the need for revolution is "virtually beyond doubt," our opportunity may be gone forever.

III.E.   Here's a challenge for your colleague: Outline a plausible scenario for the future of our society in which everything turns out alright, and does so *without* a collapse of the technoindustrial system, whether through revolution or otherwise. Obviously, there may be disagreement as to what is "alright." But in any case your colleague will have to explain, inter alia: (1) How he expects to prevent computers more intelligent than humans from being developed, or, if they are developed, how he expects to prevent them from supplanting humans; (2) how he expects to avoid the risk of biological disaster that biotechnological experimentation entails; (3) how he expects to prevent the progressive lowering of standards of human dignity that we've been seeing at least since the early stages of the Industrial Revolution; and (4) how he expects nuclear weapons to be brought under control. As I pointed out above (see I.B.6), of all our technology-related problems, the problem of nuclear weapons should be by far the easiest to solve, so if your colleague can't give a good and convincing answer to question (4)—something better than just a pious hope that mankind will see the light and dismantle all the nukes in a spirit of brotherhood and reconciliation—then I suggest it's time to give up the idea of reform.

**Letter to David Skrbina,
April 5, 2005**

First, as to the likelihood that computers will catch up with humans in intelligence by the year 2029, which I think is the date predicted by Ray Kurzweil: My guess is that this will not happen until significantly later than 2029. I have no technical expertise that qualifies me to offer an opinion on this subject. My guess is based mainly on the fact that technical experts tend to underestimate the time it will take to achieve fundamental breakthroughs. In 1970, computer experts predicted that computers would surpass humans in intelligence within 15 years,[188] and obviously that didn't happen.

I do think it's highly probable that machines will *eventually* surpass humans in intelligence. I'm enough of a materialist to believe that the human brain functions solely according to the laws of physics and chemistry. In other words, the brain is in a sense a machine, so it should be possible to duplicate it artificially. And if the brain can be duplicated artificially, it can certainly be improved upon.

Second, while I think it's highly probable that the technosystem is headed for *eventual* physical disaster, I don't think the risk of a massive, worldwide physical disaster within the next few decades is as high as some people seem to believe. Again, I have no technical expertise on which to base such an opinion. But back in the late 1960s there were supposedly qualified people who made dire predictions for the near future—e.g., Paul Ehrlich in his book *The Population Bomb*. Their predictions were not entirely without substance. They predicted the greenhouse effect, for example; they predicted epidemics, and we have AIDS. But on the whole the consequences of overpopulation and reckless consumption of natural resources have been nowhere near as severe as these people predicted.

On the other hand, there is a difference between the doomsday prophets of the 1960s and people like Bill Joy and Martin Rees. Certainly Paul Ehrlich and probably many of the other 1960s doomsdayers were leftish types, and leftish types, as we know, look for any excuse to rail against the existing society; hence, their criticisms tend to be wildly exaggerated. But Bill Joy and Martin Rees are not leftish types as far as I know; in fact, they are dedicated technophiles. And dedicated technophiles are not likely to be motivated to exaggerate the dangers of technology. So maybe I'm naïve in feeling that the risk of physical disaster is less imminent than Joy and Rees seem to think.

The foregoing remarks are intended to clarify matters that I discussed in my letter of March 17, 2005. Now I'd like to address specifically some points raised in your letters.

I. You write: "Art, music, literature, and (for the most part) religion are considered by most people to be true and important achievements of humanity…. You seem to undervalue any such accomplishments, and in fact virtually advocate throwing them away…; art and literature are nothing more than 'a harmless outlet for rebellious impulses.' "

I.A. I did write in "Morality and Revolution": "Art, literature and the like provide a harmless outlet for rebellious impulses…." (I think Ellul somewhere says much the same thing.) But I've never said that art and literature were *nothing more* than that. In any case, I don't *advocate* "throwing away" art and literature. I do recognize that the loss of much art and literature would be a consequence of the downfall of the technoindustrial system, but getting rid of art and literature is not a *goal.*

I.B. It could be argued that the arts actually are in poor health in modern society and have been in much better health in many primitive societies. You claim that in our society the arts "are considered by most people to be true and important achievements of humanity." But how often do most people visit an art museum, listen to classical music, or read serious literature? Very seldom, I think. Furthermore, even if we include commercial graphic art, television, light novels, and the like among the arts, only a small minority of people today participate *actively* in the arts, whether as professionals or as amateurs. Most people participate only as spectators or consumers of art.

Primitives too may have specialists in certain arts, but active participation tends to be much more widespread among them than it is in the modern world. For instance, among the African pygmies, *everyone* participated in song and dance. After describing the dances of the Mbuti pygmies, their "*angeborene Schauspielkunst*" (inborn dramatic art), and their music, Schebesta writes: "Here I will go into no further detail about Mbuti art, of whatever kind, for I only wanted to show what significance all of this has for their daily life. Here opens a source that feeds the life-energies of the primitives, that brightens and pleasantly adorns their forest life, which is otherwise so hard. That is probably why the Mbuti are so devoted to these pleasures."[189] Compare industrial society, in which most people participate in the arts only to the extent of watching Hollywood movies, reading popular magazines or light novels, and having a radio blaring in their ears without actually listening to it.

Admittedly, much primitive art is crude, but this is by no means true of all of it. You must have seen reproductions of some of the magnificent paintings found on the walls of caves in Western Europe, and the polyphony of the African pygmies is much admired by serious students of music.[190] Of course, no pre-modern society had a body of art that matched in range and elaborate development the arts of present-day industrial society, and much of the latter would undoubtedly be lost with the collapse of the system. But the argument I would use here is that of...

I.C. *The monkey and the peanut.* When I was a little kid, my father told me of a trick for catching monkeys that he had read about somewhere. You take a glass bottle the neck of which is narrow enough so that a monkey's clenched fist will not pass through it, but wide enough so that a monkey can squeeze his open hand into the bottle. You put a piece of bait—say, a peanut—into the bottle. A monkey reaches into the bottle, clutches the peanut in his little fist, and then finds that he can't pull his hand out of the bottle. He's too greedy to let go of the peanut, so you can just walk over and pick him up. Thus, because the monkey refuses to accept the loss of the peanut, he loses everything.

If we continue on our present course, we'll probably be replaced by computers sooner or later. What use do you think the machines will have for art, literature, and music? If we aren't replaced by computers, we'll certainly be changed profoundly. See ISAIF, ¶ 178. What reason do you have to believe that people of the future will still be responsive to the art, music, and literature of the past? Already the arts of the past have been largely superseded by the popular entertainment media, which offer intense kicks that make the old-time stuff seem boring. Shakespeare and Cervantes wrote, Vermeer and Frans Hals painted[191] for ordinary people, not for an elite minority of intellectuals. But how many people still read Shakespeare and Cervantes when they're not required to do so as part of a college course? How many hang reproductions of the Old Masters' paintings on their walls? Even if the human race still exists 200 years from now, will *anyone* still appreciate the classics of art, music, and literature? I seriously doubt it. So if we continue on our present course we'll probably lose the Western artistic tradition anyway, and we'll certainly lose a great deal more besides.

So maybe it's better to let go of the peanut than to lose everything by trying to hang onto it. Especially since we don't have to give up the whole peanut. If the system collapses before it's too late, we'll retain our humanity and our capacity to appreciate art, literature and music. It's safe to assume then that people will continue to create art, literature, and music as they always have in the past, and that works of high quality will occasionally appear.

I.D. Along with art, literature, and music you mention religion. I'm rather surprised that you regard religion as something that would be lost with the collapse of modern civilization, since modern civilization is notorious for its secularity. The explorer and ethnographer Vilhjalmur Stefansson wrote: "One frequently hears the remark that no people in the world have yet been found who are so low that they do not have a religion. This is absolutely true, but the inference one is likely to draw is misleading. It is not only true that no people are so low that they do not have a religion, but it is equally true that the lower you go in the scale of human culture the more religion you find...."[192]

Actually Stefansson's observation is not strictly accurate, but it is true that in most primitive societies religion played a more important role than it does in modern society. Colin Turnbull makes clear how much religious feeling was integrated into the daily lives of the Mbuti pygmies,[193] and the North American Indians had a similarly rich religious life, which was

intimately interwoven with their day-to-day existence.[194] Compare this with
the religious life of most modern people: Their theological sophistication is
virtually zero; they may go to church on Sundays, but the rest of the week
they govern their behavior almost exclusively according to secular mores.

However, a reservation is called for: It's possible that a resurgence of
religion may occur in the modern world. See the article by Bill Moyers[195]
that I enclosed with my last letter. But I certainly *hope* that the kind of
kook religion described by Moyers is not the kind of religion of which
your colleague would regret the loss if the system collapsed. Among other
things, that brand of religion is irrational, intolerant, and even hate-filled.
It's worth noting that a similar current has developed within Hinduism
(see enclosed article);[196] and of course we all know what's going on in
Islam. None of this should surprise us. Each of the great world religions
claims to have exclusive possession of the truth, and ever since their advent
religion has been a source and/or instrument of conflict, often very deadly
conflict. Primitive religions, in contrast, are generally tolerant, syncre-
tistic, or both.[197] I know of no religious wars among primitives.

So if your colleague believes that modern religions would be lost
with the collapse of the system (a proposition which unfortunately I think
is very doubtful), it's not clear to me why he should regret it.

II. You read me as holding that "we have now passed… the point
at which reform was a viable option." But that is not my view. I don't
think that reform was ever a viable option. The Industrial Revolution and
succeeding developments have resulted from the operation of "objective"
historical forces (see my letter of October 12, 2004), and neither reform
nor (counter)revolution could have prevented them. However, we may
now be approaching a window of opportunity during which it may be
possible to "kill" the technoindustrial system.

A simple, *decentralized* organism like a hydra is hard to kill. You can
cut it up into pieces and each piece will grow into a whole new hydra. A
complex and *centralized* organism like a mammal is easy to kill. A blow or
a stab to a vital organ, a sufficient lowering of body temperature, or any
one of many other factors can kill a mammal.

Northwestern Europe in the 18th century was poised for the
Industrial Revolution. However, its economy was still relatively simple
and decentralized, like a hydra. Even in the unlikely event that war or
revolution had wiped out half the population and destroyed half the

infrastructure, the survivors would have been able to pick up the pieces and get their economy functioning again. So the Industrial Revolution probably would have been delayed only by a few decades.

Today, on the other hand, the technoindustrial system is growing more and more to resemble a single, centralized, worldwide organism in which every part is dependent on the functioning of the whole. In other words, the system increasingly resembles a complex, easy-to-kill organism like a mammal. If the system once broke down badly enough it would "die," and its reconstruction would be extraordinarily difficult. See ISAIF, ¶¶ 207–212. Some believe that its reconstruction would even be impossible. This was the opinion of (for example) the distinguished astronomer Fred Hoyle.[198]

So only now, in my opinion, is there a realistic possibility of altering the course of technoindustrial development.

Letter to David Skrbina,
July 10, 2005

Regarding the material about monkey genes—yes, it's not uncommon to read reports of new ways of monkeying with the brain (no pun intended), and there is plenty of reason to worry about this stuff, not so much because employers might force their employees to take gene treatments to turn them into workaholics (which I think is unlikely), as because increased understanding of the brain leads to solutions that are, at the least, insulting to human dignity. See ISAIF, ¶¶ 143–45, 149–156.

Regarding Ray Kurzweil's "Promise and Peril,"[199] you write, "I'm not sure which disturb me more, his 'promises' or his 'perils'." I feel the same way. To me they are all just perils. I'm skeptical about Kurzweil's predictions, though. I'll bet that a lot of them will turn out to be just pie in the sky. In the past there have been too many confident predictions about the future of technology that have not been fulfilled. It's certainly not that I would want to downplay the power or the danger of technology. However, I do question Kurzweil's ability to predict the future. I'll be very surprised if everything that he predicts actually materializes, but I won't be a bit surprised if a lot of scary stuff happens that neither Kurzweil nor anyone else can now anticipate.

To address a few specific points from Kurzweil's article:

He asks: "Should we tell the millions of people afflicted with cancer and other devastating conditions that we are canceling the development of all bioengineered treatments because there is a risk that these same technologies may someday be used for malevolent purposes?" Kurzweil fails to note that cancer results largely from the modern way of life (see my letter of March 17, 2005), and the same is true of many other "devastating conditions," e.g., AIDS, which, assuming that it occurred at all, would probably have remained localized if it had not been for modern transportation facilities, which spread the disease everywhere. In any case, what is at stake now are the most fundamental aspects of the fate of the whole world. It would be senseless to risk a disastrous outcome in order to prolong artificially the lives of people suffering from "devastating conditions."

Throughout his essay Kurzweil romanticizes the technological way of life, while he paints a misleading and grim picture of pre-industrial life. In my letter of November 23, 2004, I pointed out some reasons for considering primitive life better than modern life. To address specifically Kurzweil's point about life-expectancy—he mentions an expectancy of 35 years for pre-industrial Swedish females and 33 for males. Let's split the difference and make it 34 years overall. This figure is correct,[200] but it is misleading because it gives the impression that few people lived beyond their mid-thirties. Actually, the low life-expectancies of pre-industrial times largely reflected the high rate of infant and early-childhood mortality. For 18th-century Sweden it appears that about 32½% of babies born alive died before reaching the age of five years. But of those who survived the difficult first five years roughly 60% lived at least to the age of 50, 36% lived at least to the age of 65, and 18% lived at least to the age of 75.[201] This shows how misleading it can be to cite the 34-year life expectancy without further explanation. It is worth noting that the survival curve for hunter-gatherers shown by Gurven & Kaplan does not differ greatly from that for 18th-century Sweden,[202] and that about 8% of a population of Kalahari Bushmen (hunter-gatherers) was found to consist of persons from 60 to 80 or more years old.[203] My recollection is that according to the 1970 census, 10% of the American population was then aged 65 or older.[204] This figure has stuck in my mind because I read it not long after reading the foregoing figure for the Bushmen.

Kurzweil states not only that technological progress proceeds exponentially but that biological evolution has always done so. Whether this is true will depend on what sort of quantitative measure of "progress" or "evolution" one uses. But Kurzweil just states flatly and without qualification: "Exponential growth is a feature of any evolutionary process...." This kind of overconfidence is apparent also in other parts of the article, and it reinforces my suspicion (which I mentioned in an earlier letter) that Kurzweil is more of a showman than a serious thinker.

Again, I myself believe that technology is carrying us forward at an accelerating and extremely dangerous rate; on that point I fully agree with Kurzweil. But I question whether he is a responsible, balanced, and reliable commentator.

Kurzweil admits that we can't "absolutely ensure" the survival of human ethics and values, but he does seem to believe we can do a lot to promote their survival. And throughout his article generally he shows his belief that humans can to a significant degree control the path that technological progress will take. I maintain that he is dead wrong. History shows the futility of human efforts to guide the development of societies, and, given that the pace of change—as Kurzweil himself says—will keep accelerating indefinitely, the futility of such efforts in the future will be even more certain. So Kurzweil's ideas for limiting the dangerous aspects of technological progress are completely unrealistic. Relevant here are my remarks about "natural selection" (see my letter of October 12, 2004). For example, "human values" in the long run will survive only if they are the "fittest" values in terms of natural selection. And it is highly unlikely that they will continue to be the fittest values in the world of the future, which will be utterly unlike the world that has existed heretofore.

A question has to be raised about the people who are promoting all this mad technological growth—those who do the research and those who provide the funds for research. Are they criminals? Should they be punished?

*　　　*　　　*

Concerning the recent [as of 2005] terrorist action in Britain: Quite apart from any humanitarian considerations, the radical Islamics' approach seems senseless. They take a hostile stance toward whole nations, such as the U.S. or Britain, and they indiscriminately kill ordinary citizens of those countries. In doing so they only strengthen the countries in question, because they provide the politicians with what they most need: a feared external enemy to unite the people behind their leaders. The Islamics seem to have forgotten the principle of "divide and conquer": Their best policy would have been to profess friendship for the American, British, etc. *people* and limit their expressed hostility to the elite groups of those countries, while portraying the ordinary people as victims or dupes of their leaders. (Notice that this is the position that the U.S. usually adopts toward hostile countries.)

So the terrorists' acts of mass slaughter seem stupid. But there may be an explanation other than stupidity for their actions: The radical Islamic leaders may be less interested in the effect that the bombings have on the U.S. or the U.K. than in their effect within the Islamic world. The leaders' main goal may be to build a strong and fanatical Islamic movement, and for this purpose they may feel that spectacular acts of mass destruction are more effective than assassinations of single individuals, however important the latter may be. I've found some support for this hypothesis:

> [A] radical remake of the faith is indeed the underlying intention of bin Laden and his followers. Attacking America and its allies is merely a tactic, intended to provoke a backlash strong enough to alert Muslims to the supposed truth of their predicament, and so rally them to purge their faith of all that is alien to its essence. Promoting a clash of civilizations is merely stage one. The more difficult part, as the radicals see it, is convincing fellow Muslims to reject the modern world absolutely (including such aberrations as democracy), topple their own insidiously secularizing quisling governments, and return to the pure path.[205]

NOTES

1. See List of Works Cited.
2. NEB (2003), Vol. 28, "Technology, The History of," p. 451.
3. Trotsky, Vol. One, pp. xviii–xix.
4. "[A]n ideology, in order to function as the basis of a successful movement, must link up the goal with the issue. This can best be accomplished by setting forth a plan in which the items are the opposite of that which is regarded as the cause of the problem-experiences." Abel, p. 350.
5. Cashdan, pp. 22–23.
6. "In every well-documented instance, cases of hardship [=starvation] may be traced to the intervention of modern intruders." Coon, pp. 388–89.
7. See, e.g., Gurven & Kaplan, pp. 342, 343, 346, 349.
8. "Social equality" here does not necessarily include gender equality.

See "The Truth About Primitive Life," in Kaczynski, *Technological Slavery* (2010), pp. 127–189. In recent decades anthropologists have attacked earlier investigators' claims of social equality among nomadic hunter-gatherers by pointing out examples of inequality in such societies. See, e.g., Shott. I'm not qualified to take sides in this debate, but it should be noted that, simply because of the physical conditions of their existence, there was no way that nomadic hunter-gatherer societies could have had anything approaching the degree of social inequality that exists in modern society, where most people are powerless while a few individuals, "maybe 500 or 1,000" out of seven billion (ISAIF, ¶ 67), make all of the world's really important decisions. If social inequalities among nomadic hunter-gatherers had been of the same order of magnitude as the inequalities of civilized societies, then the inequalities would have been so obvious that even the most superficial observers could not have missed them, and the recent efforts to prove the existence of inequality in such societies would have been unnecessary.

Slavery was rare among nomadic hunter-gatherers, NEB (2003), Vol. 27, "Slavery," p. 288, but not unknown, NEB (1997), Vol. 10, "slave," p. 873; Legros, p. 617.

9. See "The Truth About Primitive Life," in Kaczynski, *Technological Slavery* (2010), pp. 127–189.

10. "The propagandist must realize that neither rational arguments nor catchy slogans can, by themselves, do much to influence human behavior." NEB (2003), Vol. 26, "Propaganda," pp. 175–76.

11. Ibid., p. 176.

12. Ibid., p. 174.

13. China's "one-child" policy was easily circumvented. Osnos, p. 32, col. 2. Nevertheless, it "almost certainly" reduced to some extent (though it did not halt) China's population growth. *The Economist*, July 23, 2011, p. 12. But the policy aroused serious opposition, and demographers claimed it was damaging to China. Ibid., May 7, 2011, pp. 43–44; July 23, 2011, pp. 37–38. The one-child policy has now been replaced by a two-child policy. *USA Today*, Oct. 30–Nov. 1, 2015, p. 1A.

14. See Hoffer, § 65.

15. NEB (2003), Vol. 16, "Christianity," p. 261. See Freeman, p. 172 (Christians were "agreed that they must remain perpetual apostates from the approved religions"); p. 175; p. 221 ("Christians were expected to cut themselves off from all the religious rituals of civic life... . Social cohesion was achieved through defining a community that stood apart from the rest of society...").

16. Trotsky, Vol. One, p. 223.

17. Ibid., p. 324. On this subject generally see ibid., pp. 223–331.

18. Ibid., Vol. One, Chapt. VIII, pp. 136–152.

19. See Trotsky, the entire work.

20. Admittedly, one would have to stretch a point to say that (II) here is identical with the second objective for a revolutionary movement that I listed in my letter of Aug. 29, 2004: "to increase the tensions within the social order until those tensions reach the breaking point." But one thing I've learned about expository writing is that too much precision is counterproductive. In order to be understood one has to simplify as much as possible, even at the cost of precision. For the purposes of my letter of Aug. 29, 2004, the point I needed to emphasize was that a revolutionary movement has to increase social tensions rather than relieving them through reform. If I had given a more detailed and precise account of the task of a revolutionary movement, as in the present letter, it would only have distracted attention from the point that I needed to make in my letter of Aug. 29, 2004. So I beg your indulgence for my failure to be perfectly consistent in this instance.

21. "When different events are experienced as affecting personal and social values the dissatisfaction and opposition resulting therefrom must be capable of being focussed upon some object that can be regarded as the *common source* of the disturbing events," Abel, p. 349. A movement must "skilfully link[ ] dissatisfactions with its ideology." Ibid., p. 351.

22. The suggestion that a biotechnological accident could provide a trigger for revolution is in tension with my earlier suggestion (letter of Aug. 29, 2004) that it might be desirable to slow the progress of biotechnology in order to postpone any biotechnological catastrophe. On the one hand, such a catastrophe might be so severe that afterward there would be nothing left to save; on the other hand, a lesser catastrophe might provide the occasion for revolution. It's arguable which consideration should be given more weight. But on the whole I think it would be best to try to slow the progress of biotechnology.

23. NEB (2003), Vol. 28, "Union of Soviet Socialist Republics," p. 1000.

24. "[T]he most effective media as a rule... are not the impersonal mass media but rather those few associations or organizations (reference groups) with which the individual feels identified. ... Quite often the ordinary man not only avoids but actively distrusts the mass media... but in the warmth of his reference group he feels at home... ." Ibid., Vol. 26, "Propaganda," p. 176.

25. See Appendix One.

26. "All animals... derive satisfaction from the mere act of seeking a goal." *The Week*, Feb. 6, 2009, p. 23, reviewing Grandin & Johnson.

27. Seligman, p. 55. White, Kavanau, as in our List of Works Cited.

28. Morris, passim, especially pp. 160–225.

29. Ibid., pp. 189, 194.

30. Keniston, pp. 269, 296, 297.

31. Goodman, pp. 13, 17–35 (Chapt. I), 234–36.

32. Keyfitz, p. 116.

33. See e.g. Tacitus, *Germania* 46 (hunter-gatherers present in Baltic area

< 2,000 years ago); NEB (2003), Vol. 28, "Spain," p. 18 (hunter-gatherers present in Spain up to 5,500 years ago).

34. "Ten thousand years ago all men were hunters, including the ancestors of everyone reading this book. The span of ten millennia encompasses about four hundred generations, too few to allow for any notable genetic changes." Coon, p. XVII. Admittedly, it may be open to argument whether four hundred generations "allow for any notable genetic changes."

35. Robert Wright, as referenced in our List of Works Cited.

36. There is no claim here that this is an exhaustive list of the ways in which human intentions for a society can be realized on a historical scale. If you can identify any additional ways that are relevant for the purposes of the present discussion, I'll be interested to hear of them.

37. See Carrillo, pp. 201–02, 207–08.

38. The proponents of progress seem to have believed that technology would provide people with an abundance of leisure time that they would devote to intellectual and esthetic pursuits. E.g., John Adams (the future President) wrote in 1780:

"I must study politics and war that my sons may have liberty to study mathematics and philosophy. [In the 18th century "philosophy" included "natural philosophy," i.e., what we nowadays call "science."] My sons ought to study mathematics and philosophy, geography, natural history and naval architecture, navigation, commerce and agriculture, in order to give their children a right to study painting, poetry, music, architecture, statuary, tapestry, and porcelain."

Quoted by Haraszti, pp. 307–08n49. Today these beliefs about the social consequences of technological progress seem astonishingly naïve. Yet, despite all evidence to the contrary, despite the fact that for the last 250 years the utopia of universal leisure creatively employed has kept receding into the indefinite future, the same beliefs survive today in a form that is only slightly modified. See Thompson, pp. 54–58, 60, and compare ISAIF, ¶¶ 38–41, 59–86.

39. R. Zakaria, p. 59.

40. After writing this I learned of the existence of Dennett's book (see List of Works Cited), which apparently deals with the role of natural selection in shaping human culture. I have not seen Dennett's book.

41. NEB (2003), Vol. 27, "Social Structure and Change," p. 369.

42. See Appendix Two.

43. "[E]ach territorial clan had its own headman and council, and there was also a paramount chief for the entire tribe. The council members of each clan were elected in a meeting between the middle-aged and elderly men, and a few of the outstanding younger ones as well." Coon, p. 253.

44. NEB (2003), Vol. 15, "Buddhism," p. 277.

45. Ibid., Vol. 28, "Ukraine," p. 985.

46. Election of captains: Ibid., Vol. 2, "buccaneers," p. 592. For deposition of captains I'm relying on my memory of books read during the 1960s.

47. Ibid., Vol. 19, "Geneva," p. 743.

48. Ibid., Vol. 20, "Greek and Roman Civilizations," p. 294.

49. It seems clear that in WWII the soldiers of the authoritarian (or even totalitarian) regimes of Germany, Japan, and the Soviet Union fought better than Britons, Americans, or Frenchmen. Germans: Astor, pp. 914, 974. Dyson, p. 4. Jenkins, pp. 680–81, 692–93, 714. Murphy, p. 15. Ulam, p. 585. Wheeler, p. 129 (citing Creveld). Kane, p. 82, is interesting but does not contradict the proposition that German soldiers had better fighting spirit than Americans. In 1939, German generals expressed conflicting opinions about the fighting quality of their troops. Compare opinions in Kosthorst: p. 32, Bock, Leeb (unfavorable), Sodenstern (mixed); pp. 49, 169, 173, Rundstedt (favorable). But on balance the sources known to me strongly indicate Germans' fighting quality was superior to that of French & British, probably also Americans. Japanese: Astor, pp. 268, 413, 843–44. Dunnigan & Nofi, pp. 300–02, 306; Japanese soldiers usually fought to the death, ibid., pp. 39, 80–81, 119, 145, 151, 152, 191, 303, 317, 318, 338, 458. Jenkins, p. 681 (British surrender at Singapore). NEB (2003), Vol. 29, "World Wars," p. 1002 (same). Knox, p. 259. Russians: Thurston, p. 215. NEB (2003), Vol. 29, "World Wars," p. 998 ("isolated Soviet troops fought with a stubbornness that the French had not shown"). It's not clear whether the Germans fought better than the British in WWI, for the British then fought well. Hitchens, p. 101 (Ludendorff: "these British soldiers fight like lions"). Jenkins, p. 681. Liddell Hart, p. 236. Parker, Chapt. 13 by W.A. Murray, p. 259 (British were "the best soldiers, man for man, in 1914"). But if it's true that the Germans fought less well than the British in WWI, it was not by any wide margin. Hitchens, p. 104. Liddell Hart, pp. 188, 234, 476. Parker, Chapt. 14 by W.A. Murray, p. 278.

50. See Appendix Three.

51. NEB (2003), Vol. 27, "Socio-Economic Doctrines and Reform Movements," p. 413. Jenkins, pp. 457, 468–69. Gilbert, *European Powers*, pp. 191–92. In U.S.: Kaplan & Weinberg, Chapt. II. Leuchtenburg, pp. 26, 27, 30&n43, 102&n22, 182–83, 221–22 &n78, 224, 275–77, 279, 288. Patterson, p. 214.

52. NEB (2003), Vol. 25, "Political Parties and Interest Groups," p. 981: "The victory of the Allies in 1945, as well as the revelation of the horrors of Nazism, stopped the growth of the [f]ascists and provoked their decline... ." But the horrors of Nazism were important only because the fascists lost the war. If the fascists had won, their atrocities would not have prevented them from being admired and imitated. The democracies certainly committed plenty of atrocities in the course of their colonial expansion over the world, but they nevertheless are admired and imitated—*when they are proving themselves successful in competition*

with other systems. However painful it may be to humanitarian idealists, the fact is that success and power are what most people principally admire and seek to imitate. A case in point: Anti-slavery sentiment was very strong in Britain during the 19th century (see Note 109, below), but in 1861, when it appeared that the slave-holding South would succeed in maintaining its independence during the U.S. Civil War, "nearly all [Englishmen, including the arch-liberal Gladstone] were glad of it," because secession of the South from the U.S. would represent "a diminution of a dangerous power," i.e., of the U.S. "The sentiment of anti-slavery had disappeared." Adams, pp. 114–15, 165–66. The British were even poised to intervene forcibly in behalf of the South, but they dropped that idea as soon as it no longer appeared that the South was winning the war. NEB (2003), Vol. 29, "United States of America," pp. 236–37.

53.   NEB (2003), Vol. 27, "Socio-Economic Doctrines and Reform Movements," pp. 399–402.

54.   See Appendix Three.

55.   Ferris, pp. 40–41.

56.   Ibid., p. 289.

57.   Poncins, p. 78.

58.   Ibid., p. 111.

59.   Sarmiento, p. 74.

60.   See Appendix Four.

61.   O. Russell, pp. 26–27.

62.   Turnbull, *Forest People*, passim, and *Wayward Servants*, passim.

63.   Turnbull, *Mountain People*, p. 24.

64.   Turnbull, *Forest People*, p. 26.

65.   Schebesta, I. Band, p. 73.

66.   Ibid., p. 205. Also: "The economic activity of the hunter-gatherer knows neither haste nor hurry, nor agonizing worry over the daily bread." Schebesta, II. Band, I. Teil, p. 18.

67.   Poncins, pp. 212–13.

68.   Ibid., p. 292.

69.   Ibid., p. 273.

70.   Axtell, pp. 326–27.

71.   Ibid. and passim.

72.   E.g., Parkman, pp. 375–76; Washburn, pp. 51–52.

73.   Robert Wright, as referenced in our List of Works Cited.

74.   Schebesta, I. Band, p. 228.

75.   Ibid., pp. 213–14. The suicide was probably not attributable to depression, because it was a sudden and immediate reaction to an event that the individual felt was disastrous. After citing the foregoing information from Schebesta, earlier editions of this book referred to a source that claimed there

was a "virtual absence of reference to anything like depression in [classical Greek & Roman] antiquity." The source overlooked the fact that in the 2nd century AD the Greek physician Aretaeus of Cappadocia described what we now call manic-depressive disorder and therefore must have described depression. NEB (2003), Vol. 1, "affective disorder," p. 126.

 76. Poncins, pp. 169–175, 237.

 77. Coon, pp. 72, 184.

 78. Ibid., pp. 372–73.

 79. Chang, p. 80.

 80. E.g., *The Denver Post*, Dec. 30, 2003, p. 5A; *USA Today*, Feb. 7, 2013, p. 4D; ibid., Aug. 5, 2013, pp. 1A, 7A; ibid., Feb. 11, 2014, p. 3A.

 81. *Time*, June 10, 2002, p. 48.

 82. *U.S. News & World Report*, March 6, 2000, p. 45.

 83. Ibid., Feb. 18, 2002, p. 56.

 84. Gershon & Rieder, p. 129.

 85. *Funk & Wagnalls New Encyclopedia*, 1996, Vol. 24, "Suicide," p. 423.

 86. E.g., *USA Today*, Aug. 13, 2014, p. 2A; Oct. 10–12, 2014, pp. 1A, 6A; March 20, 2018, p. 3A; April 13, 2018, p. 3A; Nov. 28, 2018, pp. 1A, 4A; April 16, 2019, p. 5A. The rising suicide rate shoots down the argument (e.g., *USA Today*, Feb. 7, 2013, p. 4D, col. 4) that the growing incidence of depression is merely apparent and is only the result of more effective diagnosis. It can hardly be claimed that suicide is more effectively diagnosed today than it was in earlier decades. For a fuller picture, see also Lukianoff & Haidt, p. 45; Rosin, p. 72; Twenge, pp. 61, 64; and *The Economist*, Nov. 24, 2018, pp. 50–53. In relation to the threefold increase in suicides among young (15–24 yrs.) Americans from 1950 to 1990 (see Note 85), bear in mind that in 1950 there were no suicide hotlines or other major suicide-prevention programs and only a tiny minority of people took psychotherapy or antidepressants. And in relation to the declining suicide rates reported by the *Economist* for Russia and Asian nations bear in mind that, to the extent that the declines are a result of interventions with people who are on the verge of killing themselves or official measures such as restriction of access to poisons or alcohol—to that extent the declines do not reflect improvement in the general psychological health of the population. Also note that, even without antidepressants or suicide-prevention programs, the suicide rate in industrialized nations ought to decline over time. As natural selection through suicide progressively eliminates individuals who cannot or will not tolerate the degrading conditions to which technological civilization subjects us, such individuals are replaced by those who adjust well to modern society because they have little need for autonomy and are content to spend their lives doing only what they are told to do.

 87. *Los Angeles Times*, Sept. 15, 1998, p. A1. The study was reported at about that date in the *Archives of General Psychiatry*, according to the *L.A. Times* article.

88. NEB (2003), Vol. 29, "United Kingdom," p. 38.

89. Ibid., pp. 61–66.

90. Ibid., Vol. 27, "Southern Africa," p. 920.

91. Ibid., p. 925.

92. Ibid., pp. 928–29. Sampson, passim, e.g., pp. 148–150, 157–58, 331, 343, 353, 377, 384, 393, 458–59, 464, 476.

93. NEB (2003), Vol. 27, "Southern Africa," p. 925.

94. Poland's putative democracy perhaps is seriously flawed. See: *The Week*, Jan. 29, 2016, p. 14, "Poland in the doghouse." Strybel, pp. 1, 4. Napierala-Cowen, p. 3. Szelag, p. 3. *Polish-American Journal*, Feb. 2016, pp. 1, 4, "Poland Downplays Tensions with Germany." Bokota, p. 2. Stur, pp. 1, 3.

95. *Newsweek*, Sept. 27, 2004, p. 36.

96. *The Denver Post*, Oct. 19, 2004, p. 15A.

97. Ibid., Oct. 18, 2004, p. 15A.

98. Here I am not including Finland among the Scandinavian countries.

99. NEB (2003), Vol. 24, "Netherlands," pp. 891–94.

100. Ibid., p. 894 ("When the crisis of the 1848 revolutions broke... [a] new constitution was written...").

101. Ibid., Vol. 28, "Sweden," pp. 335–38.

102. Ibid., Vol. 24, "Norway," pp. 1092–94.

103. Ibid., Vol. 17, "Denmark," pp. 240–41.

104. Ibid., Vol. 28, "Switzerland," pp. 352–56.

105. Ibid., p. 354 ("a new constitution, modeled after that of the United States, was established in 1848...").

106. Earlier editions of this book mentioned India as a probable exception, but it may seriously be doubted whether India is a functioning democracy. See *The Week*, June 24, 2011, p. 18, "Why the middle class won't vote." In a "Letter from Delhi," broadcast on BBC and heard by this writer via Radio KRCC in Colorado Springs on March 5, 2011 at roughly 2:30 AM (Mountain Time), Mark Tully described the massive corruption that pervades the government of India. He mentioned that India had all the usual apparatus of parliamentary democracy; but, without doing so explicitly, he questioned by implication whether India could be considered a functioning democracy.

107. Sometimes a country can be intentionally and calculatedly assimilated to the technoindustrial system and the culture thereof. This falls under one of the exceptions that I noted—exception (iii) in my letter of Oct. 12, 2004—in which human intentions for the future of a society can be successfully realized.

108. "[A]ntislavery groups estimated that 27 million people were enslaved at the beginning of the 21st century, more than in any previous historical period," NEB (2003), Vol. 27, "Slavery," p. 293. I assume, however, that the *percentage* of the world's population that lives in slavery today is smaller than in earlier times,

and that the elimination of slavery from fully modernized countries is very nearly complete.

109. "The fate of slavery [in most of the world outside the British Isles] depended on the British abolition movement…," ibid.

110. The example of Brazil is instructive. At the cost of some oversimplification, we can say that the abolition of slavery there in 1888 was motivated by four factors (not necessarily in order of importance): (i) Fear of slave revolts (Priore & Venâncio, Chapt. XVIII, pp. 223, 225–26, 227; Chapt. XX, p. 246). (ii) Recognition of the inefficiency of slave-based economies in comparison with more modern systems (ibid., Chapt. XVIII, pp. 223–24, 225; Chapt. XXII, p. 269). (iii) Pressure from the British (ibid., Chapt. XVIII, pp. 223, 225; Chapt. XXI, p. 255). Pressure from the British was effective only because Britain was economically (and therefore also militarily) powerful, and Britain's economic power was due in part to the efficiency of its non-slave economy. (iv) A "civilizing," or, to put it more accurately, a liberalizing and modernizing movement that in relation to slavery was ostensibly motivated in part by humanitarian sentiments (liberalizing/ modernizing trend in general, ibid., passim, e.g., Chapt. XVIII, pp. 228–231; specifically in relation to slavery, Chapt. XVIII, pp. 223–25, 227; Chapt. XXI, pp. 254, 257, 259, 262). We need not question the sincerity of these humanitarian sentiments in order to doubt that it was mere coincidence that liberalizing movements arose throughout a large part of the world just at the time when the liberal and semi-liberal regimes of Europe and North America were achieving great prestige and power through their remarkable economic and technological success. Thus, three of the four factors that led to the abolition of slavery in Brazil were strongly related to the inefficiency of its slave-based economy.

111. NEB (2003), Vol. 27, "Slavery," p. 299.

112. Ibid., pp. 298–99.

113. Fear of a repetition of slave revolts already experienced was a factor in the abolition of slavery in Brazil. Priore & Venâncio, Chapt. XVIII, pp. 225–26. In the Danish Virgin Islands: "Slavery… was abolished in 1848 after a serious uprising in that year," NEB (2003), Vol. 29, "West Indies," p. 777.

114. Zimmermann, pp. 30–31.

115. NEB (2003), Vol. 20, "Greek and Roman Civilizations," p. 277.

116. Bolívar, letter to the editor of the *Gaceta Real de Jamaica,* Sept. 1815, in Soriano, p. 86.

117. Ibid., p. 87. Here Bolívar was not trying to justify slavery, but was arguing merely that the slaves would never rebel. See ibid., pp. 87–88. Actually Bolívar was passionately opposed to slavery. See in Soriano, Bolívar's "Discurso de Angostura," p. 120, and his "Discurso del Libertador al Congreso Constituyente de Bolivia," pp. 136–37. I'm not aware of any reason to doubt the accuracy of Bolívar's remarks about the easy conditions of servitude and the improbability

of slave revolts in those parts of Latin America that had come under his direct personal observation up to September 1815. But it should be noted that those conditions did not prevail everywhere in Latin America or even in all parts of Bolívar's native country of Venezuela. E.g., in 1795, when Bolívar would have been about twelve years old, there was unrest among the slaves in Argentina and a slave revolt in Coro, Venezuela, a couple of hundred miles from Bolívar's home town of Caracas. Humphreys & Lynch, pp. 19, 101, 107. At other times there were slave insurrections in Brazil. Ibid., p. 232. Priore & Venâncio, Chapt. XVIII, pp. 225–26; Chapt. XXI, p. 257. Notwithstanding the reported unrest, the conditions of slavery in rural Argentina were surprisingly easy. Mayo, pp. 139–150, 198–99.

118. NEB (2003), Vol. 27, "Slavery," p. 288.

119. T.H. von Laue, p. 202.

120. I don't mean to suggest that discipline as such is necessarily bad. I suspect that any successful revolutionary movement directed against the technoindustrial system will have to be well disciplined.

121. Nietzsche, p. 103.

122. For this whole paragraph see Zaccone, Fehervari, et al.; Trevelyan, Smallman-Raynor & Cliff; Nathanson & Martin; *U.S. News & World Report*, May 8, 2000, pp. 47–49; *National Geographic*, May 2006, pp. 127, 129; *The Week*, Dec. 11, 2009, p. 26; *USA Today*, Feb. 24, 2011, p. 3A and March 29, 2011, p. 3D.

123. NEB (2003), Vol. 20, "Hitler," p. 628. Rothfels, p. 230n28, cites an estimate according to which some 35% to 40% of Germans were "conscious anti-Nazis" in 1944. If accurate, this estimate would throw serious doubt on the *Britannica's* statement that the majority of Germans supported Hitler "until the very end;" for large numbers of Germans presumably would have taken great care to conceal any anti-Nazi sentiments they might have, hence would not have been included in the 35% to 40%. But the estimate appears to rest on flimsy grounds. In any case, whatever the extent of public support for Hitler may have been, no rational observer of mass politics will claim that the majority of any nation can be counted on to make consistently wise judgments on questions of public importance; and that is what matters for present purposes.

124. See, e.g., NEB (2003), Vol. 26, "Propaganda", p. 175 ("The rank and file of any group, especially a big one, have been shown to be remarkably passive until aroused by quasi-parental leaders whom they admire and trust."); Trotsky, Vol. Two, p. vii ("[T]he mere existence of privations is not enough to cause an insurrection…. It is necessary that… new conditions and new ideas should open the prospect of a revolutionary way out.").

125. China: Fallows, pp. 21–22; *The Week*, Oct. 8, 2010, p. 15; *USA Today*, Feb. 25, 2014, p. 2A. Egypt: *USA Today*, Nov. 5, 2014, p. 9A. India: *USA Today*, Dec. 8, 2015, p. 3A.

126. *Vegetarian Times*, May 2004, p. 13 (quoting *Los Angeles Times* of Jan. 13, 2004).

127. *Science News*, Vol. 163, Feb. 1, 2003, p. 72.

128. "Kids Need More Protection From Chemicals," *Los Angeles Times*, Jan. 28, 1999.

129. *U.S. News & World Report,* Jan. 24, 2000, pp. 30–31.

130. *Time*, Oct. 18, 2004, p. 29.

131. This has been massively publicized. To cite just one example: *USA Today*, Nov. 3, 2014, p. 3A.

132. *Time,* July 1, 2002, p. 57. *U.S. News & World Report*, Feb. 5, 2001, pp. 46, 48, 50.

133. Ibid., pp. 44–46.

134. *Time*, Nov. 22, 2004, pp. 72–73.

135. Ibid., Oct. 4, 2004, pp. 68–70.

136. *U.S. News & World Report,* Feb. 5, 2001, pp. 48, 50.

137. Ibid., p. 50.

138. *The Denver Post,* June 16, 2004, p. 2A.

139. Ibid.

140. *Christian Science Monitor*, March 8, 2001, p. 20. Kolbert, "Ice Memory," pp. 30–37.

141. Poncins, pp. 164–65.

142. Illich, Chapt 5.

143. Ibid.

144. This is from Ellul, *Anarchy and Christianity*.

145. Kirkham, Levy & Crotty, p. 4.

146. Schebesta, II. Band, I. Teil, pp. 8, 18.

147. Bonvillain, pp. 20 21.

148. Turnbull, *Wayward Servants*, pp. 27, 28, 42, 178–181, 183, 187, 228, 256, 274, 294, 300. *Forest People*, pp. 110, 125.

149. Schebesta, II. Band, I. Teil, p. 8.

150. Admittedly there is a gray area: Sometimes a reform is in the interest of the system only because conditions are so hard on human beings that they will rebel if there is no alleviation. E.g., the U.S. government's efforts to rectify the atrocious injustices inflicted on black people were entirely inadequate until the revolt of black Americans during the 1950s and 1960s (the "civil rights movement") forced the government to take more vigorous action. But notice that the revolt did not begin until strong leaders had emerged.

151. NEB (2003), Vol. 2, "bee," p. 42. Blau, especially pp. 16–18. *USA Today*, Oct. 9, 2014, p. 5A; Oct. 10, 2014, p. 4A.

152. See my letter of Oct. 12, 2004; ISAIF, ¶¶ 44, 58, 145.

153. Greaves, p. 16. Greaves actually writes, "overall *age-related* mortality

from the major types of cancer in Western society at the end of the twentieth century was probably more than ten times that at the end of the nineteenth century." I assume this means that cancer mortality *in any given age group* has increased by a factor of more than ten. For balance: "overall rates of new cancer cases and deaths from cancer in the U.S. have been declining gradually since 1991... ." *University of California, Berkeley Wellness Letter,* Sept. 2004, p 8. "Cancer fatality rates [in U.S.] have dropped by 23 percent in men and 15 percent in women over two decades." *The Week,* Jan. 20, 2012, p. 18. On the other hand, "The incidence of cancer worldwide is surging at alarming rates... . New cancer cases will skyrocket globally from an estimated 14 million in 2012 to 22 million cases a year within the next two decades... ." *USA Today,* Feb. 5, 2014, p. 3A.

154. From speech attributed to Gaius Memmius by Sallust, *Jugurthine War,* Book 31, somewhere around Chapt. 16 (translation of S.A. Handford; see List of Works Cited). Roman historians commonly invented the speeches that they put into the mouths of famous people, but the quotation reflects Roman attitudes whether it was spoken by Memmius or invented by Sallust.

155. Calderón de la Barca, Jornada Primera, Escena Cuarta, p. 25 ("hombre que está agraviado es infame...," etc.). Cervantes, "Novela de la Gitanilla," pp. 79–89 (with the evident approval of almost everyone, including Cervantes, a nobleman kills a soldier for striking him in the face). On Calderón's and other 17th-century Spanish attitudes concerning revenge for wounded honor, see Barja, pp. 337–347, 523, 533–34.

156. See Danner, p. 45: "The young [Iraqi] man... pushed his face close to mine, and spoke to me slowly and emphatically: '... it is a *shame* to have foreigners break down their doors. It is a *shame* for them to have foreigners stop and search their women. It is a *shame* for the foreigners to put a bag over their heads, to make a man lie on the ground with your shoe on his neck. ... This is a great *shame* for the whole tribe. [¶] It is the *duty* of that man, and of that tribe, to get revenge on this soldier—to kill that man. Their duty is to attack them, to *wash the shame.*' " See also Rubin, p. 36: "If any injury is done to a [Pashtun] man's land, women, or gold, it is a matter of honor for him to exact revenge."

157. Burr & Hamilton: NEB (2003), Vol. 2, "Burr, Aaron," p. 664. Jackson: Kunhardt, Kunhardt & Kunhardt, p. 350. For more on dueling in 19th-century U.S.: Jack Lynch, p. 77. Sanborn, p. 240. Livingston, p. 177, as quoted in *Garrison v. Louisiana,* 379 U.S. 64, 68 (1964) (this means Vol. 379, *United States Reports,* 1964, pp. 64, 68).

158. In England Wellington, the victor of Waterloo, fought a duel (1829)— of which the king himself approved. Churchill, *Great Democracies,* p. 30. In France, the brilliant young mathematician Évariste Galois was killed in a duel (1832). NEB (2007), Vol. 5, "Galois, Évariste," pp. 95–96. In Geneva, in 1864, the distinguished socialist leader Ferdinand Lassalle died as the result of a duel. Bebel, p.

91. In Germany Bismarck, the future Iron Chancellor, challenged the pioneer anthropologist Rudolf Virchow to a duel (1865)—which Virchow wisely declined. NEB (2003), Vol. 12, "Virchow, Rudolf (Carl)," p. 386. As late as 1888, the French general and politician Georges Boulanger was severely wounded in a duel with the Prime Minister of his country, Charles Floquet. Ibid., Vol. 2, "Boulanger, Georges," p. 421.

159. Graham & Gurr, Chapt. 12 by Roger Lane, pp. 475–76. NEB (2003), Vol. 25, "Police," pp. 959–960. Ortega y Gasset, p. 124.

160. See Note 124.

161. Arrhenius, as in our List of Works Cited. Apparently Arrhenius was not the first to predict the greenhouse effect, but further exploration of the origin of the prediction would be beyond the scope of this book.

162. Moyers, pp. 8, 10.

163. Some of us would add: biological engineering of other organisms (an insult to the dignity of all life).

164. *National Geographic*, Nov. 2003, pp. 4–29, had a surprisingly vigorous article on surveillance technology (e.g., p. 9: "Cameras are becoming so omni-present that all Britons should assume that their behavior outside the home is monitored... . Machines will recognize our faces and our fingerprints. They will watch out for... red-light runners and highway speeders."). For other scary stuff on surveillance, see, e.g., *The Denver Post*, July 13, 2004, p. 2A ("Mexico has required some prosecutors to have tiny computer chips implanted in their skin as a security measure... ."); *Time Bonus Section*, Oct. 2003, pp. A8-A16; *Time*, Jan. 12, 2004, "Beyond the Sixth Sense."

165. The claim here is not that governments or corporations will directly use psychoactive medications to control people, but that people will "voluntarily" medicate themselves (e.g., for depression) or their children (e.g., for hyperactivity or attention-deficit disorder) in order to enable them to meet the system's demands.

166. Mercader, pp. 235, 238, 239, 241, 282. Coon, p. 6.

167. E.g., Mercader, p. 233.

168. NEB (2003), Vol. 14, "Biosphere," pp. 1190, 1202. Ibid., Vol. 19, "Forestry and Wood Production," p. 410.

169. E.g., Coon, pp. 243–44.

170. Churchill, *My Early Life*, p. 79.

171. Smelser, p. 273 ("The peace movement is a general social movement which has been in existence since its beginning in England during the revolutionary and Napoleonic wars."). It's true that warfare has declined in quantitative terms since 1945, but this has nothing to do with the efforts of the peace movement. Warfare directly between major powers has ceased only because (i) the existence of nuclear weapons has made such warfare too dangerous; and (ii)

even discounting nuclear weapons, the nature of modern warfare has made it excessively expensive both in economic and in sociological terms. But the danger of a resumption of large-scale warfare always hangs over us, and if there is ever a third world war it will be catastrophic beyond anything previously seen in the history of civilization—even if no nuclear weapons are used.

172. García López, p. 567.

173. Unless it is rich enough to undertake a massive, long-term propaganda campaign on a national scale—a possibility too far-fetched to be considered here.

174. This is an oversimplification, but there is enough truth in it so that it can serve our purpose as an example. See NEB (2003), Vol. 29, "Work and Employment," pp. 953–56.

175. Trotsky, Vol. One, p. 223. See my letter of Aug. 29, 2004.

176. See Geertz, pp. 4–6.

177. Rees, pp. 1–2, 8, 121–24.

178. Quammen, pp. 57–69.

179. These statements about Earth First! are based mainly on my recollection of M.F. Lee, passim.

180. Turnbull, *Change and Adaptation*, pp. 89–90, 92.

181. Ibid., p. 11.

182. Diamond, passim, e.g., p. 275. See also Rostow, p. 135 ("Generally men have preferred to go down in the style to which they had become accustomed rather than to change their ways of thinking and of looking at the world.").

183. In terms of freedom and dignity I personally feel that the situation is *already* bad enough to justify revolution, but I don't need to rely on that.

184. *The Denver Post*, Jan. 25, 2005, p. 11A.

185. M.J. Webster, p. 9A, col. 2.

186. Advertisement by Honda in *National Geographic*, Feb. 2005 (unnumbered page).

187. *The Denver Post*, Feb. 18, 2005, pp. 28A–29A. *The Economist*, April 2, 2011, p. 65. Milstein, pp. 40–47. Whittle, pp. 28–33. Markoff, "Pentagon Offers Robotics Prize," p. B4. *National Geographic*, Aug. 2011, pp. 82–83. *Time*, Jan. 9, 2012, p. 30.

188. Darrach, p. 58.

189. Schebesta, II. Band, I. Teil, p. 261.

190. See Louis Sarno, *Song from the Forest*.

191. NEB (2003), Vol. 24, "The Netherlands," p. 891.

192. Stefansson, p. 38.

193. Turnbull, *Forest People*, pp. 92–93, 145; *Wayward Servants*, pp. 19, 234, 252–53, 271, 278. Turnbull's account of Mbuti religion does not seem fully consistent with that of Schebesta. But Schebesta, II. Band, III.Teil, does make clear that the religion of the Mbuti was closely integrated into their daily life and

was of great importance to them; e.g., pp. 6–8, 11, 85, 96, 159–160, 179, 214–15, 222–23.

194. E.g., Wissler, pp. 179–182, 304–09.

195. Moyers, pp. 8, 10.

196. Dalrymple, pp. 62–65.

197. See Axtell, passim, e.g., pp. 4, 19, 278, 285–86.

198. Hoyle, p. 62.

199. See Kurzweil in our List of Works Cited. Dr. Skrbina had sent me a copy of this article.

200. Gurven & Kaplan, p. 327, Table 2.

201. These figures are very rough, being merely estimated from ibid., p. 328, graph d.

202. Ibid.

203. R.B. Lee, p. 54.

204. My memory on this point is confirmed by *The Organizer's Manual* (see List of Works Cited—Works Without Named Author), p. 296.

205. Rodenbeck, p. 16.

EXCERPTS FROM LETTERS
TO A GERMAN

Excerpts from Letters to a German (2006)

These letters were originally written in German and the excerpts were later translated into English for publication in that form. Since I can't express myself in German anywhere near as well as I can in English, it would have been better to write an entirely new text based on the ideas of the excerpts, but time for that has been lacking.

There are two difficulties connected with the characteristic victimization issues of the left, such as the alleged oppression of women, homosexuals, racial or ethnic minorities, and animals.

First, these issues distract attention from the technology problem. Rebellious energies that might have been directed against the technological system are expended instead on the irrelevant problems of racism, sexism, etc. Therefore it would have been better if these problems had been completely solved. In that case, they could not have distracted attention from the technology problem.

But revolutionists should not attempt to solve the problems of racism, sexism, and so forth, because, in addressing these problems, they would further distract attention from the problem of technology. Moreover, revolutionists could contribute very little to the solution of the problems of women, minorities, etc., because technological society itself is already working to solve these problems. Every day the media teach us that women are equal to men, that homosexuals should be respected, that all races should receive equal treatment, and so forth. Hence, any efforts in this direction by revolutionists would be superfluous.

Through their obsessive concentration on victimization issues such as the alleged oppression of women, homosexuals, and racial minorities, leftists vastly increase the extent to which these issues distract attention from the technology problem. But it would be counterproductive for revolutionists to try to obstruct leftists' efforts to solve the problems of women, minorities, and so forth, because such obstruction would intensify the controversy over these issues and therefore would distract even more attention from the technology problem. Instead, revolutionists must repeatedly point out and emphasize that the energy expended on the leftists' victimization issues is wasted, and that that energy should be expended on the technology problem.

A second difficulty connected with victimization issues is that any group that concerns itself with such issues will attract leftists. As ISAIF argues, leftists are useless as revolutionists because most of them don't really want to overthrow the existing form of society. They are interested only in satisfying their own psychological needs through vehement advocacy of "causes." Any cause will do as long as it is not specifically right-wing. Thus, when any movement (other than a right-wing movement) arises that aspires to be revolutionary, leftists come swarming to it like flies to honey until they outnumber the original members of the movement, take it over, and transform it into a leftist movement. Thereafter the movement is useless for revolutionary purposes.[1] Thus, the left serves as a mechanism for emasculating nascent revolutionary movements and rendering them harmless.

Therefore, in order to form an effective movement, revolutionists must take pains to exclude leftists from the movement. In order to drive away leftists, revolutionists should not only avoid involvement in efforts to help women, homosexuals, or racial minorities; they should specifically disavow any interest in such issues, and they should emphasize again and again that women, homosexuals, racial minorities, and so forth should consider themselves lucky because our society treats them better than most earlier societies have done. By adopting this position, revolutionists will separate themselves from the left and discourage leftists from attempting to join them.

*   *   *

You seem to think that increasing the pressure to which people are subject in modern society will be sufficient to produce a revolution. But this is not correct. Certainly a serious grievance must be present in order for a revolution to occur, but a serious grievance, or even the greatest suffering, by itself is not sufficient to bring about a revolution. People who have studied the process of revolution are agreed that in addition to a grievance, some precipitating factor is necessary. The precipitating factor might be a dynamic leader, some extraordinary event, or anything that arouses new hope that rebellion can bring relief from the grievance.

Thus Trotsky wrote: "In reality the mere existence of privations is not enough to cause an insurrection.... It is necessary that... new conditions and new ideas should open the prospect of a revolutionary way out."[2]

In the opinion of the philosopher-sociologist Eric Hoffer: "[T]he presence of an outstanding leader is indispensable. Without him there will be no movement. The ripeness of the times does not automatically produce a mass movement... ."[3]

Similarly the *Encyclopaedia Britannica*: "The rank and file of any group, especially a big one, have been shown to be remarkably passive until aroused by quasi-parental leaders whom they admire and trust."[4]

Of course, the prerequisites for revolution are much more complex than the mere presence of dynamic leaders or of "new conditions and new ideas" that arouse hope.[5] The point is, however, that revolutionists cannot simply wait passively for hard conditions to produce a revolution. Instead, revolutionists must actively prepare the way for revolution.

I should add that the remarks about leftism, here and in ISAIF, are based on observation of the American left. I do not know whether the remarks can be applied without modification to the European left.

*   *   *

You write: "Let us not deceive ourselves about the real role of women." If you mean that motherhood is the *only* suitable role for women, then I disagree. Quite apart from child-rearing, women have always done very important, even indispensable work, and work that was often very hard physically or required great skill. To mention only a few examples: Among the Mbuti pygmies of Africa and exclusive of child-rearing, the women worked far more than the men, they provided the greater part of the food, they built the huts, and their work was often very hard. Among other things, they carried huge stacks of firewood into camp on their backs.[6] Though in warm countries it was the women of hunting-and-gathering societies who provided the greater part of the food, in cold countries the men provided the greater part through hunting.[7] But in cold countries the women produced the clothing,[8] which in such climates was indispensable, and in doing so the women of certain hunting-and-gathering societies showed extraordinary skill.[9] In some other hunting-and-gathering societies, the women were able to weave baskets so closely that they could be used as containers for water.[10]

Thus, without denying the importance of their role as mothers, we must also acknowledge the importance of the role of women as laborers and skilled handworkers. And moreover I maintain that women, just as much as men, need work, that is, activities directed toward a goal (the "power process").[11] And I suspect that the reason why today's women want to take up masculine occupations is that their role as mother is not enough to satisfy them now that technology has reduced other traditional feminine occupations to triviality. The modern woman doesn't need to make clothes, because she can buy them; she doesn't need to weave baskets, because she has at her disposal any number of good containers; she doesn't need to look for fruits, nuts, and roots in the forest, because she can purchase good food; and so forth.

*   *   *

You write: "The system operates so insidiously that it talks ethnic minorities into believing that the loss of their identity is a good thing. Minorities are manipulated to their own disadvantage, and entirely without any perceptible compulsion." Yes, I agree with this, except that in some countries the system is more cunning: Instead of telling ethnic minorities that the loss of their identity is a good thing it tells them to maintain their ethnic identity, but at the same time the system knows very well how to drain ethnic identity of its real content and reduce it to empty external forms. This has happened both in the United States[12] and in the Soviet Union.[13]

*   *   *

Of course, I know very little about German universities, but American university intellectuals, apart from rare exceptions, are not at all suited to be members of an effective revolutionary movement. The majority belong to the left. Some of these intellectuals might make themselves useful by spreading ideas about the technology problem, but most of them are frightened at the idea of the overthrow of the system and cannot be active revolutionists. They are the "men of words" of whom Eric Hoffer has spoken:

> The preliminary work of undermining existing institutions, of familiarizing the masses with the idea of change, and of creating a receptivity to a new faith, can be done only by men who are, first and foremost, talkers

or writers.... Thus imperceptibly the man of words undermines the established institutions, discredits those in power, weakens prevailing beliefs and loyalties, and sets the stage for the rise of a mass movement.[14]

When the old order begins to fall apart, many of the vociferous men of words, who prayed so long for the day, are in a funk. The first glimpse of the face of anarchy frightens them out of their wits.[15]

The creative man of words, no matter how bitterly he may criticize and deride the existing order, is actually attached to the present. His passion is to reform and not to destroy. When the mass movement remains wholly in his keeping, he turns it into a mild affair. The reforms he initiates are of the surface, and life flows on without a sudden break.[16]

* * *

You write: "The movement should be a completely new beginning, beyond all positions of the left and of the right." Yes indeed! I agree completely!

* * *

You're right: We need to worry about the time factor. But we also have to take into consideration the possibility that the struggle will last a very long time, perhaps many decades. We should overthrow the system as soon as possible, but we must nevertheless prepare ourselves for a long-term revolutionary effort, because it may turn out that no quick overthrow of the system will be feasible.

You point out that technological progress proceeds at lightning speed; that it will take perhaps twenty years to develop the first computers that will surpass every human brain in computing power; that genetic engineering will inevitably be applied for the "improvement" of human beings; that new drugs will be developed. All of this may be true. But the future may be different from what we expect. For example, in 1970 it was reported that many computer scientists were predicting the development within fifteen years of a machine having superhuman intelligence.[17] Obviously, what the scientists predicted has not happened. Similarly, attempts to cure certain human diseases by means of genetic technology have run into difficulties:

Gene therapy can cause cancer. Thus it is possible that computers may not surpass human beings in intelligence as soon as is believed; genetic engineering may not be so easily applied to humans; and so forth. On the other hand, it is also possible that these developments will proceed even faster than anyone now suspects. In any case the social consequences of the new technology are unforeseeable and may be different from what we expect. The social consequences of the technological progress that has occurred up to the present time are different from what I expected when I was young. Therefore we have to prepare ourselves for all possibilities, including the possibility that our struggle may last a very long time.

*   *   *

There are two mistakes that almost all people, with the exception of experienced politicians and social scientists, make when they devise a plan for changing society.

The first mistake is that one works out a plan through pure reason, as if one were designing a bridge or a machine, and then one expects the plan to succeed.

One can successfully design a bridge or the like because material objects reliably obey precise rules. Thus one can predict how material objects will react under given circumstances. But in the realm of social phenomena we have at our disposal very few reliable, exact rules; therefore, in general, we cannot reliably predict social phenomena.

Among the few reliable predictions that we can make is the prediction that a plan will *not* succeed. If you let an automobile without a driver roll down a rough slope, you can't predict the route that the automobile will take, but you can predict that it will not follow a previously selected route. If you release a group of mice from a cage, you can't predict which way each mouse will run, but you can predict that the mice will not march in accord with a previously specified plan. So it goes, in general, in the domain of social phenomena.

Social scientists understand how difficult it is to carry out any long-term plan:

> History has no lessons for the future except one: that nothing ever works out as the participants quite intended or expected.[18]

World War I… ended in various plans for peace as illusory as the plans for war had been. As the historian William McNeill wrote, 'The irrationality of rational, professionalized planning could not have been made more patently manifest.'[19]

Most social planning is short-term…; the goals of planning are often not attained, and, even if the plan is successful in terms of the stated goals, it often has unforeseen consequences. The wider the scope and the longer the time span of planning, the more difficult it is to attain the goals and to avoid unforeseen and undesired consequences…. Large-scale and long-term social developments in any society are still largely unplanned.[20]

The foregoing is indisputably true, and moreover it refers to the plan of the State. The State has power, vast quantities of information, and the capacity to analyze and utilize such quantities of information. We have no power and relatively little capacity to gather and analyze information. If it is impossible for the State to carry out a long-term social plan successfully, then all the more is it impossible for us.

Therefore I maintain that revolutionists should not commit themselves to any predetermined, long-term or comprehensive plan. Instead, they should as far as possible rely on experience and proceed by trial and error, and commit themselves only to simple, short-term plans. Of course, revolutionists should also have a comprehensive, long-term plan, but this must always be provisional, and the revolutionists must always be ready to modify the comprehensive plan or even abandon it altogether, provided that they never forget the final goal, which is to overthrow the system. In other words, the movement must be flexible and prepared for all eventualities.[21]

The second of the above-mentioned errors is that one proposes a plan (let us assume that it is a very good plan) and then believes that a sufficient number of people will follow the plan merely because it is a good one. But if the goal of a plan is to change society, then, however excellent the plan may be, its excellence is not what will move people to follow it. We have to take human motivations into consideration.

In private life pure reason may often move a person to follow a good plan. For example, if through the use of reason we can convince a person that one doctor is more skillful than another, then the person will probably consult the more skillful doctor, because he knows that in this way he will recover better from his ailment.

On the other hand, if we can convince a person that a certain plan will be useful to society on the assumption that a sufficient number of people will follow the plan, this provides the person with at most a very weak motive to follow the plan, for he knows that it is very unlikely, or even impossible, that his own individual participation will by itself have any perceptible effect on society. For example: Many people know that it would be better for the world if everyone refused to use automobiles. Nevertheless, apart from rare exceptions, each one of these people has his automobile, because he says to himself that if he refuses to drive he will suffer great inconvenience without doing any perceptible good for the world; for the world will derive no perceptible advantage unless many millions of people refuse to use automobiles.

So we must always bear in mind that, with only rare exceptions, a person joins a revolutionary movement not primarily in order to achieve the movement's objective, but in order to fulfill his own psychological or physical needs or to experience some form of pleasure. However loyal and sincerely devoted he may later be to the revolutionary goal, his devotion has in some way grown out of his own needs or out of the pleasures he has experienced. Of course, the attainment of a movement's goal can fulfill the needs of a member, but in general only the actions of a few leaders can perceptibly increase the likelihood that the goal will be attained. As previously indicated, the rank-and-file member knows that his own individual participation will have at most only an imperceptible effect on progress toward the goal. Therefore the goal by itself, and through cold reason alone, cannot motivate the rank-and-file member.

Since enthusiasm produces great pleasure, enthusiasm for a strongly desired goal can be enough to move a person to revolutionary action, but only when the attainment of the goal is very near. When the attainment of the goal appears to be improbable or distant in time, the goal by itself cannot arouse much enthusiasm.

When the attainment of the goal is not near, then the following satisfactions, for example, can motivate the rank-and-file member of a revolutionary movement: (i) Sense of purpose, the feeling that one has a goal around which to organize one's life. (ii) Sense of power. (iii) Sense of belonging, the feeling of being part of a cohesive social group. (iv) Status or

prestige within the movement; the approval of other members of the movement. (v) Anger, revenge; the opportunity to retaliate against the system.

Of course, one can also find satisfaction in one's contribution to
the future attainment of the revolutionary goal, even if one's own individual contribution has only an imperceptible effect, but in that case the
satisfaction is too weak to move anyone to make significant revolutionary
efforts—apart from rare, exceptional cases. Therefore a revolutionary
movement must be based chiefly on other motivations.

*   *   *

[My German correspondent proposed infiltrating small cells of
revolutionists into the power-holding circles of society.]

As for the sense of power—a cell consisting of ten people cannot
afford a member much sense of power. The member will gain a sense of
power only when he joins the power-holding circles of society, and then
the member receives his sense of power not from the revolutionary movement but from his position within the system. He has perhaps one chance
in a hundred of gaining a position of power, and he can reach such a
position only through efforts extending over a long period. A person will
undertake such efforts and persist in them only if he finds satisfaction in
his career. Let us assume, then, that a member of a revolutionary cell
has had a successful career and after twenty years of effort has joined the
power-holding circles. He likes his career, he now has power, and he has
achieved these satisfactions through long years of effort. Will he want to
lose all this through the destruction of the system? In rare, exceptional
cases he will, but usually he will not. History offers countless examples of
the young, hot-blooded rebel who swears to resist the system forever, but
who then has a successful career, and when he is older and richer and has
status and prestige, he comes to the conclusion that the system is not so
bad after all, and that it is better to adapt himself to it.

There are further reasons to believe that your plan cannot succeed.
The plan requires that the movement should remain secret and unknown
to the public. But that is impossible. One can be quite sure that some
member of the movement will change his mind or make a mistake, so that
the existence of the movement will become publicly known.[22] Then there
will be official investigations and so forth. In history one finds examples of
sophisticated spy networks the secrecy of which was carefully guarded, but

which nevertheless became known, though some of their cells may have succeeded in remaining secret. Likewise, the existence of the movement that you propose would surely become known.

In the fourth section of your letter you propose that leaders and agitators from the ranks of the leftists should be "instructed" by members of the movement. But, apart from exceptional cases, it is impossible to believe that members of the movement could have so much control over people who have the ability to become successful leaders and agitators.

If you succeeded in infiltrating into the power-holding circles just three or four revolutionists who, moreover, did not subsequently betray the revolution in order to keep their power and their prestige, that would be an amazing success. Such infiltrators could perhaps play a role in the revolution, but their role probably would not be decisive.

*   *   *

You say that revolutions are never planned on a drawing-board, and you are right. But I wouldn't say that revolutions have always been attributable solely to the dissatisfactions of some large segment of a society. Dissatisfaction is a precondition for revolution, but dissatisfaction by itself is not enough to bring about a revolution. I've emphasized that previously. Among other things a revolutionary myth is needed, and on this subject you write that revolutions have never chosen their ideals and myths freely, which is quite true. But then you write: "The circumstances under which people live leave them no other choice than to adopt exactly these myths and ideals and no others." I do not entirely agree with this. A myth can't be chosen arbitrarily. A myth can succeed only if it responds to the prevailing (perhaps in part unconscious) dissatisfactions and yearnings. But I'm not convinced that the circumstances under which people live always must precisely determine a single myth. For example: The Prophet Mohammed created an extraordinarily successful myth when he wrote the Koran. Would you venture to say that nothing other than precisely the Koran could have responded to the yearnings of the Arabs?

Even if you were right and for each revolution only a single myth were possible, still we would not be entitled to assume that people would develop the right myth on their own, and develop it in time. The myths of the French and Russian Revolutions were not developed by the people at large, but by a small number of intellectuals. Maybe the work of the intellectuals consisted only in giving form and structure to the formless or unconscious dissatisfactions and yearnings of the nation; nevertheless, this work was indispensable for the success of the revolution.

So I maintain that the task of revolutionists is not to increase or intensify the objective grounds for dissatisfaction. There are already plenty enough grounds for dissatisfaction. Instead, revolutionists should do the following:

(a) There are certain counterfeit grounds for dissatisfaction (e.g., the alleged problems of women, ethnic minorities, homosexuals, cruelty to animals, etc.), that serve to divert attention from the real grounds for dissatisfaction. Revolutionists must somehow circumvent or negate these diversionary tactics.

(b) Revolutionists must bring into effective operation the genuine but as yet poorly perceived grounds for dissatisfaction.

(c) To this end revolutionists must (among other things) develop a revolutionary myth. This doesn't mean that they should invent a myth arbitrarily. Instead, they must discover and bring to light the real myth that already exists in inchoate form, and give it a definite structure.

*   *   *

You are right in saying that the role of the revolutionists is only that of a catalyst. Revolutionists can't create a revolution out of nothing. All they can do is realize those possibilities that are offered by the conditions under which people live, just as a catalyst can bring about a chemical reaction only if all of the necessary reagents are available. You seem to believe that one can best play the role of a catalyst by intensifying the objective grounds for dissatisfaction. But I am convinced that the objective grounds for dissatisfaction are already sufficient. In order to play the role of a catalyst one must achieve a psychological effect; for example, by discovering and utilizing the right myth.

*   *   *

There are many young people who recognize that the technological system is destroying our world and our freedom; they want to resist it, but they know that they can't achieve anything alone, therefore they look for a group or a movement that they can join. Under the circumstances existing today, they can find no groups or movements other than the leftist or similar ones. So a young person joins one of these groups and either is converted to its ideology or else gets discouraged, leaves the group, gives up, and becomes apathetic. What is needed is a real revolutionary movement that such young people could join before they were lured by some leftist group and ruined by it.

*   *   *

You maintain that we should speed up the action of "the machine" (that is, of the system) so that the machine will destroy itself. But in destroying itself the machine will also destroy us and our world, and perhaps all higher forms of life. Remember that not all of the destructive processes initiated by the system will stop as soon as the system falls apart. Consider for example the greenhouse effect.

> [G]lobal climate systems are booby-trapped with tipping points and feedback loops, thresholds past which the slow creep of environmental decay gives way to sudden and self-perpetuating collapse. Pump enough CO_2 into the sky, and that last part per million of greenhouse gas behaves like the 212th degree Fahrenheit [212° Fahrenheit = 100° Celsius] that turns a pot of hot water into a plume of billowing steam.... 'Things are happening a lot faster than anyone predicted,' says Bill Chameides, chief scientist for the advocacy group Environmental Defense and a former professor of atmospheric chemistry. 'The last 12 months have been alarming,' adds Ruth Curry of the Woods Hole Oceanographic Institute in Massachusetts. 'The ripple through the scientific community is palpable.'... Is it too late to reverse the changes global warming has wrought? That's still not clear... .[23]

By releasing so much carbon dioxide into the atmosphere, the system has already disrupted the Earth's climate to such an extent that even specialists in the field can't predict the consequences. Even if the system immediately stopped releasing carbon dioxide, the Earth's climate probably would not revert to its previous condition. No one knows where our climate will go. We don't even know for certain whether the Earth will still be inhabitable at the end of this century. Of course, the more carbon dioxide the system releases, the greater the danger is. Yes, the system could destroy itself by progressing faster and releasing greater quantities of carbon dioxide, but in the process it would destroy everything else, too.

I have already emphasized that what could lead to a revolution would not be the worsening of living conditions, but a psychological situation conducive to revolution. And one of the indispensable psychological preconditions for revolution is that people should have hope. If there's no hope, there will be no revolution. A serious problem is the fact that many of the most intelligent people have already lost hope. They think that it's too late, the Earth can't be saved. If we speeded up the destructive action of the system, we would only spread and deepen this hopelessness.

NOTES

1.   The case of the movement called Earth First! provides a neat example of this process. See M.F. Lee.

2.   Trotsky, Vol. Two, p. vii.

3.   Hoffer, § 90.

4.   NEB (2003), Vol. 26, "Propaganda," p. 175.

5.   For an extended discussion, see Smelser, pp. 313–384.

6.   Schebesta, II. Band, I. Teil, pp. 11–21, 31, 142, 170, and, at the end of the book, Bildtafel X.

7.   Coon, pp. 72–73. Cashdan, p. 28.

8.   E.g., Coon, p. 48.

9.   E.g., Poncins, pp. 14, 15, 124.

10.   E.g., Wissler, pp. 16–18; Austin, pp. 46–47.

11.   ISAIF, ¶¶ 33–37.

12.   See ISAIF, ¶ 29.

13.   See Stalin, seventh chapter, "The Bolshevik Party in the Period of Preparation and Realization of the October Socialist Revolution," § 2, pp. 258–260; Ulam, pp. 141–42, 169, 221, 595, 649–650.

14.   Hoffer, § 104.

15.   Ibid., § 110.

16.   Ibid., § 111.

17.   Darrach, p. 58.

18.   Gordon Wood, p. 34.

19.   NEB (2003), Vol. 21, "International Relations," p. 807.

20.   Ibid., Vol. 27, "Social Structure and Change," p. 370. See also Kaczynski, *Anti-Tech Revolution*, Chapt. One.

21.   See Kaczynski, *Anti-Tech Revolution*, Chapt. Four, §§ 2–4.

22.   See Ibid., § 27.

23.   *Time*, April 3, 2006, pp. 35, 36.

EXTRACT FROM
A LETTER TO A.O.

Extract from a Letter to A.O. (June 30, 2004)

You write: "Even some primitive people from Mexico join the values of modern society (because of TV). What could make them go back to the forest?"

What could "make them go back to the forest" would be an end to the functioning of the world's industrial centers. The Mexican Indians couldn't use their TV sets if the TV stations were no longer broadcasting. They couldn't use motor vehicles or any internal-combustion engines if the refineries were no longer producing fuel. They couldn't use any electrical appliances if the electrical power-plants were no longer producing electricity. Or, even if the Indians relied on small, local, water-powered generators, these would become useless when parts of the generators or of the appliances wore out and could not be replaced with new parts produced in factories. For example, could a group of Mexican Indians make a light bulb? I think it would be impossible, but even if it were possible it would be so difficult that it would not be worth the trouble. Thus, if the world's industrial centers stopped functioning, the Mexican Indians would have no choice but to revert to simple, pre-industrial methods.

But what could make the TV stations stop broadcasting, the power-plants stop generating electricity, the refineries stop producing fuel, and the factories stop making parts? If the power-plants stopped producing electricity, then the TV stations would no longer be able to broadcast, the refineries would no longer be able to produce fuel, and the factories would no longer be able to make things. If the refineries stopped producing fuel, then the transportation of goods and people would have to cease, and therefore the factories would no longer be able to make things. If the factories were no longer able to make things, then there would be no more replacement parts to keep the TV stations, power-plants, and petroleum refineries functioning. Moreover, every factory needs things produced by other factories in order to keep operating.

Thus, modern industrial society can be compared to a complex organism in which every important part is dependent on every other important part. If any one important part of the system stops functioning, then the whole system stops functioning. Or even if the complex and finely-tuned relationship among the various parts of the system is severely disrupted, the system must stop functioning. Consequently, like any other highly complex organism, the modern industrial system is much easier to kill than a simple organism.[1] Compare a human being with a hydra. You can cut a hydra into many pieces, and each piece will grow into a whole new hydra. But a human being can be killed by a blow to the head, a stab to the heart or the kidney, the cutting of a major artery—even a psychological condition such as severe depression can kill a human being. Like a human being, the industrial system is vulnerable because of its complexity and the interdependence of its parts. And the more the system comes to resemble a single, highly- organized worldwide entity, the more vulnerable it becomes.

Thus, to your question about what could make Mexican Indians give up modernity, the answer is: the death of the industrial system. Is it possible for revolutionary action to kill the industrial system? Of course, I can't answer that question with any certainty, but I think it may be possible to kill the industrial system. I suggest that the movement that led to the Russian Revolution of 1917, and the Bolsheviks in particular, could provide a model for action today. I don't mean that anyone should look at the Bolsheviks and say, "The Bolsheviks did such-and-such and so-and-so, therefore we should do the same." What I do mean is that the Russian example shows what a revolutionary movement might be able to accomplish today.

Throughout its history up to 1917, the Bolshevik party remained small in relation to the size of Russia. Yet when the time of crisis arrived the Bolsheviks were able to assume control of the country, and they were able to inspire millions of Russians to heroic efforts that enabled them against all odds to triumph over enormous difficulties.

Of course, the Russian Revolution is accounted a failure because the ideal socialist society of which the Bolsheviks dreamed never materialized. Revolutions never succeed in creating the new social order of which the revolutionaries dream. But destruction is usually easier than construction, and revolutions often do succeed in destroying the old social order against which they are directed. If revolutionaries today were to abandon all illusions about the possibility of creating a new and better society and take as their goal merely the death of the industrial system, they might well succeed in reaching that goal.

NOTES

1.   I don't mean to say that modern industrial society is literally an organism in the same sense in which a hydra or a human being is an organism. But the analogy with an organism is instructive for some purposes.

EXTRACT FROM
LETTER TO J.N.

Extract from Letter to J.N. (April 29, 2001)

The text of the following extract has been altered only in minor ways, but the notes have been greatly expanded beyond those of the original.

You write, "Watching a documentary on a tribe of Amazon Indians, I found that their life was as ordered as any modern man's... their day seemed as regimented as an office worker's."

You reached this conclusion on the basis of one documentary that you watched. I would say you were a bit hasty. I can't comment on that particular tribe because I know nothing about it. You didn't even say what tribe it was.

I wouldn't necessarily say that the life of every primitive people is less regimented than ours is. Among the Aino (a sedentary hunting-and-gathering people who formerly occupied part of Japan), ritual obligations were so elaborate and pervasive that they imposed a heavy psychological burden, often leading to serious disorders.[1] But unquestionably many primitive societies were far less regimented than ours is. One who lived among the North American Indians early in the 19th century wrote that they consisted of "individuals who had been educated to prefer almost any sacrifice to that of personal liberty.... The Indians individually acknowledge no superior, nor are they subordinate to any government.... [I]n general, the warriors while in their villages are unyielding, exceedingly tenacious of their freedom, and live together in a state of equality, closely approximated to natural rights... [A]lthough [their governments] somewhat resemble the democratic form, still a majority cannot bind a minority to a compliance with any acts of its own."[2]

Of course, you have to understand that prior to the modern era freedom was not conceived, as it often is today, as the freedom to just fritter away one's time in aimless, hedonistic pursuits. It was taken for granted that survival required effort and self-discipline. But there is a world of difference between the discipline that a small band of people imposes on itself in order to meet practical necessities, and discipline that is imposed from the outside by large organizations.

You write, "High infant- and child-mortality must affect women in these cultures with a level of angst about their children and their own lives that we can't imagine." This is a good point. The anarcho-primitivists find it convenient to overlook the high infant- and child-mortality rate of most pre-industrial societies, including Western society up to the 18th century.[3] The basic answer to this is simply that you can't have it both ways: If you want to escape the evils of industrial society, then you have to pay a price for it. However, it's likely that the high infant-mortality rate was necessary to preserve the health of the species. Today, weak and sickly babies survive to pass on their defective genes.

How do primitive women feel about it? I don't know whether anyone has ever taken the trouble to ask them. It's presumably very painful to them (and their husbands) when one of their babies dies. But I doubt that they feel the extreme anxiety that you suggest. When people see it as normal and expected that many of their children should die during the first few years of life, they probably take it in stride and don't worry about it unduly.[4] The human race doubtless has had that high infant- and child-mortality rate for the last million years and is presumably adapted to it. For a woman to be tormented by constant anxiety about her children would be maladaptive, hence a tendency to such anxiety would probably be eliminated by natural selection. Still, a high infant-mortality rate is no joke. It's one of the hardest aspects of forgoing industrial civilization.

You ask, "Is it not possible that our culture's unhappiness stems from our lack of strong religious beliefs, not our industrial lifestyle?"

Undoubtedly *some* people are happier for having strong religious beliefs. On the other hand, I don't think that strong religious belief is a prerequisite for happiness. Whether religion is *usually* conducive to happiness is open to argument. But the point I want to make here is that the decline of religion in modern society is not an *accident*. It is a *necessary result* of technical progress. There are several reasons for this, of which I will mention three.

First, as *Mean* magazine puts it,[5] "Every curtain science pulls away is another that God cannot hide behind." In other words, as science advances, it disproves more and more traditional religious beliefs and therefore undermines faith.

Second, the need for toleration is antagonistic to strong religious belief. Various features of modern society, such as easy long-distance transportation, make mixing of populations inevitable. Today, people of different ethnic groups and different religions have to live and work side by side. In order to avoid the disruptive conflicts to which religious hatred would give rise, society has to teach us to be tolerant. But toleration entails a weakening of religious faith. If you unquestioningly believed that your own creed were absolutely right, then you would also have to believe that every creed that disagreed with it was absolutely wrong, and this would imply a certain level of intolerance. In order to believe that all religions are just as good as yours, you have to have, deep in your heart, considerable uncertainty about the truth of your own religion.

Third, all of the great world religions teach us such virtues as reverence and self-restraint. But the economists tell us that our economic health depends on a high level of consumption. To get us to consume, advertisers must offer us endless pleasure, they must encourage unbridled hedonism, and this undermines religious qualities like reverence and self-restraint.

* * *

Regarding your question, there is so much to say in reply to it that I find it impossible to keep my answer brief. I'll confine myself to three points of the many that could be made.

(a) It's true that in many societies the extended family, the clan, or the village could be very confining. The paterfamilias (the "old man" who headed the extended family), or the council of village elders, kept people on a leash. But when the paterfamilias and the village elders lost their grip on the leash as a result of modernization, it was picked up by "the system," which now holds it much more tightly than the old-timers ever did.

The family or the village was small enough so that individuals within it were not powerless. Even where all authority was theoretically vested in the paterfamilias, in practice he could not retain his power unless he listened and responded to the grievances and problems of the individual members of his family.[6] Today, however, we are at the mercy of organizations, such as corporations, governments and political parties, that are too large to be responsive to single individuals. These organizations allow us a great deal of latitude where harmless recreational activities are concerned, but they keep under their own control the life-and-death issues on which our existence depends. With respect to these issues, individuals are powerless.

(b) In former times, for those who were willing to take serious risks, it was often possible to escape the bonds of the family, of the village, or of feudal structures. In medieval Western Europe, serfs ran away to become peddlers, robbers, or town-dwellers. Later, Russian peasants ran away to become Cossacks, black slaves ran away to live in the wilderness as "Maroons," indentured servants in the West Indies ran away to become buccaneers.[7] But in the modern world there is nowhere left to run. Wherever you go, you can be traced by your credit card, your social-security number, your fingerprints. You, Mr. N., live in California. Can you get a hotel or motel room there without showing your picture I.D.? You can't survive unless you fit into a slot in the system, otherwise known as a "job." And it is becoming increasingly difficult to get a job without making your whole past history accessible to prospective employers. So how can you defend your statement that "[m]odern urban society allows one to escape into an anonymity that family and clan based cultures couldn't"?

Granted, there are still corners of the world where one can find wilderness, or governments so disorganized that one can escape from the system there. But these are relics of the past, and they will disappear as the system continues to grow.

(c) "Today," you write, "one can... adopt whatever beliefs or lifestyle one wants. One can also easily travel, experiencing other cultures...."

But to what end? What, in practical terms, does one accomplish by changing one's beliefs or lifestyle, or by experiencing other cultures? Essentially nothing—except whatever fun one gets from it. People don't need only fun, they need purposeful work, and they need to have control not only over the pleasure-oriented aspects of their lives but over the serious, practical, purposeful, life-and-death aspects. That kind of control is not possible in modern society because we are all at the mercy of large organizations. Up to a point, having fun is good for you. But it's not an adequate substitute for serious, purposeful activity. For lack of this kind of activity people in our society get bored. They try to relieve their boredom by having fun. They seek new kicks, new thrills, new adventures. They masturbate their emotions by experimenting with new religions, new art-forms, travel, new cultures, new philosophies, new technologies. But still they are never satisfied, they always want more, because all of these activities are *purposeless*. People don't realize that what they really lack is serious, practical, purposeful work—work that is under their own control and is directed to the satisfaction of their own most essential, practical needs.

You ask, "How do we know that the breakdown of technological society won't lead to a simpler but more oppressive system?" We don't know it. If the technological system should break down completely, then in areas unsuitable for agriculture—such as rugged mountains, arid plains, or the subarctic—people would probably be nomadic, supporting themselves as pastoralists or by hunting and gathering. Historically, nomadic peoples have tended to have a high degree of personal freedom. But in areas suitable for large-scale, sedentary, intensive agriculture, people would probably support themselves by that kind of agriculture. And under those conditions it's likely that an oppressive landlord-class would tend to develop, like the feudal nobility of medieval Europe or the *latifundistas* of modern Latin America.

However, even under the most oppressive conditions of the past, people were not as powerless as they are today.[8] Russian serfs, for example, had means of resisting their landlords. They engaged in deception, theft, poaching, evasion of work, arson. If a peasant got angry enough, he would kill his landlord. If many peasants got angry at the same time, there would be a bloody revolt, a "jacquerie."[9] It's not a pretty picture. But it is at least arguable that Russian serfs had more freedom—the kind of freedom that really counts—than does the average, well-trained, modern middle-class person who has almost unlimited freedom in regard to recreational activities but is completely impotent vis-à-vis the large organizations that control the conditions under which he lives and the life-and-death issues on which his existence depends.

If the technoindustrial system collapses the probable result will be a reversion to a situation roughly equivalent to that which existed several hundred years ago, in the sense that people will live under widely varying conditions in different parts of the world. There will be sickness and health, full bellies and starvation, hatred and love, brotherhood and ethnic bitterness, war and peace, justice and oppression, violence and kindliness, freedom and servitude, misery and contentment. But it will be a world in which such a thing as freedom will at least be *possible*, even though everyone might not have it.

If this were all that were involved, one might reasonably argue that it would be better to maintain the existing system rather than encourage it to collapse. If the collapse is rapid—as I think it probably will have to be— there is bound to be bloodshed, starvation, and death for many people. Though our society is a generally unhappy one, most people are not sufficiently dissatisfied to want to undergo great risks and hardships in order to achieve an outcome that will by no means be universally idyllic.

But there is much more at stake than the relative advantages of a collapse versus the *currently existing* conditions of life. We also have to ask where so-called "progress" will take us in the future. What kinds of monstrous crimes will be committed with the godlike powers of the new technology? Will human behavior be so regulated through biological and psychological techniques that the concept of freedom becomes meaningless? Will there be environmental disasters, even disasters that will make the world uninhabitable? Will we be replaced by machines or by bioengineered freaks? The future is impossible to predict. But two things are certain:

First, all of the deepest human values, and the qualities that have been most respected and admired since prehistoric times, will become meaningless or obsolete in the techno-world of the future. What is the meaning of personal identity if you are someone else's clone? What is the meaning of achievement if your innate abilities have been planned for you by biotechnicians? What is the meaning of free will if your behavior can be predicted and guided by psychologists, or explained in mechanistic terms by neurophysiologists? Without free will, what is the meaning of freedom or of moral choice? What is the meaning of nature when wild organisms are allowed to survive only where and as the system chooses, and when they are altered by genes introduced, accidentally or intentionally, by human beings?

Already we can see that the prevailing concepts of traditional values like loyalty, friendship, honesty, and morality have been seriously altered under modern conditions. Courage has been devalued, personal honor has practically disappeared. In the future, with intelligent machines, human manipulation of other humans' genetic endowment, and the fact of living in a wholly artificial environment, conditions of life will be so radically different, so far outside the range of anything that the human race has experienced in the past, that all traditional values will become irrelevant and will die. The human race itself will be transformed into something entirely different from what it has been in the past.

Second, whatever may happen with technology in the future, it will *not* be rationally planned. Technology will *not* be used "wisely." In view of our society's past record, anyone who thinks that technology will be used wisely is completely out of touch with reality. Technology will take us on a course that we can neither predict nor control.

All of history, as well as understanding of complex systems in general, supports this conclusion. No society can plan and control its own development.

The changes that technology will bring will be a hundred times more radical, and more unpredictable, than any that have occurred in the past. The technological adventure is wildly reckless and utterly mad, and the people who are responsible for it are the worst criminals who have ever lived. They are worse than Hitler, worse than Stalin. Neither Stalin nor Hitler ever dreamed of anything so horrible.

* * *

Who says I love to read and write? Of course, when you're stuck in prison you have to have some sort of entertainment, and reading and writing are better than watching television (which I do not do). But when you're living out in the mountains you don't *need* entertainment. During my best time in the mountains I did very little reading, and what writing I did was mostly in my diary and was not for pleasure but for the purpose of recording my experiences so that I would never lose my memory of them. Later, beginning roughly around 1980, I did embark on a program of reading. But that was purposeful reading, mostly in the social sciences. My goal was to understand more about human nature and about history, especially about the way societies develop and change.

* * *

I've never had anything but contempt for the so-called "60s kids," the radicals of the Vietnam-War era. (The Black Panthers and other black activists are possible exceptions, since black people had then, and still have today, more genuine grievances on the score of discrimination than anyone else does). I was a supporter of the Vietnam War. I've changed my mind about that, but not for the reasons you might expect. I knew all along that our political and military leaders were fighting the war for despicable reasons—for their own political advantage and for the so-called "national interest." I supported the war because I thought it was necessary to stop the spread of communism, which I believed was even more dangerous to freedom, and even more committed to technology, than the system we have in this country is.

I've changed my mind about the war because I've concluded that I vastly overestimated the danger of communism. I overestimated its danger partly as a result of my own naivety and partly because I was influenced by media propaganda. (At the time, I was under the mistaken impression that most journalists were reasonably honest and conscientious.) As it turned out, communism broke down because of its own inefficiency, hence no war was needed to prevent its spread. Despite its ideological commitment to technology, communism showed itself to be less effective than capitalism in bringing about technological progress. Finally—again because of its own inefficiency—communism was far less successful than it would have liked to be in strangling individual freedom. At least through the 1970s, I accepted the image of communist countries that the media projected. I believed that they were tightly regulated societies in which virtually the individual's every move was supervised by the Party or the State. Undoubtedly this was the way the communist leaders would have *liked* to run their countries. But it now seems that because of corruption and inefficiency in communist systems the average man in those countries had a great deal more wiggle-room than was commonly assumed in the West. Thurston's study of life in Stalin's Russia is instructive.[10] On the basis of Thurston's information, one could plausibly argue that the average Russian worker under Stalin actually had more personal freedom than the average American worker has had at most times during the 20th century. This certainly was not because the communist leaders *wanted* the workers to have any freedom, but because there wasn't much they could do to prevent it.

*　　*　　*

You write that you "could go on-line and learn all about" me. Yes, and to judge from the Internet postings that people have sent me, probably most of what you learned was nonsense.[11] Leaving aside the question of the accuracy of the information you get from the Internet and assuming for the sake of argument that the Internet is a wholly beneficial source of information, still it weighs very little when balanced against the negative aspects of technology.

NOTES

1.   Coon, pp. 372–73.

2.   Hunter, pp. 52, 319–320. The authenticity of Hunter's account has been questioned, but has been persuasively defended by Drinnon (see List of Works Cited). In any case there are plenty of other sources that describe the freedom of certain primitive peoples. E.g., African pygmies: Turnbull, *Forest People* and *Wayward Servants*; Sarno; Schebesta, e.g., II. Band, I. Teil, p. 8 (referring to the Mbuti's "proverbial, unbridled love of freedom").

3.   See Gurven & Kaplan, pp. 326, 328.

4.   "Only with difficulty could [Mbuti] mothers remember the number of their deceased children." Schebesta, I. Band, p. 112. This suggests that the loss of a child was less than a devastating experience for Mbuti women.

5.   *Mean*, April 2001, p. 42. *Mean* was an obscure magazine (now no longer published) for which J.N. was a writer.

6.   I think W.I. Thomas and F. Znaniecki (see List of Works Cited) make this point in regard to the paterfamilias of Polish peasant families, but I'm relying on memory and can't cite the page.

7.   It may have been commonplace for slaves and medieval peasants to escape their servitude by running away. See: Hoffmann, pp. 51–52. TeBrake, p. 8. Dorpalen, pp. 69, 81, 83, 90&n64, 158. NEB (2003), Vol. 18, "European History and Culture," pp. 618, 629; Vol. 20, "Germany," pp. 75–76, 81; Vol. 27, "Slavery," pp. 298–99.

8.   In reference to many past societies, some historians and their readers assume that people had very little freedom because the rules, laws, or institutions to which they were supposedly subject appear to us to have been oppressive. These historians forget that rules mean nothing if they can't be enforced. Freedom is limited not by a society's rules alone, but by these in conjunction with the society's mechanisms for enforcement. For example, Mayo, pp. 102–03, criticizes certain historians for overlooking this point in regard to rural Argentina of the 18th and the early 19th century, where law-enforcement was so ineffective that restrictive legislation did very little to curb the anarchic behavior of the gauchos. In pre-industrial societies generally, enforcement mechanisms tended to be highly inefficient by modern standards. See, e.g., NEB (2003), Vol. 18, "European History and Culture," p. 618. The incredibly cruel punishments applied in medieval Europe may have represented a desperate attempt by the authorities to deter law-breaking in a society that lacked efficient means of enforcement.

9.   For these forms of resistance by slaves and serfs generally (not just Russian ones), see for example: Vucinich, Chapt. 2, especially pp. 56–71; Chapt. 6, especially pp. 167–174. Hoffmann, pp. 144, 305, 356, 358. TeBrake, pp. 8–9. Dorpalen, pp. 69, 70, 90, 91, 92, 120–21, 123, 128–29, 158–59. Kjetsaa, pp.

32–33. Tuchman, p. 41. NEB (2003), Vol. 27, "Slavery," pp. 298–99. Landlords or slave-owners who abused peasant or slave women sexually may have run a grave risk of being killed by the women themselves or by their menfolk. See ibid., p. 299; Mosse, pp. 13–14 (quoting Alexander Herzen), 16–17. Earlier editions of the present work cited a *Britannica* article for a story about the alleged rape of Pancho Villa's sister, but it turns out that the authenticity of the story is debated.

    10.   See our List of Works Cited.

    11.   Anyone who thinks the Internet is even minimally reliable as a source of information should read Manjoo's book (see List of Works Cited).

EXCERPTS FROM
LETTER TO M.K.

Excerpts from Letter to M.K. (October 4, 2003)

The problem of civilization is identical with the problem of technology. Let me first explain that when I speak of technology I do not refer only to physical apparatus such as tools and machines. I include also techniques, such as the techniques of chemistry, civil engineering, or biotechnology. Included too are human techniques such as those of propaganda or of educational psychology, as well as organizational techniques that could not exist at an advanced level without the physical apparatus—the tools, machines, and structures—on which the whole technological system depends.

However, technology in the broader sense of the word includes not only modern technology but also the techniques and physical apparatus that existed at earlier stages of society. For example, plows, harness for animals, blacksmith's tools, domesticated breeds of plants and animals, and the techniques of agriculture, animal husbandry, and metalworking. Early civilizations depended on these technologies, as well as on the human and organizational techniques needed to govern large numbers of people. Civilizations cannot exist without the technology on which they are based. Conversely, where the technology is available, civilization is likely to develop sooner or later.

Thus, the problem of civilization can be equated with the problem of technology. The farther back we can push technology, the farther back we will push civilization. If we could push technology all the way back to the Paleolithic age, there would be no more civilization.

*   *   *

In reference to certain actions of mine you ask, "Don't you think violence is violence?" Of course violence is violence. And violence is also a necessary part of nature. If predators did not kill members of prey species, then the prey species would multiply to the point where they would destroy their environment by consuming everything edible. Many kinds of animals are violent even against members of their own species. For example, chimpanzees often kill other chimpanzees. In some regions, fights are common among wild bears and can have fatal consequences.[1]

Human beings in the wild constitute one of the more violent species. Carleton S. Coon's survey of hunting-and-gathering cultures provides numerous examples of violence by human beings against other human beings.[2] Professor Coon makes clear that he admires hunting-and-gathering peoples and regards them as more fortunate than civilized ones.[3] But he is an honest man and does not censor out those aspects of primitive life, such as violence, that appear disagreeable to modern people. Thus, it is clear that a significant amount of violence is a natural part of human life. There is nothing wrong with violence in itself. In any particular case, whether violence is good or bad depends on how it is used and the purpose for which it is used. So why do modern people regard violence as evil in itself? They do so for one reason only: They have been brainwashed by propaganda. Modern society uses various forms of propaganda to teach people to be frightened and horrified by violence, because the technoindustrial system needs a population that is timid, docile, and afraid to assert itself, a population that will not make trouble or disrupt the orderly functioning of the system. Whatever philosophical or moral rationalizations people may invent to explain their belief that violence is wrong, the real reason for their belief is that they have unconsciously absorbed the system's propaganda.

Power depends ultimately on physical force. By teaching people that violence is wrong (except, of course, when the system itself uses violence via the police or the military), the system maintains its monopoly on physical force and thus keeps all power in its own hands.

*   *   *

All of the groups you mention here are part of a single movement. Let's call it the "GA (Green Anarchist) Movement." Of course, these people are right to the extent that they oppose civilization and the technology on which it is based. But, because of the form in which this movement is developing, it may actually help to protect the technoindustrial system and may serve as an obstacle to revolution. I will explain:

It is difficult to achieve the *permanent* suppression of rebellion through the direct application of force. When rebellion is put down by force, it very often breaks out again later in some new form in which the authorities find it more difficult to control. For example, in 1878 the German Reichstag enacted harsh and repressive laws against the

Social-Democratic movement, as a result of which the movement was crushed and its members were scattered, confused, and discouraged. But only for a short time. The movement soon reunited itself, became more energetic, and found new ways of spreading its ideas, so that by 1884 it was stronger than ever.[4]

Thus, astute observers of human affairs know that the powerful classes of a society can most effectively defend themselves against rebellion by using force and direct repression only when these are really necessary, and relying instead on manipulation to deflect rebellion. One of the most effective devices used is that of providing channels through which rebellious impulses can be expressed in ways that are harmless to the system. For example, it is well known that in the Soviet Union the satirical magazine *Krokodil* was designed to provide an outlet for complaints and for resentment of the authorities in a way that would lead no one to question the legitimacy of the Soviet system or rebel against it in any serious way. But the "democratic" system of the West has evolved mechanisms for deflecting rebellion that are far more sophisticated and effective than any that existed in the Soviet Union. It is a truly remarkable fact that in modern Western society people "rebel" in favor of the values of the very system against which they imagine themselves to be rebelling. The left "rebels" in favor of racial and religious equality, equality for women and homosexuals, humane treatment of animals, and so forth. But these are the values that the American mass media teach us over and over again every day. Leftists have been so thoroughly brainwashed by media propaganda that they are able to "rebel" only in terms of these values, which are values of the technoindustrial system itself. In this way the system has successfully deflected the rebellious impulses of the left into channels that are harmless to the system.[5]

Rebellion against technology and civilization is real rebellion, a real attack on the values of the existing system. But the green anarchists, anarcho-primitivists, and so forth (the "GA Movement") have fallen under such heavy influence from the left that their rebellion against civilization has to a great extent been neutralized. Instead of rebelling against the values of civilization, they have adopted many civilized values themselves and have constructed an imaginary picture of primitive societies that embodies these civilized values.

*   *   *

[At this point the letter to M.K. contained a long section debunking the anarcho-primitivist myth. That section is omitted here because it only duplicates some of the material found in "The Truth About Primitive Life," which appears in the 2010 edition of *Technological Slavery*.]

*   *   *

I don't mean to say that the hunting-and-gathering way of life was no better than modern life. On the contrary, I believe it was better beyond comparison. Many, perhaps most, investigators who have studied hunter-gatherers have expressed their respect, their admiration, or even their envy of them.

But obviously the reasons why primitive life was better than civilized life had nothing to do with gender equality, kindness to animals, non-competitiveness, or nonviolence. Those values are the soft values of modern civilization. By projecting those values onto hunting-and-gathering societies, the GA Movement has created a myth of a primitive utopia that never existed in reality. Thus, even though the GA Movement claims to reject civilization and modernity, it remains enslaved to some of the most important values of modern society. For this reason, the GA Movement cannot be an effective revolutionary movement.

In the first place, part of the GA Movement's energy is deflected away from the real revolutionary objective—to eliminate modern technology and civilization in general—in favor of the pseudo-revolutionary issues of racism, sexism, animal rights, homosexual rights, and so forth. In the second place, because of its commitment to these pseudo-revolutionary issues, the GA Movement may attract too many leftists—people who are less interested in getting rid of modern civilization than they are in the leftist issues of racism, sexism, etc. This would cause a further deflection of the movement's energy away from the issues of technology and civilization. In the third place, the objective of securing the rights of women, homosexuals, animals, and so forth, is incompatible with the objective of eliminating civilization, because women and homosexuals in primitive societies often do not have equality, and such societies are usually cruel to animals.[6] If one's goal is to secure the rights of these groups, then one's best policy is to stick with modern civilization. In the fourth place, the GA Movement's adoption of many of the soft values of modern civilization, as well as its myth of a soft primitive utopia, attracts too many soft, dreamy, lazy, impractical people who are more inclined to retreat into utopian fantasies than to take effective, realistic action to get rid of the technoindustrial system.

The GA Movement may be not only useless but worse than useless, because it may be an obstacle to the development of an effective revolutionary movement. Since opposition to technology and civilization is an important part of the GA Movement's program, young people who are concerned about what technological civilization is doing to the world are drawn into that movement. Certainly not all of these young people are leftists or soft, dreamy, ineffectual types; some of them have the potential to become real revolutionaries. But in the GA Movement they are outnumbered by leftists and other useless people, so they are neutralized, they become corrupted, and their revolutionary potential is wasted. In this sense, the GA Movement could be called a destroyer of potential revolutionaries.

It will be necessary to build a new revolutionary movement that will keep itself strictly separate from the GA Movement and its soft, civilized values. I don't mean that there is anything wrong with gender equality, kindness to animals, tolerance of homosexuality, or the like. But these values have no relevance to the effort to eliminate technological civilization. They are not revolutionary values. An effective revolutionary movement will have to adopt instead the hard values of primitive societies, such as skill, self-discipline, honesty, physical and mental stamina, intolerance of externally-imposed restraints, capacity to endure physical pain, and, above all, courage.

NOTES

1.   The magazine *Bears and Other Top Predators,* Vol. 1, Issue 2, pp. 28–29, shows a photograph of bears fighting and a photograph of a bear wounded in a fight, and mentions that such wounds can be deadly. See also section 6 of "The Truth About Primitive Life," in the 2010 edition of *Technological Slavery.*

2.   Coon, passim.

3.   Ibid., pp. XIX, 3, 4, 9, 10.

4.   Zimmermann, p. 23. See also Kaczynski, *Anti-Tech Revolution* Chapt. Four, section 22.

5.   See "The System's Neatest Trick," in this volume.

6.   See "The Truth About Primitive Life," section 8.

LETTER TO DR. P.B. ON
THE MOTIVATIONS OF SCIENTISTS

Letter to Dr. P.B. on the Motivations of Scientists

In 2001 I received a letter dated July 24 of that year from a Dr. P.B. The letter was accompanied by some sheets labeled "Response to ISAIF," in which Dr. B. expressed a number of criticisms of that text. Among other things, Dr. B. disagreed with my statement (ISAIF, ¶¶ 88–89) that scientists were not motivated primarily by a desire to benefit humanity. Due to the pressure of other work, it was not until May 2009 that I got around to writing a reply[1] to Dr. B.'s contention. What follows is a heavily rewritten version of that reply.

I. Dr. B. found my discussion of the motives of scientists to be "particularly weak." He wrote: "A long discussion of why Mr. Teller is a Bad Man. Which is fine. But when we think of physicists, most of us think of Einstein before Teller, and Einstein is an exemplar of one who completely contradicts [ISAIF's statement that scientists are not motivated primarily by a desire to benefit humanity]—but by no means the only one." Dr. B. further remarked that I "essentially denie[d] moral agency to scientists," and he added, inter alia:

> In talking with people who I think have worked in what are to me genuinely negative fields of research—weapons design at Lawrence Livermore, for instance—I find that those who are directing and actively engaged in the work are there because they think they are doing the right thing for the country, even with all the risks their work entails, and that by doing the right thing for the country, they do the right thing for the world. These people are actively aware of and engaging their moral agency... .

Dr. B. conceded, however, that there were scientists who acted "more in support than in directing the work" of weapons design, and who saw their jobs as "ethically neutral."

First let's get this straight: It should have been obvious that in paragraphs 87–89 of ISAIF I was discussing the *usual* or *typical* motivations of scientists; I was not concerned with the occasional exception. Thus, if it could be proven that 1% or even 5% of scientists were indeed motivated by a desire to benefit humanity, that would not seriously affect my argument. It

275

should also have been obvious that in asking about the motives of scientists I was referring to their motives *for doing scientific work*, not to their motives in other matters. I've never claimed that the majority of scientists were unconcerned with moral issues. It is one thing to say that a scientist is concerned with moral issues and quite another to say that moral issues provide his principal motive for doing research. (One can, however, find plenty of examples of amorality among scientists, some of which we will see further on.)

Thus, the argument that scientists are not motivated primarily by a desire to benefit humanity does not deny moral agency to scientists—outside of the laboratory. Dr. B. mentioned Einstein. Einstein worked for world peace—or at least preached in favor of it—and his motive for doing so no doubt was highly moral. But that says nothing about his motive for doing research in physics.

Dr. B.'s contention presumably was that scientists acted as moral agents *in doing their scientific work*. Back in 2002 I put Dr. B.'s theory to the two prison psychologists here, able men in my opinion, who described themselves as "hard-nosed rationalists" and eschewed dubious theories such as Freudianism. I quote from my notes dated April 9, 2002:

> Because I'm planning a response to a letter I received some time ago from [Dr. P.B.], when Drs. Watterson & Morrison came by today, I asked them... whether they'd gone into the field of psychology in order to serve their own personal needs or... to do good for the human race. They both said they'd become psychologists in order to satisfy their own personal needs. Then I asked them whether they thought that most psychologists became psychologists in order to... do good for the human race, or in order to serve their own personal needs. Both Dr. Watterson & Dr. Morrison said that most psychologists bec[a]me psychologists in order to satisfy their personal needs ('especially ego needs,' said Watterson), and not to do good for the human race. Morrison added that a lot of psychologists will *say* they became psychologists in order to help people, but that's not their real motive. I told Watterson & Morrison of [Dr. B.'s] opinion that scientists were 'moral agents.' Watterson & Morrison appeared to find this amusing. Morrison suggested, tongue in cheek, that I should write to [Dr. B.]... [and] give him a one-line response that reads 'Get a life!'

II. We've seen that Dr. B., in order to support his argument, claimed to "find" that people who were "directing and actively engaged" in the design of military weapons thought they were doing the right thing for the world and were "actively... engaging their moral agency." How did he "find" this? Apparently from the mere fact that they told him so. But if these people were utterly cynical about their work, would they come right out and say so? It's hardly likely. If an individual is unscrupulous enough to do harmful work to satisfy his personal needs, he will certainly be unscrupulous enough to lie about his motives.

There are people whose opinions of scientists involved in military research are very different from Dr. B.'s. In his self-accusing postwar memoirs, Hitler's Minister of Armaments wrote:

> I exploited the phenomenon of the technician's often blind devotion to his task. Because of what seems to be the moral neutrality of technology, these people were without any scruples about their activities. The more technical the world imposed on us by the war, the more dangerous was this indifference of the technician to the direct consequences of his anonymous activities.[2]

Would any of these technicians have admitted openly to outsiders that they were indifferent to the consequences of their work? Probably not. A case in point is that of Wernher von Braun, who was Hitler's chief rocket-scientist and directed the development of the V-2 rocket that killed some 20,000 civilians in Allied countries during World War II.[3] Von Braun claimed after the war that his motives had been "patriotic."[4] But while he was working for Hitler von Braun must have known that the Jews were being exterminated, since this was "a kind of open secret in Germany from the end of 1942 at the very latest."[5] What kind of patriotism would lead a man to build weapons for a regime that exterminates entire ethnic groups from sheer spite? It is sufficiently clear that "patriotism" was merely an excuse for von Braun, and that all he really wanted was to build rockets for their own sake. "As World War II neared its end in early 1945, Braun and many of his associates chose to surrender to the United States, where they believed they would likely receive support for their rocket research... ."[6]

The point here is not that building weapons for Hitler is morally equivalent to building weapons for a democratic regime like that of the United States. The point is that scientists commonly attribute to themselves noble-sounding motives such as "patriotism" that don't necessarily have anything to do with their real motives. And, no, this practice is not limited to those who build weapons for dictatorial regimes.

In the United States, the development of the first atomic bomb was directed by a physicist named J. Robert Oppenheimer. In a speech delivered on November 2, 1945, to the scientists who had participated in the bomb project at Los Alamos, New Mexico,[7] Oppenheimer remarked: "One always has to worry that what people say of their motives is not adequate." Oppenheimer then ran through the usual excuses that scientists gave for working on the atomic bomb: The Nazis might have gotten the bomb first; there was no place in the world where the development of atomic weapons would have had a smaller chance of leading to disaster than in the United States; the real importance of the scientists' work lay not in weapons but in the benefits that atomic energy would bring to mankind; etc., etc., etc. Oppenheimer noted that all these rationalizations had more or less validity, but insisted that the real reason why the scientists had developed the bomb was that, for them, their work was a personal need, an "organic necessity." Scientists, in Oppenheimer's view, lived by a philosophy according to which the acquisition and diffusion of knowledge was an end in itself, independently of whether it brought any practical benefit to the human race.[8]

The implications of Oppenheimer's speech are evident even though Oppenheimer did not state them clearly: Scientists work not for the benefit of humanity, but in order to satisfy their own needs. While Oppenheimer probably believed that science did on balance benefit humanity, he recognized that the justification of science in terms of benefit to humanity was essentially a rationalization that did not represent scientists' real motives.

It is significant that the printed version of this speech found among Oppenheimer's papers was marked: "This material is not for public release. A revised version will probably appear soon in one of the scientific journals."[9] In fact, however, the speech seems never to have been published, in "revised" form or otherwise, prior to its inclusion in Smith & Weiner's book on Oppenheimer.[10]

III. Apparently Oppenheimer was not very comfortable with what he himself said about scientists' motives. But some scientists have stated their motives more forthrightly than Oppenheimer did and with no sign of discomfort.[11]

Werner von Siemens was a 19th-century electrical engineer who invented the self-exciting generator and made other important advances in the applications of electricity.[12] In a letter dated December 25, 1887,

Siemens described his motives:

> Certainly I have striven for profit and wealth, but not mainly in order to enjoy them; rather to gain the means for the *execution of other projects and undertakings*, and by my success to win recognition of the correctness of my procedure and the usefulness of my work. Therefore from my youth upward I have yearned to establish a world-wide firm such as that of Fugger, which would assure not only to myself but also to my successors power and esteem in the world, and the means also of raising my sisters and other near relatives to higher standards of life. ...
>
> I regard our business as only secondarily a source of wealth; for me it is rather a kingdom that I have founded and that I hope to leave intact to my successors for further *creative work*.[13] [Emphasis added.]

Not a word about the benefit of humanity. But notice the importance that Siemens puts on the execution of "projects," "undertakings," and "creative work" *for their own sake*. Thus, surrogate activities. See ISAIF, ¶¶ 38–41, 84, 87–89.

Yet, surely, scientists who work in fields having an obviously humanitarian purpose, such as the treatment of disease, are motivated by a desire to benefit the human race—aren't they? In some cases perhaps. But in general I think not. The bacteriologist Hans Zinsser wrote:

> [N]ever having had any close association with workers in the field of infectious diseases, he shared this misconception of the noble motives which impelled these queer people. And not quite understanding how anyone could be impelled by noble motives, he asked us: 'How do bacteriologists get that way?'... As a matter of fact, men go into this branch of work from a number of motives, the last of which is a self-conscious desire to do good. The point is that it remains one of the few sporting propositions left for individuals who feel the need of a certain amount of excitement. Infectious disease is one of the few genuine adventures left in the world. ... About the only genuine sporting proposition that remains unimpaired by the relentless domestication of a once free-living human species is the war against these ferocious little fellow creatures....[14]

Dr. B. mentioned Einstein as one whose work was motivated by a desire to benefit humanity, but it can be demonstrated that Dr. B. was wrong.

In 1917 Einstein wrote: "Our entire much-praised technological progress, and civilization generally, could be compared to an axe in the hand of a pathological criminal."[15] It is therefore difficult to conceive of any altruistic motive for Einstein's scientific work. Einstein must have realized that any advance in physics would be likely to have practical applications and therefore to contribute to the technological progress that he had compared to an axe in the hand of a criminal, yet he continued his work in theoretical physics until very late in life[16]—even after he had seen the development of nuclear weapons, to which his own research had contributed. So why did he continue his work? It may have been a kind of compulsion. Toward the end of his life he wrote: "I cannot tear myself away from my work. It has me inexorably in its clutches."[17]

Whether it was a compulsion or not, Einstein's scientific work had nothing to do with any desire to benefit the human race. In an autobiography[18] that he wrote at the age of 67, Einstein described his reasons for devoting himself to science. As a small child he was already oppressed by a sense of the "vanity" or "emptiness" (*Nichtigkeit*) of hoping and striving. This suggests a depressive and defeatist mentality. Einstein moreover seems to have been too delicate a child to face the workaday world, for he saw at an early age what he called the "cruelty" of the busy effort (*Treiben*) that was necessary in order to make a living. At first he tried to escape from these painful feelings by becoming deeply religious, but at the age of twelve he lost his faith as a result of reading scientific books that disproved the tales of the Bible. He then turned for solace to science itself, which provided him with a "paradise" that replaced the religious paradise he had lost.[19]

It thus appears that, for Einstein, scientific work was not only a surrogate activity, but also an escape from a world that he found too harsh. In any case, it is certain that Einstein turned to science solely in order to satisfy his personal needs; nowhere in his autobiography did he suggest any ways in which his research might improve the lot of the human race.

IV. For every scientist I can name whose stated motive has been to satisfy his personal needs, one could perhaps name many who have claimed an altruistic motive. Altruistic motives certainly are not impossible. For example, I would guess that many people who do field studies in botany and zoology are motivated at least in part by a genuine love for wild plants and animals. Nevertheless, claims of altruistic motives—or, to put it more accurately, of motives that are accounted admirable under the norms of the present society—must in general be given very little weight. While a scientist who admits to a selfish motive may lower himself in the eyes of the people around him, one who claims a "noble" motive fulfills the expectations of other people and assures himself of their approval if not their admiration. It is a truism that most people, most of the time, will say what they think will win the approval of their peers. No doubt this sometimes involves conscious dishonesty, as was certainly the case with von Braun when he claimed that his motives were "patriotic." More often, I think, scientists believe their own rationalizations. Science has its own self-congratulatory ideology, and one of the functions of ideology is to justify the believer in his own eyes. As the sociologist Monnerot explains, ideology

> offers a *different version* of the relation between the motive and what it moti-
> vates. The materials which compose an ideology, and which it organizes,
> can face the full light of day, so to speak. They are not only allowable but
> honorable, and they constantly seek to affirm their relationship with the
> recognized social values. ... The aspirations of the [believer] are translated
> into ethical and social terms by ideology... .[20]

But the ideology that represents science as a humanitarian enter-prise is belied by the actual behavior of scientists. The image of scientists as dedicated humanitarians originated at a time when to many people it seemed plausible to assume that scientific and technological progress were unequivocally beneficial, and when scientific work usually was not very remunerative. An occasional applied scientist might become rich—we've already noticed the case of Werner von Siemens, and Alfred Nobel, the inventor of dynamite, provides another example—but typically the scientist toiled in his laboratory year after year on a professor's meager salary for sheer love of the work. Hence, he gave the impression of being an unselfish idealist. A few scientists even refused opportunities to profit financially from their research. Thus Roentgen, the discoverer of X-ray photography, donated the money from his Nobel prize to a university, and both he and the Curies (who discovered radium) declined to patent the processes they had invented.[21] So there is nothing surprising about the fact that scientists acquired a reputation as unselfish benefactors of mankind—which in some cases no doubt they believed themselves to be.

But all that changed during the course of World War II, when science demonstrated its crucial importance as an instrument of power. Norbert Wiener, a distinguished mathematician and pioneer computer scientist, wrote in 1956:

> In most previous times, the personnel of science had been seeded by the austerity of the work and the scantiness of the pickings. ... Thus, an ambitious man with slightly anti-social tendencies, or, to put it more politely, indifferent to spending other people's money, would formerly have avoided a scientific career as if it were the plague itself. From the time of the war on, these adventurers, who would have started out as stock promoters or lights of the insurance business, have been invading science.[22]

The scientific community in the form in which it existed before the war could have been considered as a social movement, and from that point of view what Wiener was describing was simply the corruption that overtakes any social movement when it begins to offer its adherents such advantages as money, status, or a career.[23] Needless to say, the corrupting process has continued since Wiener's time, and by now the corruption of science should be obvious to anyone.[24]

Outright scientific fraud "has been revealed, in confidential surveys, to be much more widespread than scientists like to acknowlege."[25] The case of the Korean Cloner, for example, was well publicized in 2006: "Cloning pioneer Hwang Woo Suk admitted in court... that he falsified much of his data."[26] A major scandal involving researchers at Duke University was reported in 2011, and, significantly, journals in which the researchers' flawed papers had appeared were reluctant thereafter to publish letters critical of them.[27]

Outright fraud presumably is committed only by a small minority of scientists, but many more participate in practices that come perilously close to fraud. In order to plant a slanted article in a medical journal,

> a medical-communications agency and its pharmaceutical-company sponsors will agree on a title for an article and a potential author, usually an academic physician with a reputation as a 'thought leader.' The agency will ask the thought leader to 'author' the article, sometimes in exchange for a fee. [A] ghostwriter will write the article, or perhaps an extended outline containing the message the company wants to transmit, and send

it along to the physician, who may make some changes or simply sign it as written and submit it to a journal, usually scrubbed of any mention of the ghostwriter, the agency, or the pharmaceutical company.[28]

A meta-researcher named John Ioannidis, who is "one of the world's foremost experts on the credibility of medical research," has suggested that "an obsession with winning funding has gone a long way toward weakening the reliability" of such research.[29] Ioannidis found that many studies were biased: "Researchers headed into their studies wanting certain results— and, lo and behold, they were getting them. ... [I]t's easy to manipulate results, even unintentionally or unconsciously. ... Perhaps only a minority of researchers were succumbing to this bias, but their distorted findings were having an outsize effect on published research."[30] Attempting to call attention to the distorted findings of "respected colleagues can have ugly professional repercussions."[31] And these problems are not limited to medical research: "Other meta-research experts have confirmed that similar issues distort research in all fields of science."[32]

But that's not the worst of it. There have been many instances of cynical collaboration by scientists in the nefarious activities of governments and corporations: Think of the scientists who have helped Third World countries (India, Pakistan, North Korea) to develop nuclear weapons, or of the professional global-warming deniers in cahoots with energy companies. And in Silicon Valley, where the dividing-line between scientists and businessmen has been blurred almost to the vanishing-point, some companies, for their own advantage, collaborate with U.S. government spy agencies in snooping on the American public.[33] I don't know whether any of the scientist-businessmen involved in this collaboration would claim that their motives were "patriotic," but any such claim, if it were made, would be no more credible than Wernher von Braun's claim of patriotic motives.

V. In view of all of the foregoing, only an egregious act of self-deception could enable anyone to maintain a belief in the notion that most scientists are motivated primarily by a desire to benefit humanity. A less fatuous version of the scientific ideology represents science not as a humanitarian enterprise, but as morally "neutral": Scientists simply place certain tools at society's disposal, and if ill consequences follow, the fault is society's, for "misusing" the tools; the scientists' own hands are clean. One recalls Matthew 27:24—"... he took water, and washed his hands before the multitude, saying, I am innocent..." (Pontius Pilate).

The *Encyclopaedia Britannica* uses this "neutrality" argument in its article on technology;[34] Dr. B. alluded to the same argument in his letter of July 24, 2001 (see above, I); Albert Speer mentioned it as an excuse relied on by the technicians who built weapons for Hitler (above, II); and von Braun likewise "emphasized the innate impartiality of scientific research, which in itself has no moral dimensions until its products are put to use by the larger society."[35]

Of course, technology *in the abstract* is morally neutral. But von Braun wasn't building rockets in the abstract realm of Plato's Forms. He was building rockets for Adolf Hitler, and he knew very well that those rockets would be used to kill people in defense of a regime that was carrying out mass exterminations. However neutral technology may be in the abstract, when you develop new technology or discover a scientific principle that has technological applications, you are performing a concrete action that has a concrete effect on the society in which you live. You are not entitled to disclaim responsibility for that effect on the ground that society *could* have used the technology in some other way—any more than von Braun was entitled to disclaim responsibility for his rockets on the ground that Hitler could have used them solely for space exploration and not as weapons.[36] Von Braun was obligated to ask not what Hitler could do with rockets in theory, but what he *would* do with them in practice. Similarly, when you develop new technology today, you are obligated to consider not what society could do with that technology in theory but how the technology is likely to interact with society in practice.

Everything in the foregoing paragraph is obvious, and anyone intelligent enough to be a rocket scientist or a physicist or a molecular biologist should be able to figure it all out in five minutes of honest reflection. The fact that so many scientists resort to the "moral neutrality" argument demonstrates either that they are being dishonest with themselves or with others, or else that they simply haven't bothered to think seriously about the social and moral implications of their work.[37]

There *are* a very few scientists who do think seriously about the consequences for society of their work. But their moral scruples do not significantly interfere with their research;[38] they do the research anyway, then they salve their consciences by preaching the "ethical" use of their science. In practical terms, their preaching and their scruples are useless.

Alfred Nobel was essentially a pacifist, but that didn't prevent him from developing high explosives. He consoled himself with the hope "that the destructive powers of his inventions would help bring an end to wars."[39] We all know how well *that* worked. Einstein preached—ineffectually—about world peace, but he continued his research until virtually the end of his life, despite his opinion of technology and despite the fact that his work had contributed to the development of nuclear weapons. The scientists who participated in the Manhattan Project *first* built the atomic bomb and *afterward* preached about the need for an international agency to control nuclear energy.[40] Though such an agency was created, it proved ineffectual.[41] In his book *Behavior Control*, Perry London showed that he had thought seriously about the implications of techniques that facilitated the manipulation of human behavior. He offered certain ethical ideas that he hoped would guide the use of such techniques,[42] but his ethical ideas have had no practical effect whatever. David Gelernter, in his book *Mirror Worlds*, expressed grave concerns about the effect of computer science on society.[43] Nevertheless, Gelernter continued to promote technology, including computer science,[44] and the misgivings he expressed in *Mirror Worlds* have done nothing to mitigate the consequences of computer development.

In 2009 the AAAI (Association for the Advancement of Artificial Intelligence) held a conference that dealt with the dangers posed by the development of artificial intelligence,[45] and as possible remedies the participating scientists considered "limits on research," the confinement of some research to "a high-security laboratory," and a "cadre" that was to "shape the advances and help society cope with the ramifications" of artificial intelligence. It's hard to tell to what extent all this was a public-relations effort[46] and to what extent the scientists actually believed in it, but in any case their proposals were hopelessly naïve.

The "limits" considered by the scientists clearly were not intended to stop research in artificial intelligence generally, but only in certain narrow areas that the scientists thought were particularly sensitive. Such "limits" will not be maintained for long. If the scientists of the Manhattan Project had refused to work on weapons research they would have delayed the advent of nuclear weapons only by a few years, because once quantum theory had been developed and nuclear fission discovered, it was inevitable that someone sooner or later would apply that knowledge to make weapons. Similarly, given that research in artificial intelligence is to continue, it is certain that someone sooner or later (probably sooner) will use the developing technical knowledge to invade any areas that the AAAI may try to declare "off limits."

The "high-security laboratories" will not be controlled by ordinary citizens, but by powerful organizations such as corporations and governments. Thus the confinement of certain research to high-security laboratories will only increase the already excessive concentration of power in our society.

The "cadre" that is supposed to "shape the advances and help society cope with the ramifications" of artificial intelligence fills me with dread and loathing, because these people's conception of what is good for human beings scarcely rises to the level of that of a four-year-old child.[47] I shudder to think what kind of world they would create if they were in control. In practice, however, the "cadre" will have no more success than did the groups of scientists formed after 1945 who tried to ensure that nuclear energy would be "wisely" regulated and used only for peaceful purposes. In the long run, the way artificial intelligence is developed and applied will be determined by the needs of the people who have power and are reaching for more of it.

Thus, whatever ethical standards any scientists may profess, those standards have at most a minimal effect on the overall development of science and technology. What I wrote in paragraph 92 of ISAIF was essentially correct: "Science marches on blindly, without regard to the real welfare of the human race or to any other standard, obedient only to the psychological needs of the scientists and of the government officials and corporation executives who provide the funds for research."

NOTES

1.   By the time I got around to writing my reply, Dr. P.B. was no longer at the address from which he had written me in 2001. Since his name was an extremely common one, it proved impossible to locate him definitely. Eventually a correspondent sent me an address that he *claimed* was that of the right Dr. P.B., and I sent my reply to that address but received no answer. It was probably the wrong address.

2.   Speer, p. 212.

3.   NEB (2003), Vol. 29, "War, Technology of," pp. 569–570: 4,000 V-2s were launched against Allied cities, they killed on average about 5 persons per launch, 5×4,000 = 20,000. See also *The Week*, March 6, 2009, p. 39.

4.   NEB (2003), Vol. 2, "Braun, Wernher von," p. 485.

5.   R.J. Evans, p. 560. Apart from the extermination of the Jews, plenty of other Nazi atrocities were widely known in Germany at the time. See, e.g., Rothfels, passim.

6.   NEB (2003), Vol. 19, "Exploration," p. 47.

7.   The complete text of the speech can be found in Smith & Weiner, pp. 315–325.

8.   Oppenheimer's view on this point has been explicitly confirmed by many other physicists. Kolbert, "Crash Course," p. 76. See also Burnet, p. 81: "In today's laboratory, what is desired is usually the answer that will fill a gap in the accepted structure of knowledge. It is immaterial whether filling the gap will either directly or indirectly provide health, comfort or wealth to other members of the community."

9.   Smith & Weiner, pp. 315, 350n20.

10.   Ibid.

11   Burnet's Chapter Five doesn't directly and explicitly address the question of scientists' motivations, but the author does in effect say a great deal about his own motivations and those of other scientists. He makes clear that scientists are not motivated primarily (or at all?) by a desire to benefit the human race, and he refers repeatedly to status ("recognition," pp. 82, 91; "prestige," p. 87; dominance-ranking, passim) as a major reward for scientists. When Burnet's book was published in 1970, the concepts of "power process" and "surrogate activity" had not yet been invented, but Burnet in effect makes clear the significance of science as a surrogate activity through which people having the relevant talents can experience the power process. Thus, on pp. 90ff he discusses the importance of providing suitable work for talented people; e.g.: "One of the great social necessities of an affluent society is to ensure that as large a proportion of the highly intelligent people who are born into the community find occupation that makes use of their intelligence and *feels* worth doing" (p. 91); "the day-to-day elucidation of [meteorological phenomena] can provide high-level occupation for a steadily increasing number of scientists…" (p. 93); "an irrational technological and scientific momentum is generated on the basis that because a difficult or spectacular thing can be done, it must be done. It is the equivalent at the scientific and technological level of the famous answer as to why one should climb Everest—because it is there." (p. 98).

12.   See Zimmermann, pp. 439–442; NEB (2003), Vol. 10, "Siemens, Werner von," p. 787.

13.   Klemm, p. 353.

14.   Zinsser, pp. 12–14.

15.   Albert Einstein, Letter to Heinrich Zangger, Dec. 6, 1917, in Schulmann et al., Vol. 8, Part A, pp. 561–62. The translation given here is that of Craig, p. 14. Further on in the same letter, Einstein refers to the technological

Verseuchung (corruption, contamination, or pollution) of human life, which suggests that his comparison of modern technology to an axe in the hand of a criminal was not just an offhand remark but the expression of a definite opinion.

16. NEB (2003), Vol. 18, "Einstein," p. 157.

17. Ibid.

18. Schilpp, pp. 1–94. The autobiography is printed in the original German with an English translation on alternate pages.

19. For this entire paragraph, see ibid., pp. 2, 4. See also Warburg et al., pp. 29–32. Here, in a romantic flight of fancy, Einstein addresses the motives for scientific research. Let it suffice to say, this rhapsody makes clear that Einstein's own motives were unconnected with any desire to benefit the human race.

20. Monnerot, pp. 136, 140.

21. Urban-Klaehn, p. 10.

22. Wiener, pp. 271–72.

23. Compare Kaczynski, *Anti-Tech Revolution*, Chapt. Three, Part II, discussion of Postulate 4.

24. As will be seen from ibid., the "corruption" of a movement doesn't necessarily refer to dishonesty, though dishonesty certainly is included under the heading of corruption. When we say that a movement is "corrupt" we mean merely that most members of the movement are motivated by conventional personal goals such as money, status, or a career rather than by commitment to the putative ideals of the movement. Probably the majority of scientists today are not consciously dishonest, but that doesn't mean that their motives for doing scientific work are idealistic.

25. Freedman, p. 82. See also Kelly & Wearne, p. 13, and especially Lam, p. 19.

26. *Time,* July 17, 2006, p. 11.

27. *The Economist,* Sept. 10, 2011, pp. 91–92.

28. Elliot, p. 26. See also Lam, p. 19.

29. Freedman, p. 78.

30. Ibid., p. 80.

31. Ibid.

32. Ibid., p. 85.

33. Risen & Wingfield, pp. A1, A17.

34. NEB (2003), Vol. 28, "Technology, The History of," p. 471.

35. Ibid., Vol. 2, "Braun, Wernher von," p. 485.

36. Rothfels, p. 43, writes: "It can be argued that the believers in technology and the highly specialized experts [who worked for the Nazi regime] took upon themselves an exceptional responsibility through their so to speak 'abstract' dedication to maximum performance, a dedication that pretended to have no connection with the purpose that was being served." But this doesn't need to be argued—it's obvious!

37.   For a relevant personal experience of the author, see Appendix Eight.

38.   Some scientists do impose a token limitation on their research, as by refusing to participate in weapons development. This does not demonstrate serious thought on the part of the scientists, for weapons represent only the most crudely obvious of the negative applications of science; civilian applications are in the long run far more important in determining the future of our society. Moreover, a scientist's refusal to work directly on weapons may do little to mitigate the effect on weapons development of his research. For example, even if a researcher in aerodynamics works only in connection with the design of civilian aircraft, there is nothing to prevent the information he provides from subsequently being applied to military aircraft as well.

39.   NEB (2003), Vol. 8, "Nobel, Alfred Bernhard," p. 738.

40.   Smith & Weiner, pp. 303, 310.

41.   Kaczynski, *Anti-Tech Revolution*, Chapt. One, Part I, discussion of "Atoms for Peace."

42.   London, as referenced in our List of Works Cited.

43.   Gelernter, *Mirror Worlds*, pp. 213–225.

44.   Gelernter, "Technology Crisis."

45.   Markoff, "Scientists Worry Machines May Outsmart Man."

46.   I've been told that in recent years some scientists' organizations or their public-relations firms have been developing quite sophisticated arguments that are intended to justify the role of science in society. A study of the science establishment's propaganda, especially of sophisticated propaganda directed at intelligent audiences, would be highly desirable and important, but would be beyond my own capacity under existing circumstances. In any case, however sophisticated the propagandists' arguments may be, everything relevant that I've seen in the media up to the present (2016) seems to indicate that most scientists' thinking about the social and moral implications of their work is still at a superficial, or even a juvenile level. Of course, there are exceptions, as we've noted.

47.   Example: Apple co-founder Steve Wozniak thinks that "robots taking over would be good for the human race," because they'll be "smarter than us" and will make us like "the family pet and taken care of all the time." See S. Gibbs, as referenced in our List of Works Cited.

APPENDIX ONE:
ON LEARNED HELPLESSNESS

Appendix One:
On Learned Helplessness

At the outset of my letter of October 12, 2004 to Dr. Skrbina, I made several statements based on my memory of the 1975 edition of Martin E.P. Seligman's book *Helplessness* (see our List of Works Cited). I subsequently had an opportunity to reread Seligman's book in its 1992 edition, which appears to be identical with the 1975 edition in the pages numbered with Arabic numerals, and I found that my statements about experiments with pigeons and rats were incorrect. See Seligman, pages 35, 169 (but see also pages 58–59). I found that my other statements were adequately justified by what Seligman had actually written. See Seligman, pages 21–25, 31–34, 36, 46–47, 54–60, 65, 74, 88, 92–93, 104–06, 137, 148, 155–57, 192–93 (note 29 to Chapter Three), 198 (note 41 to Chapter Five).

The 1992 edition of Seligman's book contains an introduction that did not appear in the 1975 edition, and on several points I have to disagree with the new introduction. One of these points is worth discussing here.

Seligman makes clear (e.g., on pages 99, 137) that a person acquires resistance to depression through the experience of exercising control. In his 1992 introduction, page xx, Seligman writes: "The development of technology, mass production, and mass distribution has enabled large numbers of people to have a significant measure of choice, and therefore of personal control, over their lives." Thus it might appear that, in line with Seligman's theory, modern people ought to be highly resistant to depression. Yet, as Seligman writes on page xxxiii of his 1992 introduction: "We have experienced a tenfold increase in depression in the last two generations... ." Seligman tries to explain this primarily in terms of something he calls "meaning," or "attachment to something larger than you are" (page xxxiii). This explanation is wildly speculative, and I find it implausible. An easier and more plausible explanation can be derived from two points that are implicit in Seligman's 1975 theory without being explicitly stated there.

First, the utility of the experience of exercising control depends upon the importance to the organism of the events controlled. Control in unimportant matters does little to build the organism's resistance to depression. This is suggested by what Seligman wrote on pages 61–62 of

293

his book. Modern technology tends to give the individual control only in relatively unimportant matters, while the life-and-death issues for the most part are kept under the control of large organizations. See ISAIF, ¶¶ 67, 72, 94, and Part II.A of my October 12, 2004 letter to Dr. Skrbina.

Second, in order to be effective in building resistance to depression, the exercise of control must require a serious effort. See Seligman, pages 158–59. Much of modern technology serves to minimize the effort that we have to make in order to accomplish things, and this drastically reduces the benefit that we get from the experience of exercising control even in life-and-death matters. We no longer have to grow our own food or forage for it, we just buy it in the supermarket; when threatened by physical danger we merely dial 911; to make provision for ourselves in case we get sick, all we have to do is keep up with our insurance payments and the system takes care of the rest.

These are the reasons why the kind of control that the technological system gives us is of little use in building our resistance to depression; and notice that this explanation is practically identical to that provided by the concept of the power process as expounded in ISAIF.

I need to add that in his later work Seligman seems to have become a kind of happiness guru, as shown in such books as *Learned Optimism, Authentic Happiness*, and *Flourish: A Visionary New Understanding of Happiness and Well-Being*. But we can appreciate Seligman's early work on learned helplessness even if we don't respect his subsequent efforts.

APPENDIX TWO:
HUMAN WILL VERSUS THE "OBJECTIVE" FORCES OF HISTORY

Appendix Two:
Human Will Versus the "Objective" Forces of History

Following the first paragraph of Part III.C of my October 12, 2004 letter to Dr. Skrbina I should have pointed out that if human will can be a factor in natural selection as it acts on human societies, it is also true that human will is itself acted upon by natural selection, not only by natural selection among individuals, but also by natural selection among societies. Human beings' personalities and value-systems, and therefore the kinds of choices and decisions they make (their "will"), are to an important extent influenced by the social environment (including, but by no means limited to, systems of propaganda) in which they grow up. If a society provides a social environment that influences people to make choices and decisions conducive to the survival and propagation of the society, then that society will be favored by natural selection. Hence, such societies will tend to replace other societies. So human will is not a purely external factor that acts upon the process of natural selection among societies; it is itself to a great extent a product of that process. Viewed in this way, the evolution of societies looks more deterministic. But social environments mold human beings' wills only in a *statistical* sense; there are always individual exceptions. And under certain circumstances the decisions of individuals or small groups can have an important and long-lasting effect on the course of history.[1] See the hypothetical example of the Bering Strait in Part III.A of my October 12, 2004 letter to Dr. Skrbina. For a real-life example, the Reformation could not have occurred without the social conditions that made a religious revolution possible, but the social conditions by themselves were not sufficient; a Luther was needed to strike the spark that ignited the revolutionary process. "The phenomenon that became the Protestant Reformation is unthinkable without the sense of mission and compelling personality of Martin Luther."[2] It might be objected that if Martin Luther had never lived, some other Luther would have arisen sooner or later to strike the spark. But in Luther's time European society was already approaching the threshold of a gradual process of secularization.[3] Once the process of secularization had proceeded far enough, religious passions would no longer have been sufficiently strong for the

Reformation as we know it to have been possible. If Martin Luther had never lived, it is not certain that another Luther would have arisen *in time* to produce the Reformation.

For a further example, take Hitler and World War II. It may have been inevitable that Germany during the 1930s would fall under the control of a nationalistic dictator of fascist type, but World War II would not have been inevitable if the dictator had been anyone other than Hitler. Once he had erased the Treaty of Versailles, annexed Austria and other German-speaking areas, and occupied Bohemia, Moravia, and Slovakia, Hitler's prestige and his power were immense; he was sure to be set down in history as a "great man." A "normal" fascist dictator would have stopped at that point. Mussolini may be taken to represent the "normal" fascist dictator, and he was clearly worried about the consequences of Hitler's overweening and reckless ambition, for he wrote to the Führer on January 3, 1940 urging him to be satisfied with what he had already achieved, and to create a sovereign and independent Poland in order to deprive the Western democracies of any justification for war.[4] If Hitler had been a "normal" fascist he would have taken Mussolini's advice, or rather, he would not have invaded Poland in the first place. World War II occurred only as a result of Hitler's willingness to take extreme risks for the sake of grandiose rewards.

It is impossible to say with any confidence what the long-term consequences for human history would have been if World War II had not occurred, but some of the short-term consequences are obvious enough: The prestige of fascism would have remained high; most of Central Europe would have been governed by fascists; fascist movements throughout the world would have grown stronger; and democracy would have been seriously weakened.

Moreover, there is general agreement that it was World War II that lifted the United States out of the Great Depression.[5] War in the Pacific against Japan might well have sufficed, but it is unlikely that Japan would have dared to undertake a war against the Western powers if France and the Netherlands had not been crushed by the Germans, and if Britain had not been preoccupied with the war in Europe.[6] Without American involvement in a war, the Depression would have continued—for how long, and with what consequences, can only be a matter for conjecture.

NOTES

1. "[I]ndividual causes can produce general results, especially in revolutions." Simón Bolívar, "Contestación de un Americano Meridional a un caballero de esta isla," letter dated at Kingston, Jamaica, Sept. 6, 1815; in Soriano, p. 82.

2. NEB (2010), Vol. 20, "Germany," p. 87. Max Weber would have agreed, for he clearly implied that "the Reformation [would have been] inconceivable without Luther's entirely personal religious development." Weber, pp. 79–80. See also Note 124 to Extracts from Letters to David Skrbina, and Hoffer, § 90: "Once the stage is set, the presence of an outstanding leader is indispensable. Without him there will be no movement. The ripeness of the times does not automatically produce a mass movement... ."

3. The heliocentric theory of Copernicus (1473–1543) doubtless had something to do with the process of secularization, and the discoveries of European explorers, begun in the 15th century by the Portuguese and the Spanish, probably played a significant role in initiating the process. See Bury, pp. 40–45. A definite foretaste of the secularization process can be detected in the work of Francis Bacon (1561–1626). Ibid., pp. 58–59. On the spread of rationalism during the 17th century, see ibid., pp. 127–28.

4. Kosthorst, p. 122.

5. E.g., Rostow, pp. 77–79; NEB (2003), Vol. 29, "United States of America," p. 257.

6. Ibid., "World Wars," pp. 1000–01.

APPENDIX THREE:
WHY DEMOCRACY IS THE
DOMINANT POLITICAL FORM
OF THE MODERN WORLD

Appendix Three:
Why Democracy is the Dominant Political Form of the Modern World

The argument about democracy set forth in my letters to David Skrbina of October 12, 2004 (Part II.D) and November 23, 2004 (Part IV.A) is incomplete and insufficiently clear, so I'd like to supplement that argument here.

The most important point I wanted to make was that democracy became the dominant political form of the modern world not as the result of a decision by human beings to adopt a freer or a more humane form of government, but because of an "objective" fact, namely, the fact that in modern times democracy has been associated with the highest level of economic and technological success.

To summarize the argument of my letters to Dr. Skrbina, democratic forms of government (i.e., representative democracy) have been tried at many times and places at least since the days of ancient Athens, yet democracy did not thrive sufficiently to displace authoritarian systems, which remained the dominant political forms through the 17th century. But from the advent of the Industrial Revolution the (relatively) democratic countries, above all the English-speaking ones, were also the most successful countries economically and technologically. Because they were economically and technologically successful, they were also successful militarily. The economic, technological, and military superiority of the democracies enabled them to spread democracy forcibly at the expense of authoritarian systems. In addition, many nations voluntarily attempted to adopt democratic institutions because they believed that those institutions were the source of the economic and technological success of the democracies.

As part of my argument I maintained that the two great military contests between the democracies and the authoritarian regimes—World Wars I and II—were decided in favor of the democracies because of the democracies' economic and technological vigor. The astute reader, however, may object that the democracies could have won World Wars I and II simply by virtue of their great preponderance in resources and in numbers of soldiers, with or without any superiority in economic and technological vigor.

My answer is that the democracies' preponderance in resources and numbers of soldiers was only one more expression of their economic and technological vigor. The democracies had vast manpower, territory, industrial capacity, and sources of raw materials at their disposal because they—especially the British—had built great colonial empires and had spread their language, culture, and technology, as well as their economic and political systems, over a large part of the world. The industrial capacity of the English-speaking peoples moreover made it possible for them to build powerful navies. Consequently they had, generally speaking, command of the sea, which enabled them to assist one another in war by transporting troops and supplies to wherever they might be needed.

Whether or not Germany's industrial capacity was inferior to that of Britain at the start of WWI,[1] it certainly was vastly inferior to the combined industrial capacity of Britain and the United States. In any case, the Germans were never able to build a navy capable of facing that of Britain on equal terms, and British naval superiority in WWI was of critical importance. "[T]he outcome of [WWI]… hinged upon control of the sea by the battleship. Had superiority in battleships passed to Germany, Britain would have been lost…."[2] The British naval blockade of Germany was so effective that it prevented almost all trade from reaching German ports,[3] with the result that by the end of the war the Germans were on the verge of starvation.[4] Moreover, command of the sea by the British made it possible for American troops to be brought to Europe in 1918, and it was the arrival of the Americans that broke the stalemate on the western front and led to the Allied victory.[5] Clearly, therefore, the decisive factor in WWI was a preponderance in resources that had arisen from the superior economic and technological vigor of the English-speaking peoples—comprising Britain together with the English-speaking parts of its colonial empire and its former colonies in North America.

Authoritarian systems either had failed to build colonial empires of comparable size, as in the case of Germany[6] and Japan, or else they had indeed built huge empires but had left them relatively backward and undeveloped, as in the case of Spain, Portugal, and Russia. It was during the 18th century, as the Industrial Revolution was gathering force, that authoritarian France lost out to semi-democratic Britain in the struggle for colonization of North America and India. France did not achieve stable democracy until 1871, when it was already too late to catch up with the British. Germany as a whole was politically fragmented until

1871, but the most important state in Germany—authoritarian Prussia—was already a great power by 1740[7] and had access to the sea,[8] yet failed to build an overseas empire. Even after the unification of their country in 1871 the Germans' efforts at colonization were half-hearted at best,[9] and when they at last embarked in 1897 on a serious program of empire-building it was too late, for the economically valuable lands had already been taken by other powers.[10]

Like the English-speaking peoples, the Spanish- and Portuguese-speaking peoples colonized vast territories and populated them thickly, but the manpower of their territories could not have been used effectively in a European war, because these peoples lacked the economic, technical, and organizational resources to assemble, train, and equip large armies, transport them to Europe, and keep them supplied with munitions while they were there. Moreover, they lacked the necessary command of the sea. The Russians did not need command of the sea in order to transport their men to a European battlefield, but in WWI the Russians proved themselves to be militarily ineffectual.[11] In WWII on the other hand the Russians—or strictly speaking the Soviets—played a vitally important role. The Allies won WWII "by the mobilization of superior resources, ruthlessly and often wastefully employed against militarily more skillful foes,"[12] and those superior resources included Soviet manpower: The numerically vast Soviet armies did by far the greatest part of the fighting against the German Wehrmacht. But it's unlikely that Soviet manpower alone could have prevailed against Germany. German military efficiency was so far beyond that of the Soviets that the Germans suffered only 3½ million military deaths in WWII—*including* deaths suffered in fighting the Western Allies—as against somewhere between 6 and 20 million military deaths for the Soviet Union.[13] Undoubtedly the kill ratio in favor of the Germans would have been far higher if the Soviets had not received help from the West on a massive scale—help that was made possible only by the overwhelming economic and technological power of the English-speaking peoples. This help had three components: (i) Enormous quantities of military hardware and other products of Western industry were shipped to the Soviet Union.[14] (ii) Important resources that the Germans could otherwise have applied on the eastern front were used instead against the West.[15] (iii) Command of the sea by the Western democracies prevented the importation to Germany of resources from overseas.[16] Even with the help they received from the West, the Soviets' victory may have been a near thing;

Ulam indicates that by the end of the war "the Soviet armies had bled and were almost as exhausted as the Wehrmacht."[17]

If we were to assume nevertheless that the Soviets could have defeated Germany without help from the West, that fact would be largely irrelevant for our purposes. Without major participation by the West, the outcome of a struggle between Hitler's Germany and Stalin's Russia would only have determined which of two totalitarian systems would become the world's dominant power. What mattered for the future of democracy was the fact that in WWII *the West* was victorious and demonstrated its overwhelming military superiority—superiority that depended on the democracies' economic and technological vigor.

In view of what I've said in this appendix and in my letters to Dr. Skrbina of October 12 and November 23, 2004, it seems beyond argument that democracy became the dominant political form of the modern world as a result of the democracies' outstanding economic and technological vigor. It may nevertheless be questioned whether democratic government was the *cause* of the economic and technological vigor of the democracies. In the foregoing discussion I've relied mainly on the example of the English-speaking peoples. In fact, France, following its democratization in 1871 and even before the devastation wrought by World War I, was *not* economically vigorous.[18] Was the economic and technological vigor of the English-speaking peoples perhaps the result, not of their democratic political systems, but of some other cultural trait?

For present purposes the answer to this question is not important. The objective fact is that since the advent of the Industrial Revolution democracy has been generally associated with economic and technological vigor. Whether this association has been merely a matter of chance, or whether there is a causative relation between democracy and economic and technological vigor, the fact remains that the association has existed. It is this objective fact, and not a human desire for a freer or a more humane society, that has made democracy the world's dominant political form.

It is true that some peoples have made a conscious decision to adopt democracy, but it can be shown that in modern times (at least since, say, 1800) such decisions have usually been based on a belief (correct or not) that democracy would help the peoples in question to achieve economic and technological success.[19] But even assuming that democracy had been chosen because of a belief that it would provide a freer or a more humane form of government, and even assuming that such a belief were correct, democracy could not have thriven under conditions of industrialization in competition with authoritarian systems if it had not equaled or surpassed the latter in economic and technological vigor.

Thus we are left with the inescapable conclusion that democracy became the dominant political form of the modern world not through human choice but because of an objective fact, namely, the association of democracy, since the beginning of the Industrial Revolution, with economic and technological success.

NOTES

1.   NEB (2003), Vol. 20, "Germany," p. 113 says: "By 1914 Germany was an industrial giant second only to the United States." But ibid., Vol. 29, "World Wars," p. 963, says: "Great Britain's industrial establishment was slightly superior to Germany's...," and Liddell Hart, p. 44, says: "In munitions and other war material Britain's industrial power was greatest of all... . Britain... was to prove that the strength of her banking system and the wealth distributed among a great commercial people furnished the 'sinews of war'... ."

2.   NEB (2003), Vol. 29, "War, Technology of," p. 597. See also ibid., "World Wars," p. 963; Liddell Hart, loc. cit. ("all... depended on the security of [Britain's] sea communications").

3.   NEB (2003), Vol. 29, "World Wars," p. 969.

4.   Ibid., pp. 963, 986. Ibid., "War, Theory and Conduct of," p. 652. Ibid., Vol. 20, "Germany," p. 116. Ibid., Vol. 21, "International Relations," p. 814. *World Book Encyclopedia* (2011), Vol. 21, "World War I," p. 460.

5.   NEB (2003), Vol. 21, "International Relations," p. 814. Ibid., Vol. 29, "United States of America," p. 253. Ibid., "World Wars," p. 977. Manchester, p. 339. Parker, pp. 307–08. Patterson, p. 121. *World Book Encyclopedia* (2011), Vol. 21, "World War I," pp. 462–63.

6.   At the end of the 19th century the German colonial empire was about two-thirds the size of the French in geographical extent, but its population amounted to only a fraction of that of the French empire, which in turn had only a fraction of the number of inhabitants of the British empire. See Zimmermann, p. 113 and the map between pp. 254 & 255. Moreover, the German colonies were economically a liability rather than an asset. NEB (2003), Vol. 20, "Germany," p. 117.

7.   Ibid., p. 96. But further on in the same article the *Britannica* implies that Prussia might not have become a great power until 1763. Ibid., p. 98.

8.   To this writer the reason why Prussia did not build an overseas empire

remains obscure; clarification awaits further research. For now let the following suffice: Prussia's access was to the Baltic rather than directly to the Atlantic. The extra distance to be sailed would have mattered little during the 18th century, when round-the-world voyages were nothing very extraordinary; still less would it have mattered during the 19th century when, with sailing ships of advanced design and later steamships, voyages to all parts of the world were routine. Nor would the shallowness of the Baltic along the Prussian coast have mattered much. The Dutch built ships designed for use in shallow waters, and with such ships they created their far-flung empire. The Prussians could have done likewise. A more serious problem was the fact that the narrow strait connecting the Baltic to the North Sea could be controlled by rival powers that were capable of barring Prussia's access to the Atlantic. So why couldn't Prussia itself have controlled the strait? The reason may have been a decision by Prussian kings to use their resources to make Prussia into a land power rather than a naval one. Such a decision by Louis XIV was possibly the reason why Britain, and not France, became the world's dominant naval and colonial power. Here the crucial factor may have been that, in Prussia and France, power was concentrated in royal hands, whereas, in Britain and the Netherlands, power was shared by the commercial classes. However, my present (tentative) opinion is that even if Prussia had had free access to the Atlantic and a government that left the way to power open to the commercial classes, the Prussians would not have competed successfully with the British, the Dutch, or even the French, because Prussia lacked the economic dynamism that in the far northwestern corner of Europe can be traced all the way back to 600 AD. I suggest, tentatively, that at that time—long before the advent of the "Protestant ethic" or of worldwide colonization—the northwestern corner of Europe was already predestined to the Industrial Revolution. How the economic development of those countries was related to the development of (semi-) democratic government remains open to discussion. Because this note is informal and tentative, I omit citation of my sources. But see Lebecq; Mahan, pp. 55, 58, 98, 102, 107.

9.   Zimmermann, p. 28. NEB (2003), Vol. 20, "Germany," p. 114 ("Apart from a few colonial additions in the mid-1880s, Germany... acted as a satiated power.").

10.   Ibid., p. 115.

11.   E.g., Ulam, pp. 127–29. The Russians may nevertheless have played an important role in the Allied victory, because their invasion of East Prussia forced the Germans to send troops from the western front to the eastern and thus helped the French and the British to win the crucial First Battle of the Marne. NEB (2003), Vol. 29, "World Wars," pp. 965–67.

12.   Ibid., "War, Theory and Conduct of," p. 654. Astor, p. 975. Wheeler, p. 129 (citing Creveld: U.S. Army's style of fighting in WWII was based on superior economic and technological resources). Production by U.S. industry in WWII

dwarfed that of every other nation. E.g.: NEB (2003), Vol. 21, "International Relations," pp. 848–49, 853. Jenkins, p. 678. Parker, pp. 341, 415. Keegan, p. 219. The Battle of Britain may have been won not by superior performance of Britain's aviators, but by the fact that Britain was producing fighter aircraft at twice the rate of Germany. Jenkins, pp. 632–33. Gilbert, *European Powers*, p. 260. For Western Allies' superiority in cryptology and radar see, e.g., Dunnigan & Nofi, pp. 303, 315, 385; Parker, pp. 329–330; NEB (2003), Vol. 16, "Cryptology," pp. 869, 871. Even where the Western Allies were initially at a technological disadvantage, they had the resources to develop needed technology quickly and surpass their adversaries. E.g., at the outset of the war in the Pacific the Japanese Zero fighter was superior to anything the U.S. could put in the air, but by the end of the war the U.S. was producing fighter aircraft that easily outclassed the Zero. Dunnigan & Nofi, e.g., p. 35.

13. NEB (2003), Vol. 29, "World Wars," p. 1023, Table 7, notes ** and +. See also ibid., p. 1004, Ulam, p. 556 (up to Nov. 6, 1941, Soviet armies suffered more than four times as many casualties as Germans). According to Helmuth James von Moltke, at about the beginning of Sept. 1941, ten Russians were being killed or wounded for every four Germans. A. Read & D. Fisher, p. 88. Once Austria and other territories had been annexed, Germany had a population of 80 or 90 million. Rothfels, p. 156, quoting Churchill (80 million). Kosthorst, p. 122, quoting Mussolini (90 million). The population of the Soviet Union was about 170 million. Ulam, p. 460. In view of the kill ratio in favor of the Germans, the Soviets' roughly two-to-one advantage in manpower wouldn't have amounted to much if the Western Allies had been out of the picture.

14. Keegan, p. 215 ("[N]either the British nor the Soviet economy could have borne the strains of war without external assistance. That outside help came from the United States."), 218. NEB (2003), Vol. 29, "World Wars," pp. 997, 999, 1012, 1019. Dunnigan & Nofi, pp. 2, 276, 516. Ulam, p. 581. Scott, p. 56. Dunaway, p. 52. Tim Wright, pp. 59–64. "Post-war Soviet propaganda claims Lend-Lease aircraft [from the U.S.] did not play a significant role in the Soviet defeat of Germany because they represented only 13 percent of the aircraft the Soviets fielded." Ibid., p. 65. However, that argument overlooks the fact that the Germans' best opportunity to defeat the Soviet Union was during the early stages of the war, before the Soviet factories east of the Urals could be brought fully into production. According to Field Marshal Montgomery, "White Russia" (Belarus) and Ukraine had contained "about 60 per cent of the Russian [i.e., Soviet] industrial potential," Law, p. 455, and within six months of the German attack on June 22, 1941, all but a small part of this area—by November 1942 virtually all of it—was under control of the fascists, NEB (2003), Vol. 29, "World Wars," p. 991 (map) & p. 1011 (map). During these early stages, aid from the U.S. surely was necessary to prevent a German victory. See Ulam, pp. 561, 562. It should also

be noted that for the first couple of years of the war, Soviet production of fighter aircraft was carried out according to American designs and with tooling provided by the U.S. NEB (2003), Vol. 21, "Industries, Manufacturing," p. 538.

15.   Prior to the Western Allies' cross-channel invasion of the European continent that began in June 1944 the Germans had to fight the Allies in North Africa and Italy, and this may have been the reason for the German defeat at the great Battle of Kursk in July 1943. Ulam, p. 585. A. Read & D. Fisher, pp. 121–22, claim that Kursk, rather than Stalingrad, was the turning-point on the eastern front. In addition, a part of Germany's industrial capacity was diverted to the production of submarines for use against the West. But most importantly, the Western Allies' strategic-bombing campaign deprived Germany of air superiority on the eastern front because the Germans were forced to withdraw many of their aircraft from the east and use them instead for the defense of their cities. NEB (2003), Vol. 20, "Germany," p. 124. Dunnigan & Nofi, p. 634. "Air superiority was crucial to the outcome of most of the decisive campaigns of WWII... ." NEB (2003), Vol. 29, "War, Technology of," p. 612.

16.   Parker, p. 323. See also Ulam, p. 517. Most importantly, the Allied blockade prevented Germany from importing oil from overseas. The Germans' difficult position in regard to oil and their consequent desire to capture the Soviet oil-fields in the Caucasus may have prevented them from striking a "killer blow" at Moscow during the summer of 1941, *World Book Encyclopedia* (2011), Vol. 21, "World War II," p. 477; NEB (2003), Vol. 29, "World Wars," p. 999, and it certainly motivated their drive toward the Caucasus in 1942, ibid., p. 1004; Parker, pp. 323–24, 338. This drive led to the disastrous German defeat at Stalingrad, ibid., p. 338, which was probably the turning-point of the war on the eastern front. The Germans were mistaken in believing that they could not continue the war without the oil of the Caucasus, NEB (2003), loc. cit., but they would not have made that mistake if the Allied blockade had not prevented them from importing oil from overseas.

17.   Ulam, p. 604. Wehrmacht = the German armed forces.

18.   NEB (2003), Vol. 19, "France," p. 521.

19.   See Appendix Six.

APPENDIX FOUR:
SARMIENTO AND THE GAUCHOS

Appendix Four:
Sarmiento and the Gauchos

When I quoted Domingo Faustino Sarmiento on the subject of the gauchos in Part III.D of my letter of November 23, 2004 to Dr. Skrbina, I had read only a brief excerpt from Sarmiento's *Civilización y Barbarie*. I've now had an opportunity to read the whole book, which is of considerable interest and therefore perhaps worth the comments offered in this appendix.

Though "gaucho" is commonly translated into English as "an Argentine cowboy," the term was often applied much more broadly; anyone belonging to the rural society and culture of the livestock-raising regions of Argentina or Uruguay could be called a "gaucho," or "gaucha" if female, regardless of whether he or she ever participated personally in herding livestock.[1] It is in this sense that I use the term here.

In my letter to Dr. Skrbina I stated that "Sarmiento was not romanticizing the gaucho," but the editor, Roberto Yahni, of the edition of *Civilización y Barbarie* that I've used, connects Sarmiento with the "romantic esthetic."[2] If exaggeration and the presentation of exceptional cases as if they were typical can be called "romantic," then Sarmiento was indeed guilty of romanticization, as shown by a set of notes[3] that Valentín Alsina sent to Sarmiento following the initial publication of *Civilización y Barbarie* in 1845. In the 1851 edition of his book, Sarmiento acknowledged the justice of Alsina's criticisms.[4] It's obvious, too, that Sarmiento reported many alleged occurrences merely on the basis of hearsay. On the other hand, much of what he said about the gaucho way of life presumably was based on direct observation, for he had evidently had a good deal of personal experience among the gauchos.[5] It should be noted, however, that Sarmiento never claimed that his picture of gaucho life was fully valid after 1810, the year in which the Argentine war of independence began. Since that time, said Sarmiento, some of the distinguishing features of the rural society that he described had been modified or were slowly changing.[6]

The Argentine historian Carlos A. Mayo has carried out a sober study, based on documentary evidence, of gaucho life in the province of Buenos Aires from 1740 to 1820.[7] Is Sarmiento's account consistent with Mayo's conclusions? As noted above, Sarmiento often portrays exceptional cases as if they were typical, but if these portrayals are taken merely as vignettes descriptive of particular times and places rather than as general descriptions of gaucho life, then Sarmiento's work does not appear to be seriously inconsistent with Mayo's as far as facts are concerned,[8] though, as one would expect, Mayo's book lacks the dramatic quality of Sarmiento's.

But what about the statement that I quoted in my letter of November 23, 2004, to Dr. Skrbina? The gaucho, wrote Sarmiento, is "strong, haughty, energetic... he is happy in the midst of his poverty and his privations... ."[9] How accurate was this statement?

Sarmiento portrays the gaucho male as indolent, as hardly working at all, while the burden of providing the necessities of life fell almost entirely on the women,[10] and it's hard to reconcile this with his description of the (male) gaucho as "strong and energetic." Sarmiento's picture of the idle gaucho no doubt was accurate at some times and places, for most gauchos didn't care to work for an employer when they didn't have to[11]— some probably never worked for an employer at all[12]—and they commonly spent a good deal of time drinking and gambling.[13] But at other times they did work, and work hard, and their work often required them to be decidedly strong and energetic, as well as skillful.[14] It's possible that, in the typical case, the gaucho did not have a superabundance of leisure time, if one counts as "work" not only work done for an employer but all activities—legal or not—that were undertaken to procure the necessities of life; for many gauchos supported themselves at times by stealing livestock,[15] or else by growing crops or raising livestock on their own.[16]

Were the gauchos "haughty"? In this context, "arrogant" might have been a better translation of the Spanish *altivo*. In Mayo's account the gauchos certainly seem to have been arrogant. They were "indomitable;" they had a "stern and vindictive look;" they "knew neither fear nor submission;" they were "insolent and jealous of their autonomy;" they were "not accustomed to obey or to accept dependence."[17] On the other hand, their arrogance may have evaporated when they were brought before a judge to answer for their alleged or (more likely) their real crimes.[18]

But was the gaucho "happy in the midst of his poverty and his privations"? "Happiness" is such a vague concept that it is virtually impossible to deal with it objectively. It would be better to speak in terms of relatively definite factors such as the presence or absence of anxiety, stress, depression, or dissatisfaction. Mayo gives us no direct evidence as to anxiety, stress, or depression. What we can say objectively is that most gauchos were not seriously dissatisfied with their "poverty" and their "privations," since they made little effort to remedy these even when they could easily have done so. This is shown by the fact that there was no strong correlation between economic means and what is commonly called "material standard of living," for even relatively wealthy gauchos tended to accept and live with the same "privations" as poor ones did.[19] When, during the second half of the 19th century, those who had the means began to spend heavily on material goods, it's likely that they were seeking primarily social status rather than physical comfort or security.[20]

Beyond this, all we have is Sarmiento's personal impression that the gaucho was "happy" with his "poverty" and his "privations." This impression can't be attributed to any sort of idealization of the gaucho, for Sarmiento's hostility to gaucho values and his passionate commitment to economic and technological progress are evident throughout his book.

And there the matter rests. But let's close with a brief description, by several Argentine scholars, of the "inorganic democracy" of the gauchos:

> The human type that constituted the popular Creole strata [meaning mainly the gauchos] did not correspond with the image of the man subject to authority of the traditional kind, though in most aspects of his life he was the bearer of traditional cultural norms. Due to the peculiarities of his manner of living, he was instead an anarchic individualist, attached to his personal independence and prepared to acknowledge the authority only of those who possessed to an outstanding degree the qualities that he most esteemed; for example, personal skill and courage. The autocratic authority of the *caudillos* [rough, irregular military leaders, largely independent of any civil authority] was not based on any *traditional legitimacy*, but on its acceptance by these groups that saw in the *caudillos* their own image and the exaltation of their own values. This was called *inorganic democracy* (J.L. Romero), and the term is probably acceptable, *provided it is recognized that along with these traits all the other elements of the traditional man survived: social and ecological isolation, ethnocentrism, religiosity* (not exactly the sophisticated religion of the cities, however), *resistance to change, predominance of custom and of 'prescriptive action,' subsistence economy and the corresponding attitudes in regard to work and economic activity.*[21]

NOTES

1.   For example, this is how the Uruguayan writer Javier de Viana used "gaucho" in his stories, and Sarmiento's application of the word seems consistent with this usage. The historian John Lynch writes: "By simple definition the gaucho was a free man on horseback. But the term was used by contemporaries and by later historians to mean rural people in general." John Lynch, Chapt. 3, section "Gauchos and Peons," p. 40. Mayo, pp. 151–54&n13, discusses the vague and variable meanings of "gaucho" and is not himself consistent in applying the term, ibid., e.g., pp. 110–11, 162, 182, 203, 228. For instance, on p. 135 Mayo refers to slaves as "black gauchos," but on p. 209 he seems to distinguish slaves from gauchos. I see no point in concerning myself with these questionable distinctions, so I use "gaucho" in its most general sense. But wealthy absentee ranch-owners who lived in the city much of the time do not qualify as gauchos.

2.   Sarmiento, pp. 13, 15–16.

3.   See ibid., Nota 2, pp. 380–83; Nota 35, pp. 423–24.

4.   Ibid., pp. 184–86, editor's footnote d.

5.   Sarmiento had often watched the moon rise over the Pampas, ibid., p. 61. About 1826, Sarmiento spent a year in the Sierra de San Luis, where he taught several adults from high-status (*pudientes*) gaucho families to read, ibid., p. 70n*. In 1838, Sarmiento was staying at an isolated ranch (*estancia*) in the same Sierra, ibid., pp. 70–71. And Sarmiento reported personal observation of a gaucho's tracking skills, ibid., pp. 82–83.

6.   Ibid., p. 104.

7.   Mayo, *Estancia y Sociedad*, as in our List of Works Cited.

8.   This is all the more true when one takes into account the fact that Mayo's study is mostly confined to the province of Buenos Aires, whereas Sarmiento was born in San Juan province (Sarmiento, p. 22), therefore more than 250 miles from the nearest point of Buenos Aires province; and Sarmiento had had considerable experience in the Sierra de San Luis (ibid., pp. 70–71&n*), nearly 200 miles from the nearest point of Buenos Aires province. Nothing that Sarmiento may have observed well outside Buenos Aires province can be called inconsistent with Mayo's study, because Mayo's study is not applicable to such observations.

9.   Sarmiento, p. 74.

10.   Ibid., pp. 71–72, 74. The gaucha (gaucho woman) did indeed do a great deal of productive work, Mayo, pp. 165–178, but perhaps did not, in the typical case, work as hard as one might infer from Sarmiento's account, for Mayo, p. 178, says that a contemporary description of the rural woman as "inactive and indolent" was "only partly true."

11.   Mayo, passim, e.g., pp. 105–08, 138, 156–57, 204, 222. Duart, p. 37n53.

12. It was possible for gauchos to spend much (if not all) of their time as "vagabonds," Mayo, pp. 151–163, because there was "direct access to the basic means of subsistence" (such as meat), Brittez, pp. 198–99; Mayo, pp. 36, 104, 138, 234. Stray (Mayo, e.g., pp. 113–14) or stolen (see note 15, below) livestock were a source not only of meat but of money or trade goods. And many gauchos had small or medium-sized ranches or farms of their own, e.g., Mayo, pp. 56, 214; Cabrejas, p. 45, hence would not necessarily have had to work for an employer, though the smallest ranchers or farmers might have found it necessary to supplement their income with some wage-labor, Mayo, p. 111.

13. Mayo, e.g., pp. 115, 124, 152, 156, 157, 160, 193.

14. Ibid., pp. 124–26, 200–02, 204.

15. Ibid., e.g., pp. 73, 157–160.

16. Ibid., pp. 73–86, 157.

17. Ibid., pp. 117, 131, 193, 200, 203, 210. Duart, p. 37n53.

18. Mayo, pp. 157–160.

19. Ibid., pp. 41–43. Cabrejas, pp. 46–47, 54, 59–61, 69. Correa & Wibaux, pp. 80–81. Brittez, pp. 186–87. Mayo, "Conclusiones," in Mayo, *Vivir en la frontera*, pp. 161–62. John Lynch, Chapt. 3, section "The Social Divide," p. 38 ("indifferent to material comforts"). Here our concern is mainly with the late colonial period up to 1810; as noted in the third paragraph of this appendix, Sarmiento never claimed that his portrayal of gaucho life was fully valid after 1810. Nevertheless, there were exceptions even before 1810. E.g., Cabrejas, p. 56.

20. Brittez, p. 199 ("Social actors consciously used material goods to construct and show status..."). Even before 1850, when money was spent for anything beyond minimal physical necessities, it seems that the motive often was status rather than physical comfort or security. E.g., Correa & Wibaux, pp. 80–81 (golden buttons), 82; Brittez, p. 187 (silver horse-trappings); Mayo, "Conclusiones," in Mayo, *Vivir en la frontera*, pp. 162–63 (silver spurs).

21. Tella, Germani, Graciarena, et al., pp. 212–13.

APPENDIX FIVE:
DISPOSAL OF RADIOACTIVE WASTE

Appendix Five:
Disposal of Radioactive Waste

In Part I.A.12 of my letter to Dr. Skrbina dated March 17, 2005, I expressed the opinion, based on "the demonstrated unreliability of *untested* technological solutions," that the nuclear-waste disposal site at Yucca Mountain, Nevada likely would prove to be a failure. It may be of interest to trace the subsequent history of the Yucca Mountain site as reported in the media.

On March 18, 2005, *The Denver Post*, page 4A, carried an Associated Press report by Erica Werner according to which then-recent studies had found that water seepage through the Yucca Mountain site was faster than what earlier studies had reported. The more-rapid movement of water implied a greater risk of escape of radioactive materials from the site, and there were reasons to suspect that the earlier studies had been intentionally falsified.

The Week, January 26, 2007, page 21, reported a new study: "Special new containers designed to hold nuclear waste for tens of thousands of years may begin to fall apart in just 210 years," the study found. "Researchers... had pinned their hopes on zircon, a material they thought was stable enough to store the waste...." The scientists had based this belief on computer simulations, but they were "startled" when they discovered how alpha radiation affected the "zircon" in reality.

Zircon is a gemstone. The substance referred to in the article presumably is a ceramic called transformation-toughened zirconia. See NEB (2003), Vol. 21, "Industrial Ceramics," pages 262–63.

On September 25, 2007, *The Denver Post*, page 2A, reported: "Engineers moved some planned structures at the Yucca Mountain nuclear waste dump after rock samples indicated a fault line unexpectedly ran beneath their original location...."

On March 6, 2009, *The Denver Post*, page 14A, carried an Associated Press report by H. Josef Hebert according to which the U.S. Government had abandoned the plan to store reactor waste at Yucca Mountain. This after having spent 13.5 billion dollars on the project.

On July 15, 2011, *USA Today*, page 4A, carried an Associated Press report to the effect that the U.S. House of Representatives had appropriated funds for further consideration of the plan to store nuclear waste at the Yucca Mountain site.

As of April 2016 I've made no systematic effort to follow these developments further, but if any major, definitive action had been taken for the permanent disposal of radioactive waste it probably would have been well publicized, and we would know about it. Various alternatives have been proposed (see Wald in our List of Works Cited), but whatever solution—if any—is eventually adopted, its execution inevitably will be characterized by negligence, incompetence, and dishonesty. See, e.g., *The Economist*, March 19, 2011, page 40; Eisler, page 2A. More likely, no definitive action will *ever* be taken for the permanent disposal of radioactive waste in the U.S. The problem will be allowed to drag on indefinitely, and meanwhile new nuclear power-plants will continue to be built, the festering pools of deadly stuff will grow and grow…

APPENDIX SIX:
NATIONS THAT MADE A CONSCIOUS
DECISION TO ADOPT DEMOCRATIC
GOVERNMENT USUALLY DID SO BECAUSE
THEY BELIEVED THAT DEMOCRACY WOULD
HELP THEM TO ACHIEVE ECONOMIC
AND TECHNOLOGICAL SUCCESS

Appendix Six:
Nations That Made a Conscious Decision to Adopt Democratic Government Usually Did So Because They Believed That Democracy Would Help Them to Achieve Economic and Technological Success

The proposition that forms the title of this appendix is somewhat of an oversimplification. In any case, it is not our intention to provide a fully developed argument in favor of the proposition; we merely offer some evidence that we hope will persuade the reader to take the proposition seriously and to doubt the widely held assumption that peoples have adopted democratic governments primarily because they believed that such governments were more humane or would give them greater freedom than authoritarian systems did. Because of the need for brevity, we paint with a broad brush; for the most part we omit reservations, qualifications, and discussion of exceptions to our general statements. Our purpose is merely to outline the overall trend.

Here we do not speak of democracy in the broadest sense of the word, but only of representative democracy as that expression is commonly used in reference to a certain type of political system that exists in the modern world. Nor are we concerned with Britain, or with other countries such as the Netherlands, Switzerland, or Sweden, in which democracy was largely an indigenous development and the outcome of long-term historical processes. Instead, we are interested in those countries that made a conscious decision to adopt—or attempt to adopt—democratic political systems after that form of government had shown outstanding success in Britain and in Britain's offspring, the United States.

The ideology of modern democracy grew out of English political tradition combined with 18th-century Enlightenment thought. Enlightenment thinkers were not at first inclined toward democracy. Rather, they were concerned with progress—fundamentally with economic and technological progress, which they assumed would lead to intellectual and cultural progress—and they believed that progress could best be promoted by benevolent, absolute monarchs. The Enlightenment turned to democracy only because efforts at reform proved futile under absolute monarchies, and because progress was seen to be most rapid under the semi-democratic regimes of Britain and the United States.[1]

One should not be misled by the fact that many of the reformers and revolutionaries continually prated about "liberty" and "equality." To see what motivated them one has to look at their programs of action and understand what kind of liberty and equality they were really seeking. It's true that in many cases the common people—meaning primarily the people who worked with their hands—supported democratic revolutions, and did so because they aspired to liberty and equality for themselves.[2] But it was not the common people who created the ideology of democracy or who led the democratic reform movements and revolutions. Leadership was mostly in the hands of the bourgeoisie—a term that we use here to include not only well-to-do businessmen, but all those sectors of the population who worked with their heads rather than their hands and in large part shared the values and aspirations of the propertied classes; for example, lawyers, physicians, journalists, professors and other intellectuals, even those among them who were relatively impoverished. It was the bourgeoisie who created democratic ideology and determined the form of the democratic govern-ments, and they did so in the interests of their own class.[3] Certainly many of the reformers and revolutionaries were sincere idealists who aimed to benefit the whole society, not only the bourgeoisie, but their concept of what constituted "benefit" was shaped by their bourgeois worldview.

The creed of the Argentine politician Domingo Faustino Sarmiento can be taken to exemplify the ideology of democracy as it emerged in the late 18th and early 19th centuries from the conflicting currents of the Enlightenment. Sarmiento identified "civilization," urban life, bour-geois values (even bourgeois fashions of dress), social order, the rule of law, "liberty," and economic and technological progress as aspects of a single, unified phenomenon,[4] which we nowadays would call "modernization." It's clear that economic and technological progress (and therefore *power*[5]) played a central and indispensable role in Sarmiento's vision. His "liberty" comprised the basic elements of what we call "democracy," for "liberty" was to include a representative assembly,[6] balance of powers,[7] freedom of religion,[8] freedom of the press[9] and freedom of thought generally,[10] equality before the law,[11] and codified individual rights or "guarantees."[12] Among these guarantees he included security of *property*,[13] which, with material progress, was and is one of the two dominant values of the propertied classes.[14] Sarmiento's "liberty" was not the freedom just to do whatever one pleased; rather, it was the ordered and limited liberty to which the bourgeoisie aspired, for he distinguished "liberty" from "license"[15] and disdained the lawless freedom that characterized the "barbarism" of the Argentine gaucho of his day.[16]

It is evident that Sarmiento's "liberty" was not an end in itself, but a means to the creation of a certain kind of society, a modernizing society committed to "progress"—economic and technological progress in particular. This was characteristic of the late, democratic phase of the Enlightenment and of the following decades: Liberty was primarily a tool for achieving progress.[17] Bolívar made this explicit when he wrote, "No liberty is legitimate, except when aimed at the honour of mankind and the improvement of his lot."[18]

This same conception of democracy as a means to the achievement of economic and technological progress has persisted in democratizing movements throughout the world right down to the present. During the 19th century, according to Henry Adams, the system of government by the bourgeoisie "had proved so successful that even Germany wanted to try it, and Italy yearned for it. England's middle-class government was the ideal of human progress."[19] In Germany:

> The agents of [the] introduction of technology were the middle class[,] whose minds were filled with the liberalism that had erupted in the French Revolution... .
>
> ... A prerequisite of industrial activity for the benefit of the State was that the industrialist should have a larger share than hitherto in the destinies of the State. So industrial development and constitutional aspirations were closely linked. And the same was true of the mass of the people. Here also the co-operation of the people could be demanded only if they also were given a voice, self-respect and self-government.[20]

The other side of the coin is shown by the fact that when Bismarck demonstrated that industrialization and progress could be achieved with only very limited elements of democracy under an essentially monarchical system, the bourgeoisie by and large was satisfied and willing to put aside its liberal aspirations.[21] In Russia the businessmen never aspired to democracy in the first place, because under the tsarist autocracy they had everything they needed for their purposes; though on the other hand many Russian lawyers, physicians, professors, etc. were deeply dissatisfied.[22]

In the years following the Meiji Restoration of 1868 in Japan:

> It was believed that the West depended on constitutionalism for national unity, on industrialization for material strength... .
>
> ... True national unity required the propagation of new loyalties among the general populace and the transformation of powerless and inarticulate peasants into citizens of a centralized state... .
>
> ... Village leaders... wanted a more participatory system that could reflect their emerging bourgeois interests. ... Itagaki expanded his movement for 'freedom and popular rights'... . In 1881 he organized the Liberal Party... whose members were largely wealthy farmers... .
>
> ... Okuma organized the Progressive Party... in 1882 to further his British-based constitutional ideals, which attracted considerable support among urban business and journalistic communities.
>
> ...
>
> In [Bismarck's] Germany [Ito] found an appropriate balance of imperial power and constitutional forms that seemed to offer modernity without sacrificing effective control. ...[23]

It appears, therefore, that the Japanese democratization movement did not seek freedom for its own sake, but for the sake of modernity, national unity, and the furtherance of bourgeois interests.

Similar values appeared among political reformers and revolutionaries in China. During the earlier 20th century, reform-minded Chinese political thinkers didn't necessarily favor full democracy as we understand the term. To the extent that they did advocate steps in the direction of democracy, they did so for the sake of modernization and national power.[24] Later in the 20th century, in a secret journal that he kept, former Communist Party chief Zhao Ziyang concluded that "China must become a parliamentary democracy... . Zhao's ultimate aim was a strong economy, but he had become convinced that this goal was inextricably linked to the development of democracy."[25]Again the other side of the coin: When China showed that, apparently, it could achieve vigorous economic growth without democracy, most Chinese were satisfied with that. As long as they had progress they didn't need "liberty."[26]

In the mid-twentieth century: "The new nations [that emerged from the dissolution of the British and French colonial empires] almost invariably adopted constitutions and established parliamentary governments, believing that these institutions would lead to the same freedom and prosperity that had been achieved in Europe."[27] Needléss to say, the "freedom… achieved in Europe" was the ordered and limited freedom of the bourgeoisie, and it's safe to assume that this freedom would not have been sought if it hadn't been associated with prosperity.

The assumption that democracy is a prerequisite for progress and prosperity has had a checkered history. The assumption has been strong whenever the democracies have been demonstrating superior economic success, but has been abandoned by many people when the democratic nations have fallen into severe economic difficulties (as during the Great Depression of the 1930s[28]), or when authoritarian systems have seemed to offer a prospect of more vigorous development—as we've seen above and in Part III.D of the letter of October 12, 2004 to Dr. Skrbina. Since the collapse of the authoritarian socialist bloc of Eastern Europe the assumption that democracy represents the road to prosperity, though by no means universal, seems to have been generally dominant.[29] It's true that some people are now (2015–17) reviving doubts about that assumption, but instead of questioning the value of prosperity they question the value of democracy.[30]

So as not to oversimplify any more than necessary, let's note the following points:

1. When they have lived for a time under a dictatorship that has made extensive use of brutal methods to suppress resistance—for example, causing opponents of the regime to "disappear"—people may indeed turn to democracy because it represents a more humane alternative. But it would be hard to prove that democracy is more humane than authoritarian regimes *in general*. The benign dictatorship of Getúlio Vargas in Brazil (1930–1945) was probably more humane than a typical democracy of that period; the common people greatly appreciated what Vargas did for them.[31] In Slovakia, the end of communist rule and its replacement with democracy led to an increase in the crime rate and the rate of drug abuse.[32] Many inhabitants of eastern Germany have felt that life was better there under the communist government.[33]

2. In *some* cases people may have adopted or attempted to adopt democratic government because they have desired political freedom for its own sake. For example, political freedom per se seems to have been the main goal of many of the leading reformers who tried to liberalize the government of Czechoslovakia in 1968. But even in the Czech case the aspiration for political liberalization was inextricably entangled with a desire for economic betterment.[34]

It's worth noting, on the other hand, that Costa Ricans are proud of their democracy—the only democracy in Latin America that has demonstrated long-term stability—and they would probably retain their democratic government even if they believed that doing so would cost them something in terms of prosperity.[35]

3. It should also be recognized that political liberalization sometimes has had nothing to do with any sort of idealistic intention to benefit a whole society, whether through economic progress or otherwise, but has been motivated only by self-interest in the narrowest sense. This was the case in Brazil in 1889 when the *fazendeiros* (landowners) and the provincial oligarchies, assisted by the military, replaced the monarchy with a republic. These groups acted only in order to maintain their own power, which was threatened by the policies of the monarchy.[36]

From Cecil B. Currey's account, it seems that Benjamin Franklin had no other motive for helping to foment the American Revolution than resentment of the British government's obstruction of his schemes for enriching himself through land speculation. In fact, the schemes in which he was involved were so sordid that one is tempted to call him an out-and-out scoundrel. This may shock many people, but Currey's work appears to be based on solid documentary evidence.[37] It should be noted that Washington too was heavily involved in land speculation,[38] and so was Jefferson,[39] the most idealistic of the principal revolutionary leaders.

*   *   *

From our argument that, in most cases, people aspire to democracy (i.e., "liberty") only when it seems conducive to economic and technological progress, some readers might draw the inference that people are not interested in freedom. But such an inference would not be correct. The correct inference is that, for most people, democracy per se does not represent freedom.

By and large, people are interested only in their *own* freedom. Undoubtedly a great many people are generous enough to want freedom for everyone, but the *kind* of freedom they want for everyone typically is the kind of freedom that is most important to themselves. Those for whom freedom is most closely linked with democracy are the intellectuals: The tools of the intellectual's trade are words and ideas, therefore intellectuals commonly are strong proponents of freedom of thought, freedom of speech, freedom of the press.[40] But intellectuals generally have scant sympathy for other freedoms, e.g., economic freedom or the freedom to own weapons, when these freedoms seem to threaten the physically and economically secure environment in which intellectuals can best practice their trade. The businessman's trade is the production and accumulation of wealth, so businessmen emphasize economic freedom, property rights, and an environment conducive to the creation of wealth. But when they find that they can have these without democracy they often are willing, as we noted above, to forgo the political freedoms.

For the common people—the working class—democracy in the modern sense does not represent freedom at all. With or without democracy they remain subject to the domination of the decision-making classes. If they "believe in" democracy they do so only because they've been taught to believe in it, and they often have only a very imperfect understanding of what democracy really is.

In today's society the common people, generally speaking, seem to have lost any conception of freedom beyond the kind that comes with days off from work. But where the common people have gone feral—where they have found that they can provide for their own physical needs without subordinating themselves to any large-scale, organized society—the kind of freedom that they value has nothing to do with the ordered liberty of the bourgeoisie. Rather, it is the "inorganic democracy" described in Appendix Four, above. Not being intellectuals, feral humans have little interest in ideological freedom; they tend instead to remain attached to traditional ideologies,[41] though they may modify these to suit their own needs. In other respects the freedom that feral humans prefer is anarchy— not the gentle and more-or-less orderly anarchy of anarchist philosophers, but simple lawlessness. Sarmiento pointed out that real primitives or barbarians had a higher degree of social order than the feral and lawless gauchos of his country.[42] Colombia and Venezuela had an equivalent to the gauchos in their *llaneros*, "wild, half-naked cowboys of the hot plains," who showed the same inclination to lawlessness as the gauchos did,[43] an inclination likewise in evidence on much of the North American frontier.[44]

As for progress and prosperity as these are understood in modern society, most feral humans care nothing for them.[45] Horace Kephart described the attitude of the Appalachian mountaineer as he existed at the beginning of the 20th century:

[T]hese silly, stuck-up strangers who brag and brag about 'modern improvements'—what are they, under their fine manners and fine clothes? Hirelings all. Shrewdly he observes them in their relations to each other—

'Each man is some man's servant; every soul
Is by some other's presence quite discrowned.'

Proudly he contrasts his ragged self: he who never has acknowledged a superior.... . And he turns upon his heel.[46]

Because they care nothing for "prosperity" in the modern sense, feral humans are "shiftless"—they work only as much as is necessary to satisfy their basic physical needs and then they take it easy.[47] Work as a moral imperative, independent of any real need for the results of the work, is a bourgeois value, alien to feral humans.

It should now be clear that the ordered liberty of bourgeois democracy by no means represents the only possible conception of freedom. It only remains to point out that if humans were allowed to remain in a feral state long enough, they would probably develop—eventually—a degree of social order similar to that of real primitives, and this presumably would moderate their brutality.

*   *   *

In view of recent (as of December 2016) political developments, this writer would like to make clear that nothing he has written should be interpreted as an expression of contempt for democracy. The unqualified identification of "democracy" with "freedom" is naïve to say the least, but of all forms of government of major nations existing in the world today, it is liberal democracy that allows the freest circulation of ideas and therefore provides the most favorable environment for the development of an anti-tech movement.

NOTES

1.   For this whole paragraph see: Bury, passim, e.g., pp. 60, 113, 127–28, 134 (failure of reform under absolute monarchy), 135, 139, 169, 173–74, 176, 182, 205–06, 212, 217, 248, 324–25. Dorpalen, p. 193 (Marxist view). Haraszti, passim, e.g., pp. 28, 45, 140–41, 187, 214, 239, 307–08n49. Priore & Venâncio, Chapt. XIV, pp. 179–181. Randall, pp. 201, 203–04, 206, 417, 431–32, 486–87, 592. Smelser, pp. 331–32. Whitaker, the entire book, but especially the final essay by Charles C. Griffin, pp. 119–143. NEB (2003), Vol. 2, "Bolívar, Simón," p. 339 (well versed in Enlightenment thought); Vol. 3, "Condorcet, Marie-Jean-Antoine-Nicolas de Caritat, marquis de," p. 523; Vol. 11, "Staël, Germaine de," p. 198; Vol. 12, "Turgot, Anne-Robert-Jacques," p. 54; Vol. 20, "Germany," p. 100; Vol. 25, "Political Parties and Interest Groups," p. 980; Vol. 26, "Rousseau," pp. 939–940; Vol. 27, "Socio-Economic Doctrines and Reform Movements," pp. 423–25; Vol. 29, "Voltaire," pp. 524, 527 ("growth of material prosperity").

2.   E.g., Priore & Venâncio, Chapt. XIV, pp. 185–86; Kee, pp. 41–73.

3.   A reading of the history of any of the great democratic revolutions, the English (1642–1649 & 1688), the American, the French, or the European of 1848, will show that few of their leaders were of working-class origin, and most of those who were aristocrats were influenced by bourgeois values. Also see, e.g.: NEB (2003), Vol. 25, "Political Parties and Interest Groups," p. 980 ("liberal ideology reflected the interests of the bourgeoisie…"); Vol. 20, "Germany," pp. 105–06. Dorpalen, p. 193 (Marxist view). Elias, pp. 274–76. Haraszti, pp. 32–33, 109. Humphreys & Lynch, pp. 19, 24.

4.   Sarmiento, pp. 44, 58–68, 71, 75, 105, 108, 110, 175–180, 190, 194, 206, 210, 218–222, 248, 252, 275–76, 281–82, 298, 337, 342–48, 352–53, 363–372. Bourgeois fashions: e.g., pp. 194, 338–39.

5.   Ibid., pp. 58, 59.

6.   Ibid., p. 366. The expression that Sarmiento actually uses is "formas representativas," but it's clear that some type of representative assembly is meant; see, e.g., pp. 324–25 ("Sala de Representantes").

7.   Ibid., p. 175.

8.   Ibid., pp. 177–78, 199, 363.

9.   Ibid., p. 46.

10.   Ibid., pp. 44, 194, 252, 345, 366.

11.   Ibid., pp. 120, 222, 345.

12.   Ibid., pp. 179, 298, 337, 345, 366, 367. "Seguridad individual": pp. 342, 353.

13.   Ibid., pp. 175, 366, 367.

14.   Compare *Constitution of the United States*, Amendment V: "No person shall… be deprived of… property, without due process of law; nor shall

private property be taken for public use, without just compensation." The Fifth Amendment also contains other "guarantees" for individuals. Amendment XIV, Section 1, extends these guarantees and, in addition, prescribes equality before the law. Amendment I guarantees freedom of religion and of the press; hence, by implication, freedom of thought. The U.S. Constitution and Sarmiento's creed are two manifestations of the same ideological current.

15. Sarmiento, p. 221. See also pp. 222 (civil order), 368 (rejecting "pretensiones exageradas de libertad").

16. Freedom of gaucho: ibid., pp. 95, 104. Lawlessness of gaucho: passim; e.g., pp. 62, 68, 95, 98–100, 104, 110. Barbarism of gaucho: passim; e.g., pp. 64, 68, 70, 104, 110–111.

17. The reader who has consulted the sources cited in Note 1 will probably have concluded already that liberty was regarded primarily as a tool for achieving progress. See in particular: NEB (2003), Vol. 22, "Latin America," p. 815 ("Many... identified political institutions as sources of... economic progress..."); Vol. 27, "Socio-Economic Doctrines and Reform Movements," pp. 423–25. Bury, p. 182. Haraszti, pp. 307–08n49. Randall, pp. 203–05, 417, 431–32, 592. Humphreys & Lynch, the entire book, especially pp. 91, 276, 300. Whitaker, the entire book, especially pp. 20, 55, 56, 59, 64–67, 109–115, 119–143. See also Note 110 to Letters to Skrbina.

18. Simón Bolívar, Letter to William White, quoted by Trend, p. 114.

19. Adams, p. 33.

20. Klemm, p. 269.

21. NEB (2003), Vol. 20, "Germany," pp. 105–112. Also, during the 1920s and 1930s, important capitalists supported Hitler financially because they thought that doing so would be advantageous for business purposes. Gilbert, *European Powers*, pp. 185–86.

22. NEB (2003), Vol. 26, "Russia," p. 989.

23. Ibid., Vol. 22, "Japan," pp. 298–99. "Despite its antidemocratic features the constitution [of 1889] provided a much greater arena for dissent and debate than had previously existed. The [popularly elected] lower house could initiate legislation." Ibid., p. 299.

24. Ebrey, pp. 262–66. See also ISAIF, ¶ 97.

25. Ignatius, p. 29.

26. Bremmer, p. 11A. *The Economist*, Feb. 19, 2011, p. 46. Osnos, p. 29, col. 1; p. 30, col. 2.

27. NEB (2003), Vol. 27, "Socio-Economic Doctrines and Reform Movements," p. 426. Of course, most of these parliamentary governments either did not long survive, or else turned into mere parodies of democratic government.

28. See Kaczynski, *Anti-Tech Revolution*, Chapt. One, Part V, second paragraph.

29. See letter of Oct. 12, 2004 to Dr. Skrbina, Part III.D. In an article published in 2000, Condoleezza Rice (later U.S. Secretary of State) exhibited her conviction that it was not possible in the long run to "decouple democracy and economic progress." Freeland, p. 83.

30. Ibid., p. 86. Thrall, p. 7A. Rauch, pp. 62–63. Democracy is also being questioned on other than economic grounds. Thrall, loc. cit. Rauch, loc. cit. Beinart, pp. 15–16. Susan Page, pp. 1A–2A.

31. Priore & Venâncio, Chapt. XXVIII, pp. 325–27, 329, 331, 334.

32. *World Book Encyclopedia* (2011), Vol. 17, "Slovakia," p. 508c.

33. Kirchner, p. 11.

34. Navrátil et al., pp. 2, 3, 83, 84, 92–94. Fawn, pp. 18–20. NEB (2003), Vol. 27, "Socio-Economic Doctrines and Reform Movements," p. 407.

35. Arias Sánchez (the entire work). NEB (2003), Vol. 1, "Arias Sánchez, Oscar," p. 550; Vol. 15, "Central America," pp. 671–75.

36. Priore & Venâncio, Chapt. XXII, pp. 264–272. But compare NEB (2003), Vol. 15, "Brazil," p. 204.

37. Currey, the entire work, but especially pp. 209–219, 283–86, 304, 311, 324.

38. Currey, pp. 129, 258. Randall, pp. 99, 186, 228–29.

39. Randall, pp. 111, 228. See also p. 289.

40. This requires an important qualification. Intellectuals are strong proponents of the principle of freedom of expression as long as they feel that the principle is necessary for the protection of *their own* right to express themselves. But when a faction among the intellectuals finds itself strong enough to impose its will, it may suppress the expression of opinions that conflict with its own ideology. This is what happened during the Middle Ages when the intellectuals of that era imposed religious orthodoxy and persecuted heretics. It's what has been happening in recent decades with the imposition of political correctness in many of our universities and elsewhere in our society. Some intellectuals are just as greedy for power as politicians and capitalists are. Compare Beinart, p. 15, col. 3; p. 16, col. 1.

41. See Sarmiento, pp. 70–71; Mayo, pp. 63, 176; Cabrejas, pp. 58–59; Tella, Germani, Graciarena et al., pp. 212–13; Kephart, p. 455. Dick, p. 184 ("The people were fixed in their ideas of worship, anxious that the program be carried out in the old way…"); but see pp. 181–82 (widespread lack of interest in religion) and p. 335 ("Old customs and forms rested lightly on the pioneer").

42. Lawlessness of gauchos: See Note 16, above, and Duart, p. 37n53; Cabrejas, p. 63; Mayo, e.g., pp. 95–96, 103, 117, 124, 144, 157–160, 171, 185, 187, 198, 201, 203–04. It seems that even relatively wealthy ranch-owners of both sexes shared the tendency to lawlessness, Mayo, pp. 172–73. The available evidence suggests that in the 1740s most gauchos of the "lower" class were

of Indian ancestry, but by the early 19th century most were of predominantly (though not necessarily pure) European ancestry. Mayo, pp. 117–120, 153, 236. Since the term "feral," as used here, means "having reverted from a domesticated to a wild state," and since Indians are thought of as having been "wild" to begin with, it may be questioned whether Indian gauchos can properly be called "feral." But this application of "feral" can be defended on the ground that, as Sarmiento, pp. 67–69, remarked, real primitives or barbarians, including the Indians of the Pampas, had a higher degree of social order than the gauchos did, hence were to some extent "domesticated;" and this is supported by Correa & Wibaux, pp. 81–82.

43.   Trend, pp. 71–72, 83–84.

44.   "[T]he backwoods [North American] people of the eighteenth century did not greet the coming of law and order with joy." Alden, p. 259. Kephart, passim, especially Chapts. VI, VIII, XVIII, and pp. 152, 156, 213, 230–31, 249, 266–67, 375, 387. C. Evans, Chapt. 4. Dick, e.g., pp. 30–31, 140–41, 155–56, 225–235, 257, 321–23, 336, 338.

45.   See Note 19 to Appendix Four and: Tella, Germani, Graciarena, et al., loc. cit. ("resistance to change"). Sarmiento, pp. 73–74. Kephart: attachment to traditional ways, pp. 16, 445, 455; disinterest in "prosperity," pp. 328 ("scorn of luxury"), 379–381. Dick, pp. 112, 328, 336, reports disdain for luxury and even for comfort.

46.   Kephart, p. 455.

47.   N. American frontier: Dick, pp. 24, 25, 330–31. Appalachian mountaineers: Kephart, pp. 36–39, 43, 289, 304, 445–47. Kephart probably misses the mark when he attributes the mountaineers' traits to their Celtic heritage or to the peculiarities of their mountain environment. The traits that interest us here were mostly shared by other feral peoples such as the gauchos or the frontiersmen of the N. American flatlands, whose ethnic origins and physical environment were very different from those of the mountaineers. As for the gauchos, see Note 11 to Appendix Four. Sarmiento, pp. 64, 75, 95, repeatedly refers to the gauchos' shiftlessness (*incuria*), which on p. 64 he contemptuously contrasts with the industrious habits of the Scottish and German immigrants who had settled to the south of Buenos Aires. Here it is well to distinguish feral humans from boosters. The latter move into frontier districts—usually after ferals have paved the way—with an eye to profiting financially from undeveloped resources and raising their status in bourgeois society. The boosters of course are quite pleased with the arrival of law and order and other appurtenances of civilization.

APPENDIX SEVEN:
LOYALTY TO THE SYSTEM VERSUS LOYALTY TO TRADITIONAL SOCIAL GROUPS: SOME EXAMPLES RELEVANT TO PARAGRAPHS 51 & 52 OF ISAIF

Appendix Seven:
Loyalty to the System Versus Loyalty to Traditional Social Groups: Some Examples Relevant to Paragraphs 51 & 52 of ISAIF

A group of Argentine scholars, in discussing the obstacles that had hindered modernization and economic development in Argentina and in Latin America generally, included among those obstacles a "localist spirit," prevailing in rural Argentina during the early 19th century, that was "identified with the most restricted little community and incapable of extending its loyalty to the great national community in the modern sense... ;" as well as the fact that in 20th-century Latin America "personal ties and local factors" carried far more weight than political ideologies.[1] They also indicated the problems resulting from the fact that loyalties within certain dominant groups of families were stronger than any loyalty to political principles or to the country as a whole.[2]

Empire-builders such as the Assyrians and the Incas, and totalitarians like Stalin, have taken calculated measures to break down the solidarity of ethnic groups through mass deportations[3] or by other means.[4] Capitalists have intentionally intermingled different ethnic groups for the purpose of breaking down working-class solidarity.[5] In the West since WWII the "integration" of ethnic minorities, initially undertaken for humanitarian reasons, is one of the means by which democratic systems have wittingly or unwittingly acted against ethnic solidarity. Totalitarian systems use crude methods to break down the internal loyalty of such groups as families and labor unions and transform them into tools for securing the individual's loyalty to the system as a whole.[6] Modern democratic systems use subtler means, perhaps not calculatedly, to the same end.

In ancient Athens, "Solon's social legislation seems [to have been] generally designed to reduce the primacy of the family and increase that of the community, or polis. To that extent it can be regarded as embryonically democratic."[7] The medieval Catholic Church took measures that broke down extended families and kin groups, thus increasing the authority of the Church—though it's not clear to what extent this was done calculatedly. The result in any case was that in northwestern Europe family loyalty beyond the nuclear family was greatly weakened well before the onset of the Industrial Revolution.[8] On the other hand, in China until quite recent times, loyalty to the family was far stronger than any loyalty to the country as a whole,[9] and this may have been one of the reasons why northwestern Europe underwent an Industrial Revolution while China did not, even though China was ahead of Europe in technology at least until the end of the Middle Ages. Some of the early-20th-century Chinese thinkers who were concerned with the modernization of China recognized the necessity, for their purposes, of breaking down traditional social groups such as the family.[10] Compare Rostow's view that, in order for an economic "take-off" (i.e., an industrial revolution[11]) to occur, people "must come to be valued... not for their connexion with clan or class, or, even, their guild; but for their individual ability to perform certain specific, increasingly specialized functions."[12]

NOTES

1. Tella, Germani, Graciarena et al., pp. 212–13, 265.

2. Ibid., p. 266n15. This note is quoted in Kaczynski, *Anti-Tech Revolution*, Chapt. Three, Part III, in the discussion of Rule (ii).

3. Assyrians: NEB (2003), Vol. 23, "Mesopotamia, History of Ancient," pp. 879, 884. Incas: Ibid., Vol. 26, "Pre-Columbian Civilizations," p. 39. Stalin regime: Ulam, pp. 574n55, 595.

4. Stalin regime: Ulam, pp. 220–21, 649–650.

5. Patterson, pp. 27–28.

6. E.g., Ulam, pp. 315, 345; Fischer, pp. 226, 228–29.

7. NEB (2003), Vol. 20, "Greek and Roman Civilizations," p. 229.

8. Ibid., Vol. 19, "Family and Kinship," p. 61.

9. Hoffer, § 31, citing Hubbard, p. 170. See also Ebrey, p. 59.

10. Tan, pp. 125, 297.

11. See Rostow, p. 57 ("The take-off is defined as an industrial revolution...").

12. Ibid., p. 19. See also p. 140 ("oriented... to standards of efficient performance, rather than to graft and to ties of family, clan, or region").

APPENDIX EIGHT:
IN SUPPORT OF THE LETTER TO DR. P.B.

Appendix Eight:
In Support of the Letter to Dr. P.B.

In my experience during eleven years as a student and teacher of mathematics, professors and students talked about what was going on in various fields of mathematics, about who was doing what kind of research, and about the actions and personalities of particular mathematicians, but I never heard professors or students say anything about whatever benefits their work might bring to the human race—except on one single occasion:

During my second year at Berkeley, I notified the mathematics department that I planned to resign at the end of the academic year. Some time thereafter I received a phone call from Professor X, a big wheel in the department, who said that he and another big wheel, Professor Y, wanted to talk with me and ask me to reconsider my decision to resign. Eventually I met with X and Y in the latter's office. I had been looking forward to the meeting because I expected it would give me an opportunity to air my feelings about the pointlessness of mathematical research. In response to my effort to explain those feelings, Professor Y tried to justify mathematical research by asserting that it helped "the starving children in Asia." This was a catch-phrase commonly heard at the time (circa 1969): Americans were supposed to feel sorry for "the starving children in Asia," and our country was supposed to do something to help them.

I told Professor Y that I didn't believe my research was doing anything for the starving children in Asia. He seemed taken aback. "You mean," he replied, "you don't think your work helps the starving children in Asia!?"

My work was in an area of pure mathematics that had no foreseeable or probable connection with practical applications of any kind. Y's field was symbolic logic. If a man were genuinely interested in helping "the starving children in Asia" he would go into agricultural research, or economics, or the sociology of "underdeveloped" countries, or another field that had some known relationship to the plight of starving children. He wouldn't choose symbolic logic or pure mathematics on the wildly speculative assumption that his work might one day find an application that in some way would help starving children. Y's parroting of the hackneyed formula "help the starving children in Asia" was clear proof that he

343

had never given any serious thought to the question of how, if at all, mathematics-related research would benefit the human race. He had chosen symbolic logic simply because it served his personal needs. Then, when he was challenged (probably for the first time in his life) to explain why mathematics-related work was of value, he could think of nothing better than the platitude about "starving children in Asia."

Professor X was a vastly better mathematician than Professor Y and a far more intelligent man generally. Ignoring Y's remarks about the starving children in Asia, X told me that a couple of years earlier he might have felt the same way I did about the pointlessness of mathematical research, but, he added, "I don't feel that way now." He explained that his interest was held by the continuing discovery of new applications of his field, which was functional analysis. I think he meant applications to other parts of pure mathematics, but even if he was referring to technological applications he made no claim that his work was in any way beneficial to humanity.

My conversation with X and Y ended in an impasse. But it is interesting to note that on the only two later occasions on which I had contact with X, his behavior toward me was cold to the point of rudeness.

I wrote the foregoing account in 2009, forty years after the conversation here related, but in doing so I was not relying primarily on forty-year-old memories. I had written down the most important points in some autobiographical notes that I composed in 1979, ten years after the events.

List of Works Cited

Abel, Theodore, "The Pattern of a Successful Political Movement," *American Sociological Review*, Vol. 2, No. 3, June 1937, pp. 347–352.

Adams, Henry Brooks, *The Education of Henry Adams: An Autobiography*, Mariner Books, Houghton Mifflin Co., Boston, 2000.

Alden, John R., *George Washington: A Biography*, Louisiana State University Press, 1984.

Aleksiuk, Michael, *Power Therapy*, H&H Publishers, Seattle, 1996.

Alinsky, Saul D., *Rules for Radicals: A Pragmatic Primer for Realistic Radicals*, Vintage Books, Random House, New York, 1989.

Arias Sánchez, Oscar, *El Camino de la Paz*, Editorial Costa Rica, San José, Costa Rica, 1989.

Arrhenius, Svante, "On the Influence of Carbonic Acid in the Air upon the Temperature of the Ground," *London, Edinburgh, and Dublin Philosophical Magazine and Journal of Science* (Fifth Series), Vol. 41, No. 251, April 1896, pp. 237–276.

Astor, Gerald, *The Greatest War: Americans in Combat 1941–1945*, Presidio Press, Novato, California, 1999.

Austin, Mary, *The Land of Little Rain*, Dover Books, Mineola, New York, 1996.

Axtell, James, *The Invasion Within: The Contest of Cultures in Colonial North America*, Oxford University Press, New York, 1986.

Barca. See Calderón de la Barca.

Barja, César, *Libros y Autores Clásicos*, Vermont Printing Company, Brattleboro, Vermont, 1922.

Bebel, August, *Aus meinem Leben*, Vol. 1 (Erster Teil), Verlag J.H.W. Dietz Nachfolger, Stuttgart, 1910. The copy referenced here is a facsimile put out by the University of Michigan Library, 2019.

Beinart, Peter, "Trump's Intellectuals," *The Atlantic*, Sept. 2016.

Blau, Melinda, *Killer Bees*, Steck-Vaughn Publishers, Austin, Texas, 1992.

Bokota, Stanislaw, "PiS: Savior or Ruin of Poland?," *Polish American Journal*, April 2016.

Bolívar. See Soriano.

Bonvillain, Nancy, *Women and Men: Cultural Constructs of Gender*, Second Edition, Prentice Hall, Upper Saddle River, New Jersey, 1998.

Bremmer, Ian, "As free-market democracies flail, China is the rare 'success'," *USA Today*, May 26, 2010.

Bright, Verne, "The Folklore and History of the Oregon Fever," *Oregon Historical Quarterly*, Vol. 52, Dec. 1951, pp. 241ff.

Brittez, Fernando Rafael, "La comida y las cosas: una visión arqueológica de la campaña bonaerense de la segunda mitad del siglo XIX," in Mayo, *Vivir en la frontera*, pp. 169–199.

Burnet, Frank MacFarlane, *Dominant Mammal*, William Heinemann (Australia), Melbourne, 1970.

Bury, J.B., *The Idea of Progress: An Inquiry into its Origin and Growth*, Dover Publications, New York, 1955.

Butler, Samuel. See Jones.

Cabrejas, Laura Leonor, "Vida material en la frontera bonaerense (1736–1870)," in Mayo, *Vivir en la frontera*, pp. 41–70.

Calderón de la Barca, Pedro, *La Vida es Sueño*, Edilux Ediciones, Medellín, Colombia, 1989.

Camp, L. Sprague de, *The Ancient Engineers*, Ballantine Books, New York, 1974.

Campbell, Joseph, *The Power of Myth*, Anchor Books, Random House, New York, 1988.

Carcopino, Jerome, *Daily Life in Ancient Rome*, Yale University Press, New Haven, Connecticut, 1960.

Carlyle, Thomas, *The French Revolution*, J.M. Dent, London, 1944.

Carrillo, Santiago, *Eurocomunismo y Estado*, Editorial Crítica, Grupo Editorial Grijalbo, Barcelona, 1977.

Cashdan, Elizabeth, "Hunters and Gatherers: Economic Behavior in Bands," in Plattner, pp. 21–48.

Cervantes Saavedra, Miguel de, *Novelas Ejemplares I*, Jorge A. Mestas, Ediciones Escolares, Madrid, 2004.

Chang, Leslie T., "Gilded Age, Gilded Cage," *National Geographic*, May 2008.

Christman, Henry M. (ed.), *Essential Works of Lenin*, Bantam Books, New York, 1966.

Churchill, Winston, *My Early Life: A Roving Commission*, Thornton Butterworth, London, 1930.

Churchill, Winston, *A History of the English-Speaking Peoples*, Vol. Four, *The Great Democracies*, Bantam Books, New York, 1963.

Coon, Carleton S., *The Hunting Peoples*, Little, Brown and Co., Boston, 1971.

Correa, Carolina, and Matías Wibaux, "Sabores de la pampa: Dieta y hábitos de consumo en la frontera bonaerense," in Mayo, *Vivir en la frontera*, pp. 71–86.

Craig, Gordon A., "The End of the Golden Age," *New York Review*, Nov. 4, 1999.

Creveld, Martin van, *Fighting Power: German and U.S. Army Performance, 1939–1945*, Greenwood Press, 1982.

Currey, Cecil B., *Road to Revolution: Benjamin Franklin in England 1765–1775*, Anchor Books, Doubleday & Company, Garden City, New York, 1968.

Dalrymple, William, "India: The War Over History," *New York Review*, April 7, 2005.

Danner, Mark, "Torture and Truth," *New York Review*, June 10, 2004.

Darrach, Brad, "Meet Shaky, the first electronic person," *Life*, Nov. 20, 1970.

De Camp. See Camp, L. Sprague de.

De Cervantes. See Cervantes Saavedra.

De la Barca. See Calderón de la Barca.

De Poncins. See Poncins.

Debo, Angie, *Geronimo: The Man, His Time, His Place*, University of Oklahoma Press, Norman, Oklahoma, 1976.

Del Priore. See Priore.

Dennett, Daniel C., *Darwin's Dangerous Idea*, Simon & Schuster, New York, 1995.

Diamond, Jared, *Collapse: How Societies Choose to Fail or Succeed*, Penguin Books, New York, 2011.

Dick, Everett, *The Dixie Frontier: A Social History*, University of Oklahoma Press, Norman, Oklahoma, 1993.

Di Tella. See Tella, Torcuato S. di.

Dorpalen, Andreas, *German History in Marxist Perspective: The East German Approach*, Wayne State University Press, Detroit, 1988.

Drinnon, Richard K., *White Savage: The Case of John Dunn Hunter*, Schocken Books, New York, 1972.

Duart, Diana, "Cien años de vaivenes: La frontera bonaerense (1776–1870)," in Mayo, *Vivir en la frontera*, pp. 15–40.

Dunaway, James, "Just Shoot Me," *Air & Space*, Oct./Nov. 2010.

Dunnigan, James F., and Albert A. Nofi, *The Pacific War Encyclopedia*, Checkmark Books, an imprint of Facts on File, Inc., 1998.

Durant, Will, *The Story of Civilization*, Part 1, *Our Oriental Heritage*, Book Club Edition, Simon & Schuster, New York, 1954.

Dyson, Freeman, "The Bitter End," *New York Review*, April 28, 2005.

Ebrey, Patricia Buckley, *The Cambridge Illustrated History of China*, Paperback Edition, Cambridge University Press, Cambridge, U.K., ninth printing, 2007.

Ehrlich, Paul R. and Anne H., *The Population Bomb*, Ballantine Books, New York, 1968.

Einstein, Albert. See Schulmann et al.; Schilpp.

Eisler, Peter, "Energy official wants contractor relieved," *USA Today*, Aug. 29, 2012.

Elias, Norbert, *The Civilizing Process*, trans. by Edmund Jephcott, Revised Edition, Blackwell Publishing, Malden, Massachusetts, 2000.

Elliot, Carl, "The Ghostwriter: How to Spin Pharmaceutical Research," *The Atlantic*, Dec. 2010.

Ellul, Jacques, *The Technological Society*, trans. by John Wilkinson, Alfred A. Knopf, New York, 1964.

Ellul, Jacques, *Propaganda*, Alfred A. Knopf, New York, 1965.

Ellul, Jacques, *Anarchy and Christianity*, trans. by Geoffrey W. Bromiley, Wipf and Stock Publishers, Eugene, Oregon, 2011.

Ellul, Jacques, *Autopsy of Revolution*, Wipf and Stock Publishers, Eugene, Oregon, 2012.

Evans, Colin, *Great Feuds in History*, John Wiley & Sons, New York, 2001.

Evans, Richard J., *The Third Reich at War 1939–1945*, Allen Lane, an imprint of Penguin Books, London, 2008.

Fallows, James, "Survivor: China," *The Atlantic*, Nov. 2009.

Fawn, Rick, *The Czech Republic: A Nation of Velvet*, Harwood Academic Publishers, Gordon and Breach Publishing Group, Amsterdam, 2000.

Ferris, Warren Angus, *Life in the Rocky Mountains*, edited by Paul C. Phillips, published by F.A. Rosenstock, Old West Publishing Co., Denver, 1940.

Fischer, Markoosha, *My Lives in Russia*, First Edition, Harper & Brothers Publishers, New York, 1944.

Freedman, David, "Lies, Damned Lies, and Medical Science," *The Atlantic*, Nov. 2010.

Freeland, Chrystia, "Globalization Bites Back," *The Atlantic*, May 2015 (fold-out).

Freeman, Charles, *A New History of Early Christianity*, Paperback Edition, Yale University Press, New Haven, Connecticut, 2011.

García López, J., *Historia de la Literatura Española*, Quinta edición, Las Américas Publishing Co., New York, 1959.

Gasset. See Ortega y Gasset.

Geertz, Clifford, "Very Bad News," *New York Review*, March 24, 2005.

Gelernter, David, *Mirror Worlds*, Oxford University Press, New York, 1991.

Gelernter, David, "U.S. faces technology crisis," *The Missoulian* (newspaper of Missoula, Montana), Feb. 24, 1992.

Gershon, Elliot S., and Ronald O. Rieder, "Major Disorders of Mind and Brain," *Scientific American*, Sept. 1992.

Gibbs, Samuel, "Apple co-founder Steve Wozniak says humans will be robots' pets," https://www.theguardian.com/technology/2015/jun/25/apple-co-founder-steve-wozniak-says-humans-will-be-robots-pets, downloaded April 11, 2017.

Gibbs, W. Wayt, "Seeking the Criminal Element," *Scientific American*, March 1995.

Gilbert, Martin, *The European Powers, 1900–1945*, Phoenix Press, London, 2002.

Goodman, Paul, *Growing Up Absurd*, Random House, New York, 1960.

Graham, Hugh Davis, and Ted Robert Gurr (eds.), *Violence in America: Historical and Comparative Perspectives*, Bantam Books, New York, 1970.

Grandin, Temple, and Catherine Johnson, *Animals Make Us Human*, Houghton Mifflin, Boston, 2009.

Greaves, Mel, *Cancer: The Evolutionary Legacy*, Oxford University Press, 2000.

Gurven, Michael, and Hillard Kaplan, "Longevity Among Hunter-Gatherers," *Population and Development Review*, Vol. 33, No. 2, June 2007, pp. 321–365.

Haraszti, Zoltán, *John Adams & the Prophets of Progress*, The Universal Library, Grosset & Dunlap, New York, 1964.

Hart. See Liddell Hart.

Haviland, William A., *Cultural Anthropology*, Ninth Edition, Harcourt Brace & Company, San Diego, 1999.

Headland, Thomas N., "Revisionism in Ecological Anthropology," *Current Anthropology*, Vol. 38, No. 4, Aug.–Oct. 1997, pp. 605–09.

Hitchens, Christopher, "The Pity of War," *The Atlantic*, Nov. 2009.

Hoffer, Eric, *The True Believer*, Harper Perennial, Harper Collins, New York, 1989.

Hoffmann, Richard C., *Land, Liberties, and Lordship in a Late Medieval Countryside*, University of Pennsylvania Press, Philadelphia, 1989.

Hollander, Paul, *The Survival of the Adversary Culture*, Transaction Books, New Brunswick, New Jersey, 1988.

Hoyle, Fred, *Of Men and Galaxies*, University of Washington Press, Seattle, 1964.

Hubbard, Arthur J., *The Fate of Empires*, Longmans, Green & Company, New York, 1913.

Humphreys, R.A., and John Lynch (eds.), *The Origins of the Latin American Revolutions, 1808–1826*, First Edition, Alfred A. Knopf, New York, fourth printing, 1968.

Hunter, John D., *Manners and Customs of Several Indian Tribes Located West of the Mississippi*, Ross and Haines, Minneapolis, 1957.

Huxley, Aldous, *Brave New World*, First Perennial Classics Edition, Harper Collins, New York, 1998.

Ignatius, Adi, "Tiananmen Ghosts," *Time*, May 25, 2009.

Illich, Ivan, *Tools for Conviviality*, Harper & Row, New York, 1973.

Jenkins, Roy, *Churchill: A Biography*, Plume, a member of Penguin Putnam, Inc., New York, 2002.

Jones, Henry Festing (ed.), *The Notebooks of Samuel Butler*, The Hogarth Press, London, 1985.

Joy, Bill, "Why the Future Doesn't Need Us," *Wired*, April 2000.

Kaczynski, Theodore John, *Technological Slavery*, Feral House, Port Townsend, Washington, 2010.

Kaczynski, Theodore John, *Anti-Tech Revolution: Why and How*
European Edition: Soregra Editores, Queluz de Baixo, Portugal, 2016
First North American Edition: Fitch & Madison Publishers, Scottsdale, Arizona, 2016
South American Edition: Publit, Rio de Janeiro, 2016
Second North American Edition: Fitch & Madison Publishers, Scottsdale, Arizona, 2020

All of the first three editions listed above are very nearly identical in content, though they differ as to format and pagination. The Second North American Edition differs substantially in content from the other three. Nevertheless, the passages cited in the present work can be looked up in any of these editions.

Kane, Tim, "Why Our Best Officers Are Leaving," *The Atlantic*, Jan./Feb. 2011.

Kaplan, Jeffrey, and Leonard Weinberg, *The Emergence of a Euro-American Radical Right*, Rutgers University Press, New Brunswick, New Jersey, 1998.

Kavanau, J.L., "Behavior of captive white-footed mice," *Science*, Vol. 155, 1967, pp. 1523–1539.

Kee, Robert, *The Green Flag: A History of Irish Nationalism*, Penguin Books, London, 2000.

Keegan, John, *The Second World War*, Penguin Books, New York, 1990.

Kelly, John F., and Phillip K. Wearne, *Tainting Evidence: Inside the Scandals at the FBI Crime Lab*, The Free Press, New York, 1998.

Keniston, Kenneth, *The Uncommitted*, Harcourt, Brace & World, New York, 1965.

Kephart, Horace, *Our Southern Highlanders*, New and Enlarged Edition, Land of the Sky Books, Alexander, North Carolina, 2001. Apart from the Foreword, this appears to be a facsimile of the Macmillan edition of 1922 and 1949.

Keyfitz, Nathan, review of Piel, *Only One World*, in *Scientific American*, Feb. 1993.

Kirchner, Stephanie, "Postcard: Berlin," *Time*, Sept. 29, 2008.

Kirkham, James F., Sheldon G. Levy, and William J. Crotty, *Assassination and Political Violence: A Report to the National Commission on the Causes and Prevention of Violence*, Praeger Publishers, New York, 1970.

Kjetsaa, Geir, *Fyodor Dostoyevsky: A Writer's Life*, trans. by Siri Hustvedt and David McDuff, Fawcett Columbine, New York, 1989.

Klemm, Friedrich, *A History of Western Technology*, trans. by Dorothea Waley Singer, M.I.T. Press, Cambridge, Massachusetts, sixth printing, 1978.

Knox, Donald, *The Korean War*, Vol. I, Harcourt, San Diego, 1987.

Kolbert, Elizabeth, "Ice Memory," *The New Yorker*, Jan. 7, 2002.

Kolbert, Elizabeth, "Crash Course: Can a seventeen-mile-long collider unlock the universe?," *The New Yorker*, May 14, 2007.

Kosthorst, Erich, *Die deutsche Opposition gegen Hitler zwischen Polen- und Frankreichfeldzug*, 3. bearbeitete Auflage, Schriftenreihe der Bundeszentrale für Heimatdienst, Heft 8, Bonn, 1957.

Kroeber, Alfred L., *The Arapaho*, University of Nebraska Press, Lincoln, Nebraska, 1983.

Kunhardt, Philip B., Jr., Philip B. Kunhardt III, and Peter W. Kunhardt, *The American President: The Human Drama of Our Nation's Highest Office*, Paperback Edition, Riverhead Books, New York, 2000.

Kurzweil, Ray, "The Promise and the Peril," *Interactive Week*, Vol. 7, No. 43, Oct. 23, 2000.

Lam, Bourree, "The New Science of Bad Science," *The Atlantic*, Sept. 2015.

Laue, Theodore H. von, *Why Lenin? Why Stalin?*, J.B. Lippincott Co., New York, 1971.

Law, Bernard, Viscount Montgomery of Alamein, *The Memoirs of Field-Marshal Montgomery*, Pen & Sword Books, Barnsley, South Yorkshire, U.K., 2010.

Lebecq, Stéphane, "Routes of change: Production and distribution in the West (5th–8th century)," in L. Webster & M. Brown, pp. 67–78.

Lee, Martha F., *Earth First!: Environmental Apocalypse*, Syracuse University Press, Syracuse, New York, 1995.

Lee, Richard B., "!Kung Bushman Subsistence," in Vayda, pp. 47–79.

Legros, Dominique, Comments on Headland, *Current Anthropology*, Vol. 38, No. 4, Aug.–Oct. 1997, pp. 616–18.

Lenin. See Christman.

Leuchtenburg, William E., *Franklin D. Roosevelt and the New Deal, 1932–1940*, Harper & Row, New York, 1963.

Liddell Hart, B.H., *The Real War, 1914–1918*, Little, Brown and Co., Boston, 1964.

Livingston, Edward, *A System of Penal Law for the State of Louisiana*, 1833.

London, Perry, *Behavior Control*, Harper & Row, New York, 1969.

López. See García López.

Lukianoff, Greg, and Jonathan Haidt, "The Coddling of the American Mind," *The Atlantic*, Sept. 2015.

Lynch, Jack, "Felled on the Field of Honor," *Colonial Williamsburg*, Autumn 2005.

Lynch, John, *Argentine Caudillo: Juan Manuel de Rosas*, SR Books, Lanham, Maryland, 2006. The copy referenced here was manufactured at Lexington, Kentucky, January 9, 2017, presumably through some sort of print-on-demand system.

Maas, Peter, *King of the Gypsies*, Viking Press, New York, 1975.

Mahan, Alfred Thayer, *The Influence of Sea Power upon History 1660–1783*, Dover Publications, New York, 1987.

Manchester, William, *The Arms of Krupp, 1587–1968*, Bantam Books, Toronto, 1970.

Manjoo, Farhad, *True Enough: Learning to Live in a Post-Fact Society*, John Wiley & Sons, Hoboken, New Jersey, 2008.

Markoff, John, "Ay Robot! Scientists Worry Machines May Outsmart Man," *New York Times*, July 26, 2009.

Markoff, John, "Pentagon Offers a Robotics Prize," *New York Times*, New York Edition, Oct. 29, 2012.

Marquis, Thomas B. (interpreter), *Wooden Leg: A Warrior Who Fought Custer*, Bison Books, University of Nebraska Press, Lincoln, Nebraska, 1967.

Mayo, Carlos A. (ed.), *Vivir en la frontera: La casa, la dieta, la pulpería, la escuela (1770–1870)*, Editorial Biblos, Buenos Aires, 2000. Where our notes refer to the articles that comprise *Vivir en la frontera*, they cite the names of the authors of the articles in question. See Brittez, Cabrejas, Correa & Wibaux, Duart. Where our notes cite "Mayo," the reference is to Mayo's *Estancia y sociedad en la Pampa* (see below), except where the reader is explicitly referred to "Mayo, *Vivir en la frontera*."

Mayo, Carlos A., *Estancia y sociedad en la Pampa (1740–1820)*, Segunda edición, Editorial Biblos, Buenos Aires, 2004.

Mercader, Julio (ed.), *Under the Canopy: The Archaeology of Tropical Rain Forests*, Rutgers University Press, New Brunswick, New Jersey, 2003.

Milstein, Michael, "Pilot not included," *Air & Space*, June/July 2011.

Monnerot, Jules, *Sociology and Psychology of Communism*, trans. by Jane Degras and Richard Rees, Beacon Press, Boston, 1960.

Morgan, M. Granger, "Risk Analysis and Management," *Scientific American*, July 1993.

Morris, Desmond, *The Human Zoo*, Kodansha America, Inc., New York, 1996.

Mosse, W.E., *Alexander II and the Modernization of Russia*, Revised Edition, Collier Books, New York, 1973.

Moyers, Bill, "Welcome to Doomsday," *New York Review*, March 24, 2005.

Murphy, Audie, *To Hell and Back*, Owl Books, Henry Holt and Co., New York, 2002.

Napierala-Cowen, Agnieszka, "A Different View of Poland," *Polish American Journal*, Feb. 2016.

Nathanson, Neal, and John R. Martin, "The Epidemiology of Poliomyelitis: Enigmas Surrounding its Appearance, Epidemicity, and Disappearance," *American Journal of Epidemiology*, Vol. 110, No. 6, 1979, pp. 672ff.

Navrátil, Jaromír, Antonín Benčík, Václav Kural, Marie Michálková, and Jitka Vondrová (eds.), *The Prague Spring 1968*, trans. by Mark Kramer, Joy Moss, and Ruth Tosek, Central European University Press, Budapest, 1998.

Nietzsche, Friedrich, *Twilight of the Idols/The Antichrist*, trans. by R.J. Hollingdale, Penguin Books, 1990.

Ortega y Gasset, José, *The Revolt of the Masses*, W.W. Norton & Co., New York, 1993.

Osnos, Evan, "Letter from China: Angry Youth," *The New Yorker*, July 28, 2008.

Packard, Vance, *The Hidden Persuaders*, D. McKay Co., New York, 1957.

Page, Susan, "Tony Blair fears danger ahead for democracies of the West," *USA Today*, Dec. 6, 2016.

Parker, Geoffrey (ed.), *The Cambridge History of Warfare*, Cambridge University Press, Cambridge, U.K., 2008.

Parkman, Francis, *The Old Regime in Canada*, Little, Brown and Co., Boston, 1882.

Patterson, James T., *America in the Twentieth Century: A History*, Fifth Edition, Harcourt College Publishers, Fort Worth, Texas, 2000.

Piel, Gerard, *Only One World: Our Own to Make and to Keep*, W.H. Freeman and Co., New York, 1992.

Plattner, Stuart (ed.), *Economic Anthropology*, Stanford University Press, Stanford, California, 1989.

Poncins, Gontran de, *Kabloona*, Time-Life Books, Alexandria, Virginia, 1980.

Posner, Richard A., *Catastrophe: Risk and Response*, Oxford University Press, New York, 2004.

Priore, Mary del, and Renato Pinto Venâncio, *O Livro de Ouro da História do Brasil*, Edição revista e ampliada, Ediouro Publicações, Rio de Janeiro, segunda reimpressão, 2001. The foregoing information is provided on the title page and the reverse thereof, but the date 2001 cannot be correct; the book reports events up to 2004, and a note on the reverse of p. 407 states, in Portuguese: "This book was typeset... and printed... in 2008." The copy referenced here was manufactured in Lexington, Kentucky, on Sept. 20, 2014, presumably through some sort of print-on-demand system. The selfsame copy should be available in the Labadie Collection at the University of Michigan's Special Collections Library, Ann Arbor.

Quammen, David, "Planet of Weeds," *Harper's Magazine*, Oct. 1998.

Ramos, Samuel, *El Perfil del Hombre y la Cultura en México*, Décima edición, Espasa-Calpe Mexicana, Mexico City, 1982 (originally published in 1934).

Randall, Willard Sterne, *Thomas Jefferson: A Life*, Harper Collins, New York, 1994.

Rauch, Jonathan, "Containing Trump," *The Atlantic*, March 2017.

Read, Anthony, and David Fisher, *The Fall of Berlin*, Da Capo Press, New York, 1995.

Rees, Martin, *Our Final Hour: A Scientist's Warning*, Basic Books, New York, 2004.

Reichard, Gladys A., *Navaho Religion: A Study of Symbolism*, Princeton University Press, Princeton, New Jersey, 1990.

Risen, James, and Nick Wingfield, "Silicon Valley and Spy Agency Bound by Strengthening Web," *New York Times*, June 20, 2013.

Rodenbeck, Max, "Islam Confronts its Demons," *New York Review*, April 29, 2004.

Rosin, Hanna, "The Silicon Valley Suicides," *The Atlantic*, Dec. 2015.

Ross, Andrew C., *David Livingstone: Mission and Empire*, Hambledon Continuum, London, 2006.

Rostow, W.W., *The Stages of Economic Growth: A Non-Communist Manifesto*, Third Edition, Cambridge University Press, Cambridge, U.K., 1990, reprinted 1997, transferred to digital printing 2004.

Rothfels, Hans, *Deutsche Opposition gegen Hitler: Eine Würdigung*, Neue, erweiterte Ausgabe, Fischer Taschenbuch Verlag, Frankfurt am Main, 1986.

Rubin, Elizabeth, "Veiled Rebellion," *National Geographic*, Dec. 2010.

Russell, Osborne, *Journal of a Trapper*, Bison Books, University of Nebraska Press, Lincoln, Nebraska, 1965.

Ruthen, Russell, "Strange Matters: Can Advanced Accelerators Initiate Runaway Reactions?," *Scientific American*, August 1993.

Saavedra. See Cervantes Saavedra.

Sallust (Gaius Sallustius Crispus), *The Jugurthine War/The Conspiracy of Catiline*, trans. by S.A. Handford, Penguin Books, Baltimore, 1967.

Sampson, Anthony, *Mandela: The Authorized Biography*, Alfred A. Knopf, New York, 1999.

Sanborn, Margaret, *Mark Twain: The Bachelor Years*, Doubleday, New York, 1990.

Sánchez. See Arias Sánchez.

Sarmiento, Domingo Faustino, *Facundo. Civilización y Barbarie*, edited by Roberto Yahni, Séptima edición, Ediciones Cátedra (Grupo Anaya, S.A.), Madrid, 2005.

Sarno, Louis, *Song from the Forest*, Corgi, London, 1994.

Schebesta, Paul, *Die Bambuti-Pygmäen vom Ituri*, Institut Royal Colonial Belge, Brussels; I. Band, 1938; II. Band, I. Teil, 1941; II. Band, III. Teil, 1950.

Schilpp, Paul Arthur (ed.), *Albert Einstein: Philosopher-Scientist*, Third Edition, Open Court, La Salle, Illinois, sixth printing, 1995.

Schlissel, Lillian, *Women's Diaries of the Westward Journey*, Schocken Books, New York, 1992.

Schulmann, Robert, A.J. Kox, Michael Janssen and József Illy (eds.), *The Collected Papers of Albert Einstein*, Princeton University Press, Princeton, New Jersey, 1998.

Scott, Ken, "Restoration: 'Hawks Come Home," *Air & Space*, June/July 2007.

Seligman, Martin E.P., *Helplessness: On Depression, Development, and Death*, W.H. Freeman and Co., New York, 1992.

Selznick, Philip, *The Organizational Weapon: A Study of Bolshevik Strategy and Tactics*, The Free Press of Glencoe, Illinois, 1960.

Shakespeare, William, *Julius Caesar*.

Shakespeare, William, *As You Like It*.

Shott, Michael J., "On Recent Trends in the Anthropology of Foragers," *Man* (N.S.), Vol. 27, No. 4, Dec. 1992, pp. 843–871.

Smelser, Neil J., *Theory of Collective Behavior*, Macmillan, New York, 1971.

Smith, Alice Kimball, and Charles Weiner (eds.), *Robert Oppenheimer: Letters and Recollections*, Stanford University Press, Stanford, California, 1995.

Soriano, Graciela (ed.), *Simón Bolívar: Escritos Políticos*, Alianza Editorial, Madrid, 1975.

Speer, Albert, *Inside the Third Reich*, trans. by Richard and Clara Winston, Macmillan, New York, 1970.

Stalin, Joseph, *History of the Communist Party of the Soviet Union (Bolsheviks): Short Course*, Prism Key Press, New York, 2013. Though the authorship was attributed to Stalin, this book was mostly written by a commission of the Central Committee of the Communist Party of the Soviet Union. Selznick, p. 42n23. Ulam, p. 638. The copy referenced here was manufactured in Lexington, Kentucky on July 29, 2014, presumably through some sort of print-on-demand system.

Stefansson, Vilhjalmur, *My Life with the Eskimo*, Macmillan, New York, 1951.

Strybel, Robert, "Poland Under Fire," *Polish American Journal*, Feb. 2016.

Stur, Beata, "Poland's Government Ignores Constitutional Tribunal," *Polish American Journal*, April 2016.

Szelag, Lukasz, "There are no Threats to Democracy in Poland," letter to editor, in *Polish American Journal*, Feb. 2016.

Tacitus, Publius (or Gaius) Cornelius, *The Agricola and the Germania*, trans. by H. Mattingly, Penguin Books, 1970.

Tan, Chester C., *Chinese Political Thought in the Twentieth Century*, Doubleday & Company, Garden City, New York, 1971.

TeBrake, William H., *A Plague of Insurrection*, University of Pennsylvania Press, Philadelphia, 1993.

Tella, Torcuato S. di, Gino Germani, Jorge Graciarena y colaboradores, *Argentina, Sociedad de Masas*, Tercera edición, Editorial Universitaria de Buenos Aires, Buenos Aires, 1971.

Thomas, W.I., and F. Znaniecki, *The Polish Peasant in Europe and America*, one-volume, abridged edition, University of Illinois Press, Champaign, Illinois, 1996.

Thompson, Derek, "A World Without Work," *The Atlantic*, July/Aug. 2015.

Thrall, Trevor, "Trump's generals can't fix us," *USA Today*, Dec. 13, 2016.

Thurston, Robert W., *Life and Terror in Stalin's Russia, 1934–1941*, Yale University Press, New Haven, Connecticut, 1996.

Trend, J.B., *Bolívar and the Independence of Spanish America*, published in 1951 under the auspices of the Junta de Gobierno of the United States of Venezuela and under an arrangement made with the University Press of England and the Macmillan Company, New York.

Trevelyan, Barry, Matthew Smallman-Raynor, and Andrew D. Cliff, "The Spatial Dynamics of Poliomyelitis in the United States: From Epidemic Emergence to Vaccine-Induced Retreat, 1910–1971," *Annals of the Association of American Geographers*, Vol. 95, No. 2, June 2005, pp. 269–293.

Trotsky, Leon, *History of the Russian Revolution*, trans. by Max Eastman, Pathfinder, New York, 1980.

Tuchman, Barbara, *A Distant Mirror*, Ballantine Books, New York, 1978.

Turnbull, Colin M., *The Forest People*, Simon & Schuster, New York, 1962.

Turnbull, Colin M., *Wayward Servants: The Two Worlds of the African Pygmies*, Natural History Press, Garden City, New York, 1965.

Turnbull, Colin M., *The Mountain People*, A Touchstone Book, Simon & Schuster, New York, 1972.

Turnbull, Colin M., *The Mbuti Pygmies: Change and Adaptation*, Harcourt Brace College Publishers, Fort Worth, Texas, 1983.

Twenge, Jean M., "Has the Smartphone Destroyed a Generation?", *The Atlantic*, Sept. 2017.

Ulam, Adam B., *Stalin: The Man and His Era*, Beacon Press, Boston, 1987.

Urban-Klaehn, Jagoda, "Baba Jaga's Corner: Joy of Eve's Birth and Sorrow after Pierre's Tragic Death," *Polish American Journal*, Sept. 2012.

Van Creveld. See Creveld.

Vayda, Andrew (ed.), *Environment and Cultural Behavior*, Natural History Press, Garden City, New York, 1969.

Vestal, Stanley, *Sitting Bull, Champion of the Sioux: A Biography*, University of Oklahoma Press, Norman, Oklahoma, 1989.

Von Laue. See Laue.

Vucinich, Wayne S. (ed.), *The Peasant in Nineteenth Century Russia*, Stanford University Press, Stanford, California, 1968.

Wald, Matthew L., "What Now for Nuclear Waste?," *Scientific American*, Aug. 2009.

Warburg, E., M. von Laue, A. Sommerfeld, and A. Einstein, *Zu Max Plancks sechzigstem Geburtstag. Ansprachen, gehalten am 26. April 1918 in der Deutschen Physikalischen Gesellschaft*, C.F. Müllersche Hofbuchhandlung, Karlsruhe, 1918.

Washburn, Wilcomb E., "A Moral History of Indian-White Relations," *Ethnohistory*, Vol. 4, No. 1, Winter 1957, pp. 47–61.

Weber, Max, *Die protestantische Ethik und der Geist des Kapitalismus*, Verlag von J.C.B. Mohr (Paul Siebeck), Tübingen, 1934. This is an offprint of pages 1–206 of Weber's *Gesammelte Aufsätze zur Religionssoziologie*, I. Band, Dritte, photomechanisch gedruckte Auflage, 1922, of the same publisher.

Webster, Leslie, and Michelle Brown (eds.), *The Transformation of the Roman World AD 400–900*, British Museum Press, London, 1997.

Webster, Mary Jo, "Could a robot steal your job?," *USA Today*, Oct. 29, 2014.

Wheeler, Winslow T. (ed.), *The Pentagon Labyrinth*, Center for Defense Information, World Security Institute, 2011.

Whitaker, Arthur P. (ed.), *Latin America and the Enlightenment*, Second Edition, Great Seal Books, a division of Cornell University Press, Ithaca, New York, second printing, 1963.

White, R.W., "Motivation reconsidered: The concept of competence," *Psychological Review*, Vol. 66, 1959, pp. 297–333.

Whittle, Richard, "The Drone Started Here," *Air & Space*, April/May 2013.

Wiener, Norbert, *I am a Mathematician*, Doubleday & Company, Garden City, New York, 1956.

Wilson, Timothy D., David A. Reinhard, et al., "Just think: The challenges of the disengaged mind," *Science*, Vol. 345, No. 6192, July 2014, pp. 75–77.

Wissler, Clark, *Indians of the United States*, Revised Edition, Anchor Books, Random House, New York, 1989.

Wood, Gordon S., "The Making of a Disaster," *New York Review*, April 28, 2005.

Wright, Robert, "The Evolution of Despair," *Time*, Aug. 28, 1995.

Wright, Tim, "Lieutenant Ivan Baranovsky's P-39," *Air & Space*, Sept. 2011.

Zaccone, P., Z. Fehervari, et al., "Parasitic worms and inflammatory diseases," *Parasite Immunology*, Vol. 28, 2006, pp. 515–523.

Zakaria, Rafiq, *The Struggle Within Islam*, Penguin Books, London, 1989.

Zimmermann, G.A., *Das Neunzehnte Jahrhundert: Geschichtlicher und Kulturhistorischer Rückblick*, Zweite Hälfte, Zweiter Theil, Druck und Verlag von Geo. Brumder, Milwaukee, 1902.

Zinsser, Hans, *Rats, Lice, and History*, Blue Ribbon Books, New York, 1935.

WORKS WITHOUT NAMED AUTHOR

Archives of General Psychiatry

Bears and Other Top Predators (magazine)

Christian Science Monitor, The

Constitution of the United States

Denver Post, The

Economist, The

Federal Register, The

Funk & Wagnalls New Encyclopedia, 1996

ISAIF = *Industrial Society and Its Future*, in this volume

Los Angeles Times, The

Mean (an obscure magazine now no longer published)

Missoulian, The (newspaper of Missoula, Montana)

National Geographic

NEB = *The New Encyclopaedia Britannica*, Fifteenth Edition
> The Fifteenth Edition has been modified every few years. We put a date in parentheses after NEB—e.g., NEB (2003)—to indicate the copyright date of the particular version of NEB that we cite.

New York Times, The

Newsweek

Omni (magazine)

Organizer's Manual, The, Bantam Books, New York, second printing, 1971

Polish American Journal

Science News

Sol de México, El (newspaper, Mexico City)

Sun-Times, The (newspaper of Chicago, Illinois)

Time

United States Reports (published opinions of the Supreme Court of the United States)

University of California, Berkeley Wellness Letter

US News & World Report
USA Today
Vegetarian Times
Wall Street Journal, The
Week, The
World Book Encyclopedia, The, 2011

Index